RECLAIMING THE AMERICAS

LATINX: THE FUTURE IS NOW
A series edited by Lorgia García-Peña and Nicole Guidotti-Hernández

Books in the series

Kristy L. Ulibarri, *Visible Borders, Invisible Economies: Living Death in Latinx Narratives*

Marisel C. Moreno, *Crossing Waters: Undocumented Migration in Hispanophone Caribbean and Latinx Literature and Art*

Yajaira M. Padilla, *From Threatening Guerrillas to Forever Illegals: US Central Americans and the Politics of Non-Belonging*

Francisco J. Galarte, *Brown Trans Figurations: Rethinking Race, Gender, and Sexuality in Chicanx/Latinx Studies*

Reclaiming the Americas

LATINX ART AND THE POLITICS OF TERRITORY

TATIANA REINOZA

UNIVERSITY OF TEXAS PRESS AUSTIN

This book is made possible in part by support from the Institute for Scholarship in the Liberal Arts, College of Arts and Letters, University of Notre Dame.

Printed in the United States of America
First edition, 2023

Requests for permission to reproduce material from this work should be sent to:
Permissions
University of Texas Press
P.O. Box 7819
Austin, TX 78713-7819
utpress.utexas.edu/rp-form

♾ The paper used in this book meets the minimum requirements of ANSI/NISO Z39.48-1992 (R1997) (Permanence of Paper).

LIBRARY OF CONGRESS CATALOGING-IN-PUBLICATION DATA

Names: Reinoza, Tatiana, author.
Title: Reclaiming the Americas : Latinx art and the politics of territory / Tatiana Reinoza.
Description: Austin : University of Texas Press, 2023. | Series: Latinx: the future is now | Includes bibliographical references and index. |
Identifiers: LCCN 2022017116
ISBN 978-1-4773-2690-9 (paperback)
ISBN 978-1-4773-2691-6 (pdf)
Subjects: LCSH: Hispanic American prints. | Hispanic American prints—Political aspects. | Hispanic American printmakers. | Immigrants in art. | Colonization in art. | Colonies in art.
Classification: LCC NE539.3.H57 R45 2023 | DDC 769.97308968—dc23/eng/20220727
LC record available at https://lccn.loc.gov/2022017116

doi:10.7560/326893

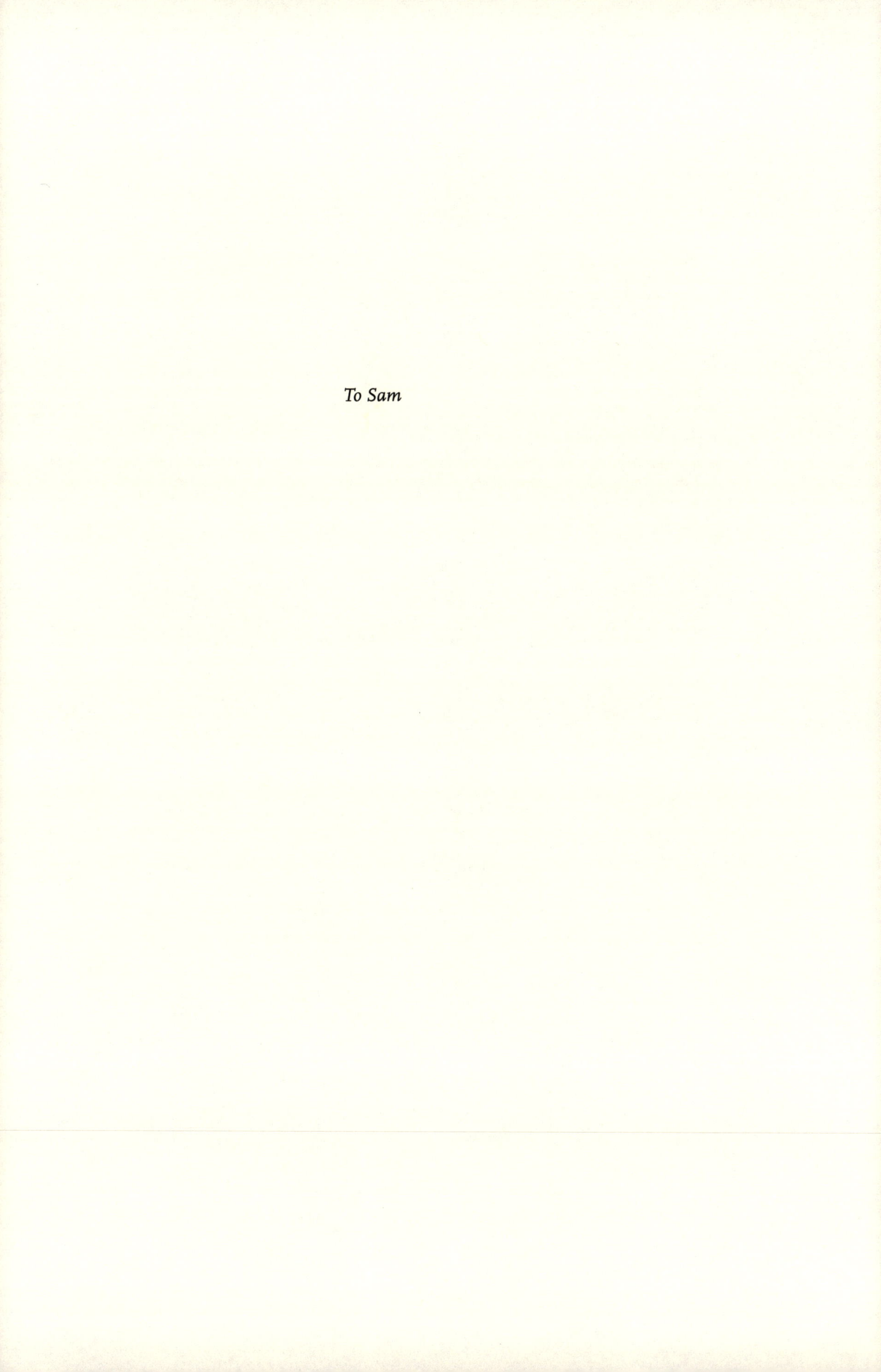

To Sam

CONTENTS

LIST OF ILLUSTRATIONS ix

INTRODUCTION 1

CHAPTER ONE Native Territorialities:
Ricardo Duffy's Border Pop and the Indigenous Uncanny 29

CHAPTER TWO Embodied Territorialities:
Enrique Chagoya and Alberto Ríos Disrupting the Western Cartographic Gaze 73

CHAPTER THREE Mestiza Territorialities:
Sandra Fernández's Migrant Justice and the Movable Border 113

CHAPTER FOUR Aqueous Territorialities:
The Dominican York Proyecto Gráfica's Island Dwellers and Water Boundaries 151

CONCLUSION Revolution on Display 191

ACKNOWLEDGMENTS 211
APPENDIX Latinx Printmaking Workshops and Collectives in the US 216
NOTES 220
BIBLIOGRAPHY 243
INDEX 259

ILLUSTRATIONS

xiv 0.1. Dalila Paola Mendez, *Corazón de la Tierra*, 2015

16 0.2. Martin Waldseemüller, *Carta Marina*, 1516

20 0.3. Philips Galle, after Jan van der Straet (Johannes Stradanus), frontispiece to *Nova Reperta*, ca. 1588

23 0.4. Sandy Rodriguez, *Rainbows, Grizzlies, and Snakes, Oh My!—Conquest to Caging in Los Angeles*, 2019

30 1.1. Ricardo Duffy, *Dig These*, 1993

32 1.2. Ricardo Duffy, *Veni Vidi Vici*, 1992

34 1.3. Emanuel Martinez, *Tierra o Muerte*, 1967

36 1.4. Ricardo Duffy, *The New Order*, 1996

37 1.5. Ed Ruscha, *Hollywood*, 1968

38 1.6. Manuel Ocampo, *Untitled (Ethnic Map of Los Angeles)*, 1987

39 1.7. Leo Burnett, *U.S.A.*, Ad No. 10338-A1

45 1.8. Ed Ruscha, *The Los Angeles County Museum on Fire*, 1965–1968

45 1.9. Andy Warhol, *Birmingham Race Riot*, 1964

48 1.10. Enrique Chagoya, *Crossing I*, 1994

48 1.11. Enrique Chagoya, *The Governor's Nightmare*, 1994

49 1.12. Rubén Ortiz Torres, *California Taco*, 1995

51 1.13. Luis C. González, aka "Louie the Foot," *1848*, 2003

53 1.14. George Franklin Cram, *Railroad and County Map of Arizona*, 1887

55 1.15. *Arizona Highways*, "How Apache Leap Got Its Name," 1935

56 1.16. Kent Monkman, *Casualties of Modernity*, 2012

59 1.17. Don Barletti, *Los Angeles Times*, Contractors in 1993 set posts for an eight-foot fence in the median of the 5 Freeway

62 1.18. Theodoor Galle and Philips Galle, after Jan van der Straet (Johannes Stradanus), "Allegory of America," *Nova Reperta*, ca. 1588

66 1.19. Andy Warhol, *The American Indian (Russell Means)*, 1976
68 1.20. Consuelo Jimenez Underwood, *Virgen de los Caminos*, 1994
72 2.1. Enrique Chagoya and Alberto Ríos, *Genome Map*, 2000
75 2.2. *Map of Tenochtitlán*, 1524
78 2.3. Enrique Chagoya and Alberto Ríos, *Theorem*, 2000
80 2.4. Enrique Chagoya and Alberto Ríos, *Asian Celestial Map*, 2000
83 2.5. Section 1 of *Map of Cuauhtinchán No. 2*, ca. 1540
84 2.6. Enrique Chagoya, *Le Cannibale Moderniste*, 1999
85 2.7. Lorenz Fries, after Martin Waldseemüller, *Terrae Novae Tabula*, 1522
87 2.8. Theodor de Bry, after John White, "Their Manner of Praying with Rattles about the Fire," 1590
88 2.9. Hans Staden, *The Dismemberment of the Flayed Body by the Men*, 1557
89 2.10. Oswald de Andrade, "Manifesto Antropófago," 1928
93 2.11. Enrique Chagoya and Alberto Ríos, *Trash World*, 2000
94 2.12. Enrique Chagoya and Alberto Ríos, *American Ocean/Cuba*, 2000
96 2.13. Gerhard Mercator, *Atlas*, 1569
97 2.14. *La Tira de la Peregrinación*, also known as Codex Boturini, sixteenth century
99 2.15. Pedro Lasch, *Route Guide—Mexico/New York—Vicencio Marquez* (*Latino/a America* series), 2003–2006
101 2.16. Enrique Chagoya, *Road Map*, 2003
106 2.17. Enrique Chagoya and Alberto Ríos, *Upside Down World Map*, 2000
108 2.18. T-O map, from Isidore of Seville's *Etymologiae*, ca. 600–625
112 3.1. Carta de la Provincia de Quito y de sus Adyacentes, 1750
116 3.2. Oswaldo Guayasamín, *Quito Azul*, n.d.
121 3.3. Felipe Guaman Poma de Ayala, Drawing 233 from *Nueva Corónica y Buen Gobierno* (1615)
126 3.4. Sandra C. Fernández, *Coming of Age* (*Transformations*), 2008
129 3.5. Oswaldo Viteri, *Caminantes Somos de la Noche y de la Pena*, 1979
130 3.6. Sandra C. Fernández, *Behind What Is Seen*, 1998

131 3.7. Codex Mendoza, title page, ca. 1541–1542

134 3.8. Ester Hernandez, *Sun Raid,* 2008

134 3.9. Ester Hernandez, *Sun Mad,* 1982

136 3.10. Sandra C. Fernández, *CAUTION: Dreamers in/on Sight,* 2013

139 3.11. Laura Aguilar, *Nature Self-Portrait #11,* 1996

140 3.12. Tony Ortega, *La Marcha de Lupe Liberty,* 2006

143 3.13. Vicki Meek, *Ida B. Wells: Telling It Like It Is,* 2002

144 3.14. Terry Ybañez, *Cutting Tongues,* 1996

147 3.15. Jonathan Rebolloso, Sandra Fernández, Sam Coronado, and Logan Hill at Coronado Studio, 2013

148 3.16. Sandra C. Fernández, *The Northern Triangle,* 2018

152 4.1. Moses Ros-Suárez, *El Reggaetón del Bachatero, 2010*

153 4.2. Members of the Dominican York Proyecto Gráfica at Bullrider Studio, 2010

154 4.3. Christopher Columbus, Hispaniola sketch, ca. 1492

156 4.4. Pepe Coronado, *Bailando con el Sol,* 1996

160 4.5. Yunior Chiqui Mendoza, *Bananhattan,* 2010

161 4.6. René de los Santos, *Cigüita Cibaeña en Nueva York,* 2010

163 4.7. Scherezade García, *Day Dreaming/Soñando Despierta,* 2010

164 4.8. Scherezade García, *Sea of Wonder,* from the series *Theories of Freedom,* 2011

166 4.9. Arturo Lindsay, *Oni of Lagos,* from the series *Children of Middle Passage,* 2001

167 4.10. Miguel Luciano, *Detrás de la Oreja,* 2010

169 4.11. Rider Ureña, *My Girl on the Floor,* 2010

171 4.12. Luanda Lozano, *Sálvame Santo,* 2010

173 4.13. Ezequiel Taveras, *Cartas III,* from the series *Cartas,* 1998

176 4.14. Luanda Lozano and Robert Blackburn at *XII Bienal de San Juan del Grabado Latinoamericano y del Caribe*

177 4.15. Luanda Lozano, *Figuras Fragmentadas por el Tiempo,* 1997

179 4.16. Reynaldo García Pantaleón, *Amarrao,* 2010

182 4.17. Pepe Coronado, *Intrépido,* 2010

187 4.18. Carlos Almonte, *Vale John,* 2010

188 4.19. iliana emilia garcía, *Dreambox,* 2010

189 4.20. Alex Guerrero, *Vista Psicotrópica,* 2010

189 4.21. Luanda Lozano, *La Musa de Blackburn,* 2017

196 5.1. Entrance to *¡Printing the Revolution!* at the Smithsonian American Art Museum

198 5.2. Wall of graphic art in *Our America: The Latino Presence in American Art* at the Smithsonian American Art Museum

199 5.3. "Urgent Images" section of *¡Printing the Revolution!* at the Smithsonian American Art Museum

203 5.4. Poli Marichal, *Santuario,* 2018

204 5.5. Jesus Barraza and Nancypili Hernandez, *Indian Land,* 2004

209 5.6. Michael Menchaca, *Cuando el Rio Suena, Gatos Lleva,* 2011

RECLAIMING THE AMERICAS

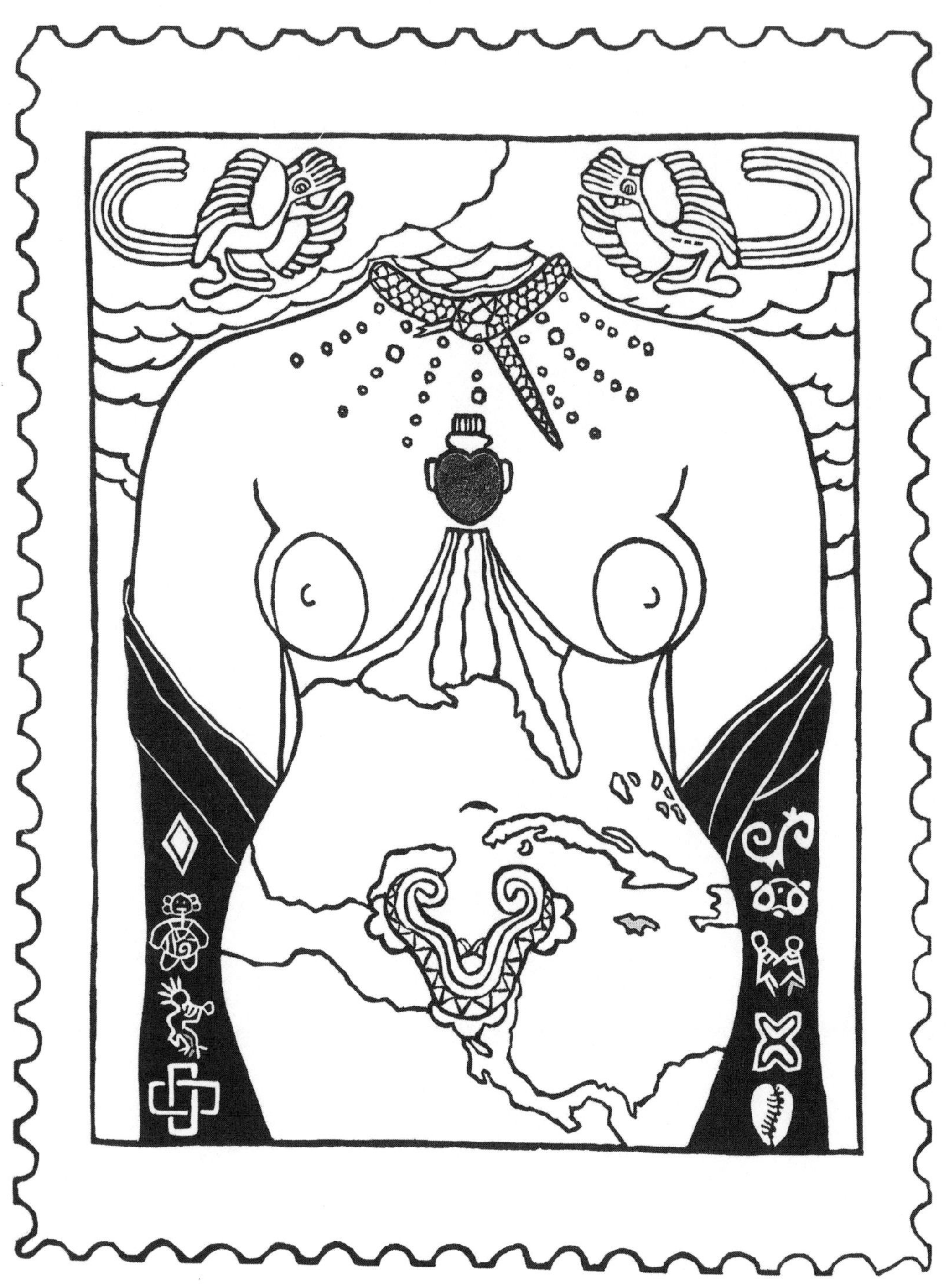

0.1. Dalila Paola Mendez, *Corazón de la Tierra*, 2015. Woodblock and gold leaf on BFK Rives, 22 × 30 inches; edition of thirty. Printed by the artist at Taller Experimental de Gráfica, Havana, Cuba. Courtesy of the artist.

Introduction

THE GODDESS APPEARS DISROBED, flanked by quetzal birds at her shoulders. A snake wraps around her neck, and its energy pulsates through her collarbone. The viewer is drawn to the gold-leaf pectoral plate in the shape of a heart, which hovers over a volcano rising between her breasts. The center of her body is a map. The geographic shape of Central America emerges out of an upside-down cave glyph placed over her uterine sacred center. Through spatial compression of the map on her body, the Gulf of Mexico narrows, and the Yucatán Peninsula nearly touches Cuba, as the Antilles at her navel draw close to the southeast tip of the United States. The robe covering her forearms contains Taíno and Yoruba symbols invoking the cardinal points, energy, freedom, and the divine intervention of Atabey and Yemaya.[1] The entire image is in the form of a postage stamp. The Los Angeles–based artist Dalila Paola Mendez created this woodcut, *Corazón de la Tierra*, at a 2015 residency at the Taller Experimental de Gráfica in Havana as part of a printmaking exchange organized by Self Help Graphics & Art (fig. 0.1).[2] *Corazón de la Tierra* was a love letter to women as a source of beauty and regenerative life, an act of reparation for the archetypal figure of America who experienced sexual violence at conquest, a way of honoring Mendez's family's multiracial origins and her matriarch's migration from El Salvador to Guatemala, Guatemala to Louisiana, and Louisiana to California. Mendez's print encapsulates many of the debates that are at the heart of this book: Why do Latinx artists turn to territorial representations? Why do they use the reproductive medium of printmaking? What do their claims to land mean in relation to their complex identities? How do they speak to the lived experience of migration in the context of growing anti-immigrant discourse? How can these alternative representations of territoriality shift how we perceive space, borders, and belonging in the twenty-first century?

Reclaiming the Americas is an interdisciplinary study that examines how Latinx artists adopted the medium of printmaking—historically used by Europeans to chart and claim New World territories—to reclaim the lands of the Americas as belonging to Indigenous, migrant, mestiza/o, and Afro-descendant people. It brings together the subjects of art, immigration, and geography to illuminate one of the most popular and yet understudied mediums for Latinx artists. Drawing from the print archives of graphic workshops across the country, I focus on artistic representations of territory that break away from traditional Western conceptions of geography. *Reclaiming the Americas* shows how Latinx artists have been at the forefront of battling the resurgence of anti-immigrant discourse, making migration histories visible, and critiquing printmaking's complicity in the colonization of the Americas.

Although exhibitions of prints have a long history in the discipline of art history, this is the first study of its kind that thematically delves into the Latinx graphic-arts movement to understand it within the tradition of art history, and to provide a much-needed pan-ethnic comparative model. In the history of Western art, printmaking has often been the domain of white male artists, from European masters such as Dürer, Rembrandt, and Goya, to contemporary art icons like Jasper Johns, Robert Rauschenberg, and Andy Warhol. This book tells a very different story, by unearthing a network of Latinx print workshops active since the 1970s in the US that adopted this medium to foster experimentation, collaboration, and political engagement. Through close readings of works by Ricardo Duffy, Enrique Chagoya, Sandra Fernández, Scherezade García, Luanda Lozano, and Pepe Coronado, I analyze how their prints reverse the Western gaze that envisioned the Americas as Terra Incognita (unknown), Terra Nullius (unclaimed), and Terra Nova (new). Unlike previous scholarship that focused on a single ethnic group, my work charts a new cognitive map for Latinx art, showing how workshop spaces became sites of interethnic and cross-racial alliances. Emphasizing the heterogeneity among artists and their practices, I pivot from the prevailing scholarship, which is often divided along cultural nationalist lines. Latinx art is born out of disparate social movements, since there is no single political platform that guides the artists' work. My research also points to the problematic legacy of Latinidad, its fraught relationship to Indigeneity and Blackness, and how it limits decolonial claims for these artworks.

The artists in this book stage an avant-garde to break with a modern tradition in Western thought that valued prints for their role in picturing and spreading knowledge production. While many academics employ the term "avant-garde" to refer to the most advanced, experimental, and provocative art of the moment, it is worth clarifying its use in art history as it highlights the stakes of the book's argument. The German critic Peter Bürger conceived of the concept in relation to the European historical avant-gardes, such as Dadaism and Surrealism, which called into question the institution of art and its privileging of aesthetic autonomy.[3] By "institution of art," Bürger meant the entire ecosystem of art, which includes galleries, museums, critics, and dealers. When these institutions embraced these works and canonized them into the pantheon of great art, Bürger read the avant-garde's attack as a failure. However, many scholars of Latin American art such as Jacqueline Barnitz, Andrea Giunta, and Gina McDaniel Tarver have shown that avant-garde and neo-avant-garde movements can thrive even while being embraced by institutions. In fact, at times, it is the institutions that create the conditions for experimental practices to flourish. This book shows how these print networks took on the role of fostering experimental print practices and encouraging political dissent.

The work of these artists recalls the Mexican avant-garde of the 1920s, a state-sponsored movement that promoted using public art, particularly muralism, to help create a national identity. Mexican artists like Diego Rivera and José Clemente Orozco adopted the Italian Renaissance technique of fresco painting popularized in the sixteenth century, but rather than using it to portray religious themes, they painted their country's history, and many of their murals became iconic manifestations of Mexicanidad. The artists in this book similarly reinvent the age-old medium of printmaking with the aims of representing their history and their struggles to define a collective identity as part of the Latinx diasporas in the United States. They do so largely without external or state-sponsored institutional support, though despite their anti-establishment practices, their graphic art has entered museum collections, as I will discuss further in the conclusion of the book. *Reclaiming the Americas* shows how these artists take on print culture's darker histories, exposing printmaking's complicity in distributing the spatial logics of colonization and revealing its pervasive Eurocentric views of land, which undergird contemporary forms of xenophobia and anti-immigrant policies.

This trend of reclaiming a medium used to inflict and justify colonial violence has been documented more closely in fields like photography. "As a new visual medium in the late nineteenth century, photography had been both witness to and agent of this process, mapping empire onto newly acquired territories by depicting Western lands as alluring, available, and—importantly—empty," writes curator Amy Scott.[4] Her study of photographic archives from *La Raza* magazine evinced the use of the camera to expose the "spatial dispossession that was inherent in the development of Western lands, from the wilderness of Yosemite to the barrios of East Los Angeles."[5] Similarly, Macarena Gómez-Barris has analyzed the photographic archive of Laura Aguilar and how she employed the mode of self-portraiture, using her mixed-race body to block the empty line of sight normalized in nineteenth-century landscape photography.[6] Ken Gonzales-Day's research on the history of lynching and its representations in photography also linked the spectacle of lynching Mexicans—and photographing their fragmented bodies—to the colonial enterprise that justified westward expansion.[7] But oddly enough, these kinds of connections have not been made in the case of printmaking, even though its history is far longer than photography's and more closely aligned with visualizing colonial territories and colonized peoples.

While many of the artists in this book critique the use of printmaking for the visualization of empire, they embrace the traditions of picturing knowledge production from the history of art of the Ancient Americas. The screenfold books known as codices from the Aztec, Maya, and Mixtec cultures recorded calendrical, religious, geographical, astronomical, and genealogical information, revealing the vast extent of Indigenous knowledge systems. The artist Enrique Chagoya laments their loss by noting: "Perhaps the most serious consequence of the war of conquest in Mexico, in terms of cultural destruction, was the burning of pre-Hispanic books and, even worse, the loss of the possibility to read, in their full richness, the few books that survived."[8] Though very few of these precolonial manuscripts survived the burning of books during the early years of the conquest, and the extant originals remain primarily in European collections, they constitute another important touchstone for Latinx artists in their search for alternative conceptualizations of territoriality. Furthermore, the colonial-era books and manuscripts, such as the Boturini and Mendoza codices, and the maps of the *Relaciones Geográficas*, which show hybrid forms of visualizing territory, are especially important sources that will be invoked in works analyzed in this book.[9]

The print workshops featured in this study emerged within what Trudy Hansen called the "golden age of the collaborative press movement in the US."[10] Between 1960 and 1990, more than three hundred graphic-art workshops transformed the landscape of contemporary art and revived printing traditions that were to some extent in danger of being lost because of the erosion of technical knowledge of these artforms. While the gendered hierarchy of art mediums still placed painting and sculpture as the pinnacle of high art, these craft-based forms of art making, which required intense collaboration and experimentation, changed notions of authorship and challenged the myth of the individual artist genius. Moreover, they were significant entry points into the art world for women and artists of color.

When the Italian American ordained nun Sister Karen Boccalero returned to her hometown of Boyle Heights and teamed up with the artistic and romantic duo Carlos Bueno and Antonio Ibañez, recent immigrants from Mexico, they envisioned an art workshop that could uphold their values of dignity for all, a preferential option for the poor, and pride in ethnic heritage. Self Help Graphics & Art began in a small garage at the height of the Chicano Movement in East Los Angeles. By 1973, the group had officially incorporated and received nonprofit status. Their widely popular art courses expanded through outreach initiatives like their annual Día de los Muertos celebration and the Barrio Mobile Art Studio, which brought art education to underserved schools. Ten years later, they launched one of the most successful printmaking residency programs in the country, still currently active, and began training hundreds of artists in the fine art of screenprinting; many of these artists have gone on to found their own workshops. Boccalero had studied printmaking with Sister Corita Kent at Immaculate Heart College and further specialized in the medium after training under Romas Viesulas at the Tyler School of Art's Rome Program. She viewed the professional printmaking program as critical to the advancement of Latinx artists in the region in order to further their careers and create modes of economic viability. While this workshop emerged within the protest politics and activist-centered mobilizations of the Chicano Movement, their printmaking program remained committed to upholding artistic freedom. Some of the biggest names of the Chicanx art canon have produced limited editions there, including Carlos Almaraz, Judy Baca, Chaz Bojorquez, Barbara Carrasco, Malaquias Montoya, Gronk, Frank Romero, and Patssi Valdez, to name just a few, and their diverse art practices attest to the organization's ethos. Formal experimentation was requisite for these artists, but political engagement was also not discouraged, as it was for their counterparts at Cirrus and Gemini GEL.

Around the time that Self Help Graphics was laying the groundwork for their Experimental Silkscreen Atelier Program, Joe Segura, a master printer trained at the Tamarind Institute, was also designing a workshop and residency program for underrepresented artists left out of the midcentury print boom in the desert town of Tempe, Arizona.[11] Arizona State University, Tempe, recruited Segura to develop a print-research facility, where he collaborated with the book artist John Risseeuw and photographer Mark Klett in reviving nineteenth-century printing processes and invited artists to come for residencies. Segura described the significance of that facility by noting: "Artists who came in were told they had the freedom to fail. So they could practice, and they could play. They were allowed to do things they had never been able to do because it hadn't been financially viable. That was another form of research. We called their investigations into media 'research.'"[12] Through his experiences in the academy and his training in the collaborative press movement, Segura noticed that Latinx, Latin American, and Southwest-based artists were not being supported by publishers. He, along with his then-spouse, Lisa Sette, opened Segura Publishing Company in 1981.[13] Their business model—both publisher and gallerist—avoided some of the limitations of nonprofit grant funding, and followed paths already established by master printers such as Kathan Brown at Crown Point Press in San Francisco. Their exclusive residency program, with access to highly technical master printers and equipment, soon included Latinx artists like the late Luis Jiménez, Luis Cruz Azaceta, and Claudia Bernardi and would eventually include canonical American artists such as Faith Ringgold, James Turrell, and Carrie Mae Weems.

While Self Help and Segura may have developed in what are primarily Mexican American communities of the Southwest, by the 1990s they were operating within inclusive models that favored racially diverse rosters of artists. Similarly, Coronado Studio emerged out of the collaborative press movement in Central Texas and an awareness of the way that "mainstream" print studios reproduced exclusionary practices. The studio's late founder and director Sam Coronado, a graduate of the University of Texas at Austin, had participated in two residencies at Self Help Graphics. He converted his painting studio into a fine-art screenprint shop in 1991, which took the name Coronado Studio and operated as a small business publisher and for-contract press that one could hire for printing. Two years later, Coronado founded a residency program named Serie Project, which eventually incorporated into a nonprofit. The program was active for twenty years, hosting over 250 (mostly Latinx) artists. For practitioners in the region, Coronado Studio became an important location to produce fine-art limited editions but also to debate life in the borderlands.

One of Coronado Studio's early master printers, the Dominican artist Pepe Coronado (no relation to Sam), would eventually move to New York and adapt these models for another context. His experiences printing in collaborative workshops and borderland communities led him to imagine that such a space was possible for the work of Dominican American artists in New York. Dominican diaspora artists decided to reclaim the pejorative label of "Dominican York" (once synonymous with an underclass) to describe the liminal space or island borderland they inhabit between the island of Hispaniola and the island of Manhattan.[14] They took up the name Dominican York Proyecto Gráfica (DYPG). Rather than establishing a brick-and-mortar workshop such as their predecessors had done, the group remained a loose organization with individual artists contributing toward themed portfolios using various printmaking techniques.[15] These print archives from Self Help Graphics, Segura, Coronado, and DYPG form the basis of this art-historical study connecting various interethnic artist networks that provide a larger picture of the Latinx printmaking field at large.

In what follows, I evaluate current debates on the new, still-emerging category of Latinx art, as it is quickly becoming the next frontier in acquisitions for mainstream institutions. My research shows how graphic-art production in workshop settings brought artists of different Latinx ethnic groups together and how the rise in anti-immigrant sentiment politically united these groups. These diverse artists and studios signal a new cognitive map for Latinx art, one based on pan-ethnic comparative scholarship or relational Latinidades that involve multiple Latinx ethnic groups. Moreover, I critique this field's resistance paradigm, which celebrated in uncritical ways what are far more nuanced and complicated artworks. This makes for a more interesting view of these relational print archives without denying their relevance in the art world or the counter-public spheres they produce. Through a discussion of print history and its visualization of territory, I return to the central premise of this book: that reclaiming the Americas has been a long-standing political project central to Latinx art. I likewise introduce my theoretical framework, which connects borderland theory, Critical Latinx Indigeneities, and decolonial aesthetics as lenses that allow readers to see these works as part of a broader intellectual history in the art of the Americas. These interventions will hopefully change how scholars, curators, and critics think about Latinx art and the complex politics of territory that inform the political subjectivities of the largest and fastest-growing minority in the United States.

LATINX ART

Latinx art is an operative construct that allows scholars, critics, and curators the ability to name, classify, and group the heterogeneous practices of artists of Latin American descent living and working in the United States.[16] The category is an umbrella term that brings together multiple diasporic art canons such as Chicano/a, Puerto Rican, Cuban American, Dominican American, and Central American–American. Chronologically, these separate art canons began their formation in the 1960s at the height of the US civil-rights movement and evolved into a more plural construct by the 1990s through mutual recognition. There is no one artistic style associated with the term, and the disciplinary range of projects varies from traditional painting and sculpture to video and digital media. The heterogeneity of the construct speaks to the diverse national origins, racial identities, class backgrounds, and shared experiences of living in the US.

As a pan-ethnic and diasporic category, the term "Latinx" speaks to the dramatic demographic shifts that took place after World War II in US cities like Chicago, Los Angeles, San Francisco, New York, Miami, and Washington, DC.[17] The combination of economic precarity, rise in authoritarianism, and US intervention during the Cold War gave way to increased migration from Latin America, even as a quota system instituted by the US government in 1965 created a problem of "illegality" for many immigrants.[18] As of the 2020 census, the Latinx population had reached a record sixty-two million, a 23 percent increase since 2010, making it the second-largest ethno-racial group in the US. But despite this growth, the Latinx population remains largely understudied in academic discourse, particularly from a humanities standpoint. Part of the challenge comes from the vast heterogeneity that constitutes this group: from the two dozen national-origin countries to the countless Indigenous languages kept alive, the variety of religious practices ranging from Catholic and Evangelical to Santería, the broadest possible spectrum of racial self-identifications, as well as the complexities of being immigrant, native-born, or multiple-generation American. By focusing on the art and cultural production of Latinx artists, I touch on various aspects of this diasporic formation that brought artists of different backgrounds into the space of printmaking workshops. Although the term only gained traction in the academy and activist circles in the last ten years, and some may object to its use for art that predates the term, the -x in "Latinx" speaks to the inclusive politics of gender neutrality espoused by younger generations invested in challenging the colonial gendering of the Spanish language. This is not about being elitist or trendy but about aligning with a particular set of values. Charlene Villaseñor Black and Emily Engel, the editors to the field's flagship journal *Latin American and Latinx Visual Culture*, explain that Latinx "draws our attention to the complexities of race and ethnicity in the twenty-first century Western Hemisphere, questions the persistence of Eurocentric ideological belief systems, confronts cultural erasure, and suggests the possibilities of border-crossing perceptual practices."[19] The artists in this study have different forms of self-identification based on their national-origin groups, yet reading their work through this categorical lens shows how they have deliberately worked in tandem to envision a collective future for Latinx art.

One of the catalysts for this sense of shared experience is the continued rise of xenophobic nationalism in the US. Although many of the artists discussed in this study are second- or third-generation American, or they were born in Latin America and have lived most of their lives in the US, they are consistently perceived as foreign in a Black-white national racial imaginary. The fear of Latinx foreignness is often expressed through economic and pathologizing terms: immigrants are taking jobs, using needed public resources, bringing drugs or crime. But these ideas, which turn into discriminatory behaviors, are codified through legal policies that favor native white inhabitants or nativism. Anti-immigrant policies and xenophobic hate speech have made Latinx communities a target of suspicion, surveillance, and ultimately unbelonging. These policies include the militarization of the border, the internal deployment of Immigration and Customs Enforcement, the racial profiling of brownness, the expansion of deportation mechanisms, and the mass detention of families and unaccompanied children seeking asylum. The 2019 El Paso Walmart mass shooting by a white supremacist stands out as an extreme expression of this immigrant phobia, but the casual racism of xenophobia is embedded into everyday conversations, such as the political theater surrounding the construction of a border wall. Social scientists and immigration historians have eagerly documented how these ideological apparatuses, which are on the rise today, have a long, drawn-out history in the US.[20] My intervention from a humanities viewpoint is to consider how this continued sense of exclusion motivated artists to unite their efforts against this fear of the foreigner and to show how prints became an ideal way to debate the colonial origins of this hatred.

As the largest subgroup within Latinx art, Chicanx artists have led the way in framing this resistant discourse against anti-immigrant sentiment. Their geographic, familial, and bicultural experiences are intimately linked to the US-Mexico border region, but in a racist white society that very border has been weaponized to question their worthiness of citizenship and belonging. The roots of anti-Mexican sentiments telescope back to nineteenth-century frontier violence, as well as xenophobic policies that enacted the repatriation of almost two million Mexican Americans during the Great Depression.[21] The art historian Jennifer González notes, "The border is not merely a physical marker or a geographical zone of contention and contact, it is a psychological condition of double-consciousness."[22] This internal conflict of being seen as marginal, subordinate, or as an other has led many Chicanx artists to theorize about their relationship to the borderlands as contested and mythical geographies, theoretical positions that I will return to later in this introduction. Their standpoint of critical engagement with visions of the border and immigration politics has likewise inspired other Latinx and Indigenous artists to raise their voices, especially as communities from the Caribbean and Central and South America become targets of a "deportation machine."[23]

The second-largest subgroup within Latinx art is the art of the Puerto Rican diaspora, known as Nuyoricans or Diasporicans. Cities like New York, Chicago, and Philadelphia were transformed by the Puerto Rican presence and the development of robust Puerto Rican art and cultural centers.[24] As a US territory under colonial control since the Spanish-American War of 1898, the island of Puerto Rico and its cultural production occupies a gray zone: it has a distinct Spanish-speaking, Latin American identity, and yet is coercively annexed to the political economy of the US. The island's industrialization in the 1940s, known as Operation Bootstrap, gave way to mass migration to US cities in search of work, a process aided by the fact that Puerto Ricans were granted US citizenship through the Jones Act of 1917.[25] Their growing politicization in the 1960s as twice-displaced migrant workers, first from their island homeland and then by the collapse of American manufacturing, inspired the parallel claim shared by Chicanos as the internal-colony thesis—a way to view their racial oppression as a consequence of US imperialism.[26] These are the political roots of Latinx art, as the field developed out of this shared resistance; its historiography can be traced in the development of Ethnic Studies and effectively documented in journals such as *Aztlán*, *Centro Journal*, and *Revista Chicano-Riqueña*.

The history of Latinx printmaking began with these two ethnic groups in the late 1960s and early 1970s. Their efforts have been historicized in the realm of exhibitions: *The Role of Paper: Affirmation and Identity in Chicano and Boricua Art* (1999), *Pressing the Point: Parallel Expressions in the Graphic Arts of the Chicano and Puerto Rican Movements* (1999), *Just Another Poster? Chicano Graphics Arts in California* (2001), *Poly/Graphic San Juan Triennial* (2004), *Estampas de La Raza: Contemporary Prints from the Romo Collection* (2012), and most recently the monumental *¡Printing the Revolution! The Rise and Impact of Chicano Graphics, 1965 to Now* (2020). These curatorial projects and associated scholarship have generated critical acclaim for artists, urgently needed art criticism, and, at times, museum acquisitions. In their efforts to map the field and its various genealogies, scholars have established the connections between the medium of printing and Latinx social movements, or what George Lipsitz calls "art-based community making."[27] They have also emphasized printmaking's radical potential to resist dominant and assimilationist paradigms through creative use of reproduction technologies that fomented cultural nationalism, feminist formations, and political viewpoints like the US Third World Left when activists of color adopted and fought for the anticolonial struggles of Third World nations.[28] My work builds on this scholarship but also differs in a number of ways.

First, printmaking is one of the most avant-garde mediums for Latinx artists, but in existing scholarship writers fail to note this, or at times actively refuse that framework.[29] Printshops were creative laboratories where artists proclaimed positions on social issues but also did what artists do: experiment, imagine, lay claim to art histories, compete with peers, and critique what came before them. For most scholars, myself included, the tendency thus far has been to emphasize these artists' central role in social movements and identity-formation processes, and to avoid looking closely at their formal interventions, associated styles, technical processes, and witty art-historical allusions. This problem is in part owed to the fact that so few Latinx art scholars have been able to train in the discipline of art history, which remains one of the most staunchly Eurocentric fields, unwelcoming to the study of artists from racialized groups.[30]

But in a more self-critical assessment, the political roots of Latinx art, which can be traced back to the Chicanx and Puerto Rican cultural-nationalist movements of the 1960s, have created dogmatic positions and binaries (art for the people vs. art for art's sake) that favor Marxist and identitarian readings, the two main analytical frameworks for Latinx art. For example, the art historian Guisela Latorre, in her reading of Chicanx Indigenist murals, noted how this movement contested modernism and "diametrically opposed . . . the prevailing discourses and practices surrounding the visual arts in the field of art history," including its periodization and primitivist colonialist rhetoric; yet she insisted that the artists' primary opposition was to viewing art as separate from everyday life, which was also the goal of the historical avant-gardes: to question the autonomy of art in bourgeois society.[31] These positions are understandable considering how much art-world racism has hurt and devalued the legitimacy of Latinx art. But when scholars writing on this work operate outside the frameworks of art history, they obscure and limit the exposure of artists working in a global contemporary art field. This book presents artists working in the medium of printmaking, who are taking great risks, experimenting with formal innovation, conversant with American and Latin American artists, and proclaiming positions on social justice. Like most contemporary artists, they are multidisciplinary and shift to different mediums depending on their concept and intended audience. Therefore, I do not isolate their work solely within this medium, instead drawing thematic comparisons to show how printmaking leads the way in the greater field of contemporary art.

Further, these exhibitions have created the illusion that workshops were strictly divided along national identity lines. But since their emergence in the 1970s, Latinx printmaking workshops have fostered interethnic and cross-racial artist networks. Mary Thomas documents the coalitional work that took place between African American, Asian American, and Chicanx artists from the early days of Self Help Graphics.[32] In Northern California, La Raza Silkscreen Center in San Francisco's Mission District fostered a pan-Latinx space; Pete Gallegos, Linda Lucero, Oscar Melara, and Herbert Sigüenza's roots are in Mexican American and Central American families, but their community-based print projects were intertwined with many other cultural organizations in the Bay Area, including the Kearny Street Workshop led by Asian American artists in San Francisco's Chinatown/Manilatown neighborhood.[33] These networks varied by location. The printshop Taller Puertorriqueño in Philadelphia was a Diasporican stronghold, owing to their community's more isolated position, but they shared resources and collaborated with African American artists at the Brandywine Workshop.[34]

I use the Latinx art construct to draw attention to the rich printmaking traditions of this particular field, which continue to be excluded from or only marginally seen in American and Latin American art exhibitions and publications. Their exclusion from these fields is not only a matter of scholars writing about them in an ethnic silo but is largely a result of the dynamics of US art-world racism, which often renders their work marginal or foreign.[35] Reflecting on this omission, the curator Carmen Ramos noted, "the term 'Latino art' [is] not a sign of cultural essence but an indicator of descent, shared experience, and art historical marginalization."[36] These exclusions take many forms, as curator Chon Noriega points out in regard to the most established subfield of the construct, "more than anything else, the term [Chicano art] effectively describes the art and artists left out of public exhibition, permanent collections, critical discourse, and canon formation."[37] Arlene Dávila's recent *Latinx Art* highlights how much of this is rooted in a political economy based on racial capitalism: "These issues are reinforced by the highly segregated and exclusive worlds of the market (art galleries, art fairs and auctions, and mainstream museums) dominated by white stakeholders, white Latinxs, and white-identified Latin American migrants from middle-class and upwardly mobile backgrounds."[38] One may assume that this connection to Latin American heritage would automatically grant entry to the larger and more established field of Latin American art, but that is rarely the case. Unless the artists possess strong ties to the Latin American cultural infrastructure based on class origins and what Dávila calls "national privilege," they will be excluded from active participation.[39]

Only more recently, in the exhibition arena, has there been more effort into placing Latinx and Latin American art in conversation. Latin American art is a geopolitical construct that arose from the imperial designs of Europe, and its vast heterogeneity speaks to the more than twenty nation-states, languages, races, religions, colonial histories, and US interventions that it purports to represent. Latinx art also speaks to heterogeneity in its effort to encompass multiple diasporic art canons. Many scholars view them as indistinct or as interrelated double-helix structures intertwined on a common axis. But that axis seems fleeting when we compare the uneven development of cultural infrastructure (galleries, museums, dealers, collectors), historiography, and visibility. As the recent volume by Alejandro Anreus, Robin Adèle Greeley, and Megan Sullivan makes clear, the relationship between these categories can be fraught, since their cultural imaginaries can differ greatly depending on the local context.[40] Despite the fact that these are imperfect, unstable categories, they reiterate how they serve a strategic purpose to differentiate the work of these artists from European and US mainstream art practices but also to claim space within an increasingly globalized art world. In the introduction to their thematic exhibition *Home—So Different, So Appealing* (2017), curators Mari Carmen Ramírez, Pilar Tompkins Rivas, and Chon Noriega observed how the categories of Latinx and Latin American art tend to be "treated as distinct," with Latinx being positioned in a "derivative relation" to Latin American art.[41] While they may share commonalities, including an anticolonial stance, Latinx art does not grow out of a Latin American context and should therefore not be considered a derivation.

Unfortunately, that has also been the case with printmaking. Scholars such as Shifra Goldman, Tere Romo, Carol Wells, and Lyle Williams trace the roots of Latinx printmaking to the longer and more established history of the medium in Mexico, Cuba, and Puerto Rico, where printmaking centers often operated with full government support.[42] However, little work has been done to document the synchronicities, collaborations, and back-and-forth that has made this field a hemispheric print network. Among these early collaborations, the first Mexican American artist to achieve the title of Master Printer at Tamarind was Ernest de Soto (1923–2014). Based in San Francisco, he cofounded Collectors Press Lithography in 1967 and opened his own workshop, The Ernest F. De Soto Workshop, in 1975. The De Soto Workshop collaborated with a number of prominent artists, including the Mexican artist José Luis Cuevas, and Costa Rican–Mexican artist Francisco Zuñiga, as well as Chicano artists Rupert García and Luis Jiménez.[43] The members of Mexico City's Grupo 65 (Arnulfo Aquino Casas, Rebeca Hidalgo, and Melecio Galván) spent almost a year in residency at La Raza Silkscreen Center and created prints such as *The Unforgettable Guerrilla Tania* (1972).[44] Not only is there a tendency to ignore how Latinx art workshops have supported American and Latin American artists, prevailing scholarship emphasizes the derivate position of Latinx artists who appropriate or visually quote Latin American art. One of these prominent cases is the Mexican artist Adolfo Mexiac. His linocut *Libertad de Expresión* (1954), which was popularized and reissued during the 1968 student movement in Mexico, inspired Chicano artist Rodolfo "Rudy" Cuellar to appropriate the padlocked figure for his bicentennial poster, *Humor in Xhicano Arte 200 Years of Oppression 1776–1976* (1976), which was recently shown in *¡Printing the Revolution!* Curators often fail to mention Mexiac's relationship with Chicanx artists, which began in the 1970s as he traveled to Austin at the invitation of Sylvia Orozco and the Mujeres Artistas del Suroeste, leading Mexiac to hold printmaking residencies and exhibitions in Texas.[45]

Furthermore, Ramírez, Tompkins Rivas, and Noriega consider the Latin American and Latinx art categories, one pan-ethnic and the other pan-national, "aesthetic and cultural fictions," and that the overreliance on them produces reductive readings of works of art. For this reason, each of my chapters follows a close reading methodology, urging the reader to focus on one object (or a particular portfolio) from multiple vantage points to see its formal and experimental qualities. However, a strictly formalist or universalist approach outside these categorical constructs would negate how much of these works hinge on social history and territorial claims linked to identity and geopolitics.

Close readings combined with social history also reveal the problematic legacy of Latinidad, including its fraught relationship with Indigeneity and Blackness. The historical development of Latinidad can be traced back to the nineteenth century, when France exported its concept of *latinité* to the fledgling new republics of South America in an effort to subvert US influence in the region. The Creole elite of Spanish and Portuguese descent embraced their postcolonial identity of Latinidad, which pan-ethnically and pan-nationally tied them to a Roman Catholic European tradition that differed from the Anglo-Saxon Protestant origins of the US. As Walter Mignolo explains, this created a new racial order: "The local creole elite translated the principle into a de facto social differentiation between Spanish Creoles on top, Mestizos/as and Mulattos/as in the next social group down, and Indios, Zambos, and Negroes at the bottom of the pyramid."[46] As a consequence, the end of external colonialism signaled the beginning of an internal colonialism that would continue to marginalize Indigenous and Black subjects in Latin America, as well as their diasporic Latinx counterparts in the US.

In their search for national identities, Latin American nation-states embraced Latinidad's desire for mestizaje, the racial mixture or "cosmic race" as espoused by the Mexican theorist José Vasconcelos, that would promote interracial marriage and procreation to counter the premise of racial purity in Europe and the US. However, much of the focus in Latin America was on combining Indigenous and European races to whiten the national makeup, while disavowing the African presence. As the art historian Tatiana Flores has argued, Latinidad enabled an instrumentalization of mestizaje giving way to anti-Black racism and the idea that Latin America's racial mixing erased the existence of racism, all the while upholding white supremacy.[47] She cited Alan Pelaez Lopez's digital campaign "Latinidad Is Canceled" as an emblematic performance in this time of racial reckoning that actively questioned Black and Indigenous erasure. Flores's comparative and hemispheric approach to Latinidad likewise elucidates how race is not fixed in Latin America: it is contingent on class, as opposed to the "one-drop rule" in the US, which makes anyone with known African ancestry Black.[48] These pervasive and complex notions of race are acutely felt by Latinx artists who remain at the crux of these racial geographies.

In the US context, Latinidad is understood as a "sociohistorical process whereby various Latin American national-origin groups are understood as sharing a sense of collective identity and cultural consciousness."[49] But as the political theorist Cristina Beltrán points out, this leads to homogenizing tendencies in the shorthand use of "Latinx" and "Hispanic" and the presumption of a shared politics for a population whose heterogeneity (race, class, language, immigration status) cannot be subsumed into a monolithic political viewpoint.[50] How else to explain that in a climate of growing xenophobia, some Latinxs voted for Proposition 187, which barred undocumented immigrants from accessing public services, and twenty years later helped elect the xenophobic forty-fifth president of the United States. According to Beltrán, the assumption of Latinidad as a unified political category obscures the historical and discursive construction of Latinx identity and forecloses its potential to be a site of inclusion and contestation.[51]

Mestizaje underwent a process of resignification for the doubly racialized Latinx artist. For the two major groups that initiated the Latinx paradigm, Chicanos and Puerto Ricans, mestizaje was a political tool uniting diverse people under the banner of cultural nationalism, distinguishing them racially from the myth of racial purity in the US and providing ancestral claims to land vis-à-vis their Indigenous heritage. The revival of Indigenous art from Mexico and Puerto Rico that took shape in the Latinx art of the 1970s was a reaction to the overt forms of racism and the limited political rights Latinxs experienced. Moreover, postmodern and queer writers of color like Gloria Anzaldúa theorized border subjectivity and "new mestiza consciousness" as the liminal spaces of racial, gender, sexual, and linguistic difference.[52] María Josefina Saldaña-Portillo has eloquently argued that mestizaje offered a sense of reparation to deal with the "psychic pain of racism and [territorial] loss" but its romanticized appropriation of Indigeneity required the erasure of living Indigenous people.[53] While mestizaje and Indigeneity were often invoked for

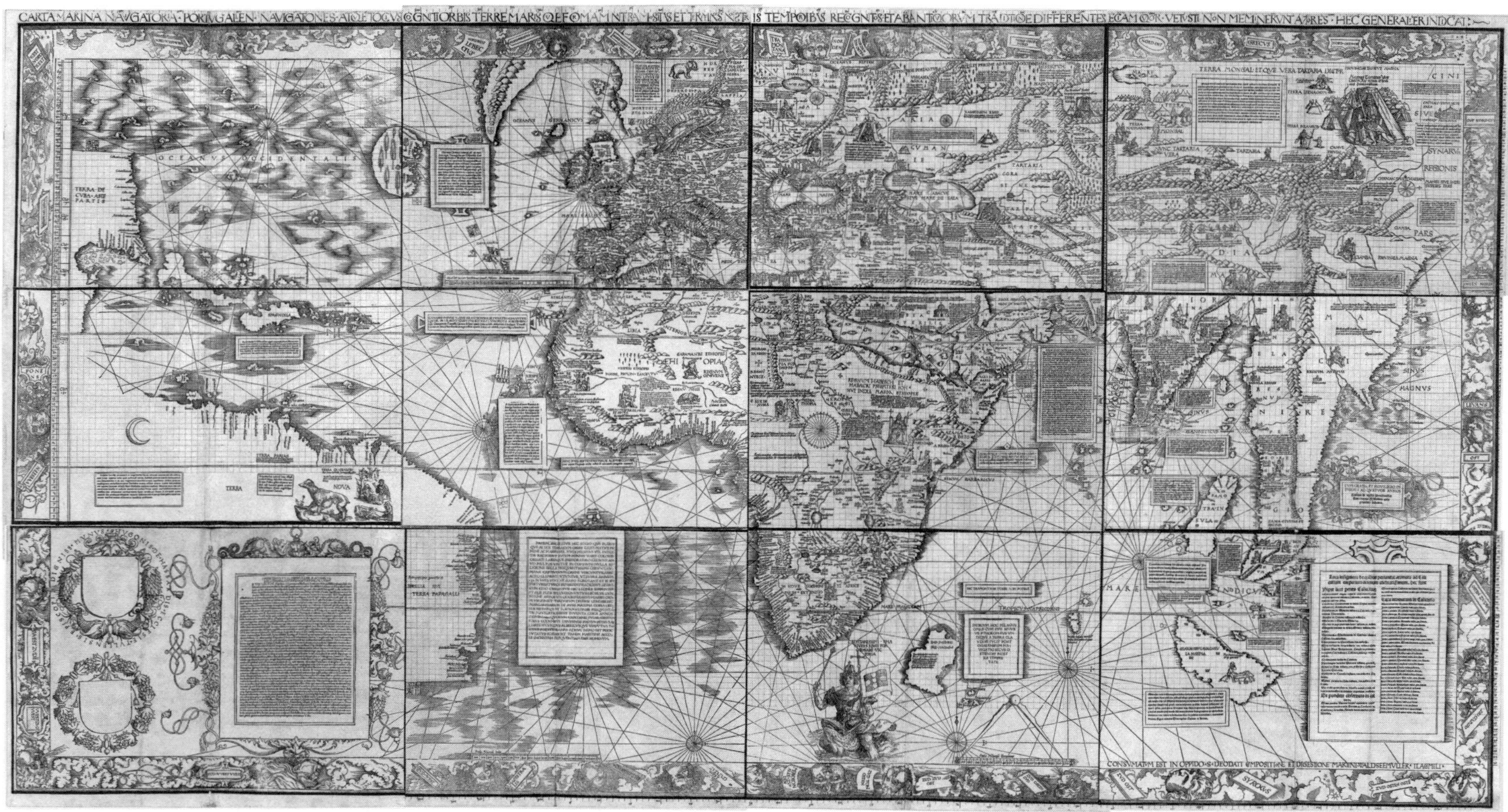

0.2. Martin Waldseemüller, *Carta Marina*, 1516. One map on twelve sheets, Jay I. Kislak Collection, Library of Congress.

their political utility in claiming sovereignty and promoting decolonization, they engaged in reactionary forms of colonial thinking that often reproduced the settler colonial logic of the vanishing Indian. These paradoxical positions will be further explored in this book as Latinx artists are de-indigenized, detribalized mestizo/a peoples unable to claim tribal affiliation or nationhood.

PICTURING THE POLITICS OF TERRITORY

Print culture became a battleground where artists wrestled with these forms of unbelonging and began creating their own narratives on the politics of territory. The interest and popularity of prints in representations of land intentionally invoked their use in early-modern Europe. During the conquest, Europeans harnessed the power of print reproduction for the making of maps and atlases that would diffuse knowledge of these New World "discoveries." Exhibitions such as *Prints and the Pursuit of Knowledge in Early Modern Europe* (2011) have shown how these cartographic projects were critical for scientific and imperial exploration, tools of persuasion that announced "discoveries," even though at times they contained inaccurate information.[54] The critic José Rabasa studied the rhetoric of these cultural products from the colonial period and argued that this new way of writing the world invented America. In the case of early-modern geographic manuscripts, maps and atlases foregrounded the secularism of science and introduced ways of seeing that became pervasive to modern conceptions of space disguised as universal, but ultimately projecting a Eurocentric viewpoint.[55] Thus when Latinx artists returned to this medium five hundred years after the conquest, they were showing how this technology was complicit in diffusing the spatial logics of colonization, as well as how it could be taken back, to reclaim the lands of the Americas as belonging to Indigenous, migrant, mestiza/o, and Afrodescendant peoples.

Martin Waldseemüller's 1516 Carta Marina, one of the earliest nautical maps of the globe, shows the most up-to-date knowledge of America's eastern seaboard at the time, while the interior of South America remains largely unknown (fig. 0.2). But rather than leave the unknown unmarked, Waldseemüller indulged in representing the travel narratives of explorers who were astonished by the sight of new animals and frightened by the practices of Indigenous peoples. He depicted an opossum—the earliest surviving European image of the creature—and titled the area "Terra Cannibalorum." The translated legend reads, "Land of Cannibals those who inhabit this land are maneaters."[56] The scale of the opossum dwarfs the size of three Natives in plumed attire who sit by a fire. The female subject bites down on an appendage, while a standing figure gestures toward the tree branches overhead, where these cannibals presumably dry human body parts. A third subject roasts the human flesh over an open flame. The large text block on the bottom right of the map tells us that one thousand copies were printed, though that number seems high, considering that only one copy remains in existence and is housed in the Library of Congress.[57] But as Waldseemüller was the most significant cartographer of the early sixteenth century, his cartographic work would influence many of the representations that followed, from Lorenz Fries to Gerhard Mercator and onward.[58]

The artists in this study employ four different approaches to delinking from Western conceptions of territory. If the West viewed land in economic terms, and that land was inhabited by those they deemed savage and racially inferior, Latinx artists have invoked those subject positions through a deployment of Indigeneity, embodiment, and racial mixing. *Native territorialities* is perhaps the most common of these approaches and draws from the Indigenous heritage of Latinx artists. Most artists of Latin American descent possess ties, and some would argue direct bloodlines, to Native cultures, and yet that connection has been obscured over time or denigrated through racialization. The Bay Area poster artist Jesus Barraza explains in his writing, "As Xicana Indigena people, we have been able to recover some of what was lost over the centuries, we are people living in diaspora who have been detribalized and deterritorialized searching for our origins."[59] From this position, Latinx artists enunciate other ways of seeing that confront hidden processes that invented Europe's discovery of the New World. But these enunciations and images can at times negate the claims to ancestral lands and the living presence of contemporary Native American groups.[60]

Embodied territorialities is another approach that these artists use to confront Western conceptions of territory. While the Western cartographic gaze often depends on disembodiment, and erasing the hand of the artist/creator, these artists stress embodiment from the position of the border dweller. They work to articulate other ways of conceiving land through our senses that diverge from male Eurocentric subjectivity. *Mestiza territorialities* is an option that invokes land rights and belonging for those racially mixed subjects (African, European, and Indigenous) who are the progeny of colonial violence. These racial mixtures are undeniable for most Latinx artists and yet one must also contend with the ideological roots of mestizaje. Its use in Latin American nationalisms (and their myths about racial democracies) served to erase the African and Indigenous presence in favor of a mixed race that could eradicate these other, less-regarded lineages. Finally, I consider *Aqueous territorial-*

ities from the position of Caribbean diaspora artists, who like the border subject recode geographic representations from the view of island dwellers who experience water boundaries. I point to a recurring use of water imagery as a space likewise loaded with Western cartography's colonial gaze, mediating the painful entry and exit of islanders, witness to the whims of repeated US intervention, and yet uncontainable and largely unmappable.

The woodcut by Dalila Paola Mendez that opened this introduction employs these methods of counter-cartography. Indigenous territorialities appear to be summoned in *Corazón de la Tierra* through powerful iconographies such as the *oztotl* cave glyph and Taíno symbology. Mendez's family is of African, European, Lenca, and Maya ancestry, making her allusions to Indigeneity less an appropriation and more of a reclamation in regard to a Central American mestizaje that shuns its Black and Indigenous heritage.[61] The allusion to the cave as a sacred center speaks to the Mesoamerican history of ritual cave use, sites that acted as portals to the underworld. In extant codices, caves could take the form of mouths or uteruses, sometimes with monstrous qualities that spoke of their divine agency. For a queer, Brown, Central American diaspora artist, these image histories also demand that artists take back the power of women that has been usurped by what the late philosopher María Lugones called the "coloniality of gender." The fusion of map and female figure references this embodiment, as well as the history of displacement and dispossession that her family carries forward. Yemaya, the mother of all Yoruba deities known as Orishas, in the symbol of the cowrie shell enacts the aqueous territorialities of island subjects who call upon the patroness that protects them in open waters.

These interventions are significant in their ability to pierce through dominant visual narratives that continue to promote Eurocentric conceptions of territorial discovery. The 2020 exhibition at the Newberry Library, *Renaissance Invention: Stradanus's Nova Reperta*, astoundingly repeated this scenario of discovery, even while conceding that war, exploration, and colonization drove the technological advancements of early-modern Europe.[62] The exhibition brought some of these issues to life through the incorporation of material objects such as armor, astrolabes, armillary spheres, glass lenses, and cannons, but the centerpiece was the influential and widely disseminated print series *Nova Reperta* (New Discoveries, or New Inventions of Modern Times) designed by Johannes Stradanus in Florence and printed in Antwerp by the Dutch engraver Philips Galle (and his son Theodoor Galle) circa 1588. The series alludes to the numerous "inventions" that transformed European cultural values: America, the compass, gunpowder, the printing press, the clock, guaiacum, distillation, silk, and stirrups (fig. 0.3).

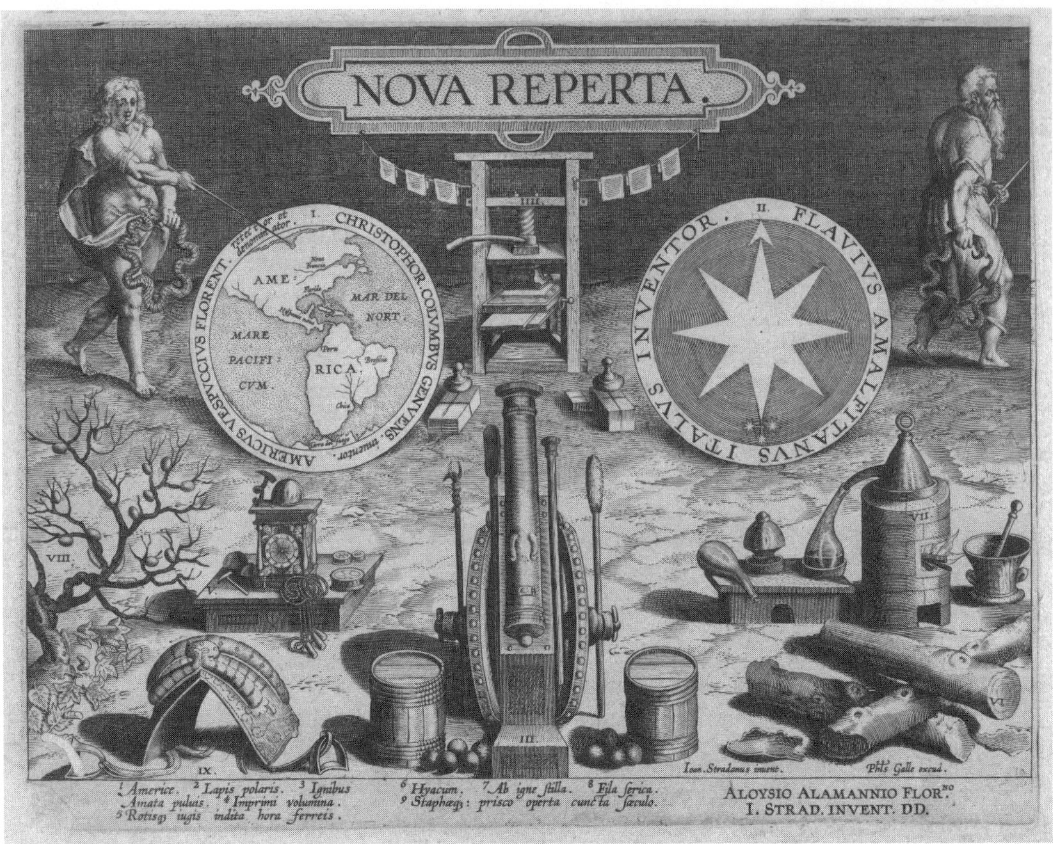

0.3. Philips Galle, after Jan van der Straet (Johannes Stradanus), frontispiece to *Nova Reperta*, ca. 1588. Engraving, Newberry Library, Chicago, VAULT Case Wing, Folio Z 412.85.

In one of the last articles published by Ernst Gombrich, the renowned art historian admitted that most of the inventions touted in the *Nova Reperta* came from elsewhere in the world, including the compass, gunpowder, and printing, which originated in China, but that what mattered was that in the West these discoveries represented the triumph of progress.[63] He concluded,

> It has become the fashion to level the charge of Eurocentricity at the West for ignoring our debt to the achievements of other civilizations. Yet while fully acknowledging this debt, we must still ask why the West, after the end of the Middle Ages, so rapidly overtook the great civilizations of the East. In the

> venerable civilizations of the East, custom was king and tradition the guiding principle. If change came it was all but imperceptible, for the laws of Heaven existed once and for all and were not to be questioned. That spirit of questioning, the systematic rejection of authority, was the one invention the East may have failed to develop. It originated in ancient Greece. However often authority tried to smother this inconvenient element, its spark was glowing underground. It was that spark, perhaps, that was fanned into flame by the awareness that our ancestors did not have the monopoly of wisdom, and that we may learn to know more than they have if only we do not accept their word unquestioned. As the motto of the Royal Society (dating from 1663) has it, *Nullius in verba*—By nobody's word.

Gombrich's comments have now been characterized as "appalling," and willfully negating the political economy of extraction that the *Nova Reperta* documents.[64] But they also reveal the larger stakes in these prints' "going viral," as we say in today's vernacular. Their historical and contemporary appeal is related not just to their aesthetic value but to the far-ranging implications of the epistemic project they promote: that European ingenuity and prowess justified the violent takeover of other civilizations.

Latinx artists have also taken vengeance on Gombrich's outlandish comments. In preparation for the five-hundredth anniversary of the fall of the Aztec empire, ten artists and writers came together to record their reflections in a podcast titled *Project 1521*. Their visual and literary descriptions enraptured audiences and offered an Indigenous perspective on the Spanish invasion. Some of their works responded directly to the Florentine Codex, a document of the sixteenth century in which Native artists and scholars, under the direction of a Spanish friar, had recorded the historical events of the conquest, including the devastating effects of European diseases and viral epidemics that claimed the lives of almost 90 percent of Indigenous populations in Central Mexico. In the first episode, Diana Magaloni, a poet and also curator of Art of the Ancient Americas at the Los Angeles County Museum of Art, read aloud a haunting poem that was an ode to *Rainbows, Grizzlies, and Snakes, Oh My!—Conquest to Caging in Los Angeles* (2019; fig. 0.4), from the *Codex Rodriguez-Mondragón*, an ongoing series of maps and paintings on amate by the artist Sandy Rodriguez that draws on the ancient Mesoamerican and colonial-era tradition of painted books, questioning master narratives of territorial discovery.[65] Magaloni's poem asked difficult and sorrowful questions about the battle waged for land and the grief of dispossession, conjuring a reimagining of those sixteenth-century artists cloistered at the peak of a dramatic plague that was taking all life, color, and words.

RAINBOW/ARCO DEL TIEMPO
¿De quién es la sangre que nutre la tierra?
¿De quién es el llanto que produce la lluvia?

¿De quién las estrellas y las conchas?
¿De quién el maíz?

¿Quiénes son los simples,
    los alegres?
¿Quiénes,
    los que necesitan poco?

¿De quién es el agua,
    la tierra y el aire?
¿De quién es el polvo
    y la muerte?

¿De quién vienes tú
    y a quién te devuelves?

Nos quedamos sin pinturas.
Sin palabras.

Esperando en silencio
que el latido de nuestros corazones
convenga la música del comienzo.

Para volver de nuevo a la raíz.
Para volar sobre el arco de colores
de un nuevo tiempo.[66]

Magaloni's words are an affront to Gombrich's view that the "spirit of questioning, the systematic rejection of authority" are the sole domain of the West. Her poem questions not only the Western conception of Terra Nullius, which justified colonial ownership of Indigenous lands, but the anthropocentric belief that humans are somehow endowed with the power to possess and conquer the very environment that sustains their life. She asks: "Whose is the water, earth, and air? To whom do we owe this dust and death? Whom do you come from, and to whom do you return?" Her poem opens up the paradoxical position in which Latinx artists find themselves, calling this impulse

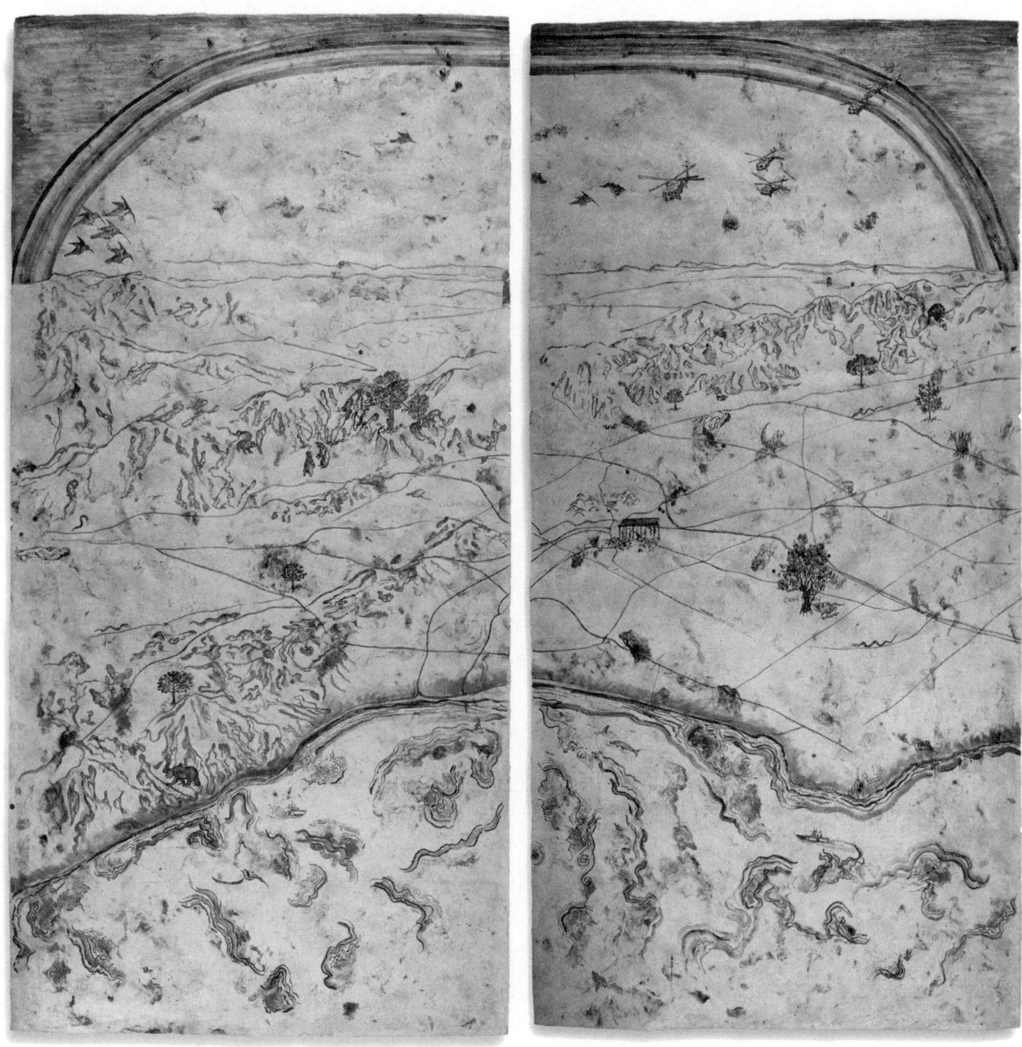

0.4. Sandy Rodriguez, *Rainbows, Grizzlies, and Snakes, Oh My!—Conquest to Caging in Los Angeles*, 2019. Los Angeles County Museum of Art, purchased with funds provided by AHAN: Studio forum, 2019 Art Here and Now. © Sandy Rodriguez. Photo by J6 Creative.

to reclaim the Americas a decolonial project when that kind of reclamation hinges on a reconquest and an underlying belief that land, water, and air can be owned, monetized, and extracted.

BRIDGING DECOLONIAL, BORDERLANDS, AND CRITICAL LATINX INDIGENEITIES

This book draws on theoretical frameworks that emphasize decolonial aesthetics in Latin American and Latinx art. Decolonial theory emerged in the early 1990s as a multisited clarion call to reckon with the legacy of colonial violence and the severe inequalities embedded in racial capitalism.[67] It was particularly important and applicable to the lived realities of marginalized communities in the United States. While decolonization denotes the process of decolonizing territories and peoples that were historically under colonial control, the decolonial references current and ongoing liberation projects aimed at delinking from a power structure still rooted in colonial ideologies. The works featured in this study engage in this practice of decolonial aesthetics by showing how printmaking diffused territorial representations from the provincial European viewpoint and, using the same medium, dispel their early-modern claims to universality. They urge viewers to consider how colonialism may have ended, but its present tense condition of "coloniality" remains in place: imposing racial classifications, creating walls, and actively working to destroy and silence knowledges outside the West.[68] From borderland, diasporic, and Indigenous subjectivities, these artists articulate decolonial options that subvert the control of how we have been taught to see and sense our relationship to geography. They aim to awaken viewers who have been inculcated in Western concepts for so long that they have erased other ways of seeing.

Their intervention in the field signals a desire to unmask printmaking's connection to envisioning territories as new, unknown, unclaimed, or inhabited by monstrous creatures, a practice complicit in the colonial violence that continues to structure racial and spatial paradigms of xenophobia, nativism, and borders in our modern era. Macarena Gómez-Barris explains that, "Before the colonial project could prosper, it had to render territories and peoples extractible, and it did so through a matrix of symbolic, physical, and representational violence."[69] During the Age of Exploration, printmaking operated as part of this matrix of representational violence. Prints helped cartographers, military officers, and admirals, as well as kings and queens, distribute the spatial logics of colonization. Through this technology, scholars document how European printers and engravers spread knowledge about the existence of a fourth continent, its flora, fauna, and Indigenous populations, and the need to civilize these far-off lands.[70] This early-modern print culture was not unidirectional, as we know from the recent turn toward a global art history,[71] and was followed by technological and political developments in the nineteenth and twentieth centuries that reclaimed printmaking as the most democratic art form.[72] I build on this radical potential of the print tradition by looking at how Latinx artists at the end of the twentieth century adopted the medium to take on print culture's darker histories.

Scholars acknowledge the role that aesthetics and the dominant field of visuality play in support of the "colonial matrix of power," aiding control of the economy, politics, and knowledge and regulating what is canonical, quality, and tasteful art.[73] This lends the decolonial theoretical framework a great deal of traction in recent Latin American and Latinx art histories.[74] In my book, the decolonial is a framework to understand artists' insistence in returning to the past to understand race and space in the present. Their prints point to colonial violence as a point of departure for the forms of xenophobia on the rise today. Not only are they invested in exposing the roots of current anti-immigrant movements and excessive territoriality, or the historical relationship between printmaking and colonization, but they gesture toward ways to outmaneuver, to dream, or to imagine other possible futures. For viewers it involves a process of unlearning, unscripting, doubting, and disobeying until their sensibilities are no longer under this imperial control. Some may say that art is futile and in vain, and perhaps that is true for a single poster or fine-art print, but taken as a whole the works in this book evince a long history of the ways printmaking has promoted decolonial thinking and how collectives of artists actively work to tear down these walls.

The genealogies of decolonial theory are multiple, and yet the contributions that US women of color and queer scholars of color have made to advancing the critique of Eurocentrism, the colonial gender system, and heteronormativity are often obscured and uncited in an academy that still privileges the work of cisgender male writers. For example, Mignolo describes how this school of thought, known as the "modernity/(de)coloniality" project, emerged in Latin America after the fall of the Soviet Union.[75] But as the cultural theorist Laura Pérez points out, feminist women of color in the US have since the late 1960s been at the forefront of critiquing essentialist and universalist notions of gender and of theorizing the intersectional nature of their identities, which involves understanding the effects of multiple forms of oppression, and dismantling the dichotomies of European theories of sexuality.[76] This book attempts to bridge these bodies of thought, integrating the important work of women writers of color like Anzaldúa, whose writing opened up possibilities for border thinking, border embodiment, mestizaje, and also reconceptualized the liminal state of being in between cultures and languages as *nepantla*, in an attempt to heal the psychic trauma that coloniality inflicted in the everyday lives of the queer, Indigenous, racialized, gendered subjects of the borderlands. However, as previously mentioned, the political project of reclaiming the Americas, while decolonial in its form and intent, can at times produce reactive forms of colonial thinking that replicate the settler colonial logic the artists seek to upend. To further nuance my close readings, I draw from the work of Critical Latinx Indigeneities scholars whose analytic reflects "how Indigeneity is defined and constructed across multiple countries and at times, across overlapping colonialities."[77] These scholars call for a hemispheric approach to the study of migration in order to see the competing colonial structures that create continuous forms of dispossession and displacement.

CHAPTER SUMMARIES

Chapter 1 examines the work of Chicano artist Ricardo Duffy, whose NAFTA-era print *The New Order* (1996), counters the resurgence of anti-immigrant legislation by revisiting the nineteenth-century ideology of Manifest Destiny. Self Help Graphics published the print during Duffy's third residency in the Experimental Silkscreen Atelier. I argue that Duffy's *New Order* contests settler mythologies through a clever appropriation of Marlboro advertising, by engaging in its own form of mythmaking and advocating for a return to Indigenous territorialities. In this chapter, I trace the development of what I call a "border pop" aesthetic that developed in the 1990s. Artists like Duffy, Enrique Chagoya, and Rubén Ortiz Torres adopted the language of pop in response to xenophobic policies, but also to question pop art's role in the production of visualizations of the West. Indigenous populations are at the center of many of these questions; themes include the resurgence of the utopian ancestral homeland Aztlán in Chicanx aesthetics, their vanishment in nineteenth-century landscape painting, and the development of folktales like that of Apache Leap. Contemporary Chicanos like Duffy reenact the loss of Indigenous land, opposing expansionism, and seeking reconquest. However, Duffy's figure of the Native mother perpetuates the comorbidities of gendering land and Indigeneity. This is considered alongside works like Andy Warhol's "The American Indian" series, and Stradanus's *Allegory of America*.

Chapter 2 focuses on the collaborative portfolio of lithographs by the Mexican-born San Francisco–based artist Enrique Chagoya and the Arizona border poet Alberto Ríos, titled *You Are Here* and published by Segura Publishing in 2000. Through their experiments in mapmaking, Chagoya and

Ríos reveal the Eurocentric fallacies of Western cartography and incite alternative ways of conceptualizing space. I argue that Chagoya and Ríos's art and language prints emphasize the role of the body in mediating a connection to geography, foregrounding an embodied territoriality opposed to European rationalism in order to counter Western cartography's hallmark of disembodied projection. This is contrasted with the recent artistic trend of experimental geography, which aims to provide "documentary" mapping to subvert technological surveillance. Chagoya and Ríos, however, seek to understand maps as forms of encounter, divested from a desire for truth or reality. Central to their compositions is physically embodied knowledge, and the lived experience of border dwellers—at times incorporating their own bodies into the experience of their works. Their maps are subversive, reimagining the global ordering of North and South, East and West, and are particularly involved in the redefinition of borders. This is echoed by performance artists like La Pocha Nostra, who enacted and created 'portable borders' through participatory projects.

Chapter 3 delves into Ecuadorian-American artist Sandra Fernández's printmaking residencies at Coronado Studio in Austin, Texas. Through panoramic prints such as *Coming of Age (Transformations)* (2008), her work offers a vivid example of the reterritorialization of the nation's borders, particularly the deployment of ICE and Homeland Security after 9/11. While Duffy makes visible the gendering of Indigenous territories, and Chagoya and Ríos use maps to contrast the knowledge of the body versus the knowledge of the archive, Fernández adds a different perspective to the historical role of the female body in print culture. Her prints evince what Mignolo calls the "colonial wound," the hurt that was left after colonialism and its social stratification, and how it manifests itself through gender and mestizaje. The chapter follows the artist back to her hometown of Quito, where she saw firsthand how this stratification manifested in the segregation of the country's Black, Indigenous, and poor mestizo population. It takes a 1750 map of the Provincia de Quito as a place of departure to consider how prints distributed the imperial designs of Europe when the colonial elite adopted these maps to forge their postcolonial identity and claim their modernity. As a US-born artist raised in the global south, Fernández eventually returned to the country of her birth only to be read as a Latin American exile. I consider how the cultural politics of this Texas-based workshop shaped Fernández's vision of the borderlands and exposed her to the exploitation of immigrant labor. Her turn toward a mestiza consciousness awakened Fernández's interest in linking the border to colonial manuscripts like the Codex Mendoza as a way to expose the historical roots of domination and inequality. She also gave voice to the vulnerable position and equally powerful voice of her students, who were Dreamers in a rapidly changing immigration apparatus. Fernández's prints such as

CAUTION: Dreamers in/on Sight (2013), build an argument against xenophobia vis-à-vis the allusions to mixed-race bodies who are the direct progeny of colonial violence. I place her work in conversation with Ecuadorian painters like Oswaldo Viteri and Chicana artists Ester Hernandez and Laura Aguilar.

Chapter 4 examines the recurring use of water imagery in the Dominican York Proyecto Gráfica's inaugural portfolio *Manifestaciones* (2010). I foreground the role of artists like master printer Pepe Coronado in forging this collective, while drawing on his experiences with Self Help Graphics and the Coronado Studio, and connecting the borderlands discourse of Chicanx artists to the liminality likewise experienced by Dominican Americans. Unlike the previous chapters, which emphasized delinking from Western conceptions of land to question the excess of current forms of territoriality and nativism, in this chapter we see Caribbean diaspora artists recode geographic representations from the point of view of island dwellers who experience water boundaries. This unique perspective, inspired by the island that was home to the first European settlement in the Americas as well as the first slave rebellion, centers the discourse of the Black Atlantic as critical to challenging the Eurocentric roots of Latinidad. The DYPG's aqueous prints demonstrate how the racialized Dominican body resists the discourse of mestizaje of the DR and the Black-white binary of the US. Their dialectical images disclose movement, liminality, and resilience, even while Dominicans face the dangers of water crossings during maritime migration.

In the conclusion of the book, I delve into the realm of exhibitions. Through a discussion of Carmen Ramos's exhibition *¡Printing the Revolution! The Rise and Impact of Chicano Graphics, 1965 to Now* (2020), I consider what happens to the avant-garde and decolonial claims of these artworks as they enter national museum collections. Is this a triumph or a failure, as Peter Bürger wrote in relation to the historical avant-gardes? How are new generations of artists countering the anti-immigrant attacks against Latinx communities? What is the role of these artists in a world that is in the midst of a climate crisis that will displace tens of millions of people and force them to migrate?

CHAPTER ONE

Native Territorialities

Ricardo Duffy's Border Pop and the Indigenous Uncanny

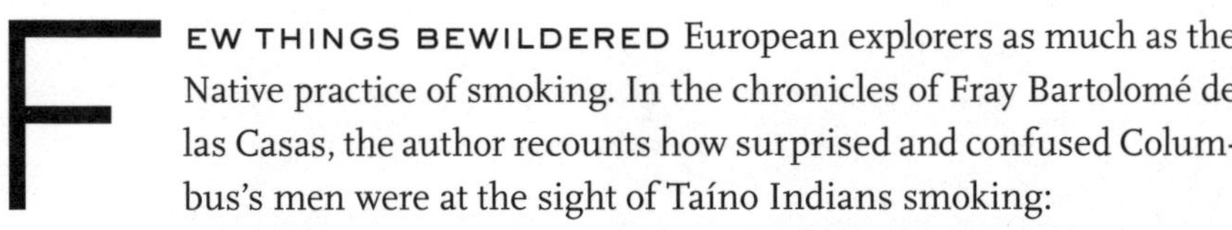

FEW THINGS BEWILDERED European explorers as much as the Native practice of smoking. In the chronicles of Fray Bartolomé de las Casas, the author recounts how surprised and confused Columbus's men were at the sight of Taíno Indians smoking:

> The two Christians met many men and women who were carrying glowing coal in their hands, as well as good-smelling herbs. They were dried plants. . . . They set one end on fire and inhaled and drank the smoke on the other. It is said that in this way they become sleepy and drunk, but also that they got rid of their tiredness. The people called these small muskets tobacco.

The strange and foreign custom must have intrigued the explorers as they observed the way it entered and exited the Indians' brown bodies, the pleasure they took in each inhale and exhale, the rich and toasted fragrance of the dried leaves, and the almost spiritual devotion to this exotic new plant. Every European voyage that followed would carry the New World leaf to Europe, and within two decades smoking would go from a "primitive" ritual among

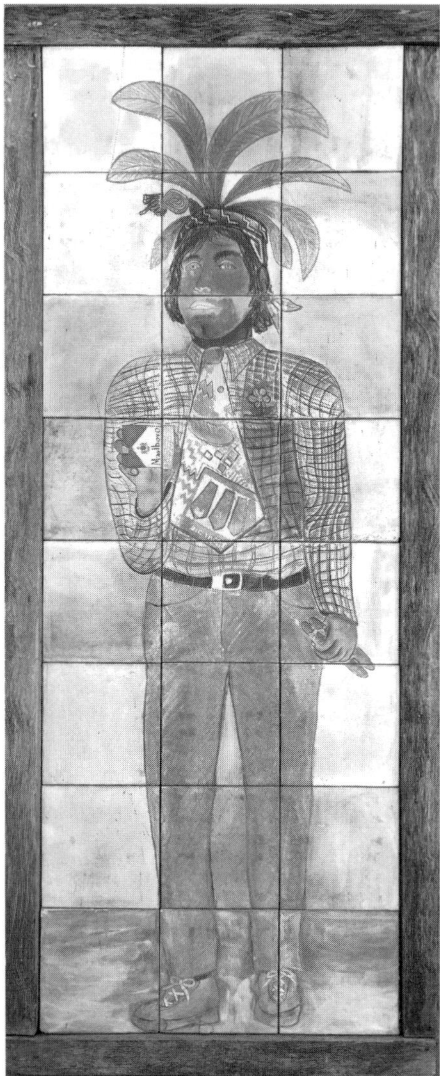

1.1. Ricardo Duffy, *Dig These*, 1993. Ceramic tile mural in wood frame, 53 × 22 × 2 inches. Courtesy of the artist.

Indians to a conventional, commonplace, even medicinal, habit for men and women the world over.[1]

The New World origins of tobacco and specifically its association with Indigenous cultures is the subject of a ceramic-tile mural *Dig These* by the artist Ricardo Duffy (b. 1951). The framed outdoor mural, which sits just outside his 1920s Spanish Colonial Revival home in San Juan Capistrano, California, portrays a young man with a pack of Marlboro cigarettes in one hand and two rolled cigars in the other (fig. 1.1). The male figure stands rather stiffly looking out into the distance. He wears contemporary clothing—a blue plaid shirt with a silly tie, a black belt, gray trousers, and matching gray shoes. A yellow flower pokes out from his shirt pocket. But the feature that inevitably catches the viewer's eye is the tall, feathered headdress that marks the copper-toned subject as Native. The large green feathers that emanate from his head (and double as tobacco leaves) form an aura over the young man. The vertical mural is a self-portrait of the artist against a backdrop of multicolored pastel tiles devoid of time and context.[2] Almost indiscernible on the cigarette box is an old Marlboro logo with two rearing horses holding the crowned crest of Philip Morris, Inc., and a banner that reads "Veni Vidi Vici" (I came; I saw; I conquered).

Born in Southern California to Elizabeth Anne Rodriguez and Richard B. Duffy, Ricardo Duffy grew up negotiating between his Mexican and Irish-Lithuanian ancestry.[3] His bicultural circumstances were further exacerbated by his parent's divorce and his mother's abandonment. Interested in drawing and surfing, as a dark-skinned and long-haired teenager he faced overt racism in segregated Los Angeles. Remarks such as "You don't need to go to school. You got a job waiting for you . . . trash collector" or "Why [are] you going surfing, 'cause you're already *mojado*?" were commonplace and often a source of fistfights.[4] The experiences of not quite fitting in, or worse, of being told to go back to Mexico, sparked Duffy's fascination with his Mexican and Indigenous roots and a deep questioning of how these borderlands, sited and embodied, had come to be incredibly fraught.

While studying art at Ventura College and California State University, Fullerton, Duffy became involved in the craft-revival movement. He excelled at ceramics, an interest owed in part to his father's employment at a porcelain factory but primarily the result of working under ceramist and sculptor Jerry Rothman, who was himself a former student of the renowned ceramic artist Peter Voulkos at Otis College of Art and Design, in Los Angeles.[5] The art-festival circuit from Ventura to Arizona, particularly in wealthy Southern California beach towns, proved quite profitable, and Duffy abandoned his studies just before completion. An extended discussion of his ceramics is beyond the scope of this study, but I would like to note that the theme of Indigeneity often began with his experiments with wheel-throwing and hand-building techniques. For example, one of his first works to touch on tobacco and Indian death, *Veni Vidi Vici* (1992), takes the form of a caravel, alluding to that year's quincentennial (fig. 1.2). He painted the body of the vessel with intricate Marlboro designs, and placed bone fragments and skulls in the interior. At the apex hang two large skulls punctured by rebar and discolored by charcoal smoke. Although many referred to Duffy as a master ceramist and compared him to contemporaries such as Robert Arneson, Duffy did not want to settle on one medium.[6] By the late 1980s, he had begun experimenting with

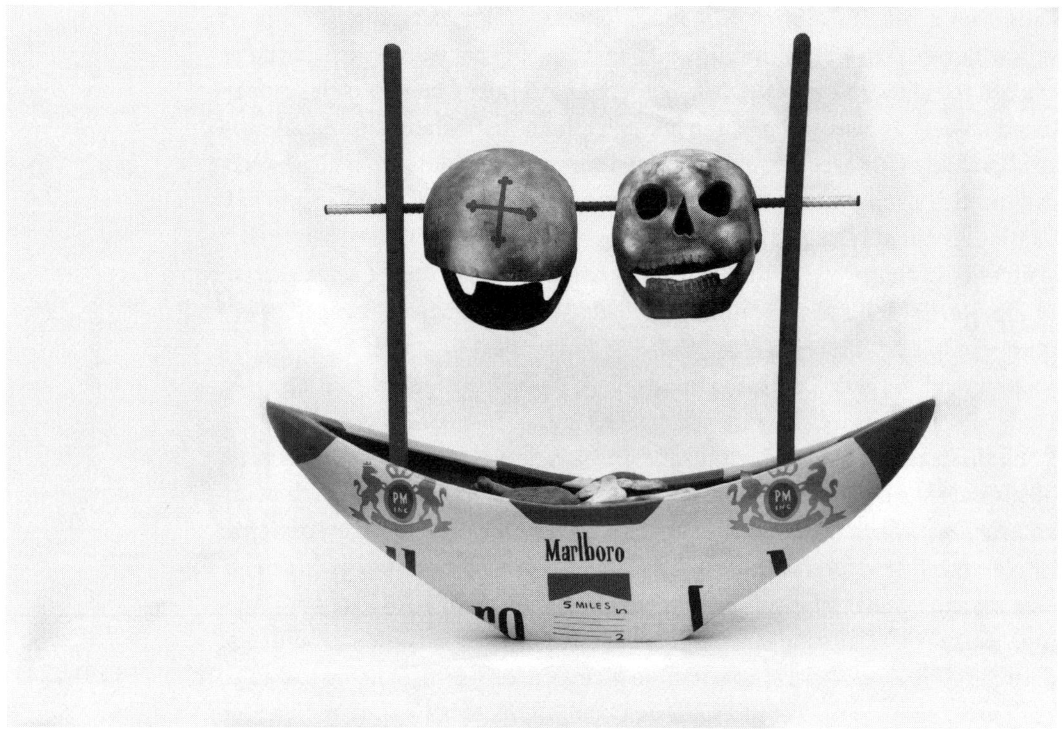

1.2. Ricardo Duffy, *Veni Vidi Vici*, 1992. Clay, charcoal smoke, acrylic paint, wood, rebar, 34 × 29½ × 12 inches. Courtesy of the artist.

painting and printmaking, a process that would eventually lead him to the East L.A. studios of Self Help Graphics & Art (hereafter referred to as SHG).[7]

Meeting Sister Karen Boccalero, director of SHG, drew him into the field of printmaking. Boccalero had studied with the graphic artist Sister Corita Kent at the now-defunct Immaculate Heart College, Los Angeles, and later specialized in printmaking in Philadelphia at Temple University's Tyler School of Art, working under renowned printmaker Romas Viesulas in their Rome program.[8] But after joining the Order of the Sisters of St. Francis, she returned to Boyle Heights in East Los Angeles, where she had grown up, and co-founded an art workshop alongside Carlos Bueno, Antonio Ibañez, and Frank Hernández. The workshop's commitment to printmaking and cultural pride in the East L.A. Mexican American community would become the cornerstone of a burgeoning Latinx graphic-arts movement, a ripple effect caused by several generations of resident artists starting their own workshops across the country.[9] "She was good. She was direct. She knew art. She knew how to see things," said Duffy of the chain-smoking Italian American nun, "and she looked at [my portfolio, and said] . . . when can you print?"[10] Duffy had never made a screenprint before. But after a few workshops, he was hooked. He was drawn to the silk screen–monotype process, not only for its speed and gestural qualities but also for its resemblance to the techniques of painting modernist ceramics.

The following year, Duffy earned an invitation to SHG's atelier, a residency program that paired artists with master printers for making of limited-edition screenprints (also referred to as silk screens or serigraphs). During his first residency, Duffy produced *Beaning Indigenous* (1991), a satirical work that exposes the racial epithet "beaner" often used to insult Mexicans. He returned to the atelier two years later to make *Primavera* (1993), its subject a fierce female jaguar that appears throughout his oeuvre, often performing as an alter ego.[11] Duffy's third printmaking residency took place three years later, when he made one of his most significant works, *The New Order.* As a sign of his growing notoriety, the Los Angeles County Museum of Art in 1997 acquired these three prints through the Art Museum Council Fund, perhaps in preparation for its exhibition, *Made in California: Art, Image, and Identity, 1900–2000* (opened in October 2000), which I will return to in my conclusion.

This book makes the argument that Latinx artists adopted the medium of printmaking to reclaim the Americas from various subject positions. In Duffy's case, the emphasis was on reorienting the conversation on land toward Native territorialities. Through collaborative workshop spaces like SHG, he gained access to a tradition of socially committed printmaking that had been nurtured in Latinx communities since the civil-rights movement. The theme of land reclamation had been present since the earliest days of a burgeoning Chicano Movement. Among the iconic examples of this trend, the Denver-based artist Emanuel Martinez produced a poster titled *Tierra o Muerte* (1967; fig. 1.3). The work is a stylized rendering of the Mexican revolutionary hero Emiliano Zapata holding a rifle and sword and looking directly at the viewer within a fisheye banner that invokes his call for land or death. Initially, Martinez printed the one-color poster as the frontispiece to a simple manila folder, inexpensive and readily available materials that could be distributed covertly among sympathizers. But over time and through its vast circulation in activist spheres it would become an icon of the "battle to reclaim communal land rights under the 1848 Treaty of Guadalupe Hidalgo."[12] While drawing on the history of photography from Mexico's Casasola archive and the vast number of prints representing the agrarian leader, such as the linocut by Francisco Mora from Taller de Gráfica Popular's *Estampas de la Revolución Mexicana* (1947), Martinez's redeployment of Zapata challenged narra-

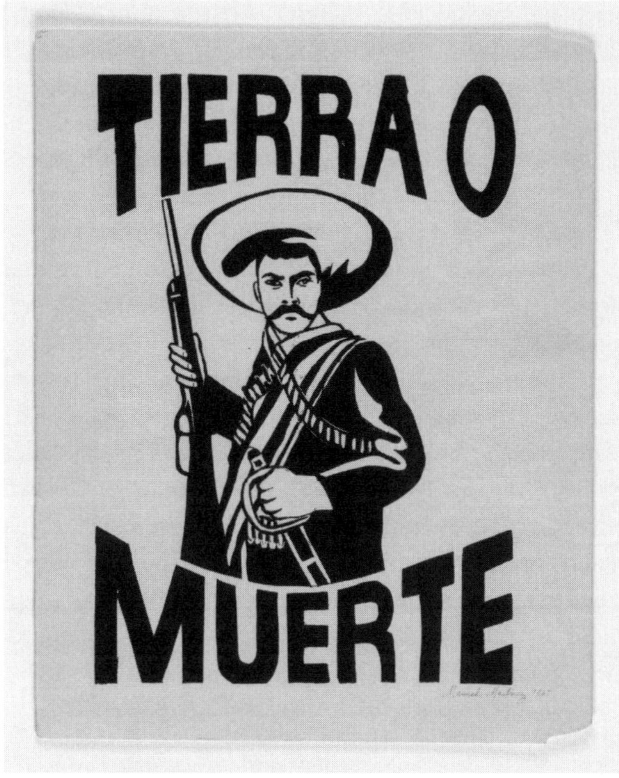

1.3. Emanuel Martinez, *Tierra o Muerte*, 1967. Screenprint on manila folder, sheet and image: 11¾ × 9½ inches. Smithsonian American Art Museum, gift of the artist, 1996.8, © Emanuel Martinez.

tives of westward expansion that erased or denied territorial links to the land lost by Mexico, and it politicized the farmworker movement in the Southwest to proclaim that the land belongs to those who work it.[13]

But the issues present in the mid-1990s were not the same as those of the late 1960s. First, the cultural infrastructure had greatly expanded. Art school–trained artists were participating in professional printmaking residency programs and producing museum-quality limited editions. It is nothing short of extraordinary to see how much changed for these artists in the two decades it took to go from raw, DIY protest posters to highly technical, multicolored, precisely printed artworks. Museums noticed, and the criterion of "quality" that had often precluded many artists of color from being considered for museum acquisitions was no longer an issue[14]—though it would still take much cultural brokering to get the proper attention from curators. Furthermore, art school had exposed these artists to the history of American and Latin American art, traditions that they drew on and formally challenged. Finally, much had been accomplished through the tireless work of those who participated firsthand in the struggles of the civil-rights movement, including the high-school walkouts and marches to end the war in Vietnam; but these advances were followed by a backlash of conservative social engineering. The major flashpoints of the 1990s—Columbus's quincentennial, the ratification of the North American Free Trade Agreement, the Zapatista Uprising, and xenophobic laws like California's Proposition 187—opened the door for new forms of contestation. The medium of printmaking, which had historically conspired with Western geography's colonial gaze, proved ideal for creating other ways of envisioning the Americas in order to outmaneuver the technologies of power that had thus far produced space in decidedly racial terms.

Blending the styles of pop art and border art with the tropes of Western landscape painting, Duffy's *The New Order* (1996; fig. 1.4) returns to the theme of New World tobacco and presents a dystopian vision of Marlboro Country. The first section of this chapter, "Border Pop," investigates how such an aesthetic came to challenge the frontier image of California through the satirical appropriation of popular culture. In a close reading of *The New Order,* Manifest Destiny—the nineteenth-century ideology of American expansionism that called for the settlement of the West as a divine right to govern the continent—is seen to inform not only the popular imagery of Marlboro advertising but also the aesthetics of West Coast pop. The second section, "Uncanny Indians in Marlboro Country," places *The New Order* in dialogue with the work of contemporary Native American artists to examine how the discourse of settler colonialism informs visions of Aztlán—the northern territories of Greater Mexico lost in the Mexican American War of 1848—that inadvertently appropriate Native traumas and territories. The third section, "Gendered Territories," considers how the gendered Native body appears in and disappears from the landscape and how this cultural practice coincides with the racialized geographies of the United States and Mexico.

This chapter aims to show that Duffy's *New Order* contests settler mythologies through a clever appropriation of Marlboro advertising by engaging in its own form of mythmaking and advocating for a return to Indigenous territorialities. I undertake this close reading through a theoretical lens that questions that formation of Aztlán as Indigenous nationhood and its redeployment of Indigenism, resuscitated from Mexico's postrevolutionary period, to recuperate the Indian "as an ancestral past rather than recognizing contemporary Indians as coinhabitants not only of this continent abstractly conceived, but of the neighborhoods and streets of hundreds of U.S. cities and towns."[15] Los Angeles is a transnational city made up of multiple Indigeneities. The original Tongva and Tatavium geography has been reshaped through multiple colonial histories of Spanish and US settlers, and through the continuous arrival of displaced Indigenous migrants who make up a matrix of diasporic geographies.[16] Duffy's avant-garde mythmaking evades the

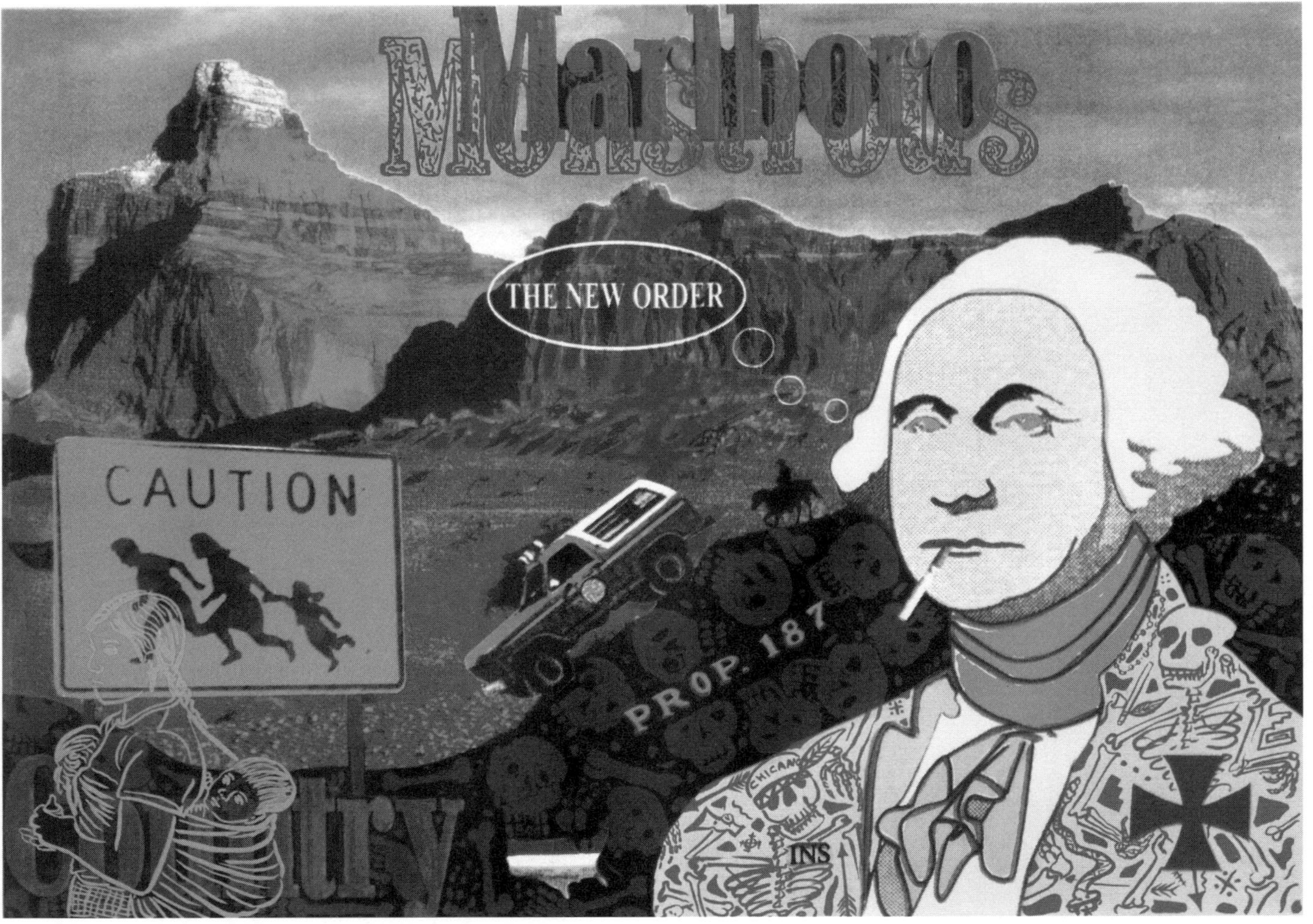

1.4. Ricardo Duffy, *The New Order*, 1996. Screenprint on paper, 20 × 26 inches; edition of seventy-five, published by Self Help Graphics, Los Angeles. Courtesy of the artist.

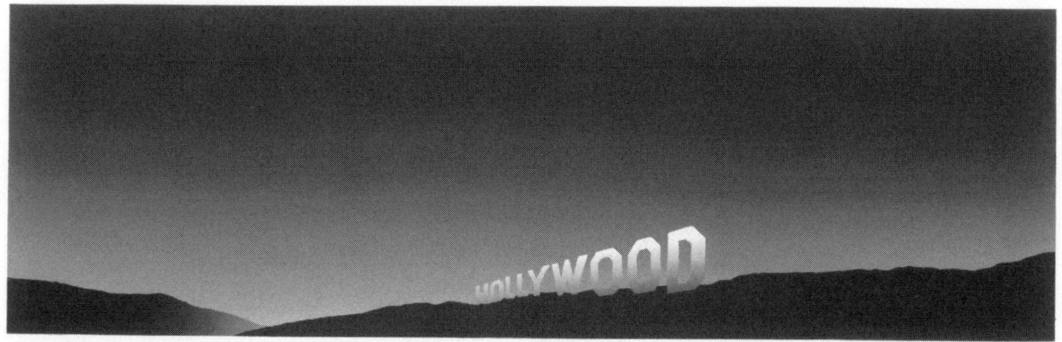

1.5. Ed Ruscha, *Hollywood*, 1968. Color screenprint, number 56 of an edition of one hundred. Image: 12½ × 40 inches; sheet: 17½ × 44⁷⁄₁₆ inches. Los Angeles County Museum of Art Acquisition Fund M.81.178. Licensed by Art Resource, NY. Courtesy of the artist and Gagosian.

question of political agency and works to unsettle the image histories, especially the art histories, that edify the western frontier.

BORDER POP

Despite the commonly held belief that New York was the birthplace of pop art, many of the movement's early proponents were artists in Los Angeles inspired by the everyday life of that city. The art historian Cécile Whiting writes about Ed Ruscha's vision of Los Angeles in the 1960s as a "city defined not by nature but commercial facades and signage seen from a moving car."[17] Ruscha's *Hollywood* (1968; fig. 1.5) is a panoramic view of the Hollywood sign seen at sunset. In its peculiar rectangularity, Whiting sees the "horizontal sweep of the movie screen" as well as a "sunset lifted straight out of a western."[18] The Santa Monica Mountains appear dwarfed at the scale, recession, and almost aural qualities of the sign, which stands in not only for the "industry" but also, perhaps more important, for the actual city. Ruscha's screenprint uplifts the popular to usher in a view of this bold West Coast cultural capital. His work, like his contemporaries', portrays the pleasure and promise of a changing western frontier.

Few artists exemplified this connection to westward expansion as much as did Ruscha (b. 1937), a Nebraska-born artist who drove west on Route 66 to settle in Los Angeles. The artist's attention to the aesthetics of commercial signage and his cinematic views of L.A. topography tapped into, in Whiting's words, a "long heritage of Western landscape painting in which the west is a

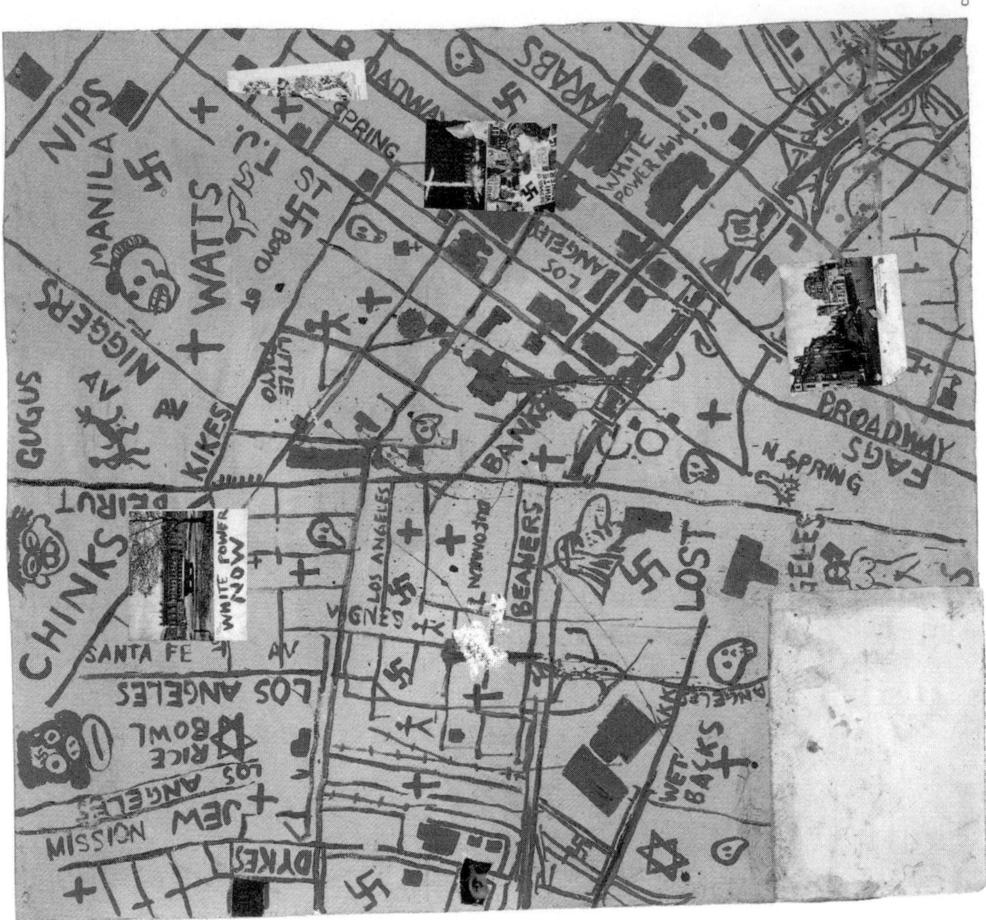

1.6. Manuel Ocampo, *Untitled (Ethnic Map of Los Angeles)*, 1987. Acrylic on canvas, 66½ × 59 inches. Courtesy of the artist and Tyler Rollins Fine Art.

place of sublime, if sometimes dangerous, beauty."[19] But this persistent image of California's sublime would not last. As the postwar economic boom faded, the influx of immigrants from Asia and Latin America—including Mexican, Korean, Cambodian, and Salvadoran refugees—created anxieties about the state's desolate frontier beliefs. What the geographer Edward Soja called a "dazzling, sprawling patchwork mosaic" of Los Angeles became even further fragmented through the spatial segregation of race, class, and ethnicity.[20]

The artist Manuel Ocampo portrayed those borders in a sardonic map known as *Untitled (Ethnic Map of Los Angeles)* (1987; fig. 1.6). The crude painting, which looks like a quickly sketched ink drawing, divides L.A. neighborhoods into territorial domains labeled with racial epithets, fascist symbols, and the slurs of sexual difference. The stark divisions Ocampo witnessed as a recent transplant from the Philippines reflected on the totalitarian origins of California's brand of white nationalism and the fear-driven desire to keep ethno-racial groups from intermixing. His grim view of the City of Angels was as much a historical reflection as it was a blueprint for the riots that besieged the city in 1992. Ocampo's map, while exaggerated in tone and gesture, represented the Los Angeles where Duffy had come of age.

Like Ocampo's parody of the street atlas, and in conversation with Ruscha's interest in the billboards and street signs, Duffy's *New Order* provides a satirical take on the western frontier of Marlboro Country. Readers will likely recall the cigarette company's widely circulated and popular ad campaign, such as AD No. 10338-A1, based on panoramic vistas of the West often with rugged cowboys on horseback (fig. 1.7). For the many of us who grew up watching those commercials and driving by those billboards, the image of Marlboro became synonymous with this country. The agency Leo Burnett Worldwide—the inspiration for the television show *Mad Men* (2007–2015)—created the Marlboro Man campaign in the mid-1950s, departing from the brand as a

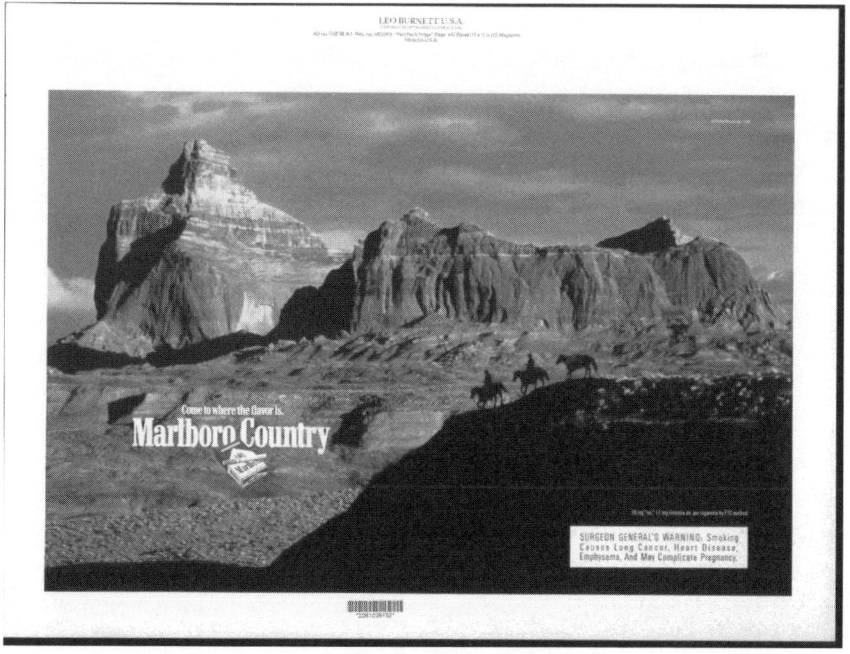

1.7. Leo Burnett, *U.S.A.*, Ad No. 10338-A1 Red Rock Ridge, 1997. Philip Morris USA Advertising Archive.

"women's" cigarette when it debuted in the 1920s with the slogan "Mild as May." When TV and print ads began to feature "groups of chisel-faced wranglers sitting around a campfire, or a solo cowboy astride a horse, cupping his smoke against the bitter winds somewhere in the red rock deserts and high plains of an ambiguous American west," as described by writer Adrian Shirk, Marlboro became the most-purchased cigarette in the United States and one of the most successful campaigns for Leo Burnett.[21]

Duffy tips his hat to the avant-garde strategies of the 1960s, which placed consumerist culture on display, often in ironic ways. The choice to return to pop in the mid-1990s, when contemporary artists were mostly focused on conceptual art methods, likely reflects a research-based approach as much as an investment in the history of the printmaking medium. On the one hand, he uses pop to revisit the occasion when big tobacco portrayed the Marlboro Man in Marlboro Country, and on the other, he gestures to the contemporary moment when Philip Morris is being held responsible for the death of innumerable smokers. In fact, the legal disputes against big tobacco in the 1990s led to a master agreement.[22] This was part of a long, drawn-out battle in the history of regulation for cigarette ads. They were banned from television and radio in 1971. The master settlement included bans on transit and billboard ads, paid product placement, sponsorship of events, and cartoons. More important, Philip Morris acknowledged that the company intentionally marketed an addictive substance to children and was forced to declassify its entire advertising archive. But in Duffy's print, the serene Marlboro landscape of cowboys and mountains becomes monstrous and, as the lettering indicates at the top, a site filled with surveillance, fleeing, and ultimately, death.

Duffy draws on the mythology of Westerns, which informed the aesthetics of Marlboro campaigns, but he flips their heroic portrayals of the cowboy by connecting this figure to the Border Patrol. His 20″ × 26″ screenprint is rather large, emulating the two-page magazine spreads or panoramic billboards now outlawed. The colors are overly saturated in a composition that is intricately layered with the sun-kissed mountains of Monument Valley in the background, a Ford Bronco and Caution sign midway, and the commanding bust portrait of George Washington, who looks toward the viewer. The bronco, Spanish for a wild or half-tamed horse, is one of the Mexican elements on which the figure of the American cowboy was conceived. As such a racial dyad emerges based on recurring tropes of the Western and enacts the myth of the frontier, the American cowboy "stands between the opposed worlds of [Mexican and Indian] savagery and [white] civilization, acting sometimes as mediator or interpreter between races and cultures but more often as civilization's most effective instrument against savagery—a man who knows how to think and fight like an Indian, to turn their own methods against them."[23] In this panoramic vista, the Border Patrol's Ford Bronco and a silhouetted cowboy ride along a ridge made of skulls and bones. Unlike the barren desert in the Marlboro commercials that make up the image of Manifest Destiny, Duffy's monstrous country evinces the death and displacement of Indigenous populations and the contemporary forms of tracking and rounding up undocumented immigrants like animals.[24]

All the figures follow the ridge from right to left, seemingly heading west or out of the country. The Bronco and cowboy look toward a yellow sign cautioning motorists to avoid pedestrian crossings. Duffy establishes a formal similarity between the silhouetted cowboy and the silhouetted family almost as if building archetypal figures that will be played out by various actors time and again. The burnt yellow of the caution sign also wraps around Washington's neck and appears to radiate off the mountain peak, creating triangular movement for the viewer. In this landscape, the caution sign takes on a double meaning as it speaks to differing constituencies: avoid pedestrian deaths and beware of the threat posed by immigrants. Below and overlapping with the sign are the faint outlines of a young Native mother with a child strapped to her back standing ready to run like the silhouettes above. The blue lines that make up her figure correspond to the blue of Washington's eyes and cravat.

With a cigarette in his mouth, and with *calaveras* and an Iron Cross on his American currency–colored coat, Washington justifies expansionism as his God-given right to spread democracy and capitalism across the North American continent. His thought bubble reads, "The New Order," perhaps in reference to George H. W. Bush's speech in 1990 on the Persian Gulf crisis. However, Duffy's use of the reference is there to signal the hypocrisy of American exceptionalism. In the words of President Bush,

> We stand today at a unique and extraordinary moment. The crisis in the Persian Gulf, as grave as it is, also offers a rare opportunity to move toward an historic period of cooperation. Out of these troubled times, our fifth objective—a new world order—can emerge: a new era—freer from the threat of terror, stronger in the pursuit of justice, and more secure in the quest for peace. An era in which the nations of the world, East and West, North and South, can prosper and live in harmony. A hundred generations have searched for this elusive path to peace, while a thousand wars raged across the span of human endeavor. Today that new world is struggling to be born, a world quite different from the one we've known. A world where the rule of law supplants the rule of the jungle. A world in which nations recognize the shared responsibility for freedom and justice. A world where the strong respect the rights of the weak.[25]

In such a view, the artist connects American foreign policy objectives in the Middle East to the Old Order, a military pursuit that required clearing the land of its original inhabitants. As he noted in our interview, "This is the way it has to be, because it's the same old story. It's the same old conquest, it's the same old condition. It's just been relabeled in a more contemporary time, but it's the same anguish. It's the same emotion."[26]

Duffy rehearsed the history of land dispossession to probe the ideologies that supported xenophobic laws such as California's Proposition 187. The ballot initiative of 1994, known as the Save Our State campaign, spearheaded by a group of Orange County right-wing activists as well as former officials of the Immigration and Naturalization Service (INS), barred undocumented immigrants from accessing public services, including education and nonemergency health care (such as prenatal services), and mandated school administrators and health aides to turn in those suspected of being in the country without papers.[27] The initiative gained widespread support, especially from the Republican Party and Governor Pete Wilson's reelection campaign.[28] Despite strong opposition from pro-immigrant activist groups, public marches, and student walkouts, the ballot measure passed by a majority 59 percent.[29] The vote signaled the consolidation of California's anti-immigrant platform, which represented a nativist sentiment that would reverberate throughout the country in the coming years. To the right of Washington, Duffy names the ballot law among a mound of skeletons. The *calaveras* appear to come alive on his coat. One wears a bandana inscribed "Chicano," the politicized Mexican American nomer the artist uses to self-identify, while another sticks his head out beyond the boundaries of the coat. Native accoutrements surround the *calaveras*: an ax, an arrow, a feathered headdress on the left, a peace pipe and rattlesnake on the right. Duffy's print suggests that the land was never Terra Nullius but rather was cleared of Native others and, moreover, that the belief in a God-given right to come, see, and conquer—recall that "Veni, vidi, vici" once graced the Marlboro corporate logo—is the same one that motivates nativist movements like Proposition 187, even when such measures are found unconstitutional.[30]

Duffy deconstructed Marlboro advertising with visual excess. In this regard, his work aligns with the origins of pop art as a critique of American consumer advertisements. Richard Hamilton's iconic collage *Just What Is It That Makes Today's Homes So Different, So Appealing?* made for the catalogue of *This Is Tomorrow* in 1956 engages a similar logic, presenting an excess of consumer items that elicit viewers to partake in the pleasures of a modern American home. The warmly lit living-room space contains furniture, rugs, lamps, plants, a tape recorder, a television, a nineteenth-century portrait next to a framed comic strip, windows that overlook an urban billboard and movie theater, tinned ham on the coffee table, and a vacuum presumably operated by a maid with an extension for cleaning the stairs. *Just What Is It . . .* appears to depict the interior of a home whose main subjects, a bodybuilder carrying an oversized Tootsie Pop and a reclined nude, enjoy a fantastical mode of leisure, free of household chores. For the British artist, this was a humorous yet satirical view of popular culture drawn from American illustrated magazines such as *Ladies' Home Journal, Life, Fortune, Look,* and *Mad.*[31] The art historian John-Paul Stonard suggests that "underlying the crowded imagery of *Just What Is It . . .* is an anxiety that this new cultural order could not, in fact, be sustained."[32] Environmental degradation, in a sea full of plastic and waterways tinged with forever chemicals, now proves how the collage was a harbinger of things to come. Similarly, Duffy draws on this tradition of satirical pop by photomontaging and screenprinting an excess of signs and icons to construct a narrative of what California represents in the 1990s, namely a paradoxical site of Marlboro Country—though in this case, it is not a new cultural order but an old one that remains harmful and unsustainable.

Duffy's art also hints at how the Marlboro image of the nineteenth-century frontiersman was an ideological foundation for West Coast pop. Ruscha and his fellow artists from the Ferus Gallery in Los Angeles enacted the male explorer in their artist personas, portraying themselves as a "homosocial community of mid-1960s frontiersmen."[33] As Whiting points out further, they cultivated the image of "Hollywood playboy" as youthful heterosexual heathens. Similarly, the frontiersman trope figured into their formal strategies of representation. In Ruscha's panoramic Hollywood sunset, a frontiersman encounters a sublime vision of Mount Lee for the first time. For the presumed male-explorer gaze, the Santa Monica Mountains seem empty, inviting, and open for a traveler willing to take in the full sunset. Unlike nineteenth-century landscape painters who imagined the terror and beauty encapsulated in the sight of the West, Ruscha stripped the work of illusionism, flattening the grandeur of the mountains and abstracting the sunset to a mesmerizing gradient. Ruscha's modern frontiersman was positioned against a mediated panorama as seen through the reproductive technologies of film, photography, and silk screen. Much like Ruscha, Duffy also looked to the city's commercial facades and street signs, but rather than abstracting their imagery or aestheticizing the experience, he deconstructed the advertisement with visual excess. Duffy's panorama warns viewers that this mediated image of California hides a desire for land that can only be satisfied through death.

To be fair, this frontiersman apolitical vision of pop art was contested from the outset. Artists such as Rupert Garcia produced early pop prints and posters in alignment with the social movements animating San Francisco in the

1960s.[34] Garcia's iconic etching *Black Man and Flag* (1967), which recently toured as part of the exhibition *Witness: Art and Civil Rights in the Sixties,* as well as *Pop América, 1965–1975*, attests to how a pop aesthetic was on the frontlines of the Bay Area's anti-racist and anti-capitalist struggles. A similar urgency accompanied the work of Chicago-based African American artist Barbara Jones-Hogu, whose bold screenprints mobilized Black radicalism in Chicago with posters such as *Unite* (1971).[35] Likewise, the San Antonio–based artist Mel Casas's "Humanscapes" series (1968–1977) reimagined the drive-in movie screen as a projection of the white anxieties and fears exposed through the civil-rights movement. In *Humanscape 68 (Kitchen Spanish)* (1973), Casas drew the curtain on those private exchanges between the ruling white elite and their Spanish-speaking servants in South Texas. Art historian Ruben Córdova, the leading specialist on Casas, ascribes agency to the caricature of the maid, whose playful use of language undermines the power of her white employer.[36] While pop art tended to reject the angst of postwar abstraction and the moral connotations of social realism, artists of color often left room for open-ended social commentary on the treatment of racialized minorities.

According to Teresa Carbone and Kellie Jones, the curators of *Witness,* many of the best-known American pop artists, such as Roy Lichtenstein, James Rosenquist, and Andy Warhol, to name a few, put forward subject matter indifferent to the social upheavals of the 1960s and 1970s. Jones questions, for example, Ruscha's series *Burning Gas Station* (1965–1966): "[Its] matter-of-factness hardly interrogates its potential commentary on the Watts Rebellion a year earlier."[37] Ruscha's large-scale canvas *The Los Angeles County Museum on Fire* (1965–1968; fig. 1.8) has likewise elicited similar critiques. Whiting contends: "The canvas is hardly a political polemic: it delivers no obvious moral verdict on the riots, the city of Los Angeles, or even the museum's mundane administrative disputes. . . . If anything, in fact, Ruscha's is a picture that flirts with prettiness—the flames light up the sky with a soft yellow glow that gently envelops the sterile building."[38] Similarly, Carbone points to the coldness with which Warhol reproduced documentary photographs of the civil-rights movement. His print *Birmingham Race Riot* (1964; fig. 1.9), based on a photograph from *Life* magazine, showed dogs and armed police attacking peaceful protesters. She notes how the reproduction undermines the authority of the photograph but observes that ultimately this dispassionate view is less about justice and more about questioning the consumption of an image seen in every American middle-class home.[39]

One of the things most critics would agree on is that pop artists had a particular investment in the medium of screenprinting. This is significant not

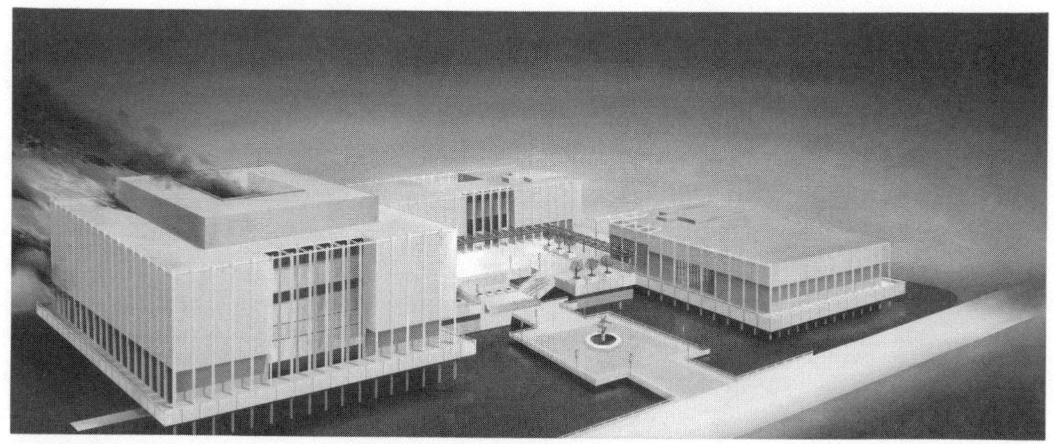

1.8. Ed Ruscha, *The Los Angeles County Museum on Fire*, 1965–1968. Oil on canvas, 53½ × 133½ inches. Gift of Joseph H. Hirshhorn, 1972, Hirshhorn Museum and Sculpture Garden, 72.252. Courtesy of the artist and Gagosian.

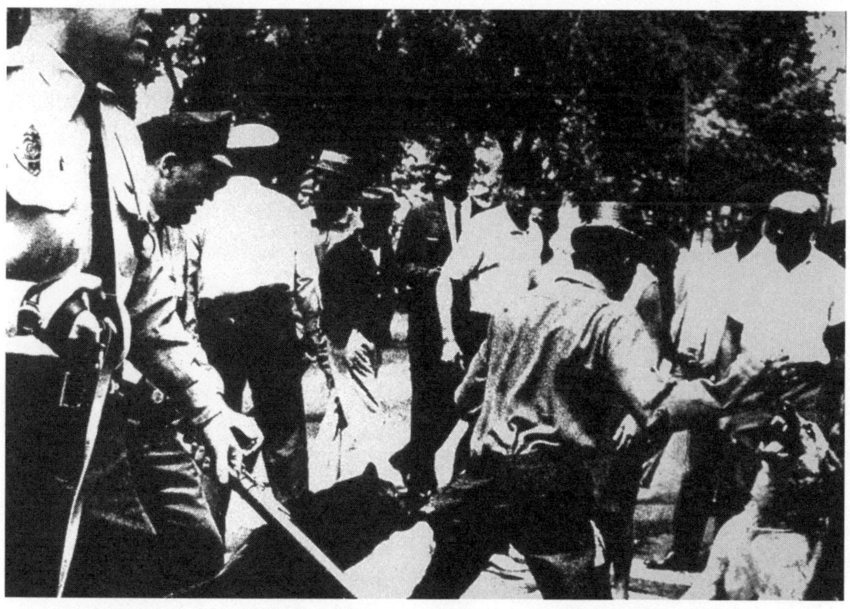

1.9. Andy Warhol, *Birmingham Race Riot*, 1964. Screenprint on paper, 20 × 24 inches. Courtesy of the Andy Warhol Foundation for the Visual Arts, licensed by Artist Rights Society.

only for Duffy's aesthetic choices but also for the workshop that produced *The New Order.* Pop artists broke with the abstract-expressionist obsession with the individual genius of the artist's hand. Curator Barry Walker noted how the medium was ideal in its portrayal of mass-produced imagery: "Pop painters like Andy Warhol and Roy Lichtenstein found the lingering taint of commercialism that was still attached to screenprinting in the early 1960s an attractive attribute that perfectly matched their particular aesthetics."[40] Unlike a previous generation of printmakers concerned with differentiating their work from the commercial or machine-made, Warhol and Lichtenstein capitalized on the consumer aesthetic. Suddenly, artworks that previously could take days or weeks could be reproduced within hours, often in collaborative workshop environments, and a photographic stencil could immediately reimage a news item from the day's paper. Warhol described the process in this manner: "You pick a photograph, blow it up, transfer it in glue onto silk, and then roll ink across it so the ink goes through the silk but not the glue. That way you get the same image, slightly different each time. It was so simple—quick and chancy. I was thrilled with it."[41] The versatile medium crossed from commercial printing into the fine-art realm in the early twentieth century, earning the distinguished moniker "serigraph" and lauded by curators such as Carl Zigrosser, who wrote: "Serigraphy is at its beginning. No one knows to what limits it will be carried. Prophecy is always hazardous. But it might well be that the serigraph will have for the twentieth century the significance and potentiality that the lithograph had for the nineteenth century."[42] It took many more years, however, before serigraphy established itself firmly in the American canon with the postwar production of artists such as Jasper Johns, Robert Rauschenberg, Ruscha, and Warhol.[43]

When Sister Karen of SHG decided in 1983 to launch the Experimental Silkscreen Atelier Program, she drew on this established tradition, owed in part to her mentor, artist Sister Corita Kent.[44] The Atelier Program coincided with the resurgence of print in the golden age of the US collaborative-press movement (1960–1990), but it emphasized cultural pride and ethnic identity at a moment when artists of color were largely excluded from access to printmaking workshops.[45] As curator Carmen Ramos points out, "Artists are nurtured by friendships, collaborations, institutions, and critics, and these connections occur in an expanded social field narrowly accessible to Latino artists."[46] Yet the cost-effectiveness and DIY ethos of screenprinting broadened accessibility, creating opportunities for young artists of color and neighborhood youth to assemble collaborative workshops, which eventually became institutions linked to new audiences and markets. While scholars in art history and art criticism have worked to document the artistic communities that revolved around workshops, such as Gemini G.E.L. in Los Angeles and Warhol's studio, The Factory, in New York, less is known about how this medium transformed the social field for artists in Latinx communities.[47] The aesthetics of screenprinting allowed SHG artists from Southern California and beyond to experiment with color, surface, and flatness; subvert the visuality of capitalism given the medium's association with consumerism; and promote pride in their Mexican American identity and neighborhood (since this was the primary audience in East Los Angeles at the time).

In a recent catalogue essay, the art historian Esther Gabara states that "Latino artists in the United States at the heart of the grandest hemispheric claim to 'America' employed Pop to reach across national borders and ethnic divides."[48] Gabara's claim not only justifies the hemispheric framework of her exhibition but also upends some of the binary thinking around a cool and detached North American pop, and a politicized pop in the South. Her point about reaching "across national borders and ethnic divides" led to a broader conversation among Latinx artists in Southern California—manifested in visual art, performance, and public actions in the 1990s—which I designate and specify as "border pop." This was not an artistic style in a strict art-historical sense but rather a way to use pop culture to humorously talk about the charged subject of immigration and border politics. Given how anti-immigrant discourse peaked in the mid-1990s following the ratification of the North American Free Trade Agreement and exemplified in the Save Our State campaign (Prop. 187), the border became a hot-button issue for right-wing conservatives who blamed Washington for lax policies and the immigrant and mixed-status families whose migration stories and separation from loved ones transformed the border into what borderlands theorist Gloria Anzaldúa called an "open wound."[49]

Satire became a way to talk about that injury. For the San Francisco–based Mexican artist Enrique Chagoya, the renewed focus on the border and the Anglo perception of Mexicans as savage invaders led him to remix and sample the archive of colonial codices. In allegorical paintings such as *Crossing I* (1994; fig. 1.10), Chagoya conceives the border war as a match between a pilgrim whose unbuttoned linen shirt exposes a Superman persona, and the Aztec deity Tlaloc, the god of rain and lightning. Likewise, he admonishes growing xenophobia in a bloody yet humorous portrayal of the Codex Magliabechiano. In *The Governor's Nightmare* (1994; fig. 1.11), Chagoya depicts a group of seated Aztec Indians enjoying the flesh, heart, and entrails of the governor while an Aztec deity seasons a hostage Mickey Mouse lying on a dinner plate. Chagoya's art practice is discussed at length in the next chapter, which follows his artist residency at Segura Publishing Company in Arizona, but the emphasis here is how the language of pop allows creative license to address the hyperbole around the border and at the same time telescopes

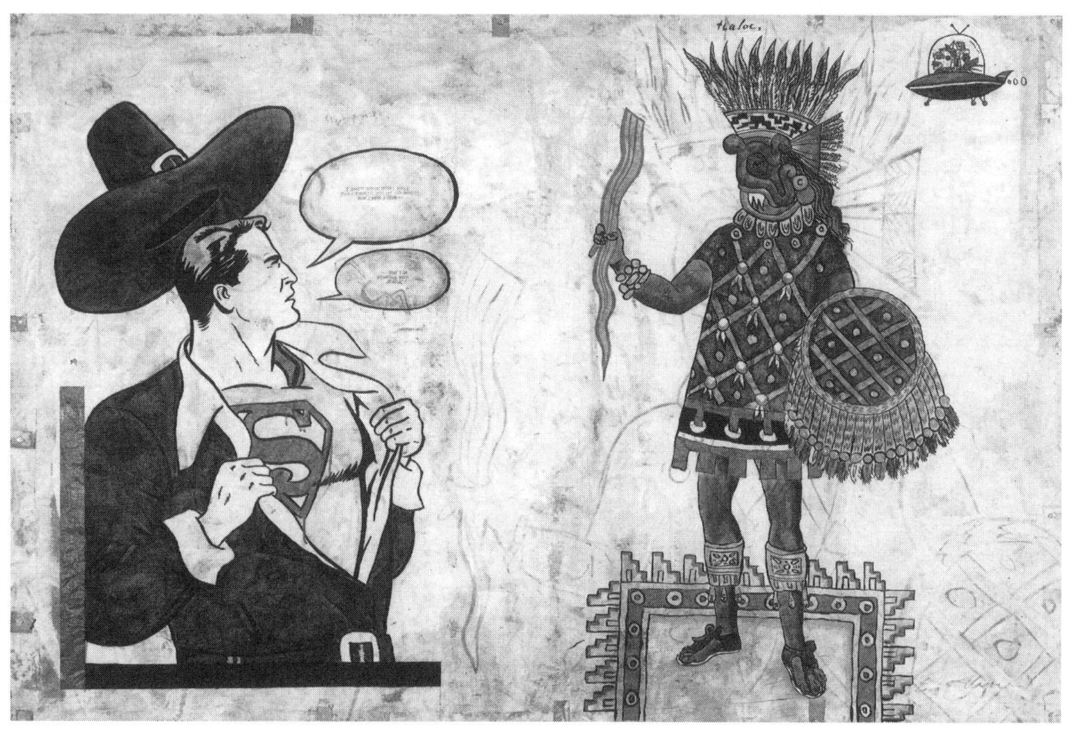

1.10. Enrique Chagoya, *Crossing I*, 1994. Acrylic and oil on paper, 48 × 72 inches. Collection of Julia and Thomas Lanigan, Upper Montclair, New Jersey. Courtesy of the artist and Anglim/Trimble.

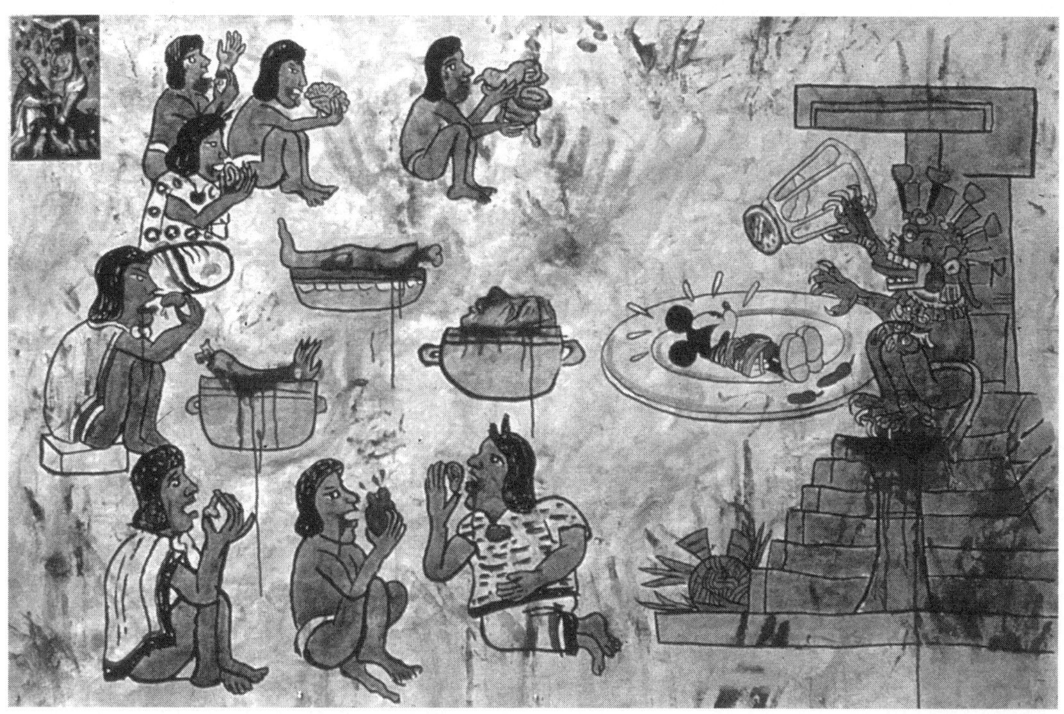

1.11. Enrique Chagoya, *The Governor's Nightmare*, 1994. Acrylic and oil on amate paper, 48 × 72 inches, Private Collection. Courtesy of the artist and Anglim/Trimble.

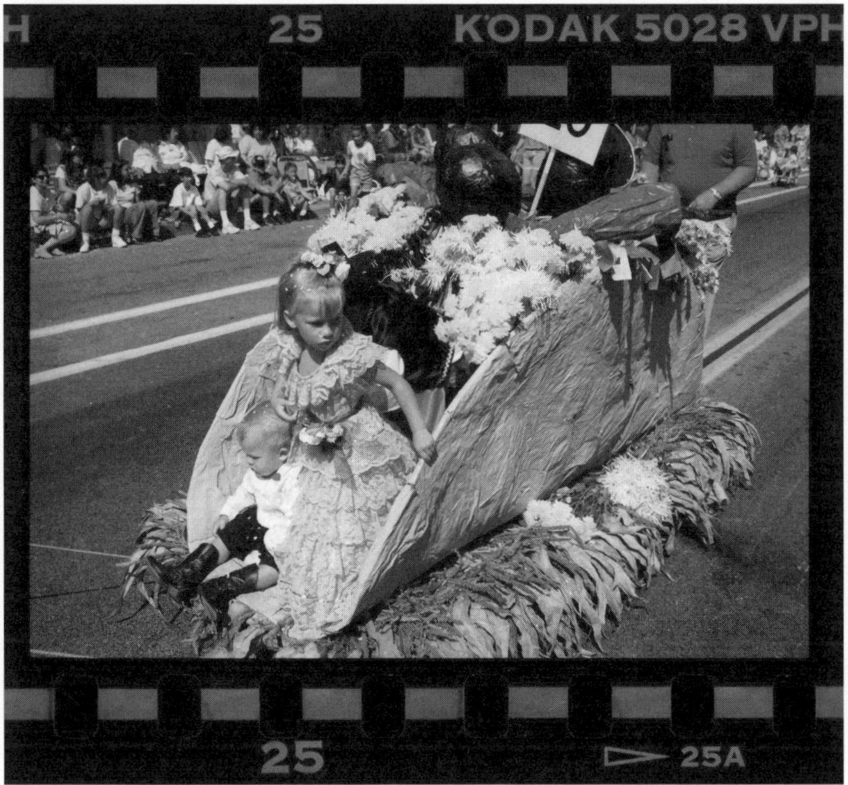

1.12. Rubén Ortiz Torres, *California Taco*, Santa Barbara, California, 1995. Fujiflex, 16 × 22 inches. Courtesy of the artist and Royale Projects.

back to the shadows of settler colonialism that pervade contemporary xenophobic movements.

The stinging satire continued in works of this post-NAFTA period such as the photographs and sculptures of Rubén Ortiz Torres.[50] The Mexico City native and Los Angeles–based artist captured a photograph titled *California Taco* (1995; fig. 1.12) that pokes fun at Southern California's parade traditions. Ortiz Torres tightly frames a parade float of blond-haired children wearing traditional Mexican dress riding atop a larger-than-life motorized taco. It is hard not to laugh at the sight of such absurdity, but in the afterlife of the photograph the viewer is hit with the irony that the state embraces Mexican food but fears actual brown-skinned Mexicans. The photograph includes a fragment of the parade audience, which acts almost like a mirror, and onlookers see how the audience's gaze gives power to the stereotypical representation. Ortiz Torres's display of Mexican culture as a commodity is perhaps intended to hark back to the days when Santa Barbara was part of Alta California and home to elite Californio ranchers.[51] But spectators likely found it humorous as the float dovetailed into the popular advertising campaign by the fast-food chain Taco Bell, especially its sombrero-wearing Chihuahua, whose Spanish catchphrase was "¡Yo quiero Taco Bell!"[52]

Duffy's *New Order* was part of the aesthetic trend of border pop in the 1990s, which contested California's nineteenth-century frontier image through the playful use of popular culture. Much like his peers' clever references to the rhetoric of colonial codices or the pageantry of Santa Barbara's taco float, Duffy dwells on Marlboro's most successful advertising campaign to lay bare its ideological origins in Manifest Destiny. In his work the same avant-garde pop strategies of the 1960s that exalted the consumable sublime are now being used to expose the paradox of Marlboro Country. Duffy was not interested in the view of the frontiersman as much as in that of the vanquished. But reorienting the gaze to contest nativism and xenophobia comes with its own risks. The next section outlines some of those issues as they relate to the uncritical appropriation of Native territorialities.

UNCANNY INDIANS IN MARLBORO COUNTRY

In a mixed-media work, part concrete poetry and part bilingual manifesto, the artist Louie "The Foot" González screenprinted a split fountain across a torn leather block titled *1848* (fig. 1.13). The soft leather appears to have been hammered to an aged piece of wood. Across vertical color fields of green, black, and red is the passage:

> 1848
> Califas
> was lost
> to the gavas
> porque oro
> tenían sus venas
> y vida
> su cuerpo sensual
> y Guadalupe
> lost Hidalgo
> and bears
> walked onto flags
> aquí
> empezó el Chicano-
> manifest destinyed.[53]

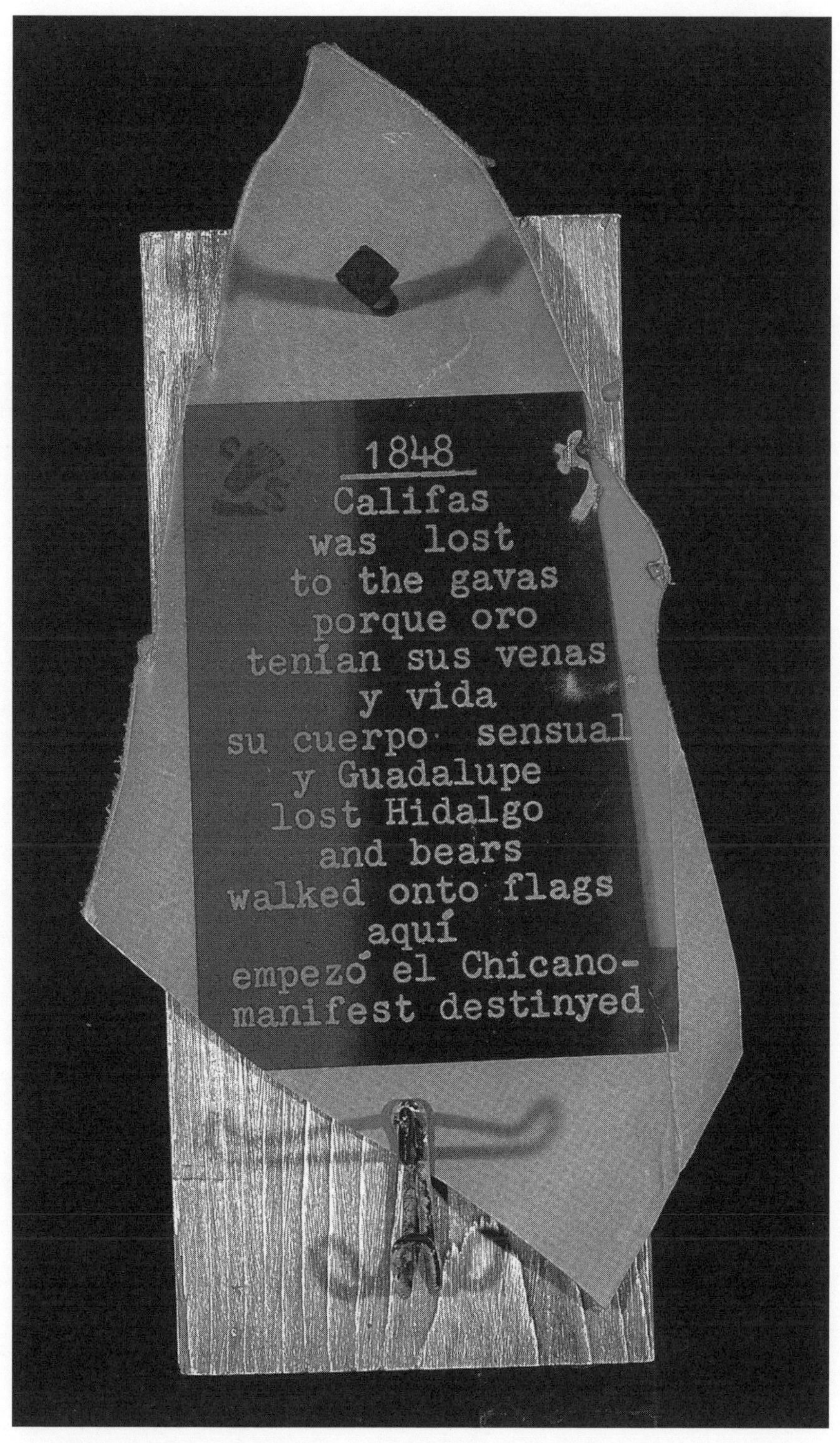

1.13. Luis C. González, aka "Louie the Foot," *1848*, 2003. Screenprint on leather, hardware and wood, 14½ × 7¼ × 4½ inches. Courtesy of the artist.

The image/text/object transports viewers back to California's Gold Rush and resembles a printed notice one might see outside a saloon. González returns to the nineteenth-century violence of the western frontier but deliberately reorients the narrative of land dispossession to one of inalienable rights to Aztlán. As the scholar Ella Diaz points out, González constructs a "verbal-visual architecture" that produces a utopian Aztlán "as a decolonial idea based on the location of an ancient, Native land with which Chicanos/as could ancestrally identify and claim their rights to US citizenship."[54] This mythical homeland lies at the heart of the Aztec empire's creation story, and its resurgence in the 1960s was how Chicanx artists negotiated their claims for a politics of territory.

Chicanx artists have long accessed "spiritual geographies" to stake a claim for sovereignty in the lands of the Southwest, and *The New Order* similarly deploys myth in the service of Native land rights.[55] In an interview, when asked about the mountain of skulls in *The New Order,* Duffy mentioned how the theme of death references Apache Leap.[56] The latter is a red bluff peak in the Pinal Mountains, east of Superior, Arizona (fig. 1.14). Legend has it that the Apaches held an outpost on this mountaintop from which they would launch raids against the white settlers, especially the farming community of Florence, which edged into Apache land. In the 1870s the federal government sent assistance to these white families in the form of a military post led by US Army Colonel George Stoneman.[57] Stoneman's troops used heliograph signals with sunlight and mirrors to scout the trails leading to the Indian lookout; once they were located, the army launched a military offensive.[58] The surprise assault on the surrounded encampment left the Apache warriors at the edge of a fatal cliff. Rather than surrender, legend claims the Apaches leaped to their deaths, the lore from which is coined the cliff's foreboding title.[59]

Noted historian Jack August and Arizona State University archivist Christine Marin question this narrative of a mass suicide. Their conversations suggest that Apache Leap is nothing but a "creation of 20th century Anglo business people . . . to gin up business in a place that offered little beyond beautiful scenery and a cyclical mining economy."[60] After sifting through old military records at the National Archives, correspondence files, and diaries of Florence settlers, August concluded that the incident does not exist in written records. It is unclear whether the attack and grisly tale of death became part of the oral histories of the Pinal Apache Indians.[61] Among the few recent mentions of the event, testimony by Wendsler Nosie, Sr., Chairman of the San Carlos Apache Tribe, describes: "The escarpment of Apache Leap . . . is also sacred and consecrated ground for our People. . . . At least seventy-five of our People sacrificed their lives at Apache Leap during the winter of 1870 to protect their land, their principles, and their freedom when faced with overwhelm-

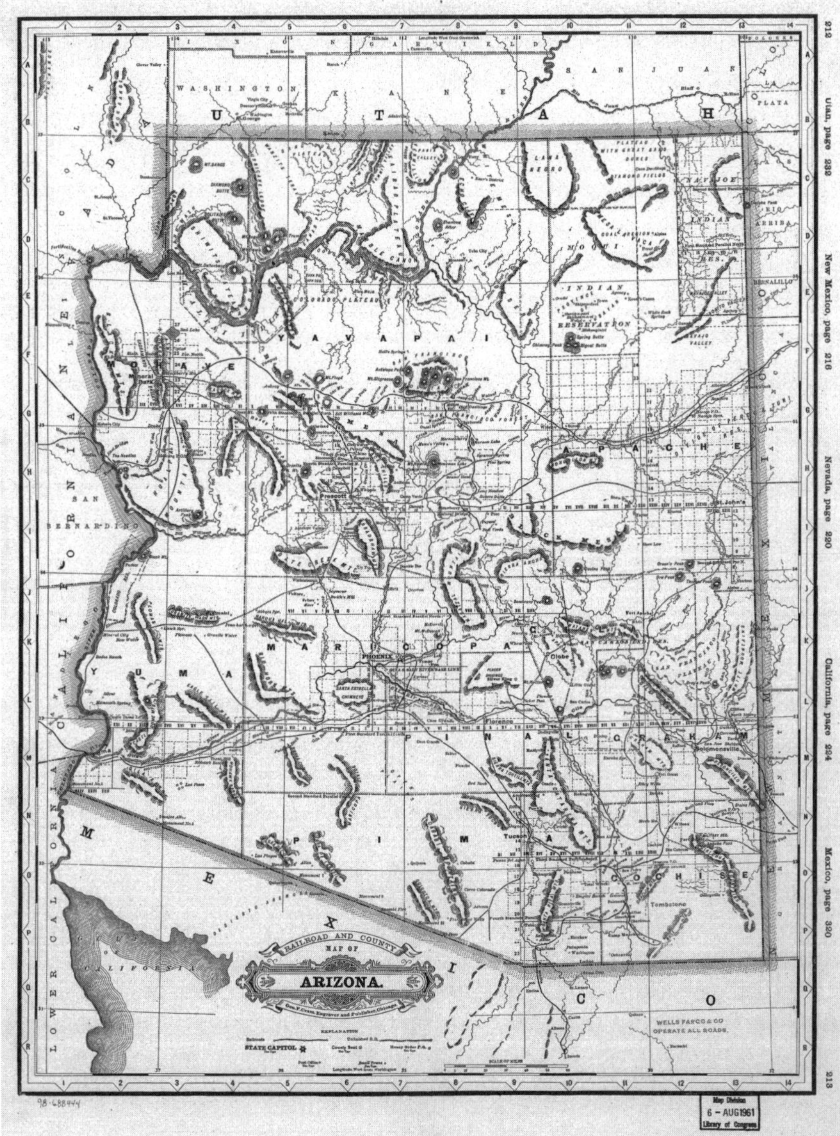

1.14. George Franklin Cram, *Railroad and County Map of Arizona*, 1887. Library of Congress.

ing military force from the U.S. Calvary [*sic*] which would have required them to surrender as prisoners of war."[62] Without a doubt, the white settlers of Arizona led punitive expeditions to kill and displace the Apaches from this region, perhaps underscoring the value of the land, home to a prominent mining district that included the Silver Queen and Silver King Mines, as well as the Magma Copper Mine.[63] But the story of Apache warriors leaping to their deaths is likely part of Depression-era folklore invested in attracting tourists into Superior, especially given that other nineteenth-century Arizona Indian massacres were greatly boasted about.

Folktales, however uncorroborated, have a way of becoming history in a place like Arizona. Columnist Sam Lowe notes that the Superior Chamber of Commerce to this day continues to hand out reprints of an *Arizona Highways* magazine that purports to tell the story of Apache Leap (fig. 1.15).[64] The piece, published by amateur historian James Mitchell Barney, attributes the offensive to the Arizona Volunteers, not the cavalry of Colonel Stoneman.[65] Organized during the Civil War, the Arizona Volunteers enlisted the help of the Pima Indians, a "friendly" tribe presumably adversarial to the Apache. The *Arizona Highways* version of the story shifts the power dynamics from white-settler aggression on Indian land to Indian versus Indian hostility. Barney wrote:

> The Florence settlers, after obtaining help from the friendly Pimas, organized a pursuing party and patiently followed the trails of the raiders for several days. . . . Those found in the Indian rancheria included women and children, but in the excitement of battle, the attacking party paid little heed to the sex or age of their enemies. When about two thirds of the band had been killed or maimed by the hail of bullets fired at them, the remainder retreated in the only direction possible: toward the westerly edge of the mountain which, on that side, broke off abruptly into sheer cliffs, hundreds of feet high.[66]

The folktale retold again and again attracted tourists craving a view of the nineteenth-century western frontier.

But the question for us is, Why would Duffy revert to the use of this myth? How could colonizing the myth of the colonizers relieve the injustices of westward expansion? How could Apache Leap as seen from this Marlboro billboard comment on the current immigration crisis? Historian Richard Slotkin, who has studied the development of the Western film genre, explains that "Myths are stories drawn from a society's history that have acquired through persistent usage the power of symbolizing that society's ideology and of dramatizing its moral consciousness—with all the complexities and contradictions that consciousness may contain."[67] Duffy appears to focus on those contradictions and to place in question their moralizing rhetoric. Some of this is driven by an autobiographical connection to Arizona. Duffy's mother, Elizabeth Anne Rodriguez, was a descendant of the Chiricahua Apache Nation, which once ruled a vast territory in what is now the borderlands of New Mexico, Arizona, Sonora, and Chihuahua. She returned to live in Superior, be-

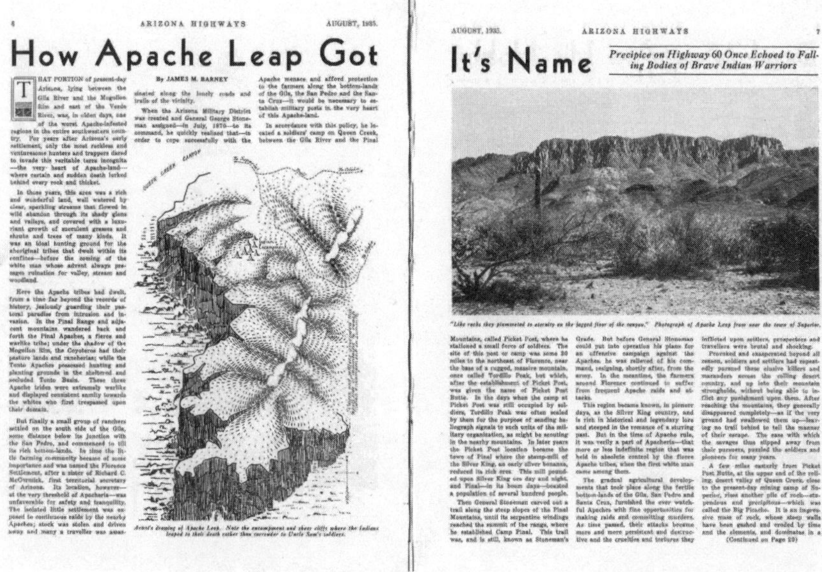

6 ARIZONA HIGHWAYS AUGUST, 1935.

How Apache Leap Got It's Name

Precipice on Highway 60 Once Echoed to Falling Bodies of Brave Indian Warriors

By JAMES M. BARNEY

THAT PORTION of present-day Arizona, lying between the Gila River and the Mogollon Rim and east of the Verde River, was, in olden days, one of the worst Apache-infested regions in the entire southwestern country. For years after Arizona's early settlement, only the most reckless and venturesome hunters and trappers dared to invade this veritable terra incognita—the very heart of Apache-land—where certain and sudden death lurked behind every rock and thicket.

In those years, this area was a rich and wonderful land, well watered by clear, sparkling streams that flowed in wild abandon through its shady glens and valleys, and covered with a luxuriant growth of succulent grasses and shrubs and trees of many kinds. It was an ideal hunting ground for the aboriginal tribes that dwelt within its confines—before the coming of the white man whose advent always presages ruination for valley, stream and woodland.

Here the Apache tribes had dwelt, from a time far beyond the records of history, jealously guarding their pastoral paradise from intrusion and invasion. In the Pinal Range and adjacent mountains wandered back and forth the Pinal Apaches, a fierce and warlike tribe; under the shadow of the Mogollon Rim, the Coyoteros had their pasture lands and rancherias; while the Tonto Apaches possessed hunting and planting grounds in the sheltered and secluded Tonto Basin. These three Apache tribes were extremely warlike and displayed consistent enmity towards the whites who first trespassed upon their domain.

But finally a small group of ranchers settled on the south side of the Gila, some distance below its junction with the San Pedro, and commenced to till its rich bottom-lands. In time the little farming community became of some importance and was named the Florence Settlement, after a sister of Richard C. McCormick, first territorial secretary of Arizona. Its location, however—at the very threshold of Apacheria—was unfavorable for safety and tranquility. The isolated little settlement was exposed to continuous raids by the nearby Apaches; stock was stolen and driven away and many a traveller was assassinated along the lonely roads and trails of the vicinity.

When the Arizona Military District was created and General George Stoneman assigned—in July, 1870—to its command, he quickly realized that—in order to cope successfully with the Apache menace and afford protection to the farmers along the bottom-lands of the Gila, the San Pedro and the Santa Cruz—it would be necessary to establish military posts in the very heart of this Apache-land.

In accordance with this policy, he located a soldiers' camp on Queen Creek, between the Gila River and the Pinal

Artist's drawing of Apache Leap. Note the escarpment and sheer cliffs where the Indians leaped to their death rather than surrender to Uncle Sam's soldiers.

AUGUST, 1935. ARIZONA HIGHWAYS 7

"Like rocks they plummeted to eternity on the jagged floor of the canyon." Photograph of Apache Leap from near the town of Superior.

1.15. *Arizona Highways*, "How Apache Leap Got Its Name," 1935. Courtesy of Arizona Highways Online.

tween the Pinetop and San Carlos Apache reservations.[68] Duffy's visits to the area and their ancestral connection sparked his interest in a Native worldview.

After a bloody war, when the Apaches officially surrendered to the US Army in 1886, they lost more than their land. Entire families were detained and relocated to Fort Marion, Florida, becoming prisoners for more than two decades.[69] From Fort Marion, the families were transferred to Alabama and eventually to Fort Sill, Oklahoma, until their release in 1913. While the logic of westward expansion and capitalism (enacted in countless treaties, including the Treaty of Guadalupe Hidalgo) demanded their land and, quite frankly, their annihilation, the Chiricahua people and their language, customs, song, and dance endured. In their story of resilience and survival, Duffy found parallels to the Native immigrants from southern Mexico and Central America clamoring for entry at the southern border.

Duffy's recognition of his own Native ancestry, as well as the connection between contemporary Native immigrants and the Indigenous nations displaced in the nineteenth century, forces the question of trauma in contemporary Native art. Reflecting on the work of (Canadian) Cree artist Kent Monkman, art historian Kate Morris notes the transhistorical effects of how the "traumas of dislocation and dispossession of Indigenous peoples are ongoing." She continues, "The legacies of colonialism are exactly that—legacies,

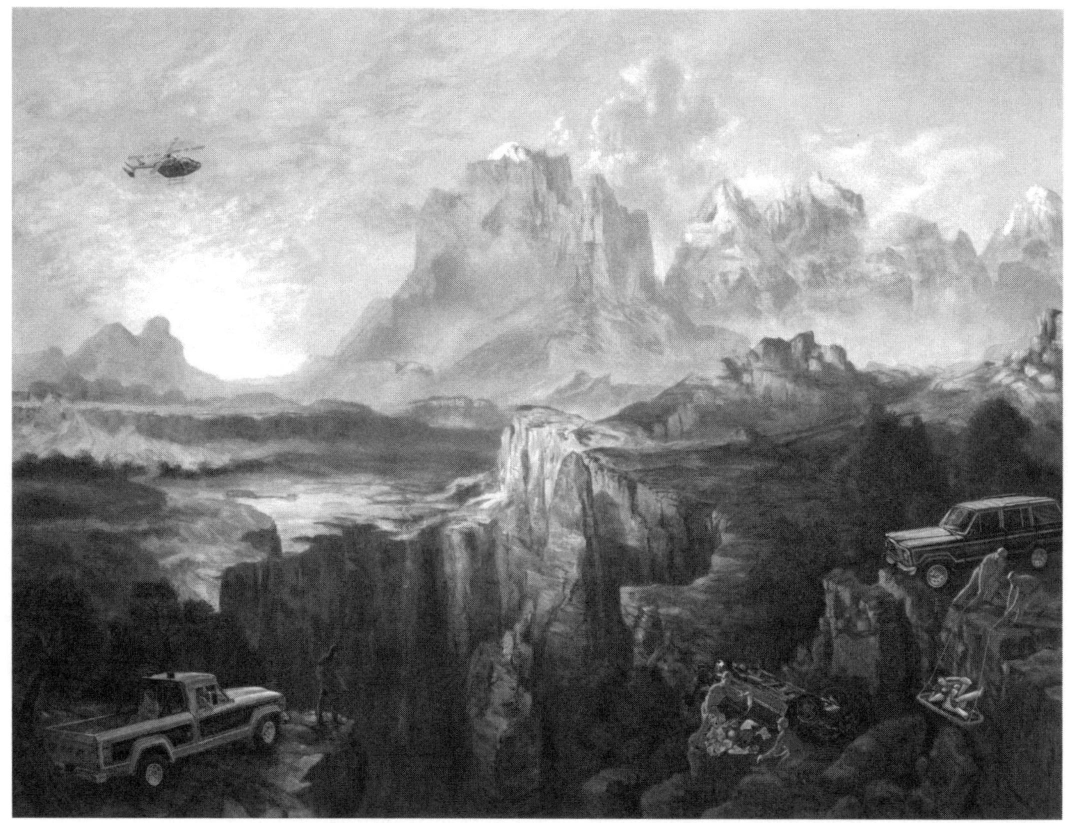

1.16. Kent Monkman, *Casualties of Modernity*, 2012. Acrylic on canvas, 36 × 48 inches. Collection of the Claridge Foundation. Courtesy of the artist.

not simply remnants of the past, but a continuation of that past into the present."[70] The palimpsestic layering of temporality, or "heterotemporality," present in *The New Order*'s Marlboro ad/urban billboard/highway sign/Border Patrol–surveilled desert hints at this ongoing suffering. The mythologies of the West seem to be the preferred site for the trauma's reenactment.

In *Casualties of Modernity* (2012; fig. 1.16), Monkman revisits the western frontier. At the edge of the void of a deep canyon, he grants viewers a bird's-eye picture of a deadly accident. A red car lies overturned on the mountainside, and four EMTs work quickly to recover the survivors. On the left, curious onlookers, perhaps eyewitnesses, survey the damage. One of them, a long-haired Native youth in red T-shirt and blue jeans, leans in to see over the cliff, assessing what could have been a worse fate. Monkman, writes Morris, is "known for his subversive interventions into the Romantic landscape painting tradition," and *Casualties of Modernity* does not disappoint in that regard.[71]

The sky is a patchwork of pink, lavender, and blue-tainted clouds. A snow-capped mountain range emits the haze and fog characteristic of extreme altitudes. The Life Flight orange helicopter on the top left flies across vanishing sunlight and presumably will airlift those hurt. Monkman juxtaposed the sublime beauty of the rugged mountain scape, including its dangerous cliffs and crevasses, with modern automobiles and bodies that appear minute and frail in comparison to their grandeur. In this way he underscored the Romantic sensibility in which human figures (and their machines) are dwarfed by the overwhelming scale and uncontrollable power of nature.

Monkman's casualties are female figures twice broken through the modernist forms of cubism and the accident but largely symbolic of a Native conquered land. The colonial gaze, interrupted, reveals the victims of a car crash (and likely alcoholism) and the passive onlookers, all mere objects of a wide-open landscape. The figure of the Indian is not just in the landscape but is the landscape—gendered female, beautiful, frightening, and open for the taking. The scholar María Josefina Saldaña-Portillo explores this logic in recent work, noting how the figure of the Indian appears and disappears in the production of national space. Saldaña-Portillo argues that national geographies are built through racialized ways of seeing, and these perceptions are shaped through colonial encounters with Indigeneity.[72] We may consider how Monkman pries open this moment precisely to reveal the logic of this learned sight and the brutality of Indian removal.

The New Order stages a similar provocation by using colonial myths against the myth of Marlboro Country. By 1963, when Philip Morris launched the Marlboro Country campaign with its focus on the cowboy and western landscape, the figure of the Indian had already vanished. Ironically, the white male cowboy had to adopt Indian ways to tame the West, had to perform a generic Indianness to clear the land of the Indigenous and barbarous. The situation is reminiscent of the pilot episode of *Mad Men* (aired 2007), in which the CEO of Lucky Strike exclaims in frustration: "What the hell are you talking about? Why not just write 'cancer' on the package? Are you insane? I'm not selling rifles. I'm *selling America*. The Indians *gave it to us* for shit's sake [author's emphasis]."[73] The racialized geography of Marlboro Country thus builds on the desire of a free land "gifted" to the colonists, a sublime terrain conquered by non-Indigenous white men. Duffy juxtaposes that racialized geography of the Indian with the history of western expansion that required the dispossession and extermination of Indigenous people. His cowboy rides atop the mountain of skulls, where his heels touch the myth of Apache Leap, the skirmish in which according to lore the US cavalry watched the desperate Indians fall to their deaths. To rid Indian savagery from Marlboro Country, the colonists justified the expendable nature of the Indigenous subjects and later reified that view through a story that claimed their rightful possession of Apache land.

To use the myth of Apache Leap against the image of Manifest Destiny is humorous and witty, but one must also consider how the narrative of settler colonialism informs the mythos of Aztlán. For artist and theorist Amalia Mesa-Bains, "The powerful symbol of Aztlan as an ancestral homeland emanated from the deep Chicana/o sense of dislocation and deterritorialization experienced in the aftermath of the Mexican-American War, which resulted in the annexation by the United States of the northern territories of Mexico, as well as the earlier Spanish colonial invasion."[74] The geographical utopia of Aztlán, which emerged from the history of territorial loss and a sense of powerlessness, invents a direct link to a pre-Columbian past, rooting itself in the Indigenous traditions of Mexico while appropriating North American Indigenous territories.[75] In *The New Order*, Aztlán also takes possession of the Southwest, mimicking the settler colonialism that grabbed this land and repopulating it with "uncanny" Indians.

The Indigenous are a simulation of those who perished in the fight for Apache land and those Chicanos who later appropriated that trauma and reenacted the loss in their mythical homeland. According to Saldaña-Portillo, Chicano Aztlán is a space produced through the melancholic incorporation of lost Indigeneity.[76] Duffy is luckier than most Chicanos in that his family can trace its lineage to the Apache, not merely generic Indianness. But the multiracial artist is many generations separated from an Indigenous specificity. His print speaks of a psychic longing, what Saldaña-Portillo calls a "Chicano racial unconscious," that makes those who are racially incomplete desire a lost Indigenous past. One can speculate that this yearning is particularly acute for an artist who is not white enough, nor Mexican enough, to fit neatly into categories. The desire is so strong, the artist surely believes the legend to be true. He has willed it so:

> The reality, because of Apache Leap, you know, 16th cavalry, all that history I've studied, and knowing people . . . from the San Carlos Reservation, which is where my mother used to live near Lake Superior. . . . So here I am and I see this Marlboro thing, and I go, "Holy macaroni moly!" And they ran away from the 16th cavalry, they didn't want to get captured, so the women and children jumped. That's pretty daring.[77]

The repressed loss creates a deep chasm between the real, the myth, the performative, and the melancholic, as deep as Monkman's canyon dividing Chicanos from present-day Native American nations. Apache Leap is not a mirror but rather is a narrative of mythical power. This appropriation puts in

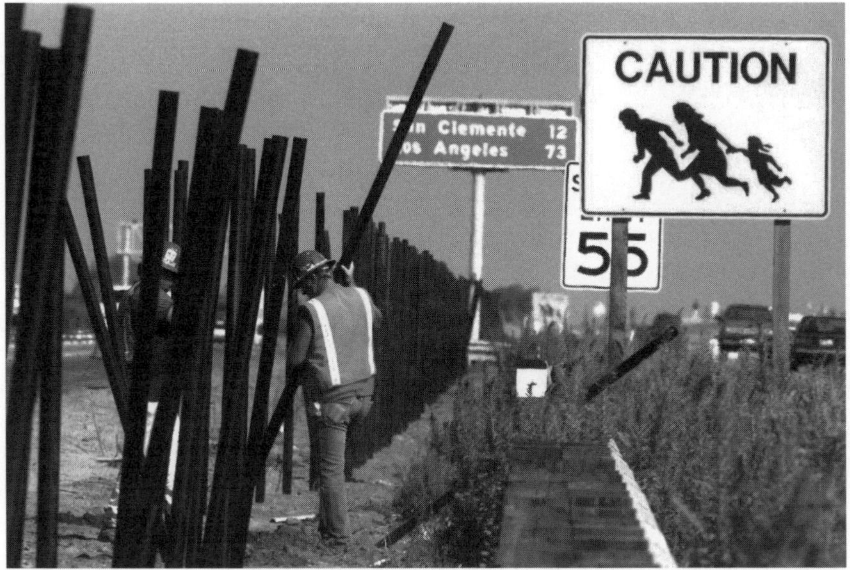

1.17. Don Barletti, *Los Angeles Times*, contractors in 1993 set posts for an eight-foot fence in the median of the 5 Freeway in the shadow of an iconic yellow pedestrian warning sign.

question the decolonial aims of Aztlán, as elaborated by Diaz earlier, and perhaps highlights the reconquest undertones of "Louie the Foot" González's "Chicano-manifest destinyed." Saldaña-Portillo would add that what further complicates this turn toward Native territorialities and bolsters this longing is that Chicanos, like many of their Mexican counterparts, are "deindigenized Indians," seeking a lost and unacknowledged history.[78]

The Indians that haunt Marlboro Country are not only a result of Duffy's play on "visual sovereignty" but also appear from the graphic unconscious of another Indigenous artist.[79] Graphic artist John Hood, who worked for California's Department of Transportation (Caltrans), made the iconic immigrants Caution sign (fig. 1.17). Hood's design of a bright yellow road sign features the silhouette of a family in flight: the father leans forward, three limbs in the air; the mother follows closely, desperately pulling on the wrist of a pigtailed girl whose feet barely touch the ground. Caltrans debuted the signs in 1990 along Interstate 5 in "danger zones" north of the border where migrants attempting to cross traffic were being killed.[80] The sign became an icon of the highly charged, undocumented immigration debate of the 1990s. Those in favor of restrictionist immigration policies viewed it as a confirmation of the out-of-control border and galvanized its potential to fuel movements like Proposition 187, as well as Operation Gatekeeper, which fenced off much of California's border crossing and drove immigrants east to more treacherous terrain.[81] The advocates for immigration rights, although somewhat disturbed at the analogy of an animal crossing, found the image to convey the vulnerability and danger that some families face at the failure of our immigration policies.

Hood was tasked with alerting drivers at the crossings to reduce the number of fatalities, but the image of a desperate family in flight perhaps also alluded to the forced removal of Indian families in the nineteenth century. Hood, who grew up on a Navajo reservation in New Mexico, attended a Bureau of Indian Affairs boarding school before enlisting in the US Marine Corps. He is a veteran of the Vietnam War. The late Native writer Roy Cook, who featured profiles of American Indian Veterans on his website, remarked on the connection between the road sign showing running immigrants and the forced removal of Native families: "As he sketched, Hood tried to imagine the despair that might drive such a family across the border and onto a forbidding foreign highway. He drew from his own experience fighting in Vietnam, where he had seen families run for their lives as villages were attacked. He remembered stories his Navajo parents had told him about ancestors who died trying to escape as U.S. soldiers marched them onto reservations."[82] Speculating on the "Chicano racial unconscious" that haunts *The New Order* illuminates the repressed and lost Indigenous past, while also making visible the "Indian racial unconscious" that Hood conjured in the silhouetted figures. He writes, "They were marched about 400 miles to Fort Sumner just beyond Albuquerque. . . . A treaty was signed in 1868, and the Navajos returned to their burned homes, cornfields, and livestock."[83] As if confinement to the reservation were not enough, two uranium mines, discovered adjacent to the Navajo Reservation, had exposed the residents to a lifetime of illness.[84]

Freud viewed the uncanny as "nothing new or foreign, but something familiar and old—established in the mind that has been estranged only by the process of repression."[85] When the repressed returns involuntarily or comes to light after being concealed, it produces that unsettling feeling. For Duffy, the specific moment came when the repressed loss of Apache Leap and the Marlboro billboard merged with the Arizona desert landscape. *The New Order* ventures to place us in the uncanny Indian country through the return of the dead. He used animism to move that mound of skull and bones, and the *calaveras* that practically rattle on the coat of George Washington. He revealed a psychic reality that, although based primarily in his own borderlands experience, also gestures to a larger American racial unconscious, an American psyche that insists on repressing the figure of the Indian and dreads the return of the dead who may bring about vengeance. This is Duffy's America.

Through the medium of prints, he invokes the recurring nightmare, bombarding us with its most cherished and monstrous images: the dollar bill, the Marlboro billboard, the road sign of silhouetted running immigrants, which appear estranged for us to ponder.

GENDERED TERRITORIES

In *The National Uncanny* (2000), literary theorist Renée Bergland argues that American nationalism sustains itself through writings that "conjure spectral Native Americans."[86] These ghostly representations attest to the shame and guilt associated with the murder and displacement of Indians as well as the pride and triumph of nationalism. The phenomenon is present in *The New Order* when the viewer connects George Washington's gaze to the spectral Indian mother and child. The blue of Washington's eyes, perhaps a reference to Toni Morrison's *The Bluest Eye*, is the same blue that shapes her vanishing figure. Bergland adds: "When European Americans speak of Native Americans, they always use the language of ghostliness. . . . They insist that Indians are able to appear and disappear suddenly and mysteriously, and also that they are ultimately doomed to vanish."[87] Perhaps the Indian mother is simply another Indian fulfilling the prophecy of reinscribing US nationalism, as Bergland explains. Of interest here, however, is making her body explicit, to learn what it may tell us about the production of gendered geographical knowledge of the borderlands.

The mother and child evoke a gendered reading of land and Indigeneity. Placed in the bottom left corner of the composition, between the running-immigrants sign and the lettering of "Country," the phantom figures emerge and merge with the landscape. The profile portrait is a freehand stenciling technique that Duffy developed in the monotype process and demonstrates his draftsmanship. The line drawing shows a mother carrying a child strapped to her back. Her hair is pulled back into a braid, and the textiles of her traditional rebozo and skirt evince Native origins. She is the bearer of life, the one who continues Native knowledge and tradition amid a landscape that speaks of Indian death and removal. But she is also nomadic as the sign above her indicates, and the politics of her maternal body say something about how gender operates in the landscape. Much like Monkman's female casualties of modernity, Duffy suggests the figure of the Indian mother is symbolic of a Native conquered land.

The Native mother's ghostly presence reveals the masculinist epistemology of Manifest Destiny. To understand how gender operates in this ideology,

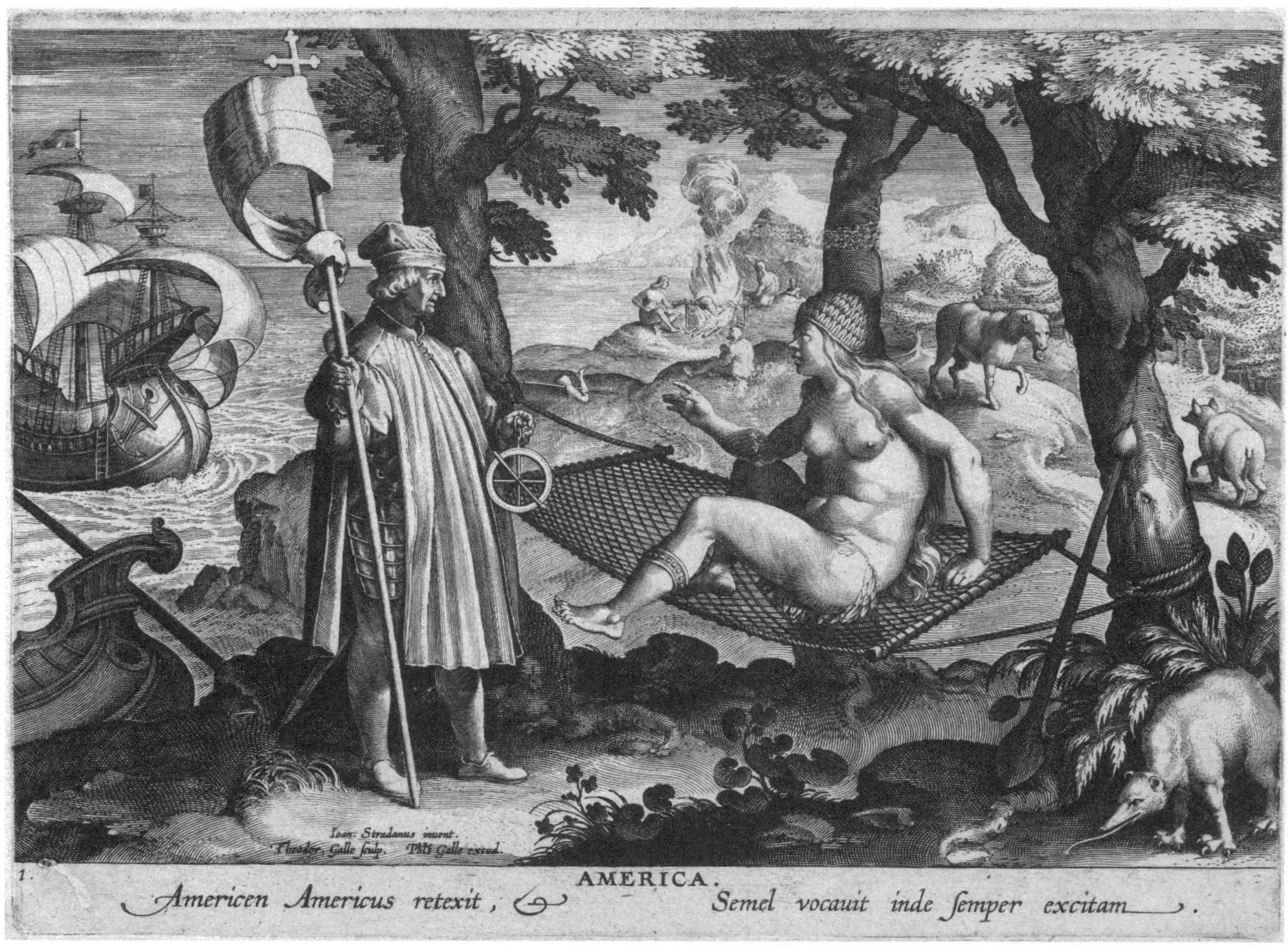

1.18. Theodoor Galle and Philips Galle, after Jan van der Straet (Johannes Stradanus), “Allegory of America,” *Nova Reperta*, ca. 1588. Engraving, sheet: 10 5/8 × 7 7/8 inches, Harris Brisbane Dick Fund 1934, 34.30, The Metropolitan Museum of Art.

it is useful to return to the writing of journalist John L. O'Sullivan, who in 1845 coined the term "Manifest Destiny" in an article that argued for the annexation of Texas. He wrote:

> Texas is now ours. . . . Her star and her stripe may already be said to have taken their place in the glorious blazon of our common nationality; and the sweep of our eagle's wing already includes within its circuit the wide extent of her fair and fertile land. She is no longer to us a mere geographical space—a certain combination of coast, plain, mountain, valley, forest and stream. . . . She comes within the dear and sacred designation of Our Country.[88]

This territorial ambition, which he considered the "fulfillment of our Manifest Destiny," gendered land and nation as female and fertile. It is worth establishing this formal connection in the pale blue color that connects Washington and the Native mother. She is the ghostly counterpart to the "father of our country." As such they become the second family portrayed in *The New Order* and an allegory for the mestizaje, or racial mixtures, that will populate this land's future.

O'Sullivan's association between territory and the female body was certainly not new but rather was part of a long tradition in Western thought based on colonial encounters. The iconic work by the Flemish artist Johannes Stradanus, *Nova Reperta: America*, engraved by Theodor Galle circa 1588 (fig. 1.18), is perhaps the most exemplary image to produce this foundational fiction.[89] The engraving portrays the female figure of America being awakened by the landing of the Florentine explorer Amerigo Vespucci. Her partly nude body rises out of a hammock to greet the Italian explorer, whose European accoutrements bear the marks of science and Christianity. America's Native body, though rendered within European notions of beauty, is a representation of the imperial subject's other. In this system, Vespucci appears to transcend embodiment, having endowed his subject with objectivity, rationality, and universality. But America's body is also characterized as geography's other—untamable, irrational, out of order. Her hand gestures toward cannibalistic rituals, originating out of Native savagery. This personification of America responds to the gaze of white male settlers, whose chronicles imagined the New World as both a nurturing mother and a wilderness awaiting incursion and mastery.[90]

Among the recurring female archetypes used to celebrate the triumph of US nationalism, Sacagawea stands out as the maternal Indian mother ushering the civilizing and imperial mission.[91] One of the possible sources for Duffy's Native mother may be this Shoshone woman, and her child Jean-

Baptiste, who served as guide and translator for the Lewis and Clark expedition (1804–1806). Sacagawea, the subject of statues, paintings, novels, films, music, coins, and stamps, has become a legendary figure in frontier mythology.[92] Her role in the national epic is that of the Indian princess who rescues and complies with the white male explorer. Literary scholar Donna Kessler, who has studied the development of this icon, writes, "The Indian princess stereotype has actually operated as a composite portrait, a wedding of idealized womanhood and of noble savagery."[93] Both sex object and ideal nurturer, she is considered the heroine who "fosters the invasion of the wilderness by a superior 'civilization.'"[94] In Duffy's *New Order* the connection between her blue-outline vanishing figure and Washington's blue-eyed gaze supports this interpretation. Both are symbols of US mastery over the gendered land, characters personifying the frontier myth to secure the continent and assimilate or eliminate the savage. While portraits of Washington flourished during the expansionist period (1840–1890), the icon of Sacagawea gained traction during the Progressive Era (1890–1920), when the country had fully redrawn the national space, claiming the lands west of the Mississippi and severely eroding Native sovereignty.[95]

On the other hand, the rebozo and patterned skirt evince southern origins for this maternal figure. Unlike Sacagawea's Shoshone leather dress, Duffy's Native mother summons the vision of a woman from southern Mexico or Guatemala. The nomadic figure perhaps gestures to the influx of rural peasant farmers from Indigenous communities, who migrated north after the neoliberal reforms of NAFTA crushed their small farming economies. Duffy's Indian ghost clearly straddles both racialized geographies. The spectral icon is flexible enough to contain references to female archetypes of Mexican and US nationalism. As such, the icon also conjures the legend of Malinche—interpreter, guide, and mistress to Spanish conquistador Hernán Cortés—who is commonly portrayed as the treacherous Native mother who helped bring down the Aztec empire and gave birth to Cortés's mixed-race child.[96]

Her maternal and racialized body begins to unravel the politics of this sight. Washington performs the expansionist gaze, making the body of the Native mother coterminous with the land. Yet the Marlboro Country campaign must erase all traces of this Indian mother, relegating her to the vanished past, replacing her with a white male cowboy who will conquer the hostile terrain. Aztlán likewise builds on the masculinist epistemology by calling for the political and spiritual retaking of this conquered land, a motherland conflated with a lost Indigeneity, as discussed in the previous section. The trend is most evident in the first stanza of Louie "The Foot" González's concrete poem, wherein he states, "the land was lost to the gavas [from *gabachos*, a slur for whites], because gold ran through *her* veins and life moved *her sensual body* [emphasis the author's]" (fig. 1.13).

Cultural critic Amy Sara Carroll recently tackled the trope of the body of Mexico as woman. She notes how Latin American foundational fictions, "time and again cast the European explorer as male and the indigenous populations with whom he came into contact as fantastically female or effeminate."[97] Rape is central to the repeated scripts of colonial encounters and extends from Native women to an effeminized landscape. Carroll goes on to consider how this ideology embeds itself within the paradigms of economic globalization in the 1990s and, further, how artists employ the female form to question the NAFTA view (penetration/domination) of the land. In particular, she considers the work of female performance artists such as Lorena Wolffer and Nao Bustamante, whose art alludes to the "allegorical slippage between Woman-as-Nation and Woman-as-Border," gesturing to how their work genders territory to expose the violence against its female citizenry as well as the neoliberal market's aggressive restructuring of the Mexican social fabric.[98] Duffy's Native mother evokes these allegorical slippages that point to the effeminized border but retain the patriarchal view of a gendered land linked to Indigeneity.

The cultural logic is not all that different from Warhol's portrait of Russell Means (fig. 1.19). In 1976, Warhol embarked on a new series, which he eventually titled "The American Indian Series," as a collaborative venture with West Coast art dealer Douglas Chrismas.[99] With Warhol's interest in pop portraiture, Chrismas sought out a model that personified the contemporary Indian at the critical juncture of the nation's bicentennial. He found Means's activism and pop-culture celebrity to be the perfect combination to appeal to Warhol's aesthetics. In exchange for Means's participation, Chrismas made a $5,000 donation to the American Indian Movement, which at that point was still reeling from the highly publicized occupation of Wounded Knee.[100] Means was an Oglala Lakota Indian from the Pine Ridge Reservation in South Dakota and was thought to be one of the leaders of the Wounded Knee Occupation, an armed resistance that lasted seventy days in 1973 (and involved hostages, two deaths, and numerous injuries); he called on Washington to recognize Oglala Sioux sovereignty (and restrict the meddling of the Bureau of Indian Affairs).[101] Most readers will recall his performance as Chingachgook in the film *The Last of the Mohicans* (1992), in which he played the role of Indian warrior and adoptive father to the white protagonist played by Daniel Day-Lewis.[102]

The American Indian (Russell Means) demonstrates how the excess of the stereotype has consequences for the reading of Native land. The bust portrait is a triangular composition with a vivid palette. Means stares directly at the

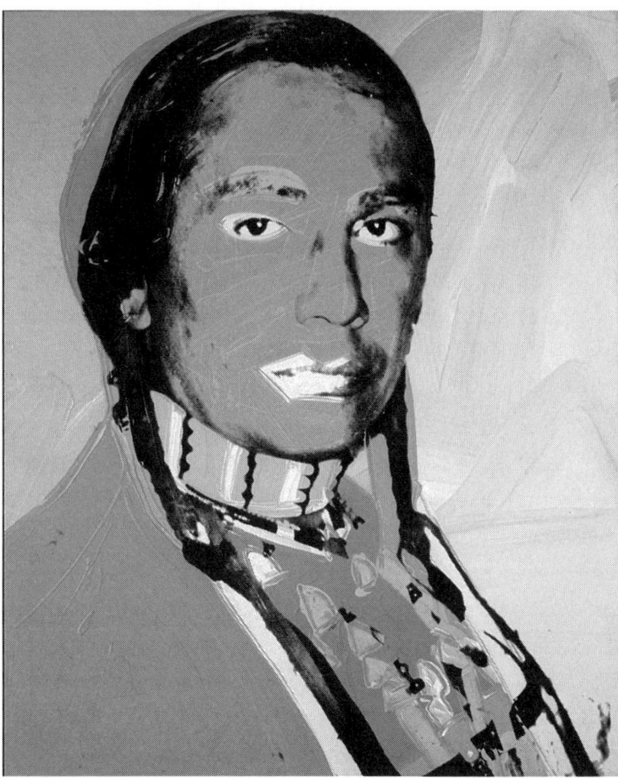

1.19. Andy Warhol, *The American Indian (Russell Means)*, 1976. Acrylic and screenprint on canvas, 50 × 42 inches. Courtesy of the Andy Warhol Foundation for the Visual Arts, licensed by Artist Rights Society.

viewer, and the photographic stencil adds gravity to the sitter's gaze. Much like Warhol's portraits of Mao, here color conveys the aura of the figure. Using saturated tones, Warhol covered Means's face in a coral red. His palette knife is evident in lines and scratches that perhaps suggest the imagery of Indian war paint. A blue line touches Means's jet-black hair and follows the curve of his head to open into the triangle of his shirt. Warhol's work captivates the viewer in the intricacies of Means's braids and jewelry, which cascade down into soft neon shapes that almost vibrate off his chest. In this extravagance, the product of an American pop-culture view of Indian celebrity, Warhol invokes American mythmaking, only this time he plays the part of Vespucci, while Means is "fantastically female and effeminate." The camp gesture flaunts liberatory sexual politics, but it drags the figure of Means and symbolically genders the territory that witnessed the massacre at Wounded Knee. It follows the logic of a masculinist vision that neutralizes the power of the other by making them perform in a female fashion.

Invoking René Magritte's *Ceci N'Est Pas une Pipe* (1929), the writer Gerald Vizenor cautions, "This is not an Indian," in reference to Warhol's portrait of

Means.[103] Vizenor's work theorized how the word "Indian," and the icon of Indian, operated as a simulation, notably as a colonial enactment that came to stand in for the real. According to Vizenor, these re-creations rely on the shallowness of stereotypical characters who continue to perpetuate the myth of Native savagery. Yet he sees a possibility for disrupting replications in those whose tribal presence challenges the simulacrum. The practice of contestation is at the core of what he calls "survivance" as it reveals the superficial surface of the racialized (and gendered) stereotype. In Vizenor's view, Means is one of these "post-Indian warriors" because he challenges the empty signifier with his Oglala Lakota affiliation, but he also warns that even the post-Indian can traffic in these inventions (perhaps referring to Means's Hollywood celebrity) for personal gain.

Warhol's simulation is part of a long tradition in Western landscape painting of inventing the noble and ignoble savage. In her essay in the catalogue *The West as America*, art historian Julie Schimmel concludes, "Real Indians never inhabited the paintings of white artists."[104] Retracing nineteenth-century depictions of Indians in the work of painters such as George Catlin and Charles Bird King, she notes how the binaries of noble and ignoble resulted in images of laziness, lasciviousness, naivety, exoticism, primitivism (via flesh, fur, tattoos), and impressive physiques that bordered on European notions of male beauty. But the most damaging of these pictorial strategies were the conflict scenes. This is where Warhol's war paint stands out, where "Indians were cast as villains who prevented a peaceful appropriation of western lands."[105] Such conflict paintings reflected and bolstered the animus behind federal legislation such as the Indian Removal Act (1830).

Duffy's border-pop print relies on these established tropes in American art that reproduce a gendered reading of land and Indigeneity. Although *The New Order* espouses a view directly opposed to the ideology of American expansionism, Duffy's Native mother still evinces a masculinist epistemology that genders the border as female and is tied to an Indigenous heterotemporality (lost past, migrant present, Indigenous future). "This is not an Indian," but a product of the colonial legacies that the geospatial turn in Latinx art must contend with if it is to challenge geography's hold on the structure of language and visuality.

A counterpoint to the gendering of land and to the use of the Native mother as an allegory for territory can be found in the work of Consuelo Jimenez Underwood. Her textile practice recovers Indigenous aesthetics and the "craft" of women's work in sensuous fabric sculptures and installations. Her 1994 *Virgen de los Caminos*, for example, is a delicate embroidered quilt made in honor of the child in the running-immigrant sign (fig. 1.20). At center, the emblem of a Virgin of Guadalupe, Patroness of the Americas, is surrounded

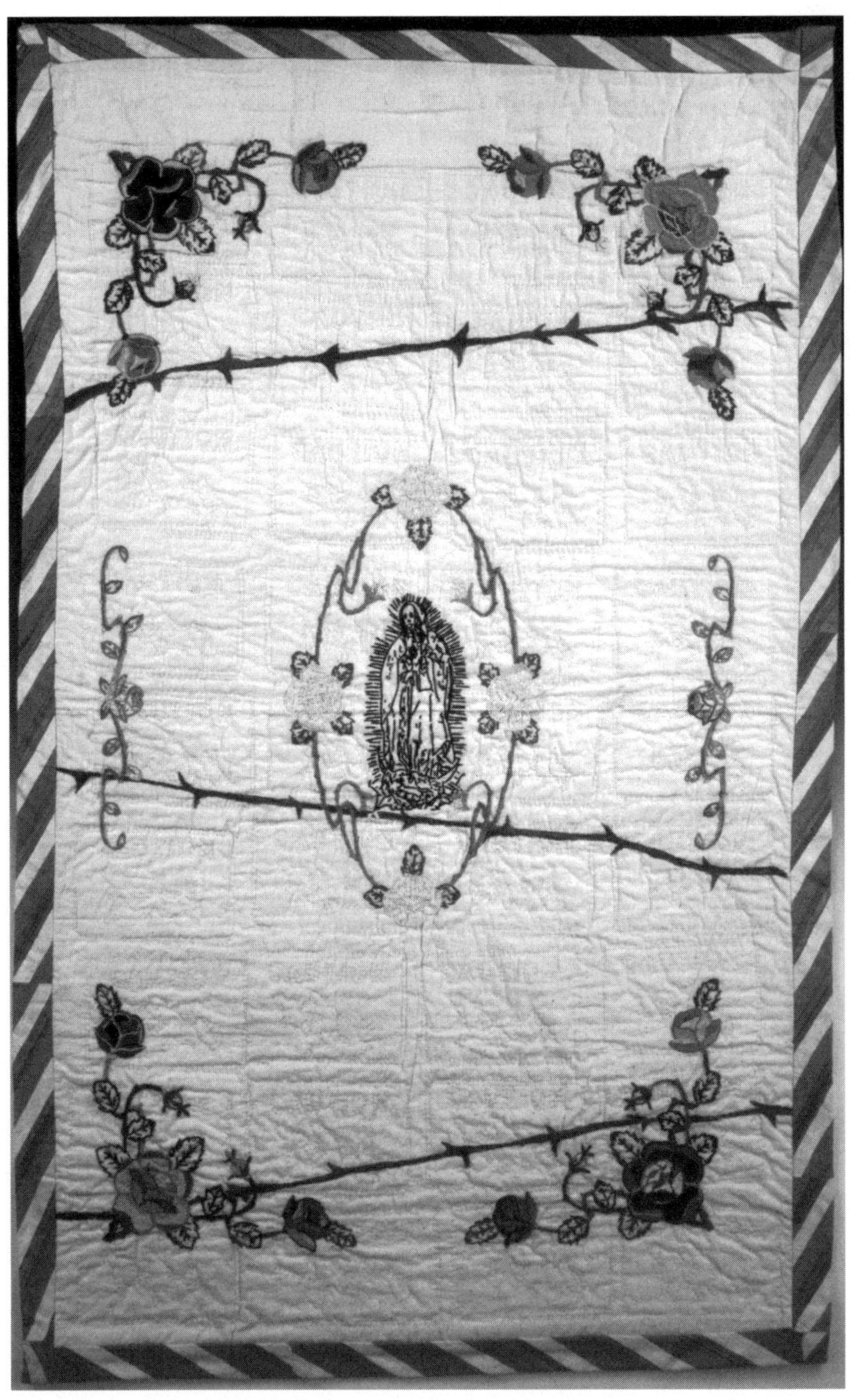

1.20. Consuelo Jimenez Underwood, *Virgen de los Caminos*, 1994. Embroidered and quilted cotton and silk with graphite, 58 × 36 inches. Courtesy of the artist and Smithsonian American Art Museum, Museum Purchase, 1996.77.

by colorful flowers, which are crossed by strands of barbed wire. The border of the blanket is made up of brown and white diagonal lines that create movement and keep the viewer at attention. Almost indiscernible is the running-pedestrian Caution sign which forms the patchwork of the quilt in the background. Jimenez Underwood carefully stitched the sign in metallic thread and, appealing to seriality, repeated the sign until it made a quilt of the family as "ghosts, stitched forever in the running position."[106] In this case, the artist gestures toward the continuous forms of Indigenous displacement that will uproot communities from southern Mexico and Central America and transform Los Angeles into a matrix of multiple Indigeneities. However, the fact that they remain vanishing figures indicates how little political agency they exert under this existing and oppressing social order.

CONCLUSION

This chapter laid the groundwork for understanding how Latinx artists reclaimed the tradition of printmaking and set out to contest the rise in anti-immigrant discourse in the 1990s. It followed the residency of Ricardo Duffy at Self Help Graphics as one paradigmatic example of how artists responded to the rise in xenophobic policies. My close reading of the work revealed the clever appropriations of a border-pop aesthetic, the cultural politics of SHG and how it nurtured experimentation and anti-assimilationist viewpoints. But as impactful as it was in countering the myth of the frontier as the conquest of wilderness and displacement of the savage, *The New Order* makes manifest troubling allusions to a reconquest of twice-stolen, gendered land. I close this chapter by thinking about the work's reception in California at the turn of the century that would lead to only a greater number of calls to close the borders to the foreign and nonwhite.

In the fall of 2000, the Los Angeles County Museum of Art (LACMA) opened one of its largest exhibitions to date, *Made in California: Art, Image, and Identity, 1900–2000*, which examined how artists explored the changing image of the Golden State in the twentieth century. Landscape was a central theme throughout the exhibition. As curator Stephanie Barron noted, "Although the Edenic image of California continued to be celebrated, even in artist's depictions of freeways and swimming pools, landscape increasingly came to signify a *contested territory* in which pollution, environmental disasters, and monotonous urban sprawl prevailed" [author's emphasis].[107] This critical questioning in the mythical image of California opened the door for a number of artists, including Duffy, a Native Californian whose bicultural experiences revealed the frailty of paradise.

Art critics concerned with aesthetic autonomy and modernist notions of quality expressed ire with LACMA's massive millennial blockbuster. Unorthodox in its approach, the curatorial team assembled by Stephanie Barron presented art objects within particular social and political contexts. These "environments" consisted of art interspersed among furniture, postcards, fashion, cars, surfboards, orange-crate labels, and media stations with relevant film and music clips. In short, the LACMA galleries mediated an exchange between high art and vernacular pop culture. For *New York Times* critic Roberta Smith, the exhibition demonstrated "that elaborating an object's context or dismantling the so-called canon requires the suspension of notions of quality."[108] Christopher Knight, from the *Los Angeles Times*, went even further in pointing out, "There's some great art, but the show features more third-rate (and worse) painting, sculpture and photography than any local exhibition in memory."[109] Their appeal to quality, as well as the general dislike of the inclusion of cultural artifacts and accompanying wall text, revealed a racially coded ambivalence toward the diversity of California images the exhibition boasted that looked to answer the questions: Which California? Whose California?

If Smith's readers had heeded her call to skip the fifth and final section of the exhibition, which she described as a "really, really bad Whitney Biennial" where the curators felt the need to "right a century's worth of social wrongs," they would have missed a number of remarkable works including Duffy's *New Order.* The last section of the exhibition covered the years 1980 to 2000, when the image of California became synonymous with disaster-fiction genres that reflected real-life events such as the L.A. riots, the O. J. Simpson trial, and the never-ending cycles of earthquakes, floods, wildfires, and droughts. It was within this context that many LACMA visitors encountered Duffy's work for the first time in a section that dispelled California's idyllic Eden and signaled the contested territory that it had become through narratives of racial segregation, embodied marginalities, and immigration crossings. Curator Howard Fox meditated on how California's art and ideas had reoriented the national conversation, often in profound ways. He wrote, "California—especially the inchoate megalopolis of Southern California, with its ever-mutating mosaic of territories and neighborhoods and its polyglot cultural matrix—may be, for better or for worse, a model of the world to come."[110] Eerie as it may seem, expressed through the lens of borderland futures, that world to come is here now.

The dystopian prediction outlined in Fox's text sets the stage for tracking the continued rise in xenophobic discourse that has characterized the last two decades in the US, but also the creative ways artists responded by returning to the print medium and asking questions about how these current forms of anti-immigrant hatred and territoriality telescope back to colonial times. Not all Latinx artists approach the subject with the same fury that is palpable in Duffy's palette. The next chapter turns to imaginative cartography in a collaborative portfolio of maps by Enrique Chagoya and the poet Alberto Ríos. Whereas Duffy advocates for a return to Native territorialities as a decolonial gesture to delink from Western conceptions of territory, including the national mythos of Manifest Destiny, Chagoya and Ríos take a different approach. They consider the ways hegemonic projects of mapping emphasize Western science, technology, and disembodiment. Their experiments in art and language creatively counter Eurocentric rationalism with the knowledge of the body.

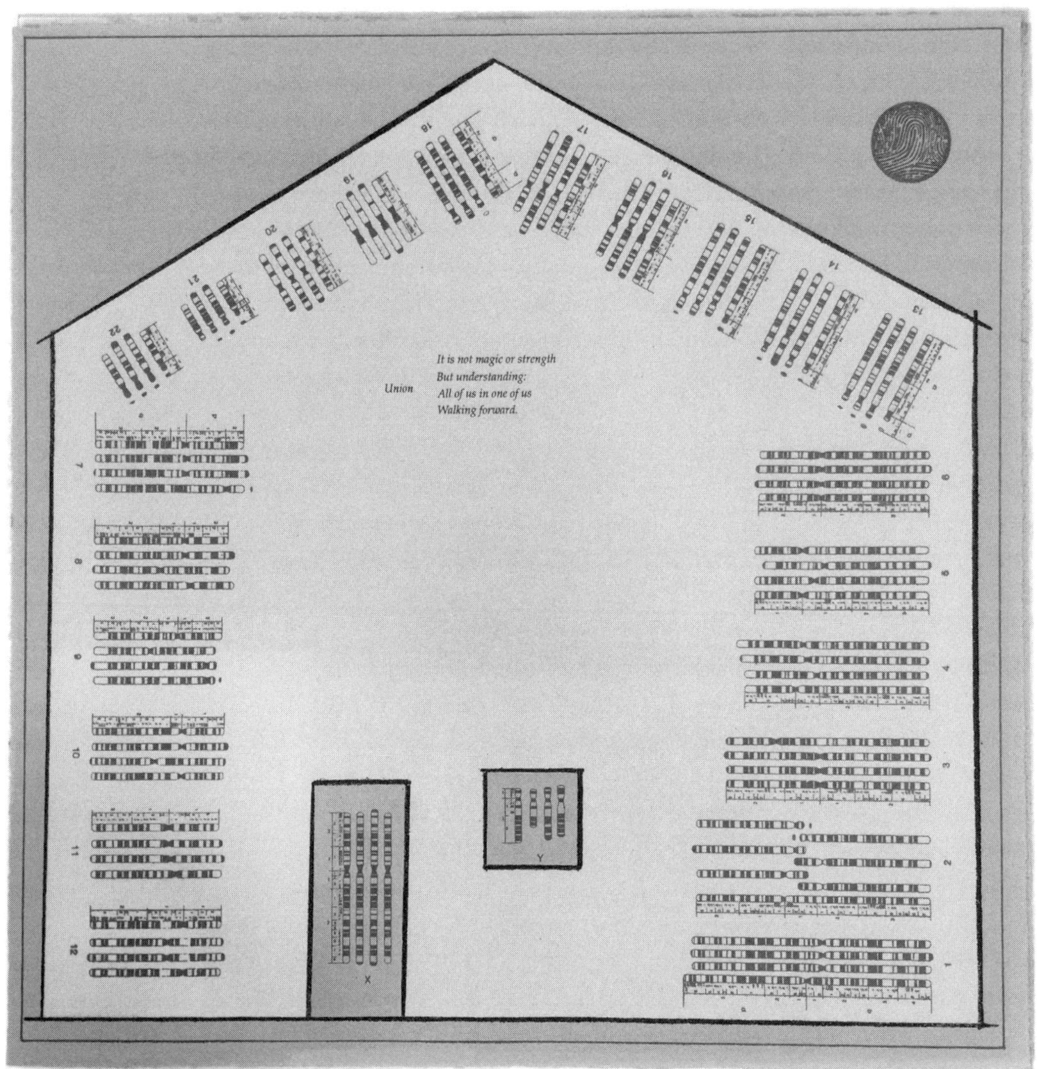

2.1. Enrique Chagoya and Alberto Ríos, *Genome Map*, from the portfolio *You Are Here*, 2000. Lithograph on Rives BFK Tan, 17 × 17 inches; edition of sixty printed by Joe Freye and John Altomare and published by Segura Publishing Company, Arizona. Courtesy of the artist, Anglim/Trimble, and the Snite Museum of Art, 2019.068.024.006.

CHAPTER TWO

Embodied Territorialities

Enrique Chagoya and Alberto Ríos Disrupting the Western Cartographic Gaze

THE LITHOGRAPH RESEMBLES an architectural plan (fig. 2.1). At center, the artist placed a beige house-shaped structure with a small door and window offering an entry point for the viewer. But this is not a regular house with a schematic layout. Instead, we find twenty-three pairs of chromosomes nestled tightly against the exterior walls, each one numbered from longest to shortest. The last pair of chromosomes, relating to sex, appear on the door and window. Inside the house, the writer placed a poem under the apex that reads: "Union / It is not magic or strength / But understanding: / All of us in one of us / Walking Forward." The red stamp overhead and to the right is a red circular mark resembling a thumbprint but doubles as a celestial object—a blood moon or setting sun. *Genome Map* is a collaboration by the artist Enrique Chagoya (b. 1953) and poet Alberto Ríos (b. 1952). It was made in the summer of 2000 when the world was witnessing a historic event, the long-awaited publication of the human genome sequence by the scientific community, which included major funding from the US Department of Energy, the National Institute of Health, and the private sector.

During a press briefing at the White House, President Clinton explained the significance of this international effort:

> Nearly two centuries ago, in this room, on this floor, Thomas Jefferson and a trusted aide spread out a magnificent map—a map Jefferson had long prayed he would get to see in his lifetime. The aide was Meriwether Lewis and the map was the product of his courageous expedition across the American frontier, all the way to the Pacific. It was a map that defined the contours and forever expanded the frontiers of our continent and our imagination. Today, the world is joining us here in the East Room to behold a map of even greater significance. We are here to celebrate the completion of the first survey of the entire human genome. Without a doubt, this is the most important, most wondrous map ever produced by humankind.[1]

It should be no surprise to the reader, at this point in the book, that the myth of the frontier would be invoked in the service of ideological formulations that equated scientific discovery with progress and the conquest of the unknown wilderness, even if in this case that wilderness was inside the human body, which is made up of about one hundred trillion cells and twenty-five thousand genes. Chagoya portrayed the race to unlock human DNA as a search for the structures inside our house, an apt metaphor for the human body as a vessel that carries all our ancestral history and dictates physical characteristics, health, and disease before birth. The poem "Union" by Ríos reflects the fact that more than 99.9 percent of a human DNA sequence is exactly the same as that of any other member of this species: *All of us in one of us*, even though at times it feels as if we could not possibly be more different.

Genome Map was part of a larger portfolio of prints titled *You Are Here*, which Chagoya and Ríos produced at Segura Publishing in Arizona. They had come at the invitation of master printer Joe Segura. Opening in 1981, Segura Publishing, the brainchild of Segura and his then-wife Lisa Sette, specialized in fine-art printmaking and promoted the work of underrepresented, politically minded artists.[2] Segura had a history of working with Chagoya since the early 1990s, and as a faculty member of Arizona State University (ASU) in Tempe he was also familiar with Ríos, who had taught creative writing at ASU since 1982. Chagoya and Ríos were highly acclaimed artists. Segura, perhaps seeking to test their authorial limits, devised a collaboration through which the two artists would chart verbal and visual encounters in relation to mapmaking. This concept had preoccupied Segura for years. He was drawn to the visualization of space through the teachings of Buckminster Fuller, the architect-inventor who taught design at Southern Illinois University, Carbondale, where Segura earned his master's degree in fine arts.[3] In addition to Fuller's philosophy, Segura was intrigued by the pictorial function of maps, which had launched and popularized various methods of printmaking. The splendorous *Map of Tenochtitlán* (fig. 2.2), a woodcut printed

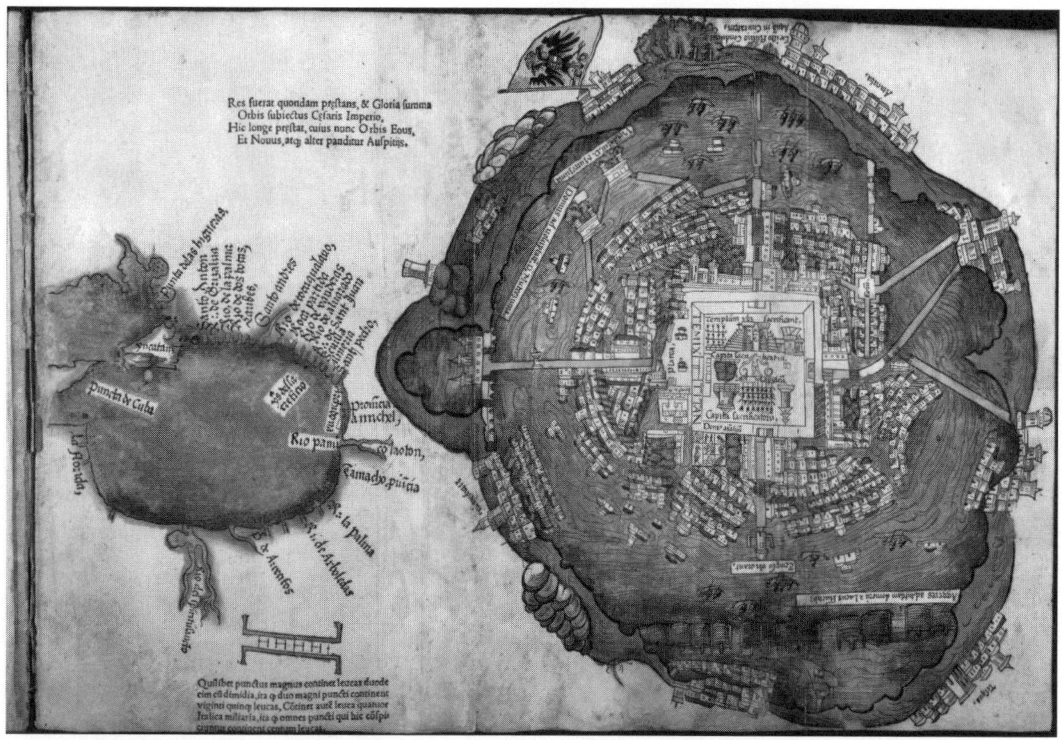

2.2. *Map of Tenochtitlán*, 1524. Woodcut printed in Nuremberg to illustrate Hernán Cortés's second letter to Charles V, 18.9 × 18.9 inches, Newberry Library, Chicago.

in 1524 by Nuremberg craftsmen, for instance, provided European audiences with the first view of the sprawling American metropolis. But as cultural theorist José Rabasa points out, it was an idealized perspective, a "territorialization of amorphous space," described in "paradisiacal terms," of a city already in ruins.[4] The spatial text of Tenochtitlán projected the colonial desire to impose order and appropriate Indigenous knowledge of the land into a form that would appeal to his majesty Charles V and ensure the Crown of its divine mission to colonize New World nations. In Segura's workshop, the epistemic and rhetorical nature of mapmaking proved irresistible for the poet and artist. They eagerly took up the challenge and in the span of a weeklong residency produced a portfolio of six lithographs.[5]

The artists had a lot in common: proximity in age, similar political beliefs, and more important, they were easygoing enough to sustain a joint project.[6] They also shared a relationship to borders: Alberto ("Tito," as Segura calls him) was raised by an English mother and a Mexican father in the border town of Nogales, Arizona; Enrique, born and raised in Mexico, immigrated to the United States as a young adult. They were artists, but also academics: Alberto taught at ASU, and Enrique in the art department at Stanford. Segura explained how he set up the partnership. He called each one. "[I said] I'd really like you to think about working with the other. They both said yes . . . and then they both almost immediately said, 'But I don't want to illustrate his work.'"[7] The concern over authorship was certainly not unfounded, but it established an expected reciprocity. Chagoya later explained, "I think poetry itself is its own end, and to me it would be some kind of an insult to say to a poet, 'You need an illustration for people to understand your poem.' Instead I thought [the project] would be more like a duet—two musical instruments, independent from one another, but they cannot play the same tune."[8] To engage in the exchange and complement but not "illustrate" the other's work, Chagoya and Ríos each gave up something of himself in the process. Over the course of the project their imagery and poetry produced increasingly abstract gestures that differed greatly in form and intent from their single-authored works. Whether straying from figuration or rearranging language as if it were furniture, their abstractions emphasized how geometric rationalization failed to translate into embodied experience.

This book argues that Latinx artists adopted the medium of printmaking with the twofold purpose of explicitly showing how this form of making art had been complicit in visualizing the colonization of the Americas and also how it could be used to reclaim these lands for Indigenous, migrant, mestiza/o, and Afro-descendant peoples. In the case of *You Are Here* readers will learn about a collaborative portfolio of poems and images that engage in ludic gestures that destabilize our understanding of Western cartography and incite alternative ways of conceptualizing space. The portfolio emphasizes that the body is the subject and agent of reterritorialization and is shown to have the means to counter Western cartography's hallmark of disembodied projection. This visual-verbal avant-garde strategy eschews the overt politics of socially committed Latinx printmaking in favor of reaching a wider audience and cultivating doubt and disobedience in hegemonic projects of mapping. When I asked Chagoya whether he considers his art to be a form of activism, he responded: "It would be too pretentious to think that art changes people's consciousness, but you could arrive to a point where your art is a departure for thinking, and the world changes through other actions."[9]

In these experiments, Chagoya and Ríos foreground the inaccuracy of maps and by doing so make the imperfect a productive threshold. Readers may recall that when European cartographers encountered maps by Amerindian artists, they were confounded by their imprecision. It is tempting to see the work of these borderland artists as reversing the gaze of Western cartography, reinscribing the spatial concepts of those who were once deemed cannibals and savages without necessarily claiming affiliation to Indigeneity. I contrast their portfolio with a trend in contemporary art that Trevor Paglen calls "experimental geography."[10] The chapter ends with a discussion of performance practices that are more closely and conceptually aligned with Chagoya and Ríos's art, not only to probe the role of the viewer but also to demonstrate the anima behind their enterprise, a way to bring prints to life.

PERFORMING THE IGNOBLE SAVAGE, OR UNSCRIPTING WESTERN CARTOGRAPHY

Early-modern geographers used an ancient mathematical theorem to measure the distance between two points. The Pythagorean theorem was a tool for mapping navigational routes during the time of Europe's colonial expansion, but the margin of error remained high. Columbus's first voyage is an obvious case in point, although countless others come to mind, such as those that saw their doom in the search for the Northwest Passage. Chagoya and Ríos chose the theorem as a subject for one of their maps to wrestle with the philosophical underpinnings of Western cartographic reason. Chagoya's geometric representation imposes an order that we may associate with scientific truth, yet Ríos's narrative poem hints at its imperfection. The work asks viewers to consider how phenomenological perception cannot be subsumed into arithmetic calculations.

Theorem (fig. 2.3) gestures to the misunderstandings between the material body and the scopic regime, cultivating a certain distrust in the hegemonic projects of mapping. In his rendering of the Pythagorean theorem, Chagoya revisits the history of nonobjective art. Monochromatic squares float about in various arrangements over a water-stained paper surface that resembles historical navigational maps. The bold squares in primary colors recall the Constructivist paintings of the Russian avant-garde as well as the geometric compositions of the Dutch movement De Stijl, modernist styles of the early twentieth century that advanced abstract art's utopian ideals. In the upper left corner, Chagoya arranged three squares whose points of contact produce a right triangle. Dotted lines emerge from the triangle to bisect the larger square into two tones. Thus begins Chagoya's illustration of the Euclidean proof of Pythagoras's theorem showing that "the area of the square built upon the hypotenuse of a right triangle is equal to the sum of the areas of the squares upon the remaining sides."

Countless mathematicians have created their own proofs of this theorem, so much so that historians of mathematics describe it as an old parlor trick.[11] The association that Chagoya makes between nonobjective art and geome-

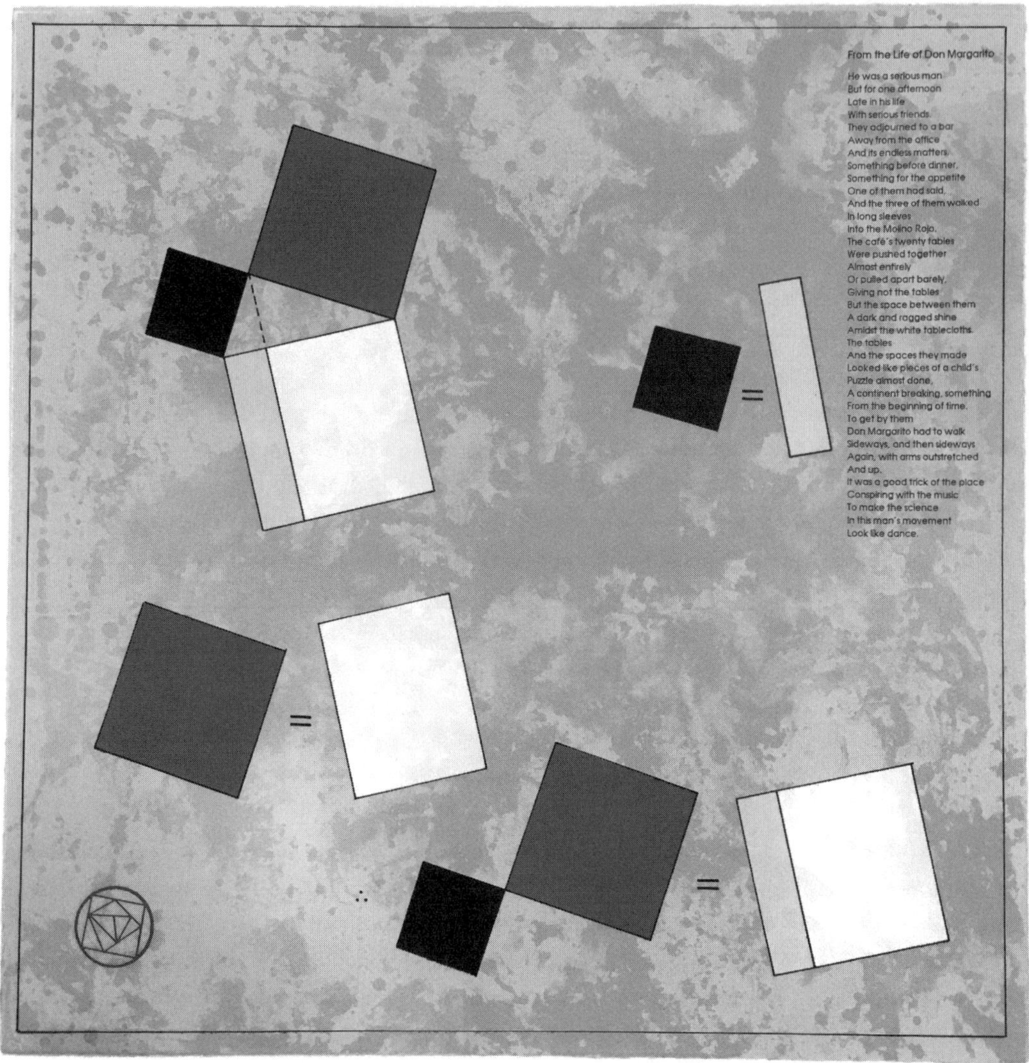

2.3. Enrique Chagoya and Alberto Ríos, *Theorem*, from the portfolio *You Are Here*, 2000. Lithograph on Rives BFK Tan, 17 × 17 inches; edition of sixty printed by Joe Freye and John Altomare and published by Segura Publishing Company, Arizona. Courtesy of the artist, Anglim/Trimble, and the Snite Museum of Art, 2019.068.024.004.

try, however, is worth further unpacking, because it helps us understand the relationship between geometry and Western cartography. Nonobjective art emerged during the rise of totalitarian regimes in the West. It was an aesthetic that hinged on the equilibrium of form and space. Artists as diverse as Kazimir Malevich, El Lissitsky, Theo van Doesburg, and Piet Mondrian saw utopian possibilities in a visual art that countered the chaos of the Great War. For an artist like Mondrian, abstraction was the "expression of pure reality."[12] In his writings he affirmed that humanity is "doomed to disequilibrium" and that art must restore this relationship through the dynamic movement of oppositions. He championed a geometric abstraction based on right angles that could produce a measure of reality not unlike that of mapping. The relationship between geometry and truth/reality was built on an episteme. Unearthing the darker side of the Renaissance, Walter Mignolo explains, "Geometric projections during the sixteenth century became a new model of a Eurocentric conception of the world."[13] The fact that this episteme became a dominant model was a matter of political power, which by the time Mondrian was painting had become a "universal" value. What is at stake in *Theorem* is how this provincial point of view succeeded in establishing its hierarchy but never fully suppressed other forms of territoriality.

Another map from the portfolio, *Asian Celestial Map*, pursues this point further by unearthing Chinese cosmology in a star map (fig. 2.4). The print shows the image of an open atlas with two circular sky maps. The blue maps display a variety of constellations, but their astronomical measures are almost illegible as Chagoya overlayed the drawing of a female figure on one side and a skull on the other. The multiple eyes, ears, and mouths on the figures, and the inclusion of the poem "The Venus Trombones" by Ríos, appeal to surrealism to question the rationalism of such a map. Since the fifth century BCE, the Chinese produced cosmography that showed how the events in heaven mirrored those on Earth. Royal astrologers carefully recorded any abnormal occurrence (comet, eclipse, meteor, or nova) and worked to interpret its possible forecasting of famine, plague, war, or an emperor gone astray.[14] Chinese imperial cartography of the sky did not change significantly until the arrival of the Jesuits in the sixteenth century.

Spatial paradigms shifted radically when explorers mapped a fourth continent during the sixteenth century and Europe began its project of colonization in earnest. Although different conceptions of territoriality existed among various cultures, including Chinese, African, Native American, and European, it was European geometric rationalizations that helped dissociate ethnic centers as well as a concept of space attached to the body. Mignolo's comparative study explains that "within an ethnic rationalization of space . . . the sacred place establishes the *axis mundi*, where space and time meet."[15] Examples of this phenomenon, which some scholars call "the omphalos syndrome," were widespread: Medieval Christians viewed Jerusalem as the navel of the world; Chinese cosmographers believed their emperor's royal palace was the center of it, and the Aztec empire's axis mundi where sky, earth, and underworld meet corresponded with the body. *Theorem* signals how Euro-

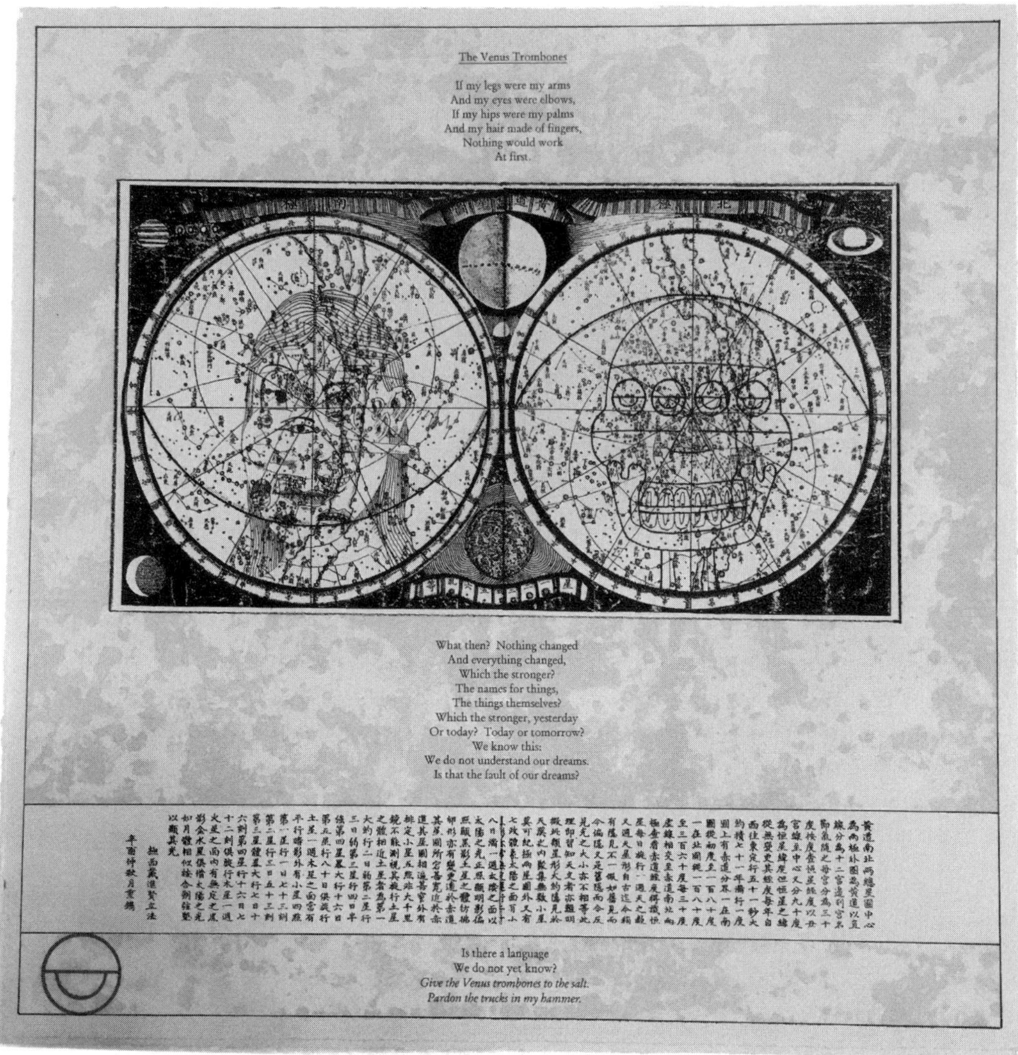

2.4. Enrique Chagoya and Alberto Ríos, *Asian Celestial Map*, from the portfolio *You Are Here*, 2000. Lithograph on Rives BFK Tan, 17 × 17 inches; edition of sixty printed by Joe Freye and John Altomare and published by Segura Publishing Company, Arizona. Courtesy of the artist, Anglim/Trimble, and the Snite Museum of Art, 2019.068.024.001.

pean colonization suppressed other forms of territoriality, diffusing through printed maps a geometric axis that created the illusion of universality and objectivity. The visual representation of Pythagoras's theorem may wink at Mondrian's utopian compositions, but on a deeper level it enacts the power of geometric projection during colonial expansion.

Ríos's narrative poem offers a powerful juxtaposition to the cool, detached forms of geometric abstraction or perhaps what they symbolize more broadly, the cartographic gaze. Geographer John Pickles describes the cartographic gaze as one based on a Cartesian commitment to vision as the privileged source of knowledge, an observer epistemology that represents nature through a technical practice of modeling a God's-eye-view and a dominant way of seeing that shapes social thought in the West.[16] Ríos's poem on the upper right, "From the Life of Don Margarito," appears quietly, seemingly disinterested in the bright shapes of Euclidean geometry that float about the surface. Ríos invites the viewer to read the poem and reflect on the themes of space, mobility, and the materiality of our bodies.

FROM THE LIFE OF DON MARGARITO

He was a serious man
But for one afternoon
Late in his life
With serious friends.
They adjourned to a bar
Away from the office
And its endless matters.
Something before dinner,
Something for the appetite
One of them had said,
And the three of them walked
In long sleeves
Into the Molino Rojo.
The cafe's twenty tables
Were pushed together
Almost entirely
Or pulled apart barely,
Giving not the tables
But the space between them
A dark and ragged shine
Amidst the white tablecloths.
The tables
And the spaces they made
Looked like pieces of a child's
Puzzle almost done,
A continent breaking, something
From the beginning of time.
To get by them

Don Margarito had to walk
Sideways, and then sideways
Again, with arms outstretched
And up.
It was a good trick of the place
Conspiring with the music
To make the science
In this man's movement
Look like dance.

In the setting of the Molino Rojo, like the Moulin Rouge, Ríos advances a provocative view of space, one that cannot be measured as easily but rather depends upon experiential knowledge. He describes a dimly lit room where the odd arrangement of tables (pushed together almost entirely or pulled apart barely) forces an older gentleman, Don Margarito, which happens to be the name of Ríos's grandfather, to navigate a puzzlelike terrain.[17] In the tables and the spaces they make, Ríos evokes a correspondence to the geometric forms in Chagoya's visual *Theorem*. But in the domain of language, they become playful geographic metaphors, "pieces of a child's puzzle almost done, a continent breaking, something from the beginning of time," and thus subject to chance and much less stable than the proof pictured on the right. Don Margarito does not rely solely on visuality, nor does he measure the distance to his favorite table; instead, he acts upon the space through the movement of his body, walking sideways with arms outstretched. Ríos refers to the dancelike movement as a "good trick of the place" that elevates its epistemic and ontological maneuver as a science.

The mischievous juxtaposition between the knowledge of the body and of the archive recalls a question that cultural theorist Diana Taylor had previously posed: "What might the shift in genres—from the scripted genres associated with the archive to the live embodied behaviors that are the repertoire of cultural practices—enable?"[18] Genres are discursive frames in which we organize knowledge, and maps are one such genre that we may consider scripted by virtue of their maker, publisher, or patron. Maps diffuse codified behaviors through their ease of archivability. In her quest to remap genre, Taylor argues that "embodied behaviors can reveal histories that fail to make it into the archive."[19] She constructs her argument from an analysis of Amerindian maps, specifically the sixteenth-century *Map of Cuauhtinchán* (fig. 2.5). The document, created around 1540 in the Valley of Puebla, narrates the journey from the sacred site of Chicomoztoc to the founding of Cuauhtinchán in 1501.[20] In Taylor's reading of the footprints, she contrasts the Native phenomenological approach to territory with the European invocation of a disembodied viewer

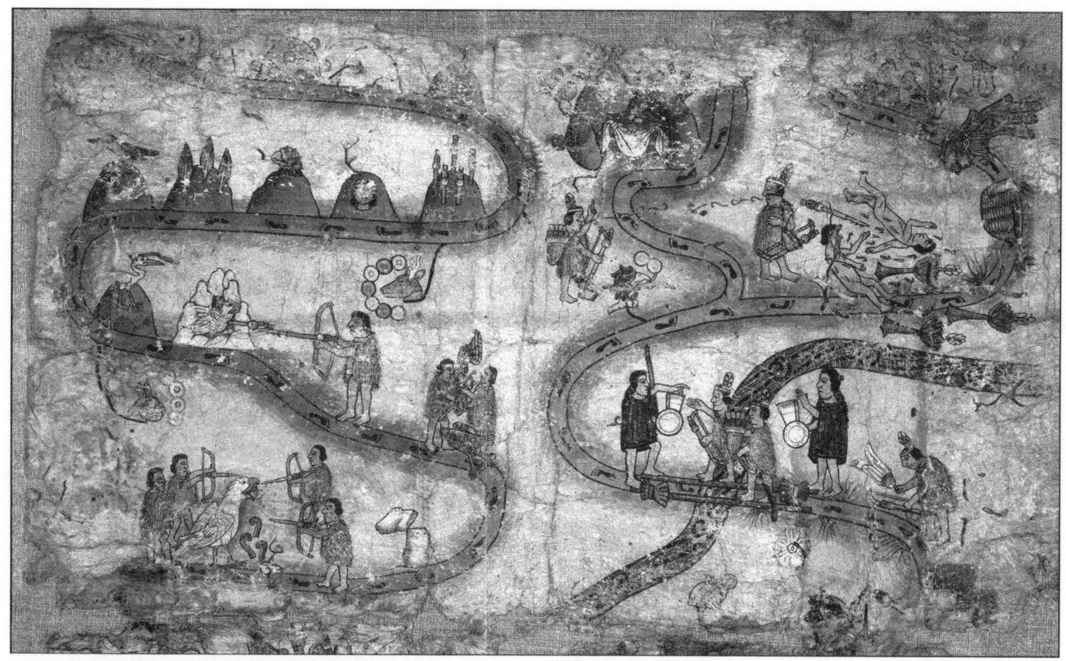

2.5. Section 1 of *Map of Cuauhtinchán No. 2*, ca. 1540. Polychrome painting on amate, 80.3 × 42.9 (ends)/44.1 (midsection) inches.

who oversees and controls territory. Chagoya and Ríos place these spatial epistemologies (the body and all-seeing eye) in conversation. Whether the viewer chooses to play along, the artists provide the tools to unscript the map.

The process of unscripting the map beckons us to consider that the colonization of space, the spread of Western cartography and its literacy, did not eradicate alternative conceptualizations of territory. Those practices and beliefs in a cosmology may have been forgotten or erased from the archive, but our body nonetheless remembers. In *Theorem* viewers vicariously experience the unscripted, or what Taylor calls "animatives," through the character of Don Margarito, who walks "sideways, then sideways again, with arms outstretched." In such a minor, everyday behavior, Don Margarito counters the perfect geometry of Pythagoras's theorem and makes room for alternative ways of understanding and moving through space. These different ontologies in relation to space are cunning acts intended to outwit the colonial logic of Western cartography, if ever momentary and brief.

Around this time, Chagoya had begun to experiment with what he calls "reverse modernism" or "reverse anthropology," mining the European modernist canon and overturning the power dynamics on its objects of colonial gaze. "Reverse modernism is doing the exact opposite of what Picasso did

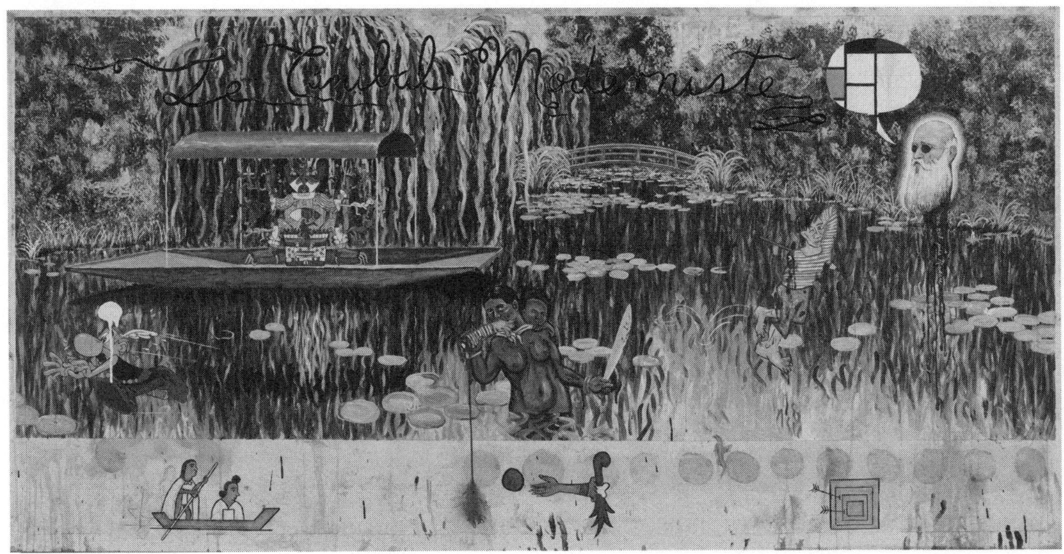

2.6. Enrique Chagoya, *Le Cannibale Moderniste*, 1999. Mixed media and paper on linen, 48 × 98 inches. Sheldon Museum of Art, University of Nebraska–Lincoln, Gift of Alexander Liberman and Frances Sheldon by exchange, U-5081.2002. Courtesy of the artist, Anglim/Trimble, and Sheldon Museum of Art, University of Nebraska–Lincoln.

with the African masks," he argued. "When he appropriated the African masks to develop his Cubist paintings, people asked him if he cared about the content, and he said, he didn't care about the content or the context of where the masks were from; he was only interested in the form."[21] In *Le Cannibale Moderniste* (1999; fig. 2.6), Chagoya depicted a verdant lagoon with water lilies and a mix of art-historical and pop icons. A brown Madonna with child stands at the center of the horizontal composition wielding a bloody machete. She feasts on Pablo Picasso's hand. The dismembered Cubist painter hovers above the water, while Claude Monet's thought bubble suggests he should have opted for Mondrian's clean-edged abstraction.

Not only does Chagoya cannibalize European art history; he also appropriates Aztec iconography to create nonlinear and transcultural narratives. An Aztec deity seated on a barge likely references the fertility goddess Mayahuel. Codexlike characters in the lower register shoot arrows at a Joseph Albers square. These are presumably obvious references for the art-history literati, but the viewers' act of reading and the work's materiality—paint on handmade amate paper—suggest the artist's reframing of European colonization as a form of cultural cannibalism. The critic Sarah Kirk Hanley explains that the work reflects a millennial shift toward a more global frame of reference and points to an incident that drew the artist's ire, when the Bibliothèque Nationale in Paris denied his requests to see the Maya manuscript known as the Paris Codex after the theft of another manuscript, presumably by a Mexican national, a few months earlier.[22] Chagoya channeled that anger into a trope that was significant in relation to cartography, based on a long history of depicting the other as grotesque and monstrous.

Mignolo writes about how the fear and desire for fantastical creatures that were thought to inhabit the outermost corners of the world captured the imagination of European cartographers before they even set foot on the continental Americas.[23] Lorenz Fries's map *Terrae Novae Tabula* (1522; fig. 2.7), for example, imagined wild animals and naked people living in the wilderness as a distinctive feature of the New World. Fries based his representation on Martin Waldseemüller's 1516 Carta Marina (see introduction, fig. 0.2), which depicted South America through symbolic and mythological characters such as

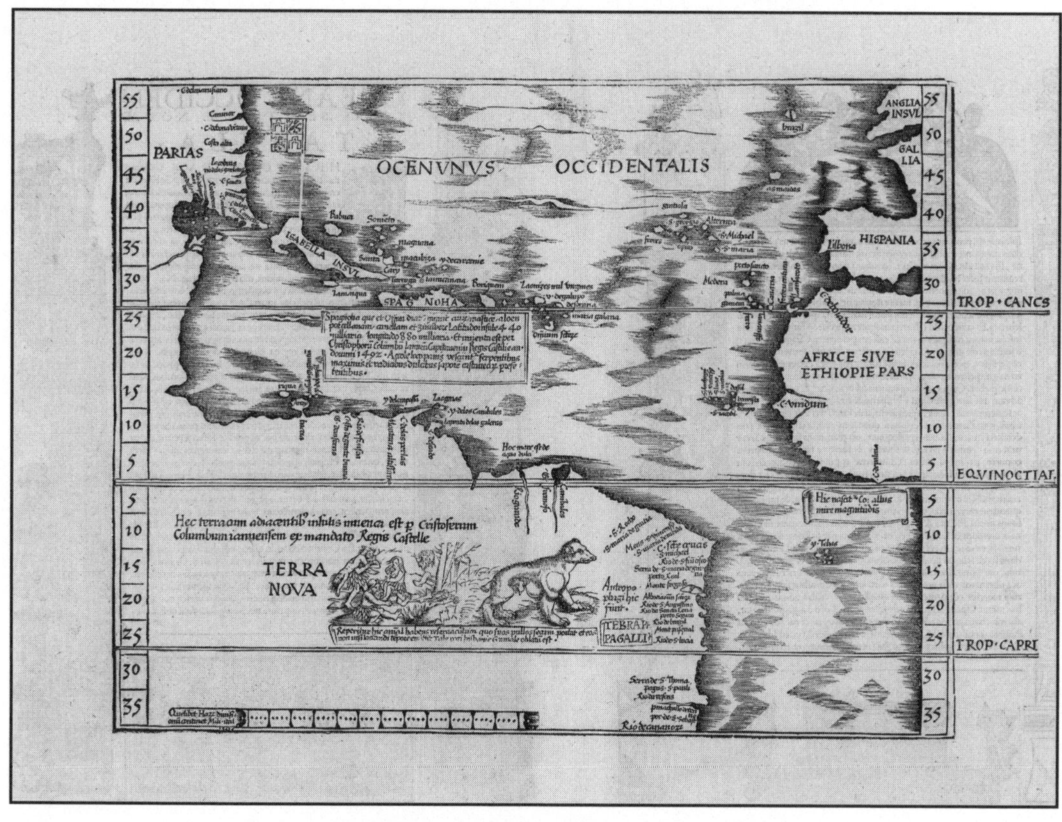

2.7. Lorenz Fries, after Martin Waldseemüller, *Oceani Occidentalis seu Terrae Novae Tabula (The Admiral's Map)*, 1522. Printed in Strasbourg, 15 × 11 inches.

Native cannibals feasting on human flesh around a fire and a large possum. Art historian Michael Schreffler has demonstrated how this pictorial rhetoric of the "fantastic" pervades representations of the allegorical figure of America as seen in the *Nova Reperta* (see chapter 1, fig. 1.18). As I described in the previous chapter, the print narrates the arrival of Amerigo Vespucci on the shores of the New World, where he awakens a nude figure seated on a hammock. The open waters and anchored caravels are on the left, while the "encounter" scene unfolds in a lush forest filled with wondrous creatures unknown to Europe. Stradanus (Jan Van der Straet) persuasively beckons viewers with an image that juxtaposes the figure of America with an almost-hidden vignette of cannibalistic activity in the background. In this rhetoric, which separates the figure from flesh-eating others, Schreffler theorizes a "transformation in European conceptualizations of the Americas and, more generally, of early-modern colonialism, in which the notion of 'America' as a consumer of human flesh is minimized and subsequently recast as the object of European consumption."[24]

Almost a century later and after sufficient explorations had discredited the tales of flesh-eating cannibals and chimeric monsters, the Flemish engraver Theodore de Bry illustrated Thomas Harriot's *A Briefe and True Report of the New Found Land of Virginia* (1588) based on the watercolor paintings of the English colonist John White.[25] The widely circulated engravings showed nude and tattooed barbarians practicing foreign rituals associated by European audiences with paganism and witchcraft (fig. 2.8). Art historian Michael Gaudio's study of Renaissance engravings examines de Bry's efforts to decode the "savage." Gaudio breaks apart the civil/savage dichotomy through a materialist approach by pointing to the importance of metals, with engraving as the metallic art par excellence, and their association with the humanist notion of civility.[26] De Bry's engravings engage in the taming of savage otherness while they enhance their exoticness and foreignness and simultaneously bolster an idealization and hierarchy of European whiteness.

The chronicles of early explorers such as the German sailor Hans Staden emboldened cartography's interest in difference. According to legend, the Indigenous Tupinambá people captured Staden in the mid-sixteenth century while he was working for the Portuguese on the coast of Brazil. Staden's sensationalist account, published in 1557, chronicles his nine months of captivity among Tupi Indians, who engaged in ritual cannibalism. Through thick descriptions of how they kill and eat their enemies, he narrated savagery in vivid detail.

> The executioner then strikes him on the back of his head and beats out his brains. The women immediately seize him and put him over the fire, where

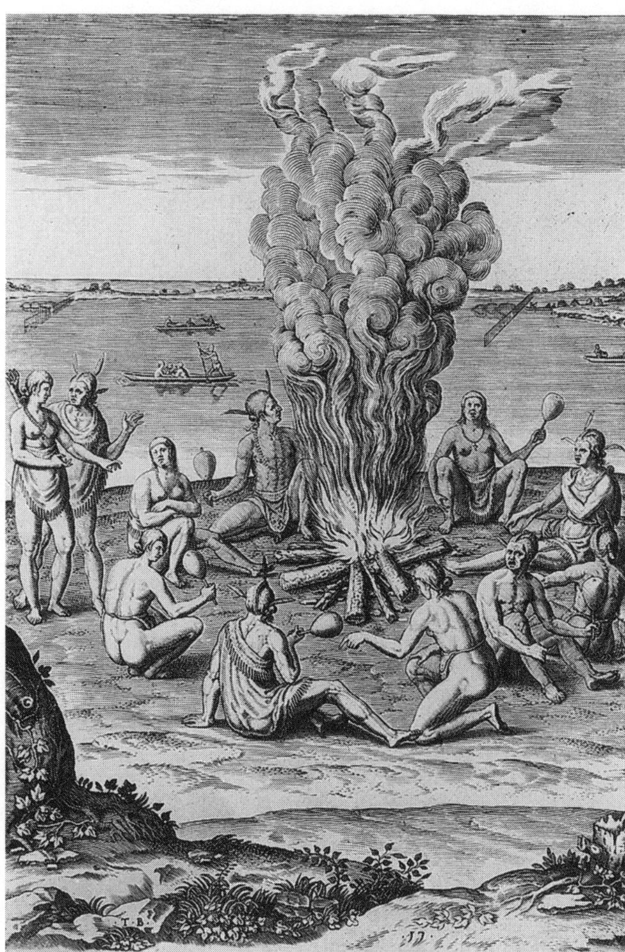

2.8. Theodor de Bry, after John White, "Their Manner of Praying with Rattles about the Fire," from *A Briefe and True Report of the New Found Land of Virginia*, 1590. Engraving, printed in Frankfurt.

> they scrape off all his skin, making him all white; they place a piece of wood in his arse to prevent a discharge. When he has then been skinned, a man takes him and cuts off the legs above the knees, and the arms at the body. Then the four women come and seize the four pieces and run around the huts with them, screaming loudly and with joy.[27]

The first-person accounts of Amerindian groups practicing human sacrifice, and a few engaging in cannibalistic ritual, provided European audiences their introduction to ethnographic knowledge of Native American groups. Over time and through widespread dissemination of these stories, the texts became foundational for understanding the other through a scenario of discovery based on fear of their idolatrous and violent practices and desire for

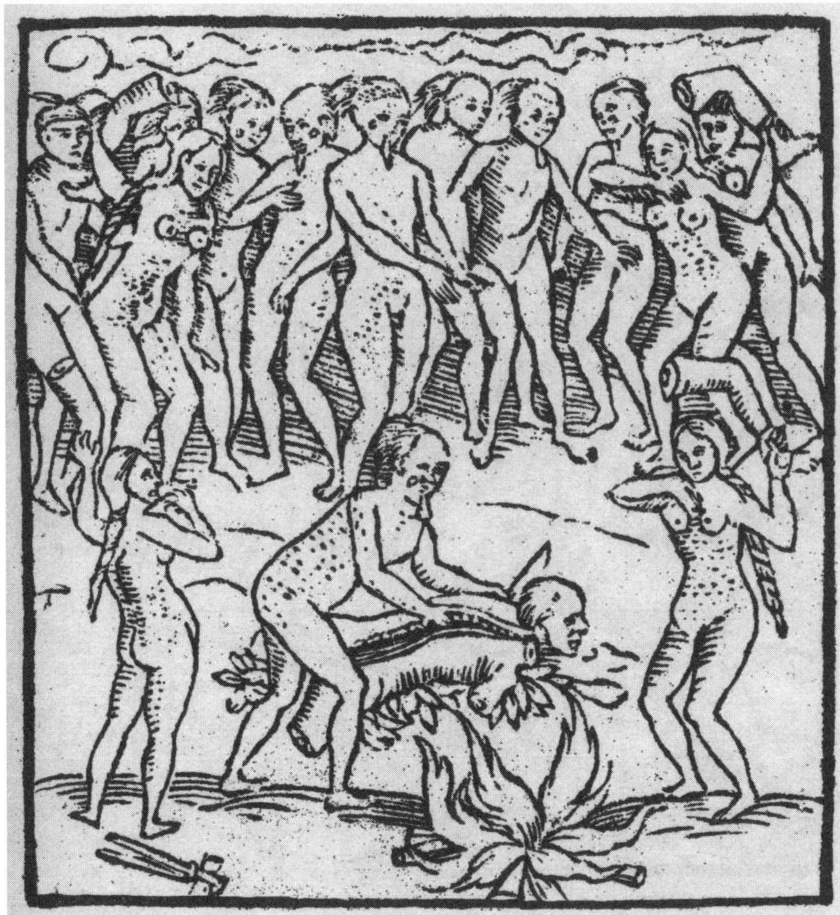

2.9. Hans Staden, *The Dismemberment of the Flayed Body by the Men*, from *True History: An Account of Cannibal Captivity in Brazil*, pl. 52, 1557. Woodcut.

mythical storytelling. The fifty-six woodcuts that appeared in Staden's chronicle were just as powerful in portraying savagery, with instances that showed Natives dismembering bodies over an open flame (fig. 2.9). Scholars such as Mignolo attribute the excesses of this kind of travel and ethnographic writing (among authors such as Staden, André Theve, and Jean de Léry) to a European-humanist ethical concern with controlling sexual behavior; one can speculate racial mixing as a driver for their anxiety, not to mention the authors' need to reiterate the superiority of European cultures.[28]

Centuries later the Brazilian avant-garde revisited this foundational myth to rebel against European cultural hegemony. In 1928 the São Paulo–based poet Oswald de Andrade penned "Manifesto Antropófago" (Cannibal Manifesto, fig. 2.10). Teasing the rhetoric of *Hamlet* and the sixteenth-century chronicles, he expounds, "Tupi or not Tupi, that is the question."[29] In a stream-of-consciousness, fractured cadence, he calls upon Brazilian modernists to cannibalize the culture of the colonizers and absorb their power: "But they were not crusaders who came; they were fugitives of a civilization that we are devouring, because we are strong and vengeful, like the Jabuti [Amazon land tortoise]. . . . Anthropophagy. The absorption of the sacred enemy."[30] Andrade built on the fear, sensationalism, and desire for primitivism of Staden's narrative and positioned Brazilian artists as equipped to unchain themselves of Europe's cultural dominion. Andrade built upon the myth of savage otherness and turned it against its creators. "Tupi or not Tupi" constructs a politics of identity for Brazilian art as an aggressive coeval that need not look across the Atlantic for approval.

Revisiting the chronicles of cannibalism and the "Manifesto Antropófago" allows us to consider how Chagoya and Ríos prompt viewers to perform as the ignoble savages. The methodology the artists invoke in unscripting West-

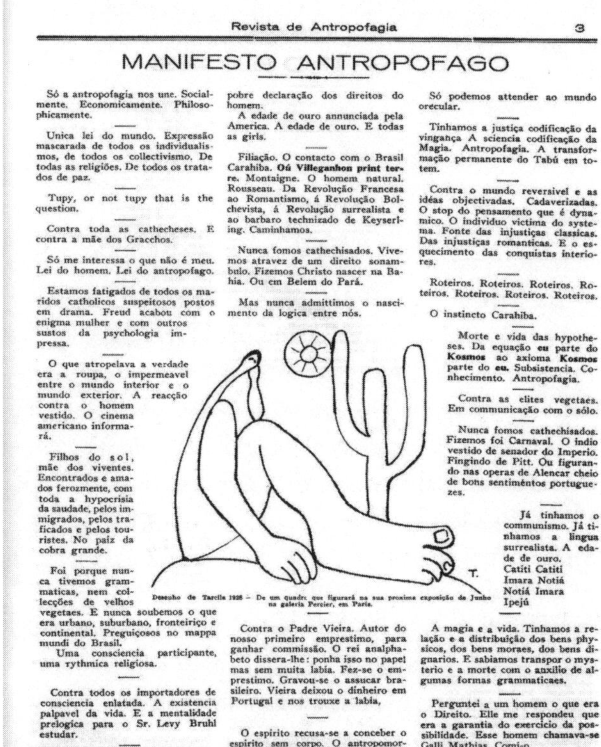

Revista de Antropofagia 3

MANIFESTO ANTROPOFAGO

Só a antropofagia nos une. Socialmente. Economicamente. Philosophicamente.

Unica lei do mundo. Expressão mascarada de todos os individualismos, de todos os collectivismo. De todas as religiões. De todos os tratados de paz.

Tupy, or not tupy that is the question.

Contra toda as cathecheses. E contra a mãe dos Gracchos.

Só me interessa o que não é meu. Lei do homem. Lei do antropofago.

Estamos fatigados de todos os maridos catholicos suspeitosos postos em drama. Freud acabou com o enigma mulher e com outros sustos da psychologia impressa.

O que atropelava a verdade era a roupa, o impermeavel entre o mundo interior e o mundo exterior. A reacção contra o homem vestido. O cinema americano informará.

Filhos do sol, mãe dos viventes. Encontrados e amados ferozmente, com toda a hypocrisia da saudade, pelos immigrados, pelos traficados e pelos touristes. No paiz da cobra grande.

Foi porque nunca tivemos grammaticas, nem collecções de velhos vegetaes. E nunca soubemos o que era urbano, suburbano, fronteiriço e continental. Preguiçosos no mappa mundi do Brasil.

Uma consciencia participante, uma rythmica religiosa.

Contra todos os importadores de consciencia enlatada. A existencia palpavel da vida. E a mentalidade prelogica para o Sr. Levy Bruhl estudar.

Queremos a revolução Carahiba. Maior que a revolução Francesa. A unificação de todas as revoltas efficazes na direcção do homem. Sem nós a Europa não teria siquer a sua pobre declaração dos direitos do homem.

A edade de ouro annunciada pela America. A edade de ouro. E todas as girls.

Filiação. O contacto com o Brasil Carahiba. **Oú Villeganhon print terre.** Montaigne. O homem natural. Rousseau. Da Revolução Francesa ao Romantismo, á Revolução Bolchevista, á Revolução surrealista e ao barbaro technizado de Keyserling. Caminhamos.

Nunca fomos cathechisados. Vivemos atravez de um direito sonambulo. Fizemos Christo nascer na Bahia. Ou em Belem do Pará.

Mas nunca admittimos o nascimento da logica entre nós.

Desenho de Tarcila 1928 – De um quadro que figurará na sua proxima exposição de Junho na galeria Percier, em Paris.

Contra o Padre Vieira. Autor do nosso primeiro emprestimo, para ganhar commissão. O rei analphabeto dissera-lhe: ponha isso no papel mas sem muita labia. Fez-se o emprestimo. Gravou-se o assucar brasileiro. Vieira deixou o dinheiro em Portugal e nos trouxe a labia,

O espirito recusa-se a conceber o espirito sem corpo. O antropomorfismo. Necessidade da vaccina antropofagica. Para o equilibrio contra as religiões de meridiano. E as inquisições exteriores.

Só podemos attender ao mundo orecular.

Tinhamos a justiça codificação da vingança A sciencia codificação da Magia. Antropofagia. A transformação permanente do Tabú em totem.

Contra o mundo reversivel e as idéas objectivadas. Cadaverizadas. O stop do pensamento que é dynamico. O individuo victima do systema. Fonte das injustiças classicas. Das injustiças romanticas. E o esquecimento das conquistas interiores.

Roteiros. Roteiros. Roteiros. Roteiros. Roteiros. Roteiros. Roteiros.

O instincto Carahiba.

Morte e vida das hypotheses. Da equação **eu** parte do **Kosmos** ao axioma **Kosmos** parte do **eu.** Subsistencia. Conhecimento. Antropofagia.

Contra as elites vegetaes. Em communicação com o sólo.

Nunca fomos cathechisados. Fizemos foi Carnaval. O indio vestido de senador do Imperio. Fingindo de Pitt. Ou figurando nas operas de Alencar cheio de bons sentiméntos portuguezes.

Já tinhamos o communismo. Já tinhamos a lingua surrealista. A edade de ouro.
Catiti Catiti
Imara Notiá
Notiá Imara
Ipejú

A magia e a vida. Tinhamos a relação e a distribuição dos bens physicos, dos bens moraes, dos bens dignarios. E sabiamos transpor o mysterio e a morte com o auxilio de algumas formas grammaticaes.

Perguntei a um homem o que era o Direito. Elle me respondeu que era a garantia do exercicio da possibilidade. Esse homem chamava-se Galli Mathias. Comi-o

Só não ha determinismo - onde ha misterio. Mas que temos nós com isso?

Continua na Pagina 7

2.10. Oswald de Andrade, "Manifesto Antropófago," *Revista de Antropofagia* 1:1 (São Paulo, May 1928).

ern cartography juxtaposes the knowledge of embodiment versus the archive. Ríos cannibalizes the value of Western literacy and commands viewers' attention. To read aloud "From the Life of Don Margarito" is to embody the savage, devouring the forms of the theorem until their very existence and meaning come into question. Not unlike the Native codices filled with abstract pictograms indecipherable to Europeans and feared by the friars for their idolatrous power, viewers sense discomfort and unease in the precision claimed by this abstract geometry as they personify the elder Don Margarito. Ríos's phenomenological approach to territory recalls Amerindian conceptualizations of space, or what the sixteenth-century explorers saw as these savage imprecisions. In the extant early-modern Mesoamerican maps, land was coterminous with embodiment, footprints indicated journeys, and territory hinged on ancestral lineage rather than geographic landmarks. Native cartography called upon viewers to "project themselves as bodies among bodies, both to make their way physically and to place themselves genealogically or historically."[31] Shifting to and from these discursive genres (the map of the theorem and the repertoire embedded in the poem), Chagoya and Ríos place in doubt the mastery of vision so central to Western cartography. They leave viewers with unresolved questions about the reality and fiction of mapping, the multiple epistemologies of space, and how these manuscripts and our unyielding faith in them delimits belonging.

MAPPING IN THE NEW MILLENNIUM

In the fall of 2008, the curator Nato Thompson opened the exhibition *Experimental Geography* at the Richard E. Peeler Art Center, DePauw University, in Greencastle, Indiana. The show surveyed contemporary art created since 2000 that focused on "human interaction with the land."[32] Through a careful selection of works from artists as diverse as Francis Alÿs, The Center for Land Use Interpretation, Lize Mogel, Trevor Paglen, and Raqs Media Collective, Thompson made several curatorial claims: cultural production has a spatial corollary; the geographic produces our sense of self; culture is a product of economic forces; and artists shape environments as much as they are shaped by those environments. Situating the works between the poetic and the pedagogical, the geological and the urban, or Guy Debord's "psychogeographic" collages of Paris and Adrian Piper's Mythic Being alter-ego, Thompson characterized the current aesthetic interest in the geographic as a theoretic rupture that responds to the impact of globalization and neoliberalism.[33] The exhibition traveled primarily to university art museums, and the catalogue generated interest from art-world enthusiasts as much as geographers.

Strategically positioned between these disciplines, the artist-geographer Paglen coined the term "experimental geography" in 2002. Paglen earned a master's in fine arts from the Art Institute of Chicago and a PhD in geography from the University of California, Berkeley, and is known for photographing prison complexes and secret military operations occluded from public eyes. In his view, "Experimental geography means practices that take on the production of space in a self-reflexive way, practices that recognize that cultural production and the production of space cannot be separated from each other, and that cultural and intellectual production is a spatial practice."[34] His definition underscores the importance of analyzing practices versus analyzing objects, which runs counter to traditional art history and criticism. From geography, Paglen draws on materialism as an empirical approach to understanding social phenomena and, relatedly, the production of space as a philosophical viewpoint inseparable from materiality. From European modernism, he adopts "experimental" to foster utopian possibilities and concede its trials and failures. Pointing to the rise in consumer-based mapping technologies, Paglen asserts that, "In our own time, another cartographic renaissance is taking place."[35]

Paglen and Thompson are right to sense that a "theoretical rupture" is underway from the collision of the geographic and the visual in everyday life, but it would be ahistorical to assume that mapping in art is new or somehow inherently radical. There are a number of post-1960s artists' works that turned toward geography, including Joyce Kozloff's *Boys' Art* series, Ingo Günther's *World Processor*, Nancy Holt's experiments in land art, and Guillermo Kuitca's soiled and painted mattresses, to name but a few.[36] Paglen's and Thompson's claims to radicalism likely depend on breaking with established aesthetic practices, fueling the rhetoric of social-justice movements, and/or countering the effects of advanced capitalism. Geographer Margaret Wickens Pearce critiqued the loftiness and vagueness of the sentiment: "I also feel compelled to defend my discipline when I read that a bus tour, accompanied by maps, to visit the hidden structures of the military-industrial complex is a radical act. I would counter that such a tour is simply a good human geography field trip."[37] While she conflates two different projects, the bus tours of the Center for Land Use Interpretation with Paglen's photographs of black sites (secret CIA prisons) in Afghanistan, her assessment suggests that radicalism is highly dependent on the perspective of the viewer.

But if these practices are neither new nor inherently radical, what could account for the current artistic interest in mapping? Most US critics, curators, and theorists cite the rise of corporate neoliberalism, the advancement in mapping technologies, and the disenchantment with postmodernist discourse as part of this moment of reckoning. Speaking to the epistemological posture of artists like Paglen, the art critic Hal Foster, for example, points to the infrastructure of neoliberalism as driving cultural producers from a deconstructive to a reconstructive posture: "In large part, this shift was a response to the increased control by corporations and governments, through satellite imaging and information mining, of what is given to us as the real in the first place—what can be represented, known, disputed, proved—at all scales, from the individual pixel to the vast agglomerations of big data."[38] Despite financial capitalism's promise of greater freedoms and its associated DIY technologies and navigation systems, Foster implies that we are less free through constant surveillance. The task at hand for these artists is, in Foster's view, "concerned less with exposing a given reality behind representation than with reconstructing an occluded reality."[39] Foster's theory works particularly well for artists such as Paglen who engage in the "documentary" genre, but the critic still associates the object with what Mondrian would call "pure reality." Paglen appropriates mapping and lens-based technologies to pinpoint precise locations hidden from public eyes and uses these alternative cartographies to contest the dynamics of power.

Chagoya and Ríos take a different approach in *You Are Here* by deliberately distancing themselves from a Eurocentric episteme that sees mapping as a measure of truth/reality. Their verbal and visual encounters rely on imprecision, irony, and fiction to reveal how the claims to truth are absurd and often one-sided. Chagoya adds, "For the most part, these are referential to maps, but they are not real maps, they are in the imagination. . . . Mapping is an exercise of power and . . . every time there is a shift in power, these maps, they change."[40] Even when they engage scientific concepts from the microcellular level of DNA to the macro field of outer space, they rely on pictorial and linguistic strategies of irony to humorously incite doubt. Their lithograph *Trash World*, for instance, shows a terrestrial globe at center, a pale blue marble with cloud formations swirling on the surface (fig. 2.11). The Western hemisphere is a faint outline almost indiscernible with the black dots that cover the planet. According to NASA, an estimated twenty-seven thousand pieces of orbital debris circle the Earth, traveling at extremely high speeds.[41] These can often collide with spacecraft and cause severe damage. Chagoya's *Trash World* is set within a gray background speckled with bright constellations. Satellites appear farther out in space along with human tools including wrenches and toothbrushes that seem to be in orbit. Ríos's poem does not reference the "space junk"; instead it addresses air traffic as if each dot represented a body in motion: "I have an idea. I've been reading / At any given time there are 100,000 / People in the Air / In airplanes above us. / Who is the mayor of the city of air?"[42] I do not mean to suggest that they incite doubt in the existence of space junk; on the contrary. But rather than represent the phenomenon as an abstraction that we cannot see, they once again invoke the body as a way

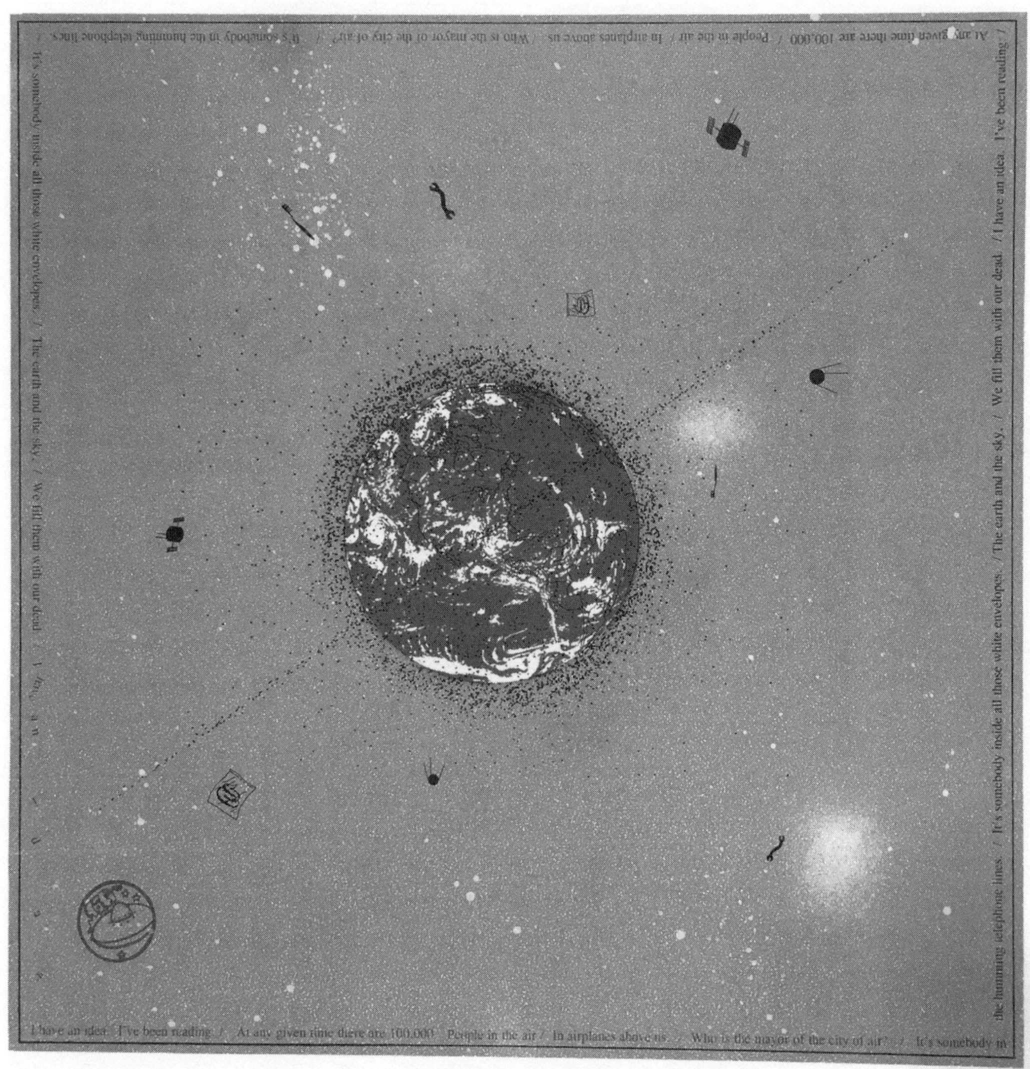

2.11. Enrique Chagoya and Alberto Ríos, *Trash World*, from the portfolio *You Are Here*, 2000. Lithograph on Rives BFK Tan, 17 × 17 inches; edition of sixty printed by Joe Freye and John Altomare and published by Segura Publishing Company, Arizona. Courtesy of the artist, Anglim/Trimble, and the Snite Museum of Art, 2019.068.024.002.

to imagine from a phenomenological perspective this chaos and disorder that NASA must constantly surveil.

In their *American Ocean/Cuba* (fig. 2.12), from the aforementioned portfolio, Chagoya and Ríos explicitly contend with mapping as an exercise of power. The artists revisited the contentious relationship between Cuba and

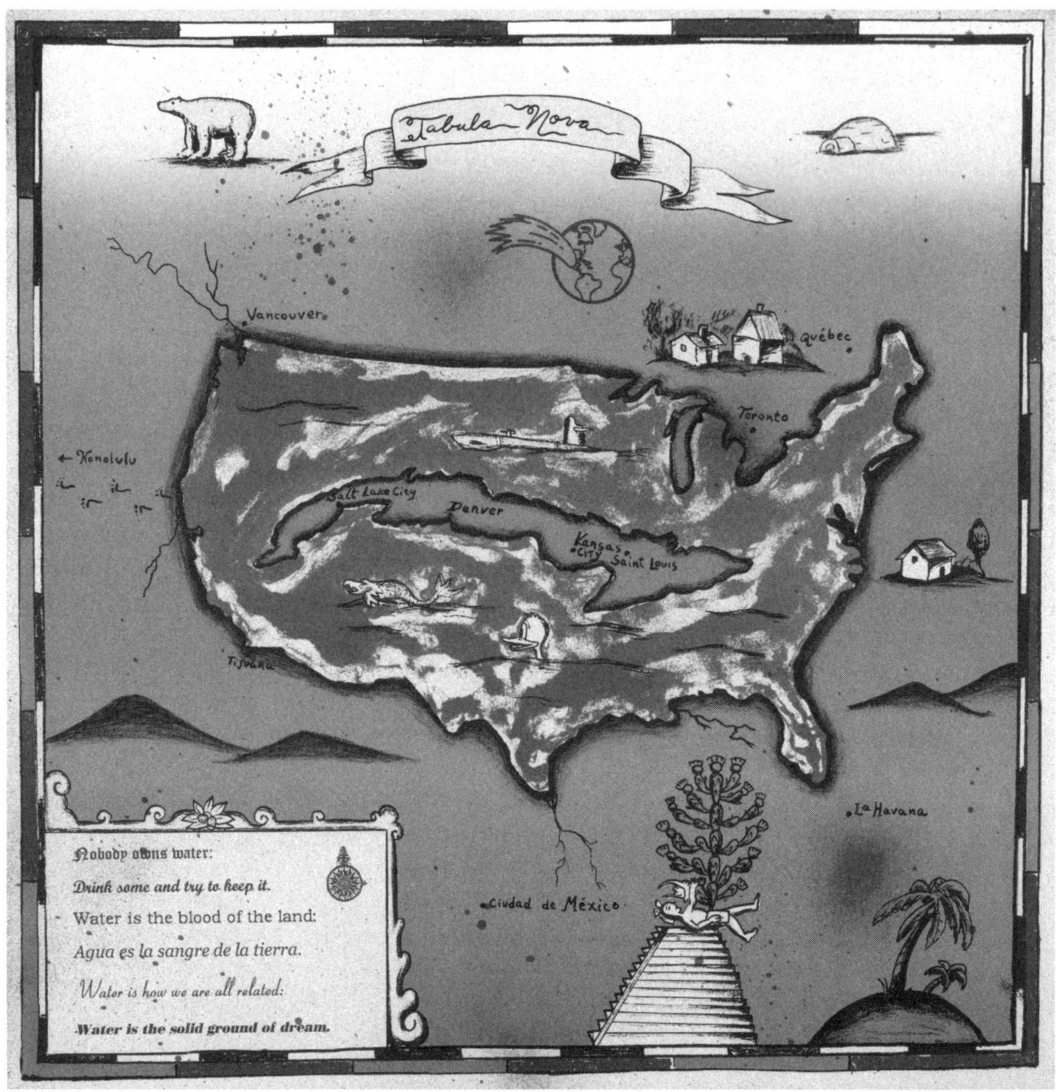

2.12. Enrique Chagoya and Alberto Ríos, *American Ocean/Cuba*, from the portfolio *You Are Here*, 2000. Lithograph on Rives BFK Tan, 17 × 17 inches; edition of sixty printed by Joe Freye and John Altomare and published by Segura Publishing Company, Arizona. Courtesy of the artist, Anglim/Trimble, and the Snite Museum of Art, 2019.068.024.003.

the United States, hemispheric powers considered mortal enemies during the Cold War. The map, with the island superimposed over a water-filled United States, invokes an alternative ending to the Cuban Missile Crisis of 1962. The half-submerged submarine vessel at the center recalls the tense moments when the US Navy chased the nuclear-armed Soviet submarine B59 bound for Cuba. *American Ocean/Cuba* suggests that such a nuclear attack would not only have reoriented the geopolitical order of the Western hemisphere but would also have called for a radical reversal between land and sea. South of the island at center, Donald Duck's head emerges from the water, mouth agape, looking toward an odd creature with the head of an eagle and the body of a fish, much like the mythical sea creatures of Renaissance maps.[43] The frightened Donald is likely one of the vestiges of Yankee imperialism.[44] By suggesting an imperfect past, the map makes present an alternative future, one that viewers are aware is a fiction but willingly partake in simulation. Geographer Denis Wood argues that maps, even the most historical, gesture to a potential future: "The World we take for granted—the real world—is made like this, out of the accumulated thought and labor of the past. It is presented to us on the platter of the map, *presented*, that is, *made present*, so that whatever invisible, unattainable, erasable past or future can become part of our living . . . *now* . . . *here*."[45] With this imagery viewers are left to ponder the absurdity of a map that places more value on fiction than on truth.

The work's incongruity reveals another factor overlooked in the recent literature on the rise of mapping in contemporary art, the profound effects of the critique of colonialism that emerged during the quincentennial celebrations in 1992. At that juncture cultural theorists revisited sixteenth-century cartographies to question how Eurocentrism consolidated power to arrogantly claim the "discovery" of a new continent. José Rabasa, for example, read Gerhard Mercator's *Atlas* (1569; fig. 2.13) as a palimpsest that drew on Spanish, Amerindian, and Northern Europe's epistemologies to produce an image of the world that is a "series of erasures and overwritings."[46] At stake in this new form of writing the world was that lands and peoples outside Europe acquired spatial meaning only after Europe had inscribed the region into a map.[47] Rabasa pointed out how through the rhetoric of the objective and the universal, viewers are made blind to the ideological dimensions of the map and equally beckoned to participate in the process of signification, complicit to the production of meaning.[48] But the theorist felt optimism in that the palimpsest cannot hide its semiotic and visual excess, noting, "The imperfect erasures are, in turn, a source of hope for the reconstitution or reinvention of the world from Native and non-Eurocentric points of view."[49]

In *American Ocean/Cuba*, the imperfect erasures depart from a fictional spatiotemporal realm, but semiotically they elicit a phenomenological relationship to geography. The map's legend contains a short poem by Ríos that addresses the immense ocean.

> Nobody owns water:
> Drink some and try to keep it.
> Water is the blood of the land:

> *Agua es la sangre de la tierra.*
> Water is how we are all related:
> Water is the solid ground of dream.

Ríos's poem is not a description but an abstraction that creates an equivalence between land and sea. If we cannot own or contain water, then why do we desire to own and contain land? Diana Magaloni echoed the sentiment in her poem "Rainbow/Arco de Tiempo," discussed in the introduction of this book, which questions the ethics of land reclamation. In the imagery Ríos conjures, land is a body, and water its blood. He notes, "we are all related," based on our dependence to this element, recalling the bloodletting rituals of Mesoamerican nations. Ríos reinforces the reversal of land and sea by positioning the water as a "solid ground" where dreams take shape. In his short poem, he provides tools to unscript the map. Viewers turn to phenomenological perception to counter disembodied projection. His use of language reinforces Native conceptualizations of territory abstracted into metaphors of ownership

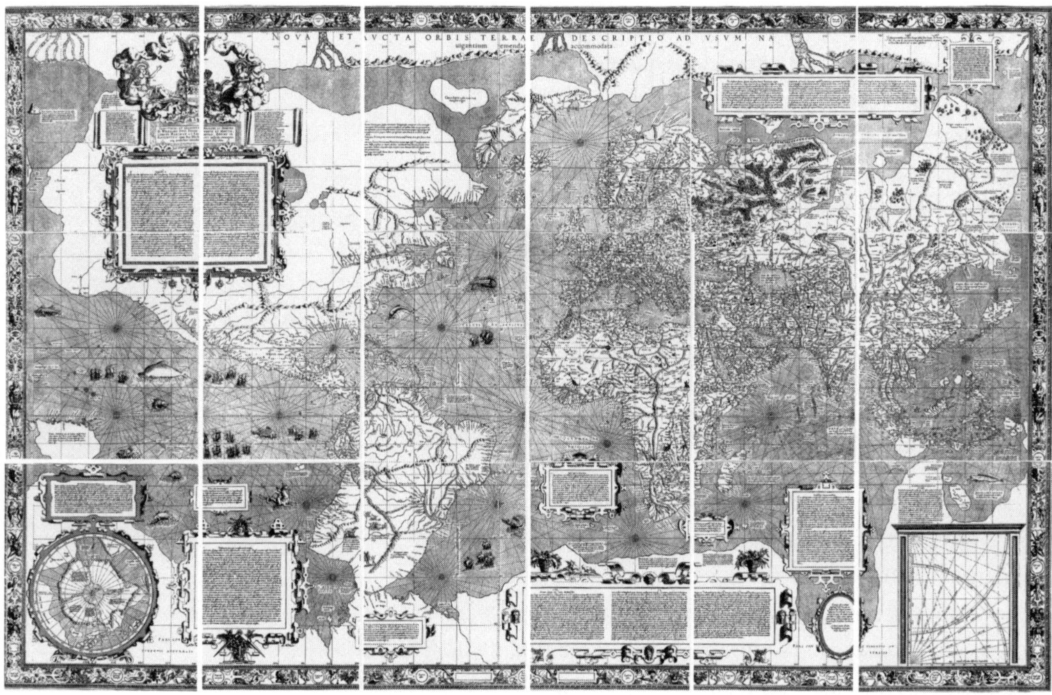

2.13. Gerhard Mercator, Nova et Aucta Orbis Terrae Descriptio ad Usum *Navigantium* Emendate Accommodata [*Atlas*], 1569. Map composite of eighteen sheets, complete map 202 × 124 cm.

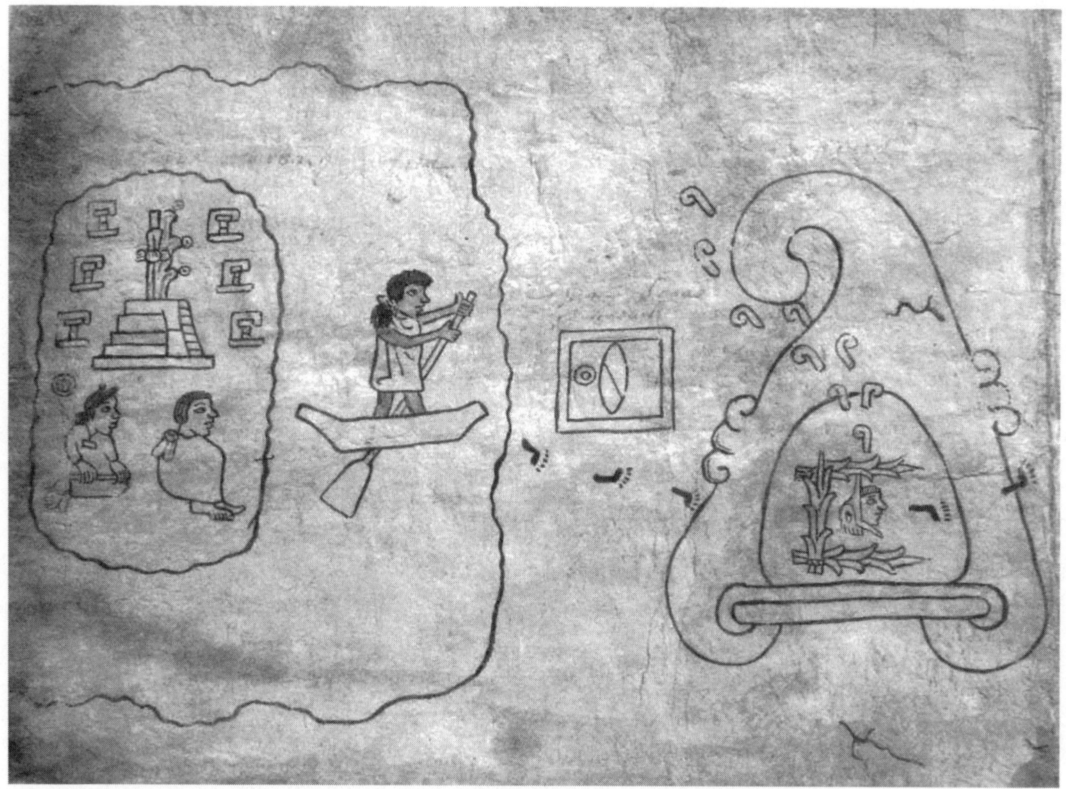

2.14. *La Tira de la Peregrinación* (also known as Codex Boturini), sixteenth century. Hand-painted on amate paper, 546 × 205 cm (extended), 26 × 20.5 × 2.2 cm (folded). Museo Nacional de Antropología, Mexico City.

and sacrifice. Chagoya also echoed those forms of map embodiment. On the southern border of the map, a pre-Columbian temple appears with a Native lying upright as if awaiting a sacrificial rite. A thorny cactus emanates from the subject's genital area. Such sacrificial rites appeased the gods who provided bountiful harvests in Mesoamerican belief systems. He also utilized embodied movement, recalling the footsteps in Mexica codices, such as the sixteenth-century *La Tira de la Peregrinación* or Codex Boturini (fig. 2.14), that document the migration of the Aztecs from Aztlán into the Valley of Mexico. Upon transforming the Atlantic and Pacific into solid land, Chagoya noted sites of interest such as Quebec, Ciudad de Mexico, and a trail of human feet leading to Honolulu.

The artist and poet's insistence on embodied knowledge questioned Eurocentric conceptions of territory and how cartographies based on this episteme reinscribe what Diana Taylor calls "scenarios of discovery." Based on foundational myths such as Columbus's first voyage, these scenarios reenact the European encounter with savages and monstrous creatures of the "new" continent. Replicated through travel narratives, maps, encyclopedias, and prints, they acquire the status of historical truths and create a dominant framework from which to approach difference. Taylor positions the scenario "as an act of transfer, as a paradigm that is formulaic, portable, repeatable, and often banal because it leaves out complexity, reduces conflict to its stock elements, and encourages fantasies of participation."[50] We may consider how those sixteenth-century documents of the "discovery," which resurfaced during the quincentennial, embed themselves in this paradigm, such as those previously mentioned by Fries, Mercator, Stradanus, de Bry, and Staden. But Taylor insists there is a way out of this formula, "The body in the scenario, however, has space to maneuver because it is not scripted."[51] This beckoning for embodiment appears through the figure of Don Margarito in *Theorem*, and it does more subtly in the footprints and poetry of *American Ocean/Cuba*. Chagoya and Ríos compel us away from the mastery of vision and the measure of reality, transporting us to a place where nothing is certain.

In contrast to trends in experimental geography that respond to new mapping technologies, big data, and surveillance, *You Are Here* is part of a critical cartography concerned with eliciting the body as an agent of destabilization. In the movements of Don Margarito, for example, the body maneuvers and breaks from the *Theorem*'s occluded script. Similarly, the transposition of the body of water with the body of land, and the transformation of water into blood in *American Ocean/Cuba*, calls upon a phenomenological perception to undo disembodied projection. *You Are Here* calls for viewers' bodies to maneuver past formulaic narratives of "discovery." Their experiment suggests that our bodies can outwit mapping's colonial origins. Without naming the neoliberal policies and trade agreements that spawned new waves of migration or the xenophobic anti-immigrant rhetoric that followed, the artists' transcultural representations of territory affirm how territory is constantly being remade and how its remaking is always an embattled process.

For *An Atlas of Radical Cartography* (2007), a publication that reproduces ten politically engaged maps from around the world with corresponding texts, editors of the project Alexis Bhagat and Lize Mogel define radical cartography as the "practice of mapmaking that subverts conventional notions in order to actively promote social change."[52] Among the maps in *An Atlas* are those contributed by Pedro Lasch recording the migrants' physical journey. In 2003, Lasch designed a simple hemispheric map of the Americas in red ink, with "Latino/a" written over the north and "America" over the south (fig. 2.15). The bold inscription over the continental landmass redefines the notion of "Amer-

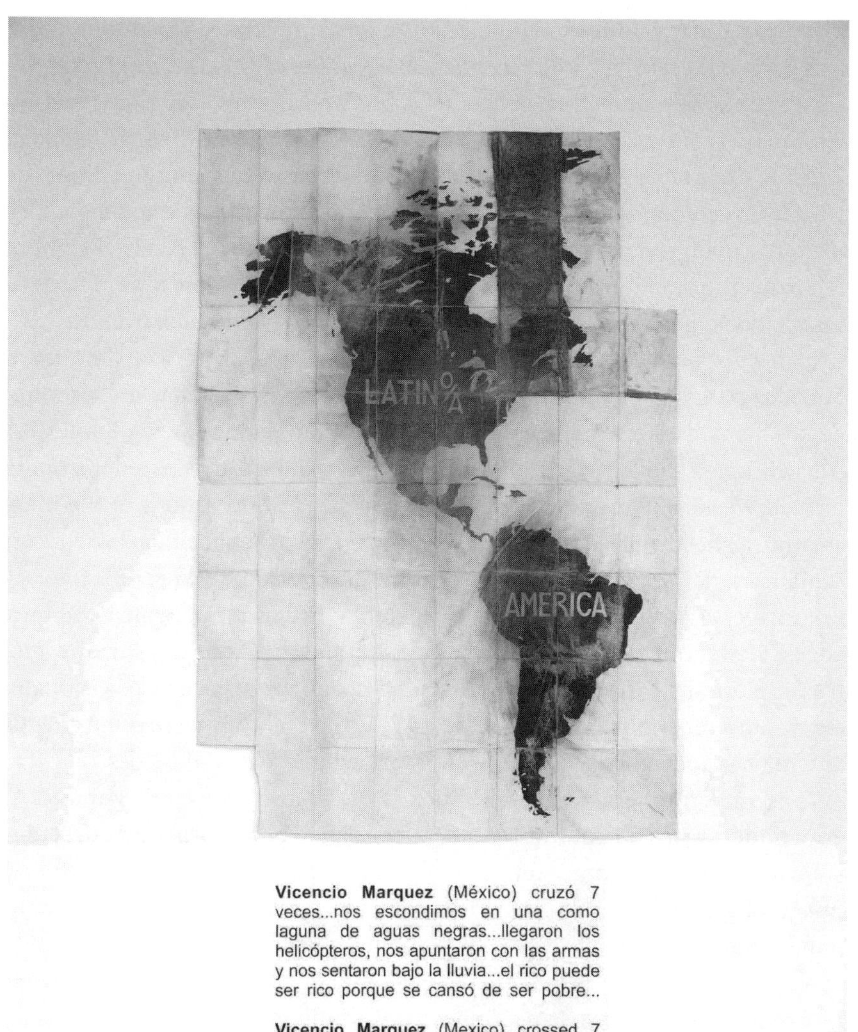

2.15. Pedro Lasch, *Route Guide—Mexico/New York—Vicencio Marquez* (*Latino/a America* series), 2003–2006. Courtesy of the artist.

ican," particularly for those of the English-speaking United States who claim it as a national category, and recenters the position of Latina/o migrants who are continuously transiting geopolitical borders in search of work, and often safety. The Mexican-born New York–based artist gave two of these folded maps to each of the twenty migrants he knew were attempting to cross the US-Mexico border. They were asked to keep one for themselves and mail back the other upon reaching their destination. Lasch eventually received eight of the maps imprinted with the ravages of the contributors' journeys. Through installations, he displays the maps along with short anecdotes from his participants' experience. The person who carried this map, Vicencio Marquez, a Mexican national, crossed the border seven times, presumably after several deportations. He recalled hiding in a lagoon of raw sewage as the Border Patrol helicopters circled overhead. In the map he mailed back, the red ink of the printed Western hemisphere has bled and rubbed over portions of the map, creating a ghostly, aged appearance. The upper-right section of the folded map contains dark brown stains the viewer will likely associate with the scatological imagery in the description. Looking at the materiality of soiled and torn edges, viewers project their own bodies into the psychogeography of transborder movement. The narratives that accompany the maps invoke a mimetic entry into a repertoire unknown to most of us, namely how to maneuver with or without papers through a highly militarized international border.

The strategy of embodied projection is one shared by Chagoya and Ríos, even if their maps do not involve this public action or performative spectatorship. The artists spent a week in Tempe, Arizona, arranging language and image, choosing inks and paper. Then printers Joe Freye and John Altomare pulled the edition of sixty onto soft and buffered tan cotton paper. The size of each print, 17″ × 17″, is too large to hold with one hand and looks oddly inaccessible when framed. I imagine what it would feel like to run my hands through the lithographs in a university map room. Would any of my students confuse these maps with those that purportedly hold truths? Would they read the poems aloud and giggle as they work to decode the signs? The distribution of these maps also differs. The production of Lasch's *Latino/a America* series presumably rejects the market, though a museum could easily acquire the installation. As the publisher investing in the production costs, Segura Publishing had high hopes of placing the limited editions in public and private collections. Still the question remains whether a project of participatory engagement can truly bring about social change, or whether that is simply a pretentious notion. The tongue-in-cheek playfulness of Chagoya and Ríos' maps will potentially reach more audiences.

In the decade after the ratification of the North American Free Trade Agreement (NAFTA), the borders may have softened for the free flow of

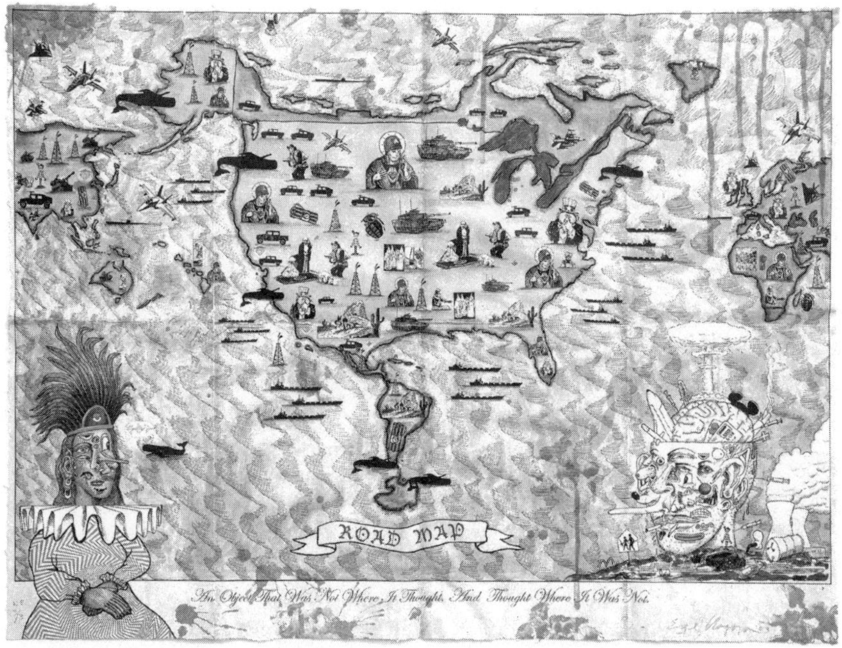

2.16. Enrique Chagoya, *Road Map*, 2003. Color Lithograph with folds, 22 × 30 inches; edition of thirty printed and published by Shark's Ink, Lyons, Colorado. Courtesy of the artist and Anglim/Trimble.

goods and capital, but Lasch's maps show how they proved to be much harder for the movement of people. Art historian Robin Greeley similarly extends that view to Chagoya's interest in maps. "From the Spanish Conquest in the Americas, to the 1848 Treaty of Guadalupe Hidalgo (in which the US moved Mexico's border, taking half its territory), to NAFTA, standard maps have attempted to coerce reality into a series of fixed lines and boundaries. Chagoya exposes the mythic and abstract nature of those lines, at the same moment he visualizes their very real, concrete and bizarre results."[53] These overt references to economic globalization altering visualizations of geography appear in Chagoya's *Road Map*, 2003 (fig. 2.16). In this colorful lithograph, the artist adopted the rhetoric of economies of scale—increasing production to lower product costs—and this notion gives way to an enlarged United States whose continental landmass is teaming with the iconographies of Christianity, oil, and militarism. In place of the allegory of America, we see the figure of Pocahontas seated on the bottom left. Her face contains multiple mouths, noses, and ears, which links it back to the female figure in the *Asian Celestial Map*. The work responded to the 2003 invasion of Iraq.

EMBODYING THE MAP

The concept of map embodiment, and perhaps more specifically border embodiment, became critical for discussing territory and sovereignty at the turn of the twenty-first century. In the case of Chagoya and Ríos, embodied geography indirectly addresses not only the geopolitical effects of neoliberalism but also a long view of how American space has been drawn and redrawn since 1492. Their map embodiment stresses a physical connection to land and more specifically to the US–Mexico border, perhaps as an aftereffect of NAFTA, which placed great emphasis on the movement of bodies (workers) through this borderline. But the attacks of September 11, 2001, that occurred far from these borderlands displaced the focus from the physical geography to a new border that became decentralized and portable. The geopolitical shifts, however, would continue to be felt vis-à-vis the body.

These shifts were felt more acutely in the realm of performance art. Following the proclamation of the war on terror and the United States' subsequent invasion of Iraq in 2003, the performance troupe La Pocha Nostra developed an interactive participatory work titled *Mapa Corpo* (2003–2009). Led by Michelle Ceballos, Violeta Luna, Roberto Sifuentes, and the acclaimed *performancero* Guillermo Gómez-Peña, the troupe turned its attention to an embodied geography that questioned the veiled interests of an allied military intervention in the Middle East. The parallel practice of performance art is enlightening, especially given the close relationship between Chagoya and Gómez-Peña, who have collaborated on a number of projects, most notably *Codex Espangliensis* (2000), an artist book published the same year as *You Are Here*. Comparing their artistic trajectories and respective relationships to the Chicano art movement, the art historian Jennifer González notes,

> As Mexicans, however, they were not really Chicanos, as U.S. residents they were not really Mexican anymore, and as former Mexicans, they were not really "American" in the hegemonic meaning of the term. . . . Unsurprising, then, that each artist's work explores the complexity of relationships between cultures that are sometimes in conflict and sometimes in collusion; that each has developed a strategy of reading across real and artificial borders.[54]

Chagoya and Ríos likewise shared the notion of living in-between. But the modalities of performance resemble the creative interplay of imagery and text that evokes in the viewer/reader a bodily repertoire often missing from the archival logic of maps. In La Pocha Nostra's work the body became a metaphor for territory and the actions of the occupier and the occupied. Unlike Chagoya and Ríos's long, abstract view, the group's performance was explicit in denouncing the use of military force as enacting forms of neocolonialism based on economic interests in the region.

Performed in more than twenty countries, *Mapa Corpo* transported viewers into an immersive environment of fear and desire that mimicked the Orientalist nature of the allied intervention. Viewers were encouraged to wander about the theatrical space. The performers were on elevated platforms where ominous tableaux unfolded: exotic dancing, shamanic incantations, the washing of a male body for burial, the healing of a female body through acupuncture. As the live action continued, sound and video projections further unsettled the audience's gaze. The central image, and the one that caused most scrutiny from critics, involved the full-frontal nudity of a female actress, often played by Violeta Luna, whose body was reimagined as occupied territory. An acupuncturist pressed needles into her flesh while she lay motionless on a gurney. The slow, repetitive nature of the actors' movements was a testament to their endurance. Each acupuncture needle carried the flag of an occupation force, and by the time all forty needles were inserted, her brown body transformed into the territory under siege, recalling the gendering of territory observed in chapter 1. Toward the end of the performance, the audience was invited to extract the pinned flags from the woman's body as an allegory for decolonizing the territory. At the same time, they were encouraged to write on the male body (the Brown immigrant archetype performed by Sifuentes) as if assuming the role of the geographer who uses writing to rename territory.

Despite its global success and some critical approval for the work's decolonial gestures, *Mapa Corpo* faced censorship in the United States. The critic Laurietz Seda spoke of the pain endured by the colonized body (the female actress with forty needles in her body) and how that pain resisted verbal language, and she praised the "metaphorical healing ritual" when the work took on a participatory element.[55] With the overt critiques of the Bush Administration's War on Terror, the artists struggled to find US venues. In an open letter published in 2006, Gómez-Peña explained that dozens of US museums and universities had rejected staging the performance: "Let's face it, overt censorship is happening throughout the United States, and not just in 'red America.' My performance art colleagues and fellow spoken-word poets are being monitored, interrogated, defunded, watered down, ignored, and un/disinvited by our cultural institutions, many of which perceive themselves as 'liberal.'"[56] Fears of losing public funding or, worse, of alienating wealthy patrons brought back the censorship and self-censorship that defined the culture wars of the Reagan era.

For art historian Ila Sheren, *Mapa Corpo* mirrored a movable cartography that responded to the dynamics of a changing global economy. She positioned the performance of embodied geography as the "twenty-first century culmination of the portable border."[57] In her *Portable Borders: Performance Art and Politics on the U.S. Frontera since 1984* (2015), she argues that performance artists advanced an abstract and itinerant representation of territorial or political conflict, and through these dynamics, "the border became uprooted from its physical location while maintaining its connection to the body as a mythical site."[58] The critic Claire Fox had noticed this shift in the oeuvre of Gómez-Peña years earlier because in performance, the border transformed into a "phenomenological category . . . something that people carried within themselves . . . [and this view] facilitated his later expansion of the border to encompass 'the world.'"[59] In enacting the globalization of the border, the artists used the body to destabilize Western cartography, much like Chagoya and Ríos. But they also reinforced the view that if land is coterminous with embodiment, and land is under siege, then we must feel that experience in the flesh.

The shift in the border's portability that Fox and Sheren traced signaled something else interesting in the context of participation: that is, the transformation of each viewer into a border crosser. This intention is loud, perhaps even obnoxious, in the context of *Mapa Corpo*. In addition to writing on one body and extracting needles from another, Gómez-Peña asks the audience to repeat after him.

> "Mexico es California" "*Mexico es California.*"
> "Marruecos es Madrid." "*Marruecos es Madrid.*"
> "Pakistan es Londres." "*Pakistan es Londres.*"
> "Argelia es Paris." "*Argelia es Paris.*"
> "Cambodia es San Francisco." "*Cambodia es San Francisco.*"
> "Turquia es Frankfurt." "*Turquia es Frankfurt.*"
> "Puerto Rico es Nueva York." "*Puerto Rico es Nueva York.*"
> "Centro America es Los Angeles." "*Centro America es Los Angeles.*"
> "Honduras es Nueva Orleans." "*Honduras es Nueva Orleans.*"
> "Argentina es Paris." "*Argentina es Paris.*"
> "*Beijing es San Francisco.*"
> "*Haiti es Nueva York . . .*"
> "Your House is also mine." "*Your House is also mine.*"
> "Your Language mine as well." "*Your Language is mine as well.*"[60]

In this call and response, the audience is asked to consider how our cities are made up of multiple geographies, especially in immigrant enclaves, and how our bodies redraw the map as we move through them. Working within a duality of violence and healing, the *Mapa Corpo* performance placed viewers in the shoes of the occupier and the occupied, perhaps testing the absurdity of these untenable positions. In contrast, Chagoya and Ríos's maps of the imagination offer a much more subtle way to experience border embodiment. Through their playful gestures, we perform the map without even knowing it.

Although the body is the medium central to performance art, we rarely consider its relationship to printmaking and mapmaking. *You Are Here* insists on phenomenological perception to counter disembodied projection. One of the ways it does so is by revealing the embodiment of the mapmaker. The unorthodox approach challenges the truth/objectivity claims of Western cartography, which operate from a detached visuality and thus obscure the mapmaker's hand. Mercator's *Atlas* (fig. 2.13) transforms the spherical world into a flat, two-dimensional, and gridded surface. The geographer surrounds the continental landmasses with bodies of water that are crisscrossed with innumerable diagonals whose points intersect in major navigational routes. Brief descriptions accompany each location, but the system of representation tells us little about Mercator's body. The precision of his lines and their measurements privileges visuality—the geographer's eye—as the one and only source of true knowledge. Chagoya and Ríos experiment with map embodiment to expose the Eurocentric nature of this epistemology.

In *Upside Down World Map* (fig. 2.17), Chagoya emphasized the primacy of the body as a reference point for territoriality. He eschews his usual cast of popular culture icons and the impending sense of conflict in his work. No less ideological, but certainly more abstract, Chagoya's world map, most likely based on a Mercator projection, as well as an art-historical reference to Joaquín Torres García's *America Invertida*, inverts the well-known form and flips it upside down. The simple gesture reverses the geopolitics of Western cartographic practice, as Bhagat and Mogel argue in *An Atlas of Radical Cartography*: "The modern north-oriented map continually reproduces the idea of the global North and the global South. The 'inverted' map calls into question our ingrained acceptance of this particular 'global order.'"[61] Chagoya's continents appear to be drawn through imprecise and rudimentary means as if mocking the detailed and ornately crafted maps of early-modern cartographers. His world map resembles a child's finger painting, and we imagine the artist's hand moving about the aluminum plate, covered in brown ink of the consistency of chocolate. His fingerprints float about the surface, making his own body a matrix whose ghostly, agitated marks emphasize movement and messiness, a carelessness antithetical to not only the map genre but also the technical precision of printmaking. By revealing the process, as if documenting a performance, Chagoya reiterates the chasm between what we know and what we sense. The faint lines in his fingerprints, unique identifiers, are far more trustworthy and measurable than those on any world map.

While Chagoya reveals the embodiment of the mapmaker, Ríos calls upon the reader to consider one's body as a source of truth. His narrative poem in

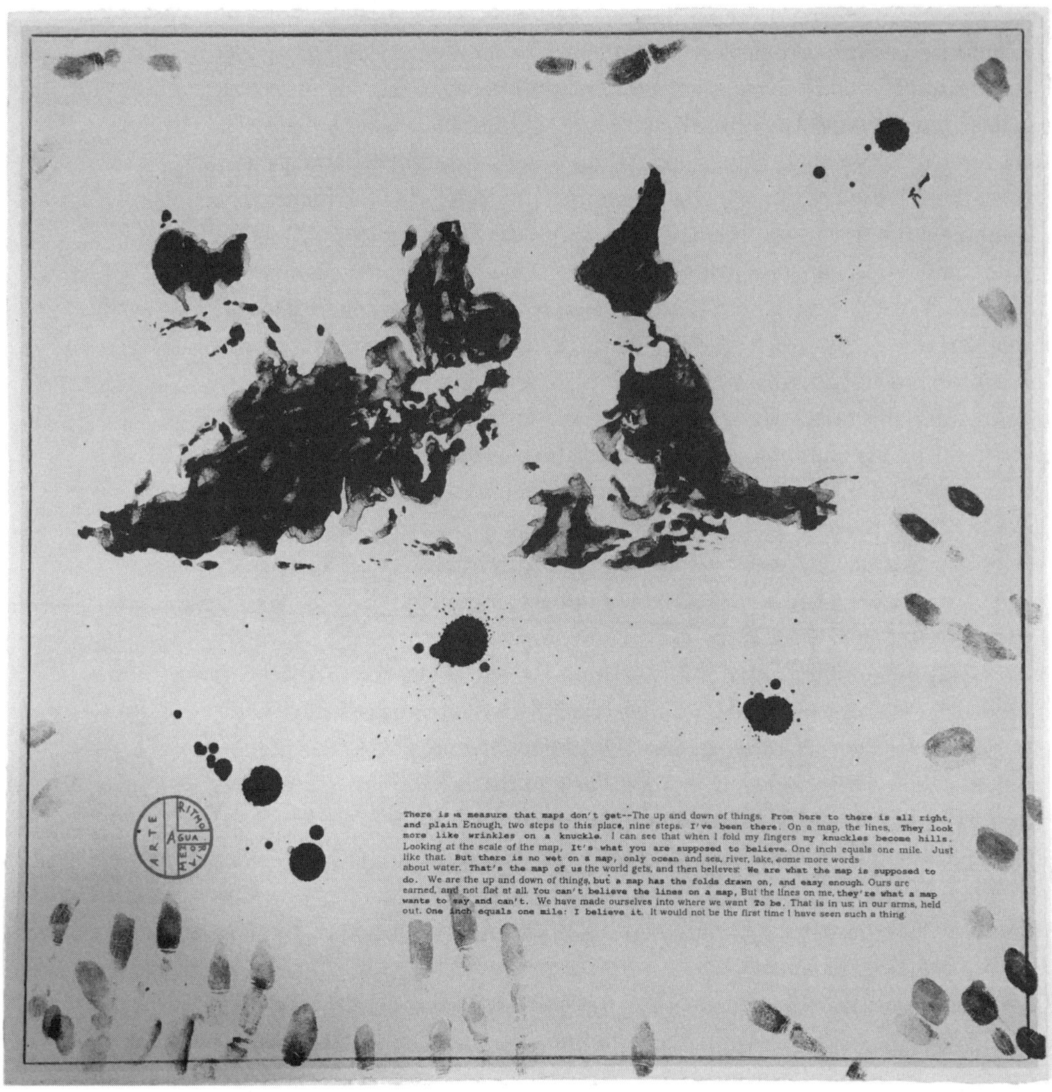

2.17. Enrique Chagoya and Alberto Ríos, *Upside Down World Map*, from the portfolio *You Are Here*, 2000. Lithograph on Rives BFK Tan, 17 × 17 inches; edition of sixty printed by Joe Freye and John Altomare and published by Segura Publishing Company, Arizona. Courtesy of the artist, Anglim/Trimble, and the Snite Museum of Art, 2019.068.024.005.

Upside Down World Map guides viewers to a haptic-based knowledge by which measurements and scales depend on their bodies:

> There is a measure that maps don't get—The up and down of things. From here to there is all right, and plain Enough, two steps to this place, nine steps. I've been there. On a map, the lines, They look more like wrinkles on

> a knuckle. I can see that when I fold my fingers my knuckles become hills. Looking at the scale of the map, it's what you are supposed to believe. One inch equals one mile. Just like that. But there is no wet on a map, only ocean and sea, river, lake, some more words about water. That's the map of us the world gets, and then believes: We are what the map is supposed to do. We are the up and down of things, but a map has the folds drawn on, and easy enough. Ours are earned, and not flat at all. You can't believe the lines on a map, But the lines on me, they're what a map wants to say and can't. We have made ourselves into where we want to be. That is in us: in our arms, held out. One inch equals one mile: I believe it. It would not be the first time I have seen such a thing.

Not only does the poem disrupt our belief in scale and geometry, it also insists in the body's perfection—"We are what the map is supposed to do." Ríos's words exalt embodied knowledge as a powerful reference point for geography that can equal or exceed the accuracy of the detached cartographic gaze. His poem incites doubt in measurements and scales that we cannot experience. His claim that "we have made ourselves into where we want to be" speculates that we carry that geography in our bodies and can use that knowledge to elicit alternative conceptions of territoriality.

Ríos's interest in the human body and its sense of perfection resurfaces in a poem published a couple years later, "Some Extensions on the Sovereignty of Science" (2002). Dedicated to his late father, the poem reflects on failing health and our inability to turn away from nature's dramatic force. But the last stanza proposes that the body possesses the kind of knowledge that can shield us from ourselves. He writes,

> The smallest muscle in the human body is in the ear.
> It is also the only muscle that does not have blood vessels;
>
> It has fluid instead. The reason for this is clear:
> The ear is so sensitive that the body, if it heard its own pulse,
>
> Would be devastated by the amplification of its own sound.
> In this knowledge I sense a great metaphor,
>
> But I do not want to be hasty in trying to capture or describe it.
> Words are our weakest hold on the world.[62]

What is this great metaphor if not a meditation on how perfect our bodies are even in their ability to protect us from what would overwhelm us? In an interview, Ríos noted, "There are many things in life we are protected from hear-

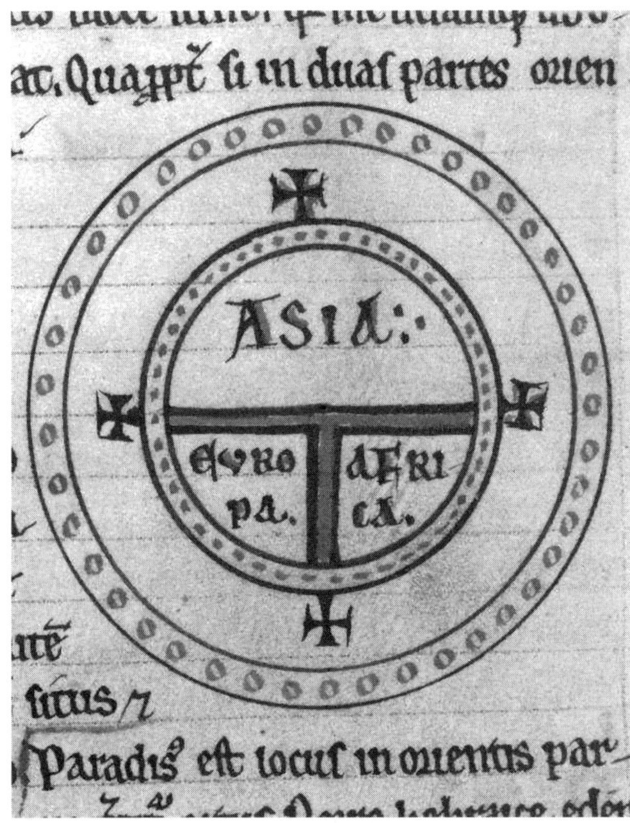

2.18. T-O map, from Isidore of Seville's *Etymologiae*, ca. 600–625.

ing, seeing, smelling, tasting, touching, and feeling." He also offered that his practice as a poet hinged on revealing the very thing "we've been protected from experiencing."[63]

The stamp in *Upside Down World Map* is a T-O map (pronounced "T and O map") that recalls medieval geography manuscripts.[64] The T-O maps represented half of the spherical earth that by the seventh century was known to consist of Africa, Asia, and Europe. The T formed the shape of the Mediterranean Sea, the Nile, and the Don, and the O was the surrounding ocean. Isidore of Seville's *Etymologiae*, among the first encyclopedic manuscripts, shows a T-O map with Asia as the largest continent at the top, Europe on the bottom left, and Africa on the bottom right (fig. 2.18). In these representations, Jerusalem, the Holy Land, served as the axis mundi. But in Chagoya's red stamp, art, rhythm, and memory replace the three known continents. The body of water remains. The only inhabitable sites in his T-O map are the most intangible registers that we experience physiologically—the things that resist being mapped or, better yet, are unmappable. Art, rhythm, and memory are also what the archive of Western cartography has asked us to forget.

You Are Here creates a sense of irony by reverting to the techniques of colonization, mainly Western literacy and cartography, to expose the epistemic violence in hegemonic projects of mapping.[65] If it is true, as Audre Lorde wrote, that "the master's tools will never dismantle the master's house," then why return to mapmaking? It is as if they mean to suggest that the tools of colonization can also be used in decolonial maneuvers that bring to light the underside of modernity. More important, Chagoya and Ríos infer that the tools we seek are already within us. Embodying the map, as much as embodying the border, is about unscripting how we typically read maps. *You Are Here* invites us, in other words, to learn how to read again in a way that cannot unsee the body of the mapmaker and our phenomenological connection to territory.

CONCLUSION

Although the outcome of this artistic collaboration between Chagoya and Ríos was unpredictable, the publisher Joe Segura considers *You Are Here* one of his most successful projects. He said in an interview:

> They came and they figured out how to not illustrate each other's work, but how to make it make sense. Alberto went to his office every day and would fax us stuff. Enrique would go to the studio and make drawings. Then they would meet at the end of each day for about an hour and then at the end of the week, they got together and they put six images together with six writings and that became the form.[66]

The portfolio is compelling, not only for its subject matter but also because it is emblematic of the kinds of projects Segura undertook for more than thirty years. Unlike Self Help Graphics & Art, which originated as a community-based workshop, Segura Publishing came out of the midcentury American print renaissance. Segura was among the first Mexican American printers trained at the Tamarind Institute (formerly Tamarind Lithography Workshop), and his own workshop and publishing projects give us a window into the multiple genealogies that make up the field of Latinx printmaking. This collaboration between artist, poet, printer, and publisher allows us to see how workshops are vibrant intellectual spaces.

In 2013, Segura Publishing left its home in Arizona and relocated to South Bend, Indiana, at the invitation of the University of Notre Dame. They changed their name to Segura Arts Studio and relaunched their residency program along with a community outreach component that would serve this underprivileged neighborhood in the rust-belt city. The Notre Dame administration invested a great deal in the relocation and remodeling of a building for a state-of-the-art workshop that could compete with renowned atelier spaces like the University of South Florida's Graphicstudio. However, their investment did not involve long-term sustainability. The workshop was given three years to become financially independent, but without access to art-market infrastructures in this isolated location that dream never materialized. Citing financial deficits, the University of Notre Dame closed Segura Arts Studio in December of 2018, and that decision effectively shuttered one of the most important Latinx printmaking studios in the country.[67] But its legacy has not been forgotten, and I hope this chapter inspires others to pursue more research.

In its creative interpretation of space and embodiment, *You Are Here* calls on the viewer to identify with the savage, a recurring trope from modern art in Latin America, and to return the gaze to Europe's project of mapping. The portfolio revisits the complicity of printmaking in the spread of Western conceptualizations of space that aided the colonization of New World nations and helped obscure archival traces of Native territorialities. Chagoya and Ríos prompt viewers to engage in small acts of disobedience and to question how the world was rewritten as a result of these visual cultures of contact, how this provincial epistemology became a dominant form of knowledge, how it continues to structure social thought even in the realm of the digital, where the reproductive technology of printmaking has been replaced with a far more powerful propagative tool. With the rise of digital mapping technologies in the twenty-first century comes the techno-utopian belief in a democratization of the power of maps. But despite the proliferation and everyday use of GPS technology, such as the rapid deployment of contact-tracing apps during the Covid-19 pandemic, maps continue to be instruments of power.

Although Chagoya and Ríos share many of the values espoused by experimental geography—practices that take on the production of space in a self-reflexive way and that foster utopian possibilities—they also differ in how radically they break away from an episteme that sees mapping as a measure of truth. Since this dominant way of seeing shapes social thought in the West, they use everything at their disposal—humor, irony, surrealism—to subvert the power of the cartographic gaze. They do not reveal truths; most of the prints hinge on fiction, and yet they cultivate these anarcho-possibilities for thinking of space and territory beyond what is given to us by the dominant culture. Chagoya muses, "I'm looking for the irrational side, like in the work of crazy minds. . . . The irrational way of looking is a very important way to understand the invisible essences of the world."[68] Unlike the other case studies in this book, which reclaim the Americas from various subject positions—Indigenous, migrant, mestizo/a, and Afro-Latinx—these artists are able to subvert the paradox of reconquest and gesture to a potential future where multiple ways of knowing and envisioning territory can productively coexist. The *Genome Map* that houses the rich shared histories of our fraught species certainly demands we try.

The chronology of the project taking place in a post-NAFTA era is also indicative of how neoliberalism rewrites geography. Despite the hemispheric and borderless rhetoric of free trade, the movement of workers through the US–Mexico border became much more restricted in the 1990s. The maps that Chagoya and Ríos imagined, although timeless, responded to these economic shifts. The next chapter takes us from Arizona to the Texas borderlands and contemplates the effects of neoliberalism after September 11, 2001, when under the threat of terrorism the nation once again redrew its borders. It begins in the place where these artists left off but considers how changing dynamics of the global economy created a movable cartography that restricted movement and visibility inside the American metropolis.

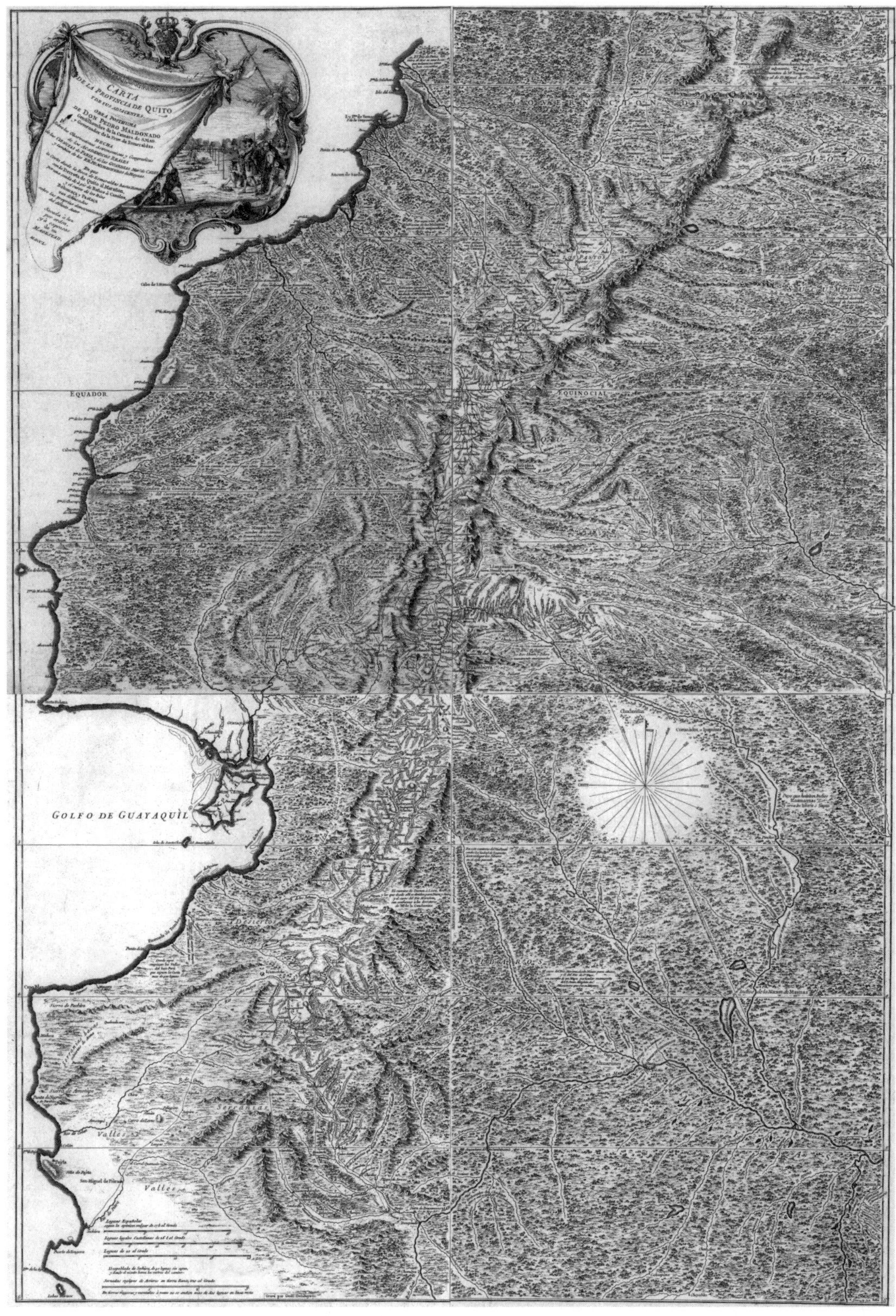

3.1. Carta de la Provincia de Quito y de sus Adyacentes, 1750. One map engraved on four sheets, 53 × 30 inches if joined. Library of Congress, Geography and Map Division. Restrike edition printed in Quito by Roberto Arnoldo Sicles Garzón and published by Estampería Quiteña in 2019.

CHAPTER THREE

Mestiza Territorialities

Sandra Fernández's Migrant Justice and the Movable Border

IN THE EARLY EIGHTEENTH CENTURY an international team of scientists traveled to the equator to try to answer one of the daunting questions of Enlightenment science. The Geodesic Mission to the Equator (1735–1744), as it came to be known, launched a cartographic expedition to discern the exact shape of the earth. French geographers Charles-Marie de La Condamine, Pierre Bouguer, and Louis Godin were joined by Spanish naval officers Jorge Juan y Santacilia and Antonio de Ulloa. But in order to traverse this vast and uncharted region of the Andes, which included coastal lands, jungles, volcanic peaks, and malarial swamps, they enlisted the help of local scientist and explorer Pedro Vicente Maldonado. The latter, having undertaken several missions, possessed an unrivaled knowledge of the terrain. After the scientists completed these extensive triangulated surveys of the region, Maldonado traveled to Europe with the results. His manuscript took the form of a monumental map that represents a landmark of Enlightenment-era cartography.

The story of this map, Carta de la Provincia de Quito y de sus Adyacentes (1750; fig. 3.1), coincidentally intersects with the work of a contemporary artist that this chapter follows, the Ecuadorian-American artist Sandra C.

Fernández. The two of us traveled to Quito in January of 2019 and visited the printmaking workshop Estampería Quiteña. When we arrived at the studio, we observed master printer Roberto Arnoldo Sicles Garzón working with large copper plates. He told us the story of the map, how the plates had recently been rediscovered, and how, to his surprise, the Office of the President had asked him to restore them and pull a new, limited edition from the refurbished plates. For Sicles Garzón and the workshop, the President's request was a great honor, as it focused on the momentous scientific discovery and awe-inspiring vastness of the lands that became the Republic of Ecuador in 1822. I use this chance encounter with an object from colonial history to signal what this map represents for Fernández, who grew up straddling the line between modernity and its underside, coloniality. Like most Ecuadorian schoolchildren, she learned about the fantastical voyages of the Franco-Hispanic Geodesic Mission in her grade school, which informed her interest in geography but also in the uneven relationships that develop between imperial powers and colonial subjects.

This chapter focuses on Fernández's prints and how they portray the geography of the borderlands and the (in)visibility of undocumented immigrants. As a paradigmatic example of how artists from Latinx communities contest territoriality and nativism, her representations of the border question the imaginary lines drawn on colonial maps such as those produced by the eighteenth-century Geodesic Mission. Fernández's work provides this distinct insight through a view from the south. The Carta de la Provincia de Quito offers many parallels to consider how geographic representations fuel discourses of colonization, science, and nationalism. In the previous chapter, contemporary artists took to unscripting the Western cartographic gaze through bodily performance. Those verbal and visual experiments by Enrique Chagoya and Alberto Ríos counter the repetitive gestures of Enlightenment scientists who traversed the equatorial line. The knowledge that these scientists produced in their travel writing, maps, and public monuments often obscures "that European empirical practices and instrumental observations were socially embedded performances."[1] This spectacle of data collection and measurement was hidden away in representations of geographic space like the Carta that stressed disembodiment. Fernández finds alternative ways to challenge this Cartesian projection.

This chapter follows her printmaking residencies at the Austin-based workshop Coronado Studio between 2008 and 2013. During this time, Central Texas experienced an economic and population boom as the country recovered from a recession and many West Coast and East Coast companies relocated to more affordable localities. Rapid urbanization gave way to informal economies, low-wage labor, and a growing service sector that brought immi-

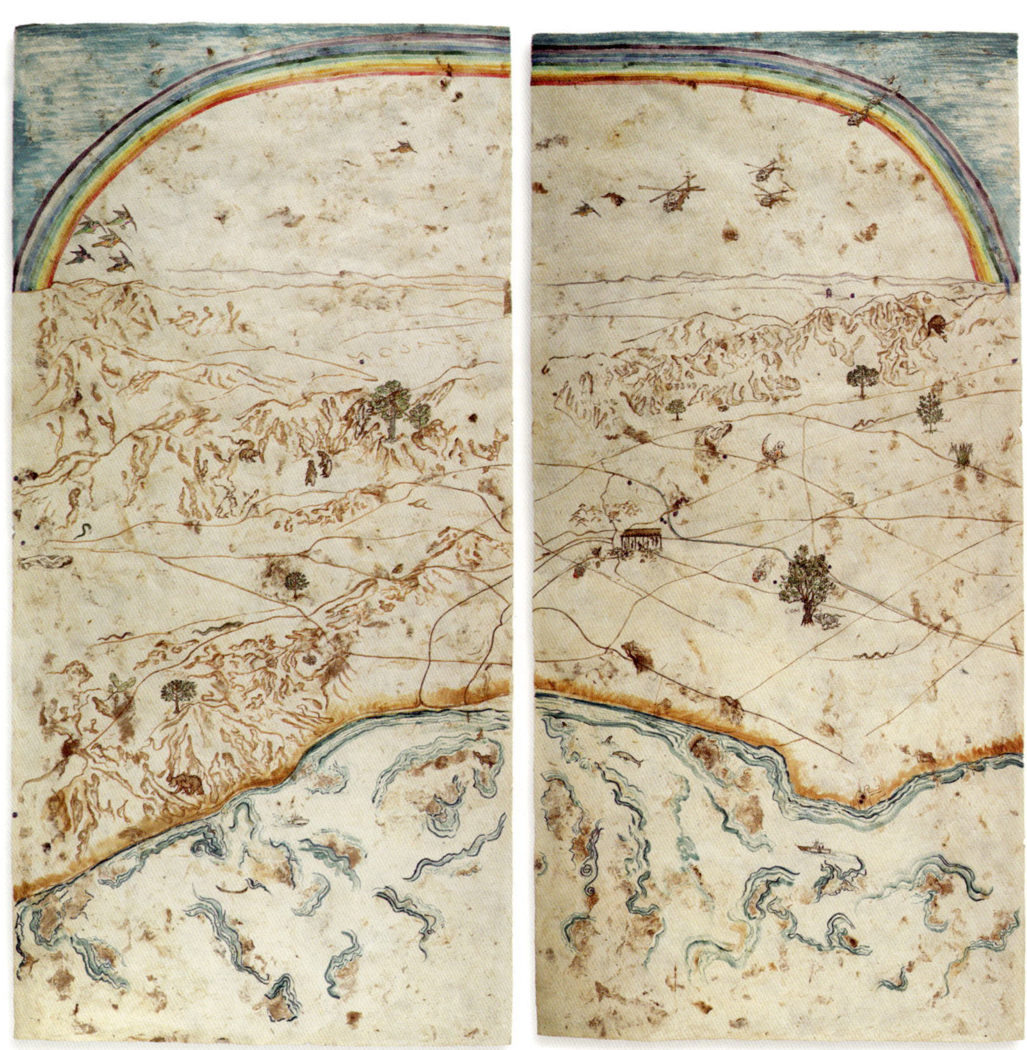

Sandy Rodriguez, *Rainbows, Grizzlies, and Snakes, Oh My!—Conquest to Caging in Los Angeles*, 2019. Los Angeles County Museum of Art, purchased with funds provided by AHAN: Studio forum, 2019 Art Here and Now. © Sandy Rodriguez. Photo by J6 Creative.

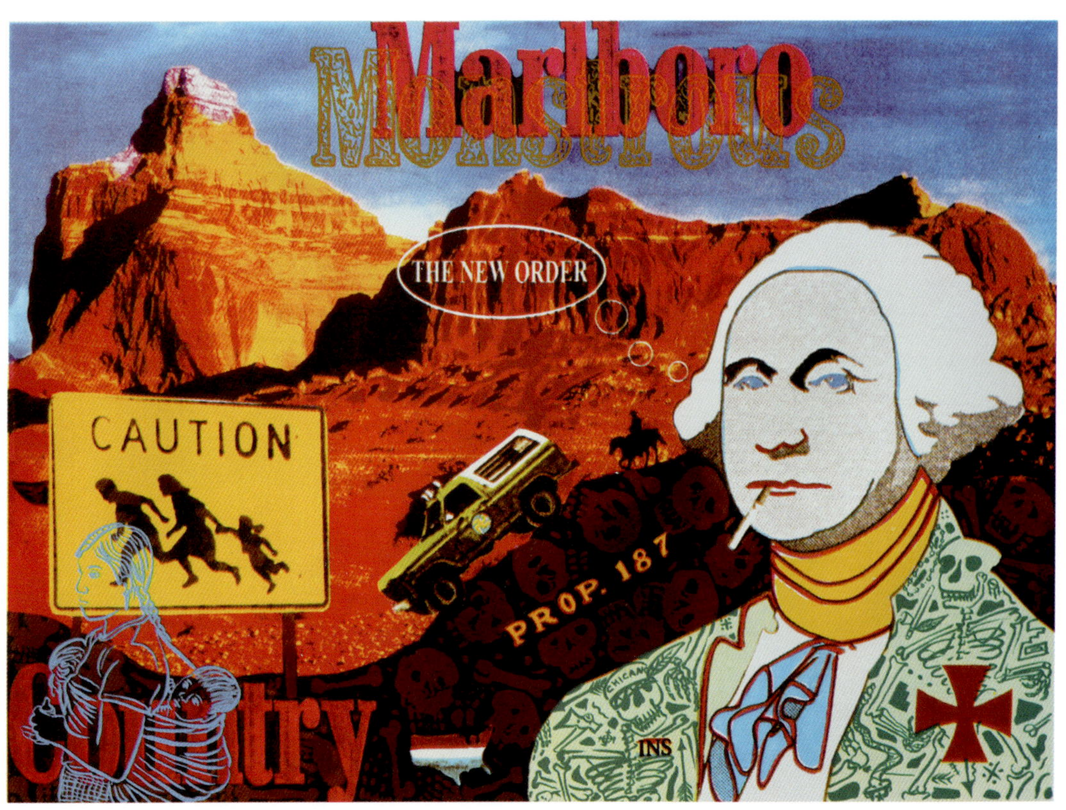

Ricardo Duffy, *The New Order*, 1996. Screenprint on paper, 20 × 26 inches; edition of seventy-five, published by Self Help Graphics, Los Angeles. Courtesy of the artist.

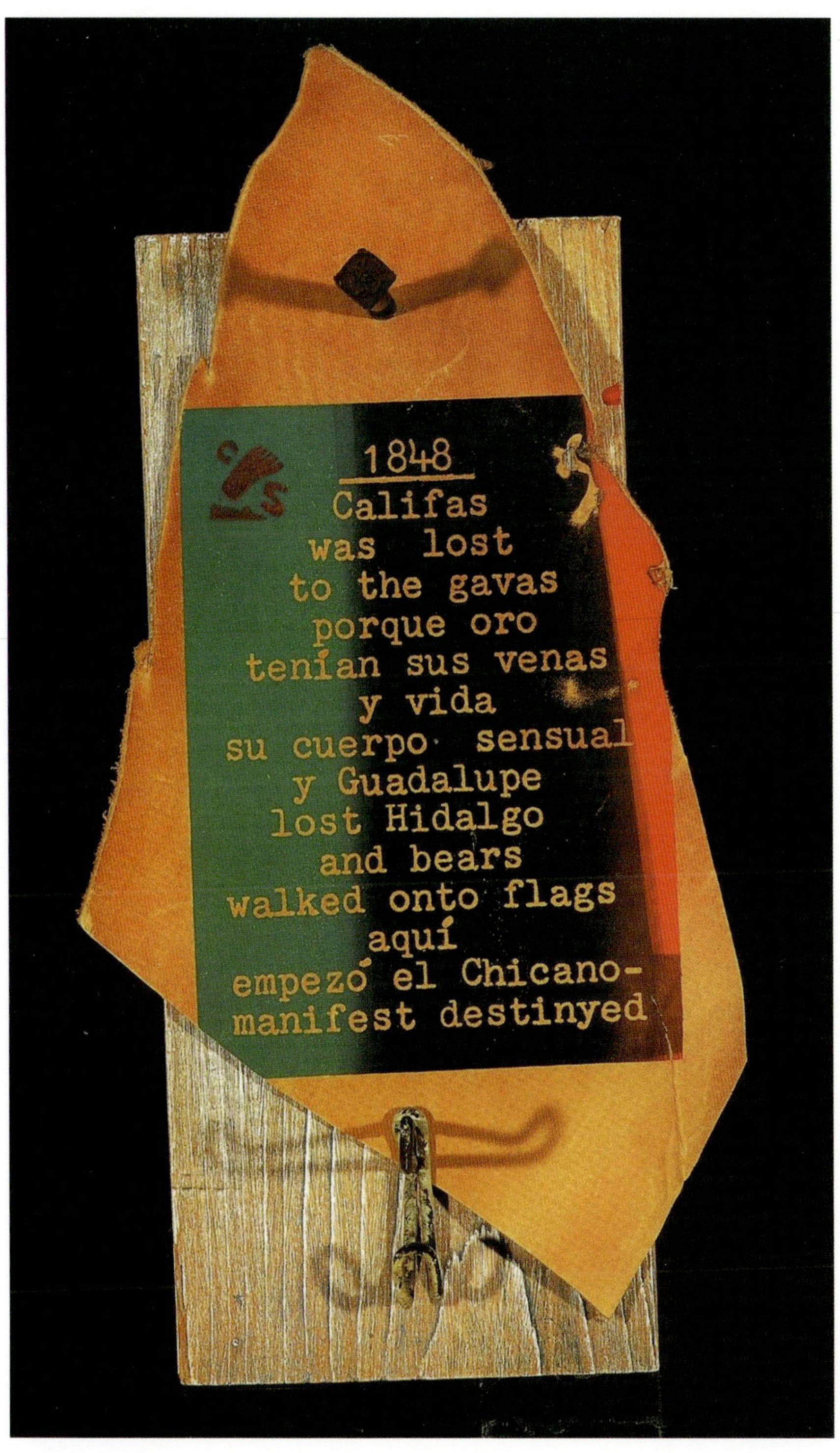

Luis C. González, aka "Louie the Foot," *1848*, 2003. Screenprint on leather, hardware and wood, 14½ × 7¼ × 4½ inches. Courtesy of the artist.

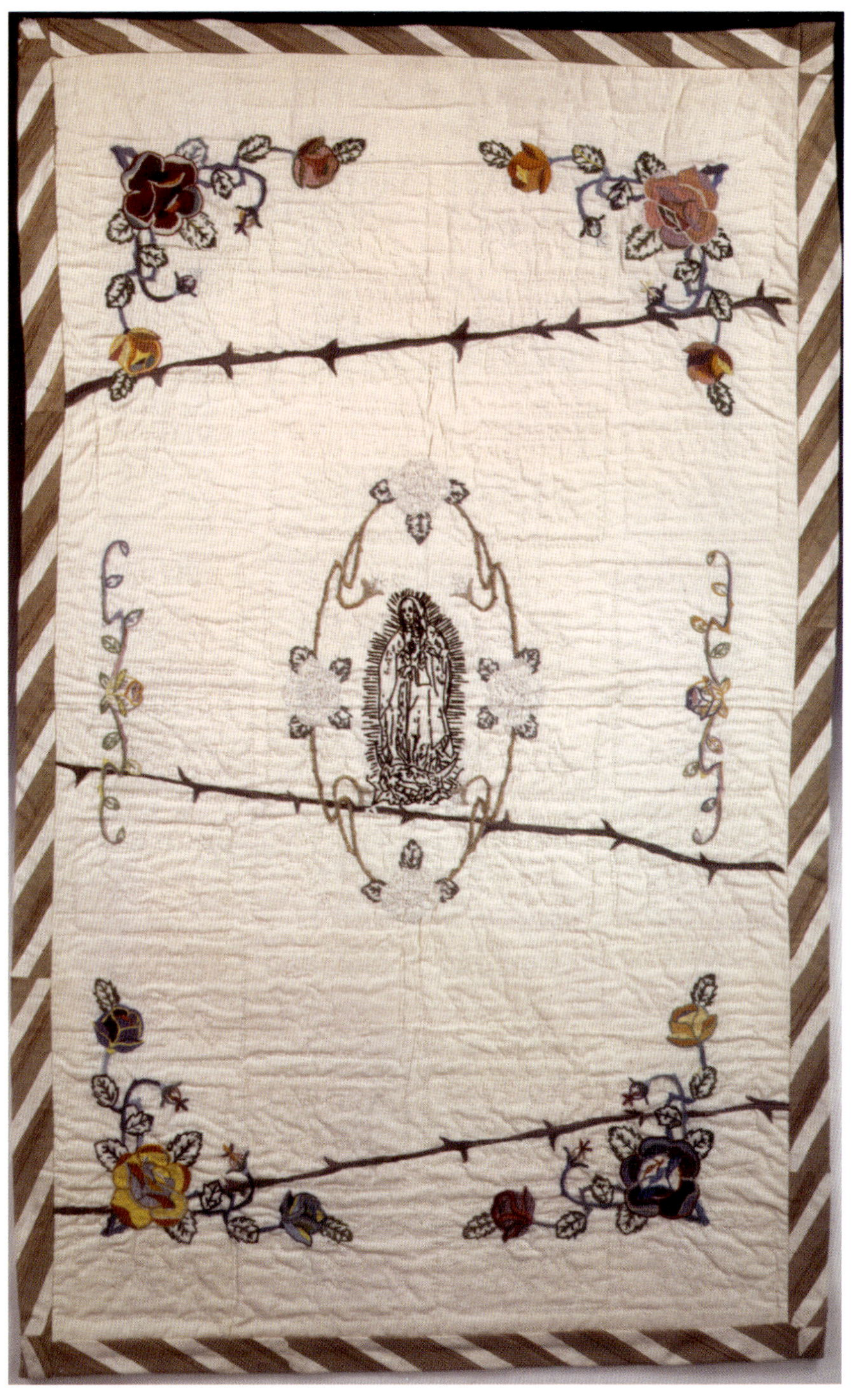

Consuelo Jimenez Underwood, *Virgen de los Caminos*, 1994. Embroidered and quilted cotton and silk with graphite, 58 × 36 inches. Courtesy of the artist and Smithsonian American Art Museum, Museum Purchase, 1996.77.

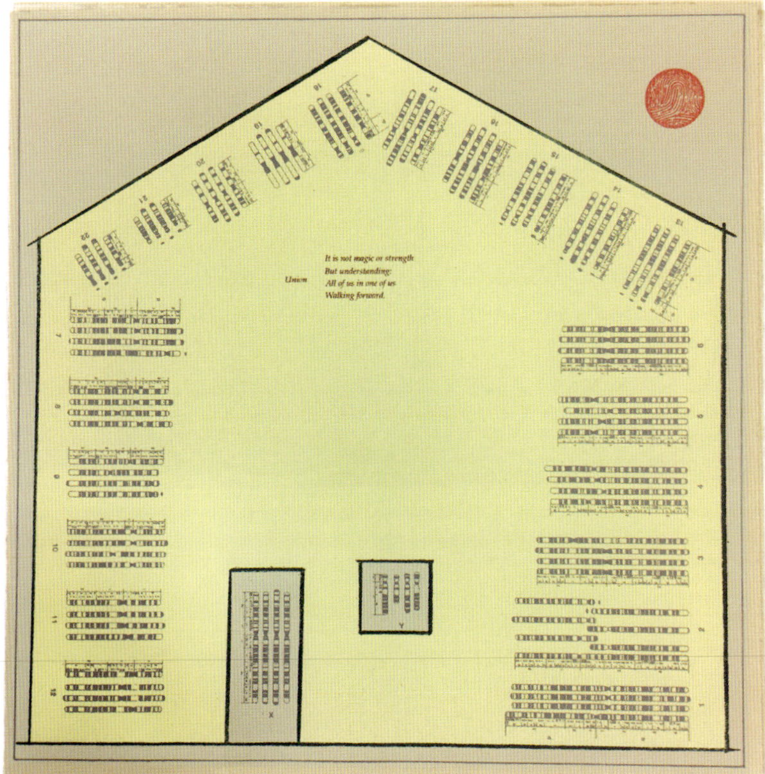

Enrique Chagoya and Alberto Ríos, *Genome Map*, from the portfolio *You Are Here*, 2000. Lithograph on Rives BFK Tan, 17 × 17 inches; edition of sixty printed by Joe Freye and John Altomare and published by Segura Publishing Company, Arizona. Courtesy of the artist, Anglim/Trimble, and the Snite Museum of Art, 2019.068.024.006.

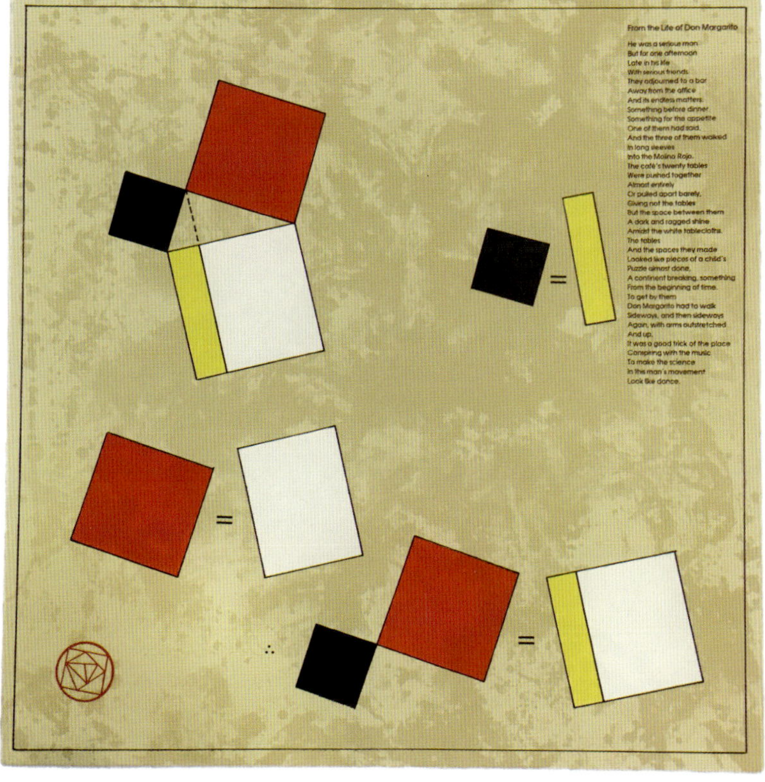

Enrique Chagoya and Alberto Ríos, *Theorem*, from the portfolio *You Are Here*, 2000. Lithograph on Rives BFK Tan, 17 × 17 inches; edition of sixty printed by Joe Freye and John Altomare and published by Segura Publishing Company, Arizona. Courtesy of the artist, Anglim/Trimble, and the Snite Museum of Art, 2019.068.024.004.

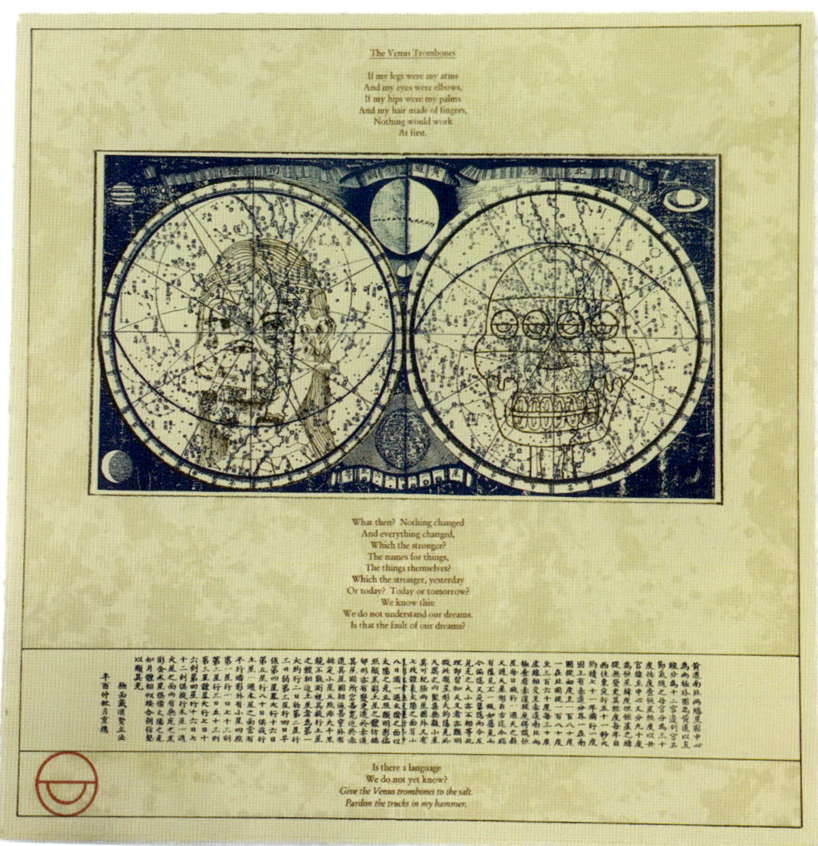

Enrique Chagoya and Alberto Ríos, *Asian Celestial Map*, from the portfolio *You Are Here*, 2000. Lithograph on Rives BFK Tan, 17 × 17 inches; edition of sixty printed by Joe Freye and John Altomare and published by Segura Publishing Company, Arizona. Courtesy of the artist, Anglim/Trimble, and the Snite Museum of Art, 2019.068.024.001.

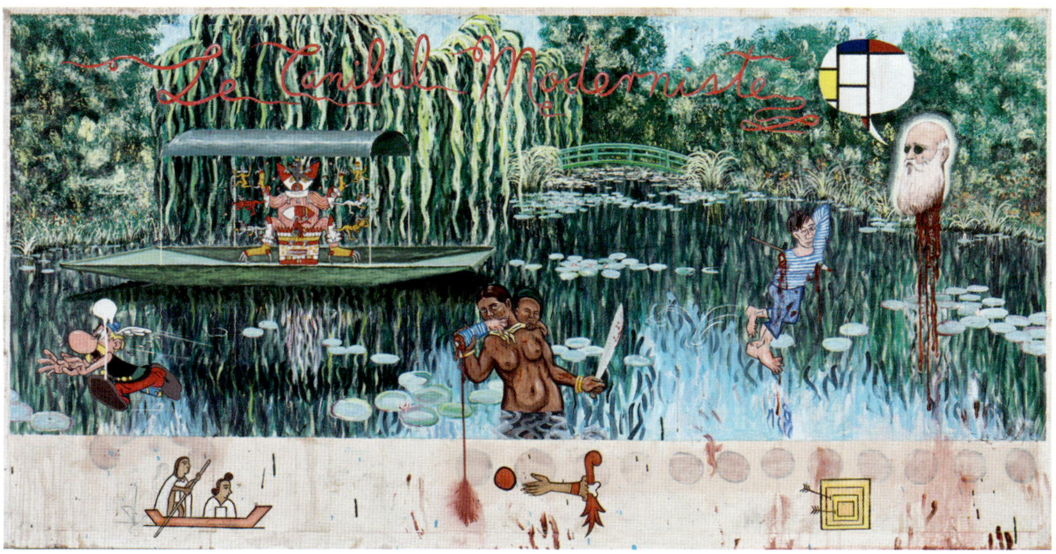

Enrique Chagoya, *Le Cannibale Moderniste*, 1999. Mixed media and paper on linen, 48 × 98 inches. Sheldon Museum of Art, University of Nebraska–Lincoln, Gift of Alexander Liberman and Frances Sheldon by exchange, U-5081.2002. Courtesy of the artist, Anglim/Trimble, and Sheldon Museum of Art, University of Nebraska–Lincoln.

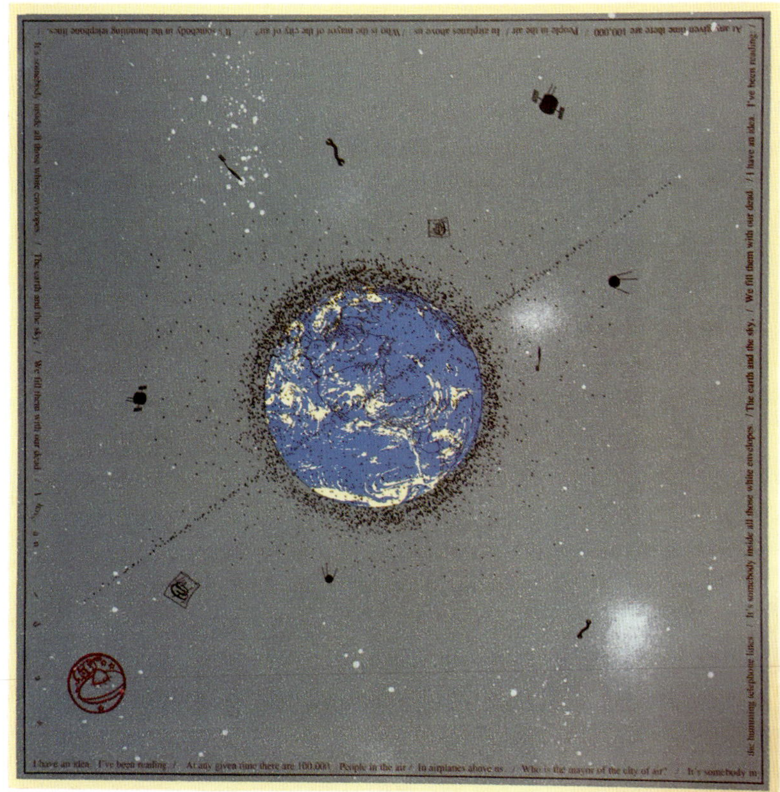

Enrique Chagoya and Alberto Ríos, *Trash World*, from the portfolio *You Are Here*, 2000. Lithograph on Rives BFK Tan, 17 × 17 inches; edition of sixty printed by Joe Freye and John Altomare and published by Segura Publishing Company, Arizona. Courtesy of the artist, Anglim/Trimble, and the Snite Museum of Art, 2019.068.024.002.

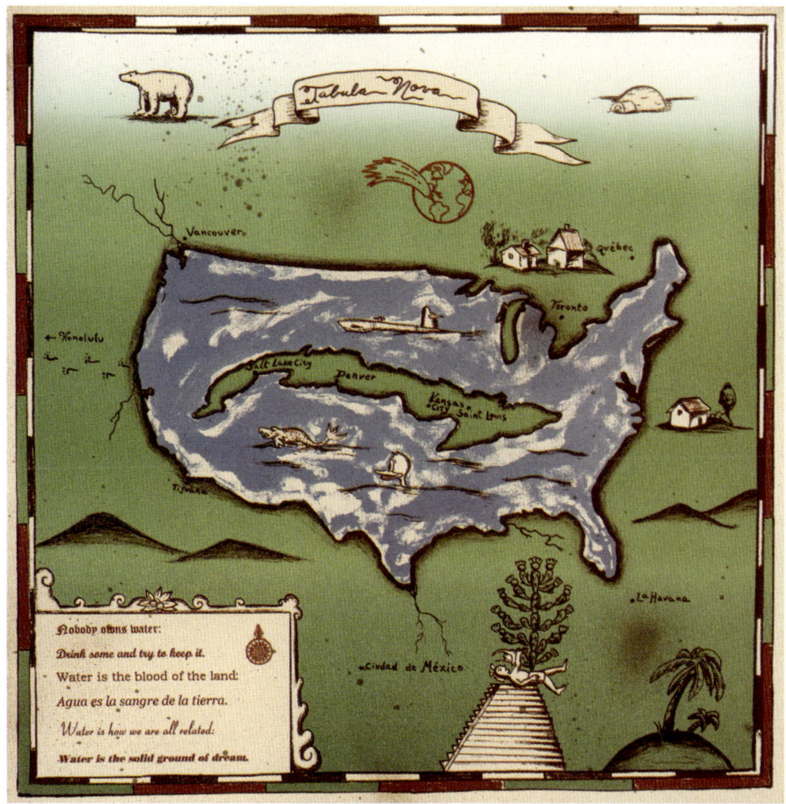

Enrique Chagoya and Alberto Ríos, *American Ocean/Cuba*, from the portfolio *You Are Here*, 2000. Lithograph on Rives BFK Tan, 17 × 17 inches; edition of sixty printed by Joe Freye and John Altomare and published by Segura Publishing Company, Arizona. Courtesy of the artist, Anglim/Trimble, and the Snite Museum of Art, 2019.068.024.003.

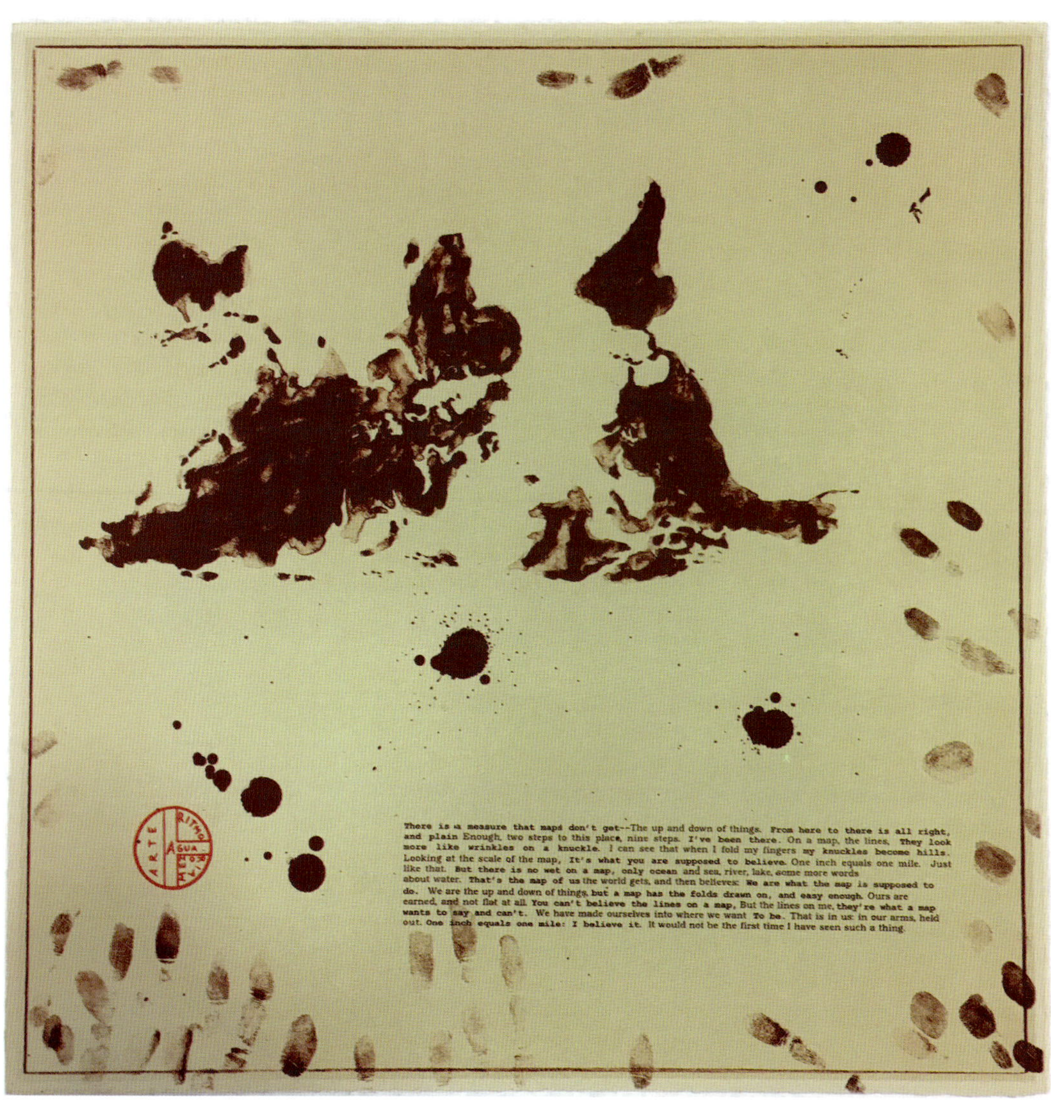

Enrique Chagoya and Alberto Ríos, *Upside Down World Map*, from the portfolio *You Are Here*, 2000. Lithograph on Rives BFK Tan, 17 × 17 inches; edition of sixty printed by Joe Freye and John Altomare and published by Segura Publishing Company, Arizona. Courtesy of the artist, Anglim/Trimble, and the Snite Museum of Art, 2019.068.024.005.

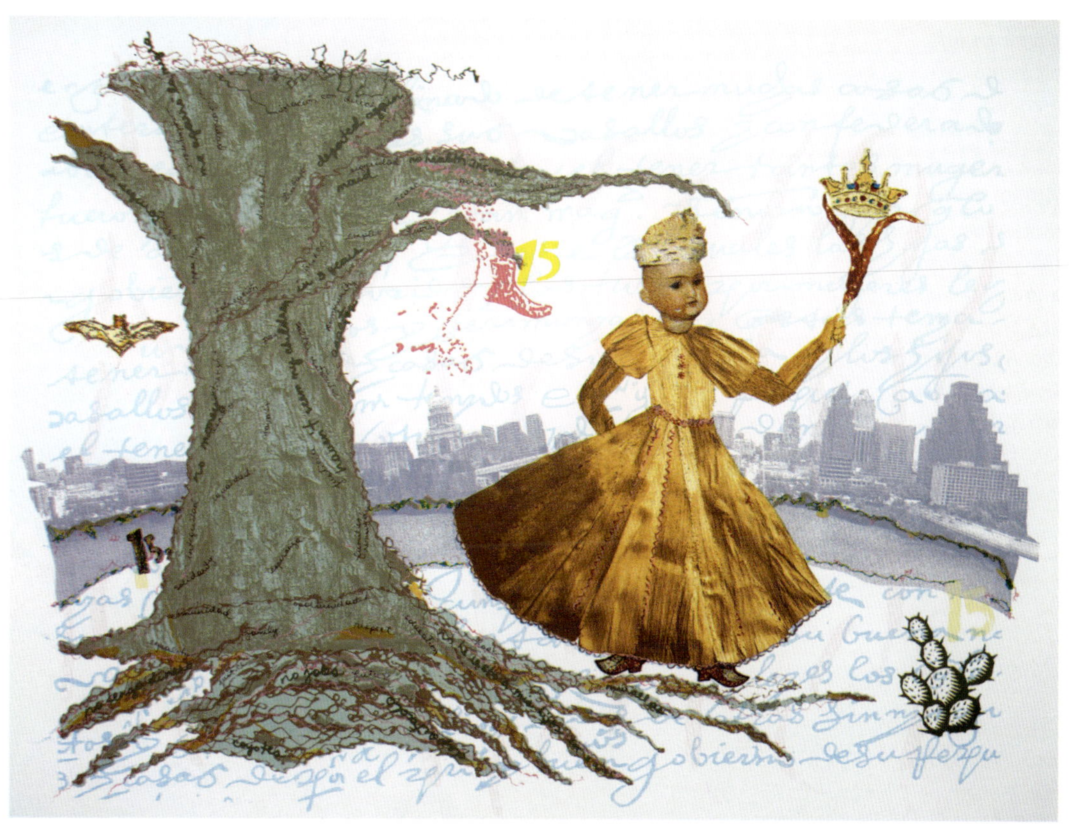

Sandra C. Fernández, *Coming of Age (Transformations)*, 2008. Screenprint on paper, 24 × 30 inches; edition of fifty. Printed by Brian Johnson at Coronado Studio, Austin, Texas. Courtesy of the artist.

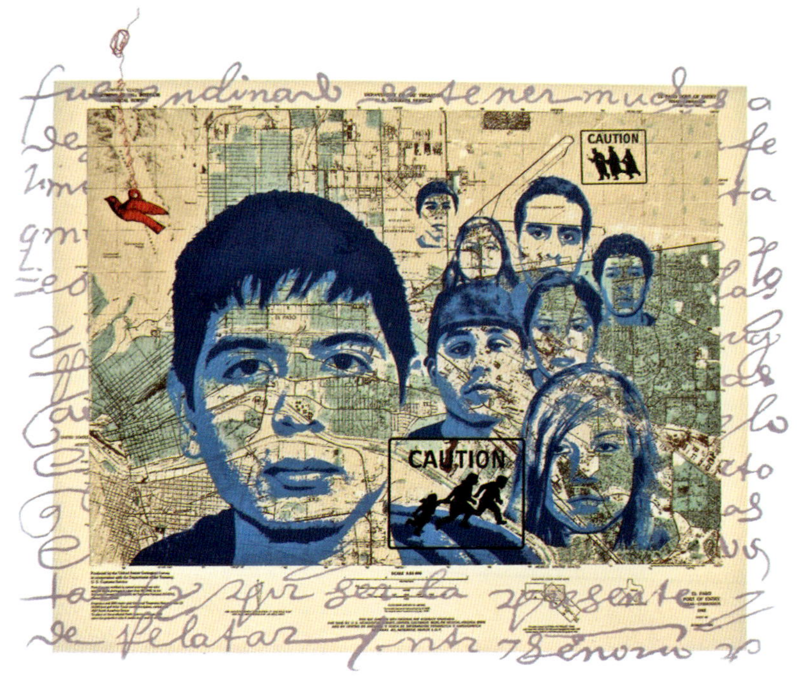

Sandra C. Fernández, *CAUTION: Dreamers in/on Sight*, 2013. Screenprint and thread on paper, 22 × 30 inches; edition of fifty, printed by Jonathan Rebolloso and Logan Hill at Coronado Studio, Austin, Texas. Courtesy of the artist.

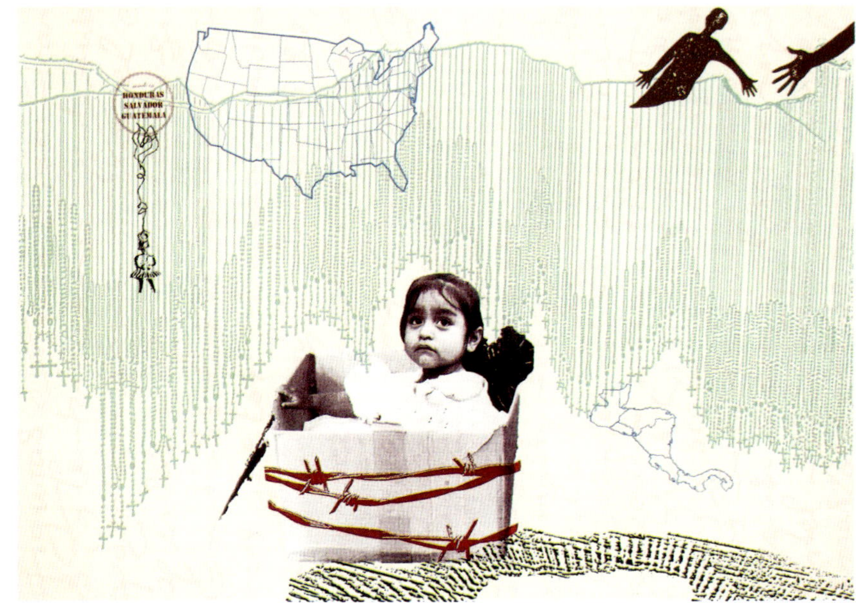

Sandra C. Fernández, *The Northern Triangle*, 2018. Screenprint on paper, 22 × 30 inches; edition of sixty-four printed by Oscar Duardo and published by Self Help Graphics, Los Angeles. Courtesy of the artist.

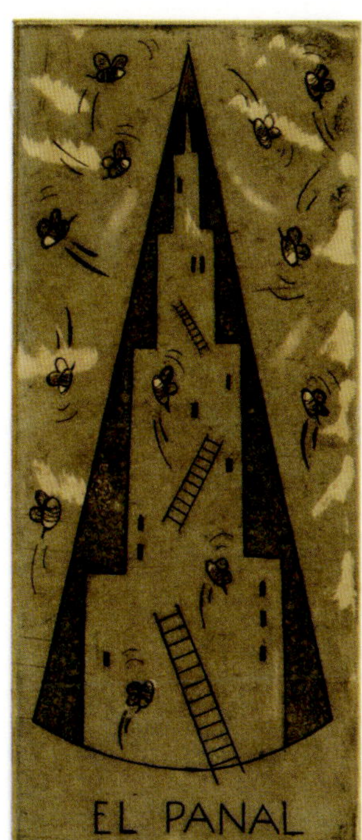

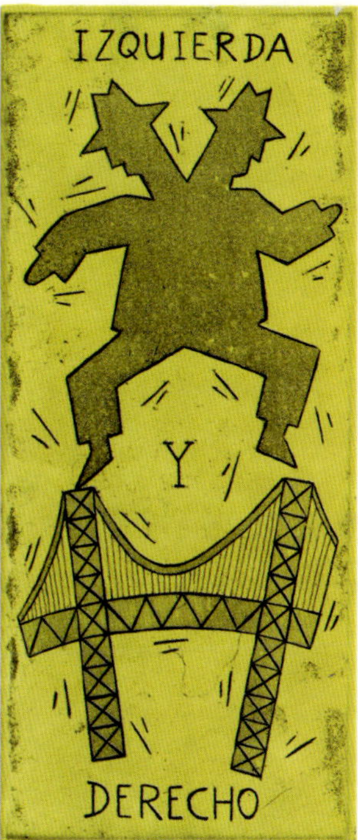

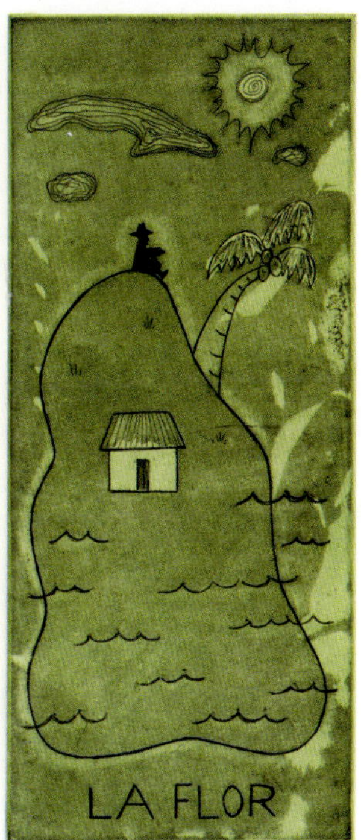

Moses Ros-Suárez, *El Reggaetón del Bachatero*, 2010. Silk aquatint and chine collé on BFK Rives, image: 7 × 9 inches; sheet: 12 × 15 inches; edition of twenty-five printed by the artist and Luanda Lozano at Manhattan Graphics Center and the Robert Blackburn Printmaking Workshop for the portfolio *Manifestaciones* by the Dominican York Proyecto Gráfica. Courtesy of the artist.

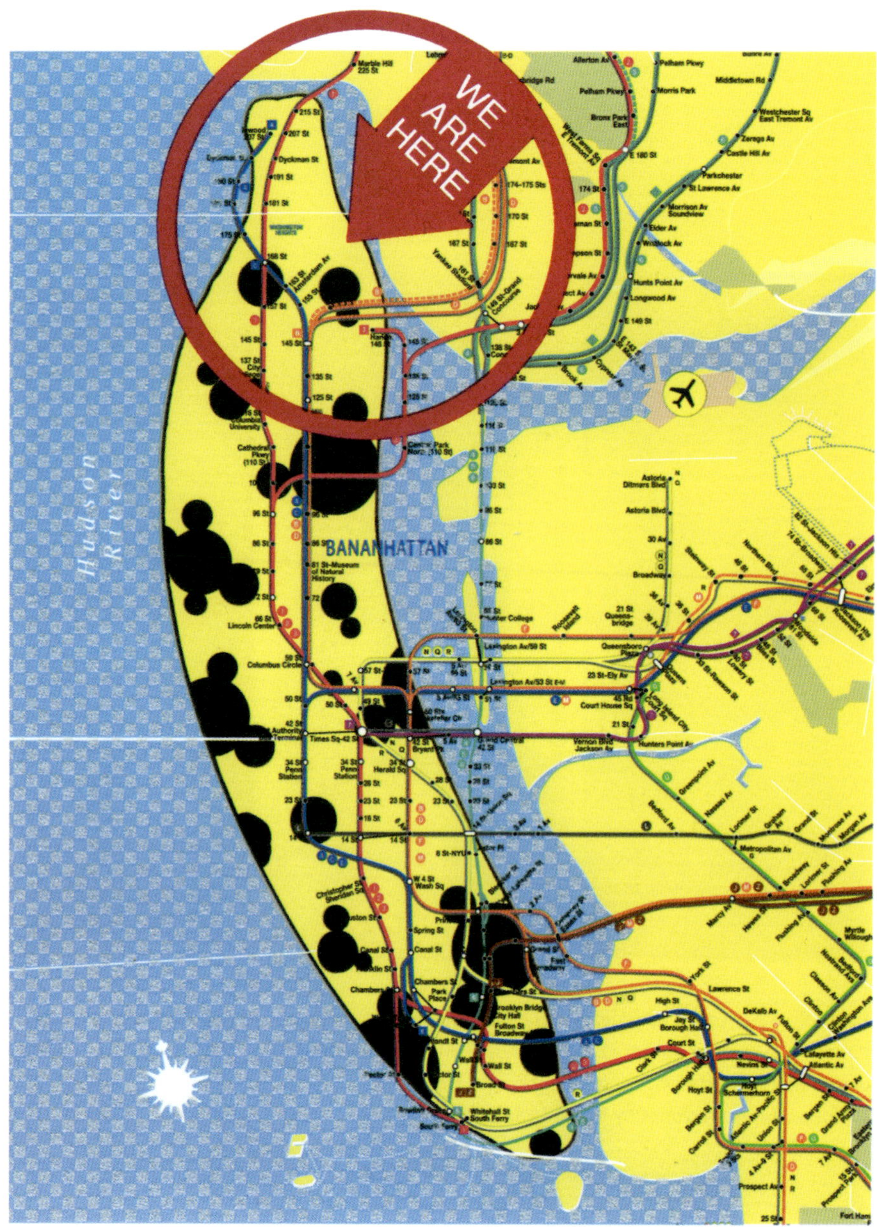

Yunior Chiqui Mendoza, *Bananhattan*, 2010. Inkjet and screenprint on BFK Rives, image: 9½ × 7 inches; sheet: 15 × 11¼ inches; edition of twenty-five printed by the artist, Reynaldo García Pantaleón, and Pepe Coronado at Coronado printstudio for the portfolio *Manifestaciones* by the Dominican York Proyecto Gráfica. Courtesy of the artist.

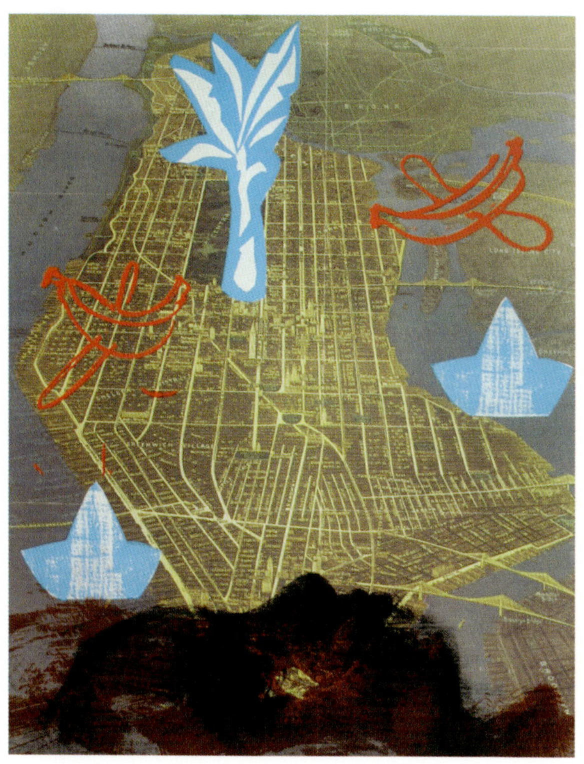

Scherezade García, *Day Dreaming/Soñando Despierta*, 2010. Screenprint and inkjet on BFK Rives, image: 9 × 7 inches; sheet: 15 × 12 inches; edition of twenty-five printed by the artist, Alex Guerrero, and Pepe Coronado at Coronado printstudio for the portfolio *Manifestaciones* by the Dominican York Proyecto Gráfica. Courtesy of the artist.

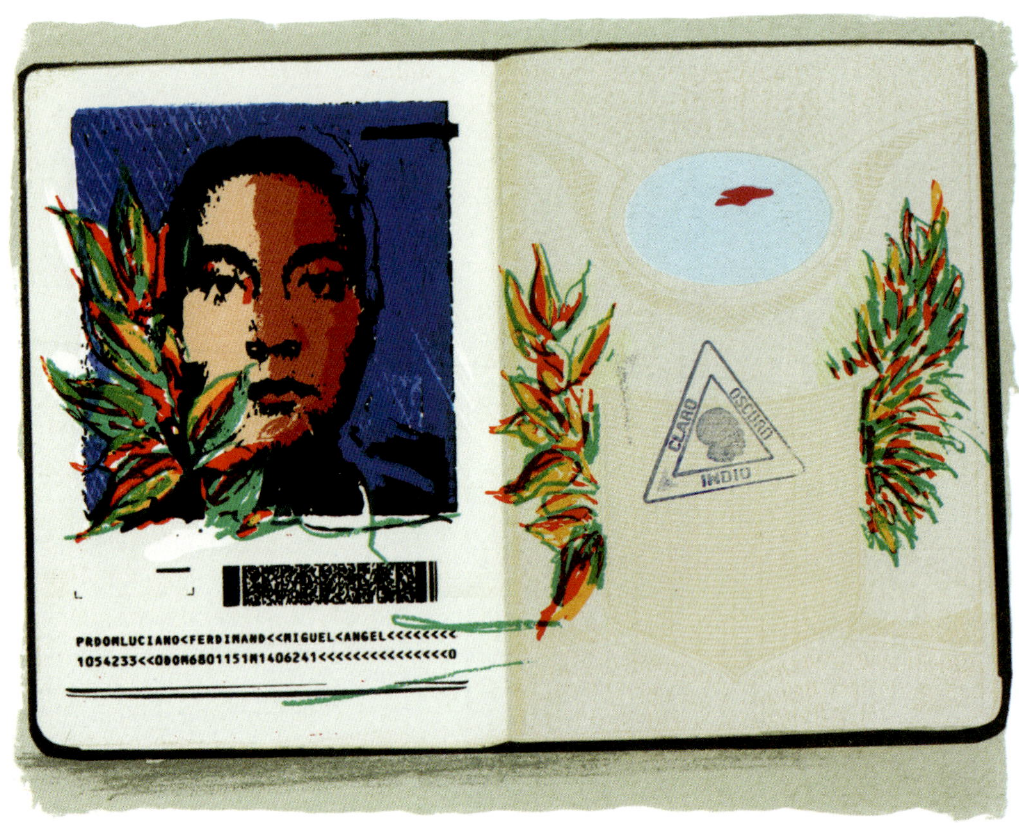

Miguel Luciano, *Detrás de la Oreja*, 2010. Screenprint and rubber stamp on BFK Rives, image: 7 × 9 inches; sheet: 12 × 15 inches; edition of twenty-five printed by the artist and Alex Guerrero at Bullrider Studio for the portfolio *Manifestaciones* by the Dominican York Proyecto Gráfica. Courtesy of the artist.

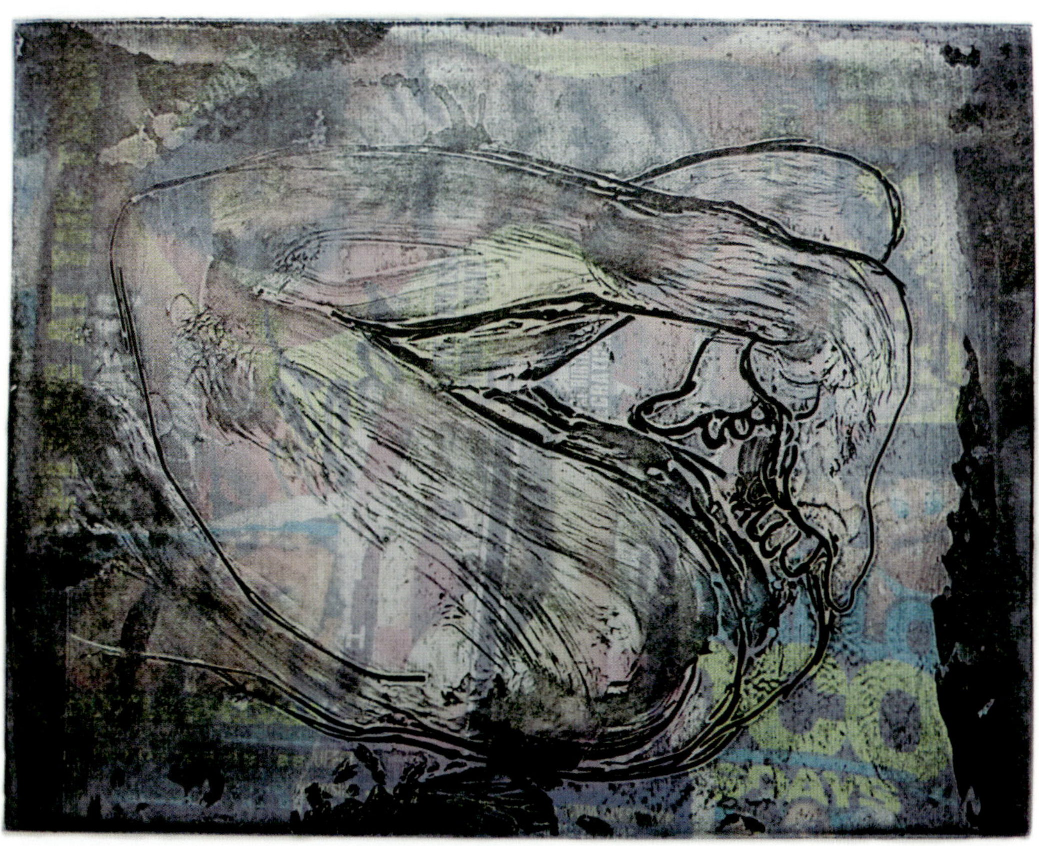

Rider Ureña, *My Girl on the Floor*, 2010. Inkjet and silk aquatint on BFK Rives, image: 7 × 9 inches; sheet: 12 × 15 inches; edition of twenty-five printed by the artist and Pepe Coronado at Bullrider Studio for the portfolio *Manifestaciones* by the Dominican York Proyecto Gráfica. Courtesy of the artist.

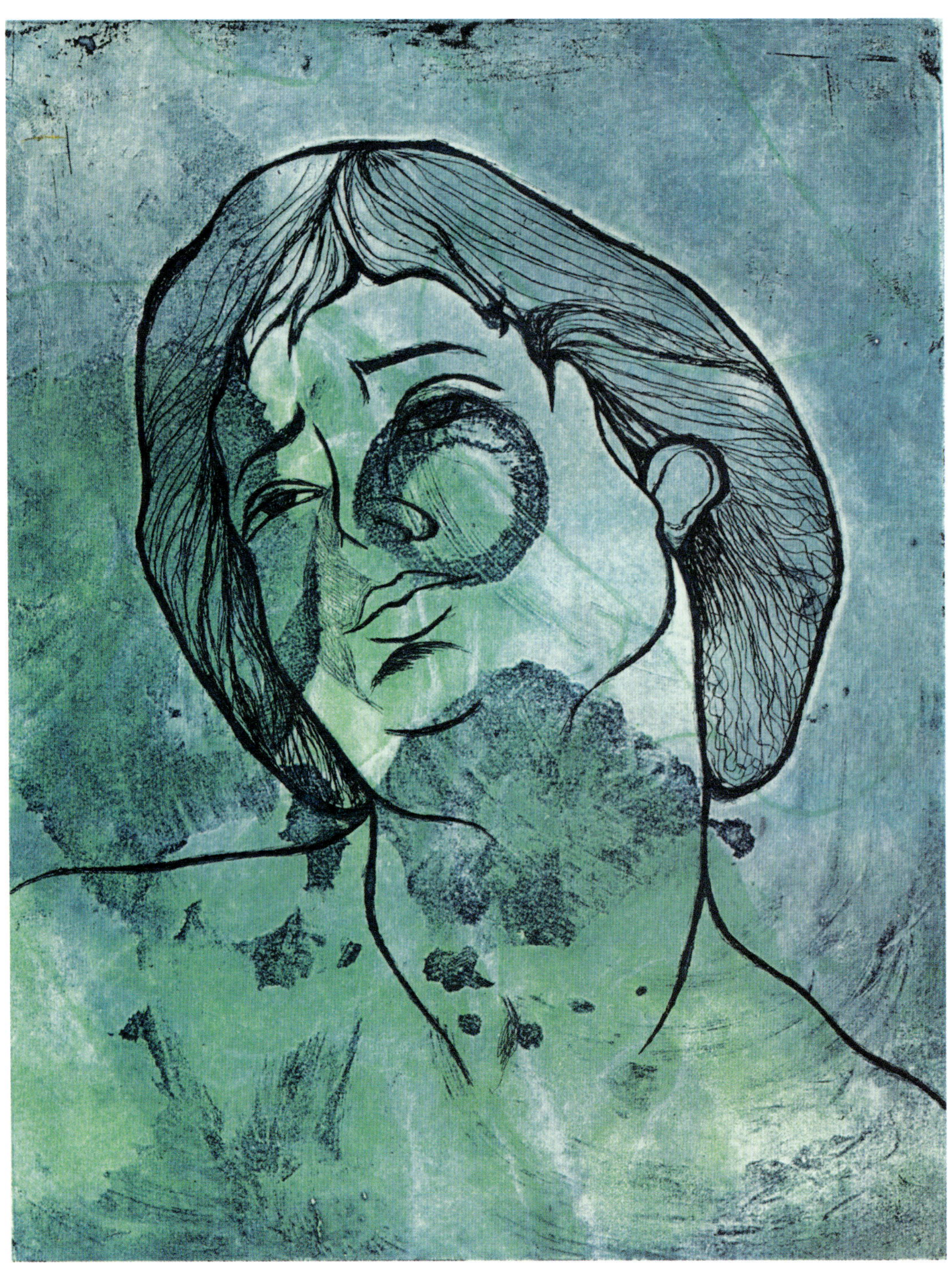

Luanda Lozano, *Sálvame Santo*, 2010. Etching and chine collé on BFK Rives, image: 7 × 9 inches; sheet: 12 × 15 inches; edition of twenty-five printed by the artist at Manhattan Graphics Center and the Robert Blackburn Printmaking Workshop for the portfolio *Manifestaciones* by the Dominican York Proyecto Gráfica. Courtesy of the artist.

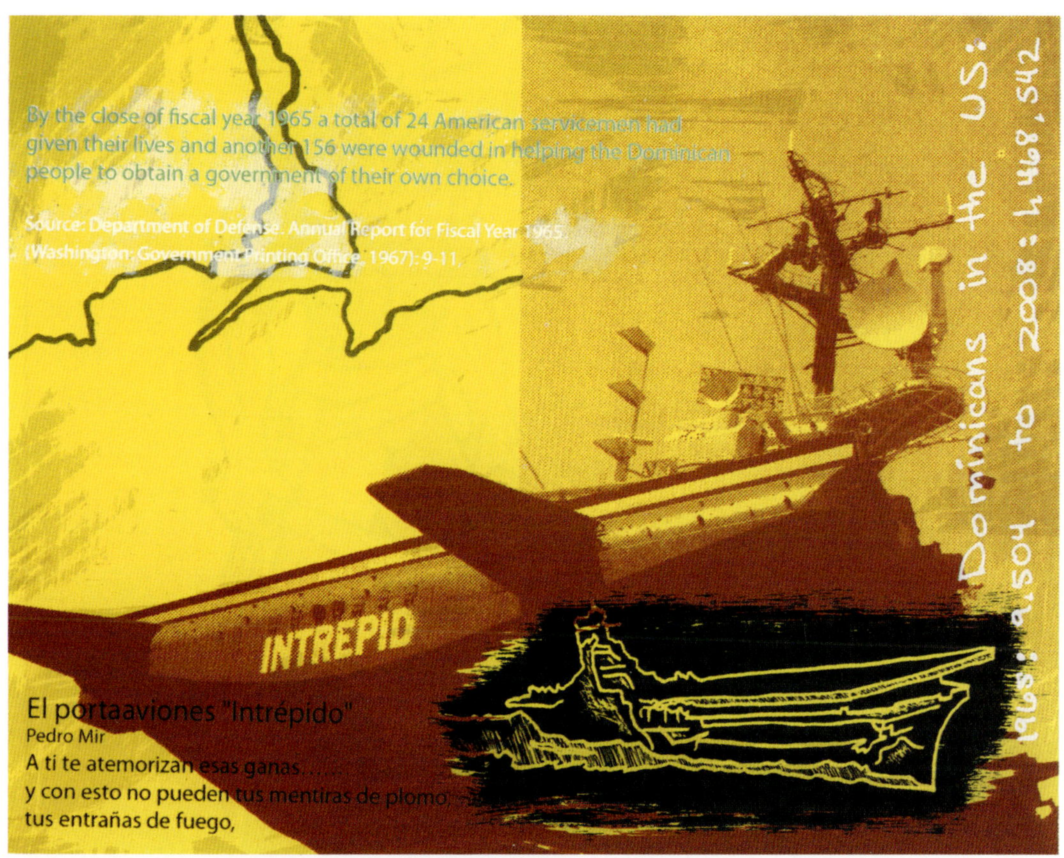

Pepe Coronado, *Intrépido*, 2010. Screenprint on BFK Rives, image: 7 × 9 inches; sheet: 12 × 15 inches; edition of twenty-five printed by the artist at Coronado printstudio for the portfolio *Manifestaciones* by the Dominican York Proyecto Gráfica. Courtesy of the artist.

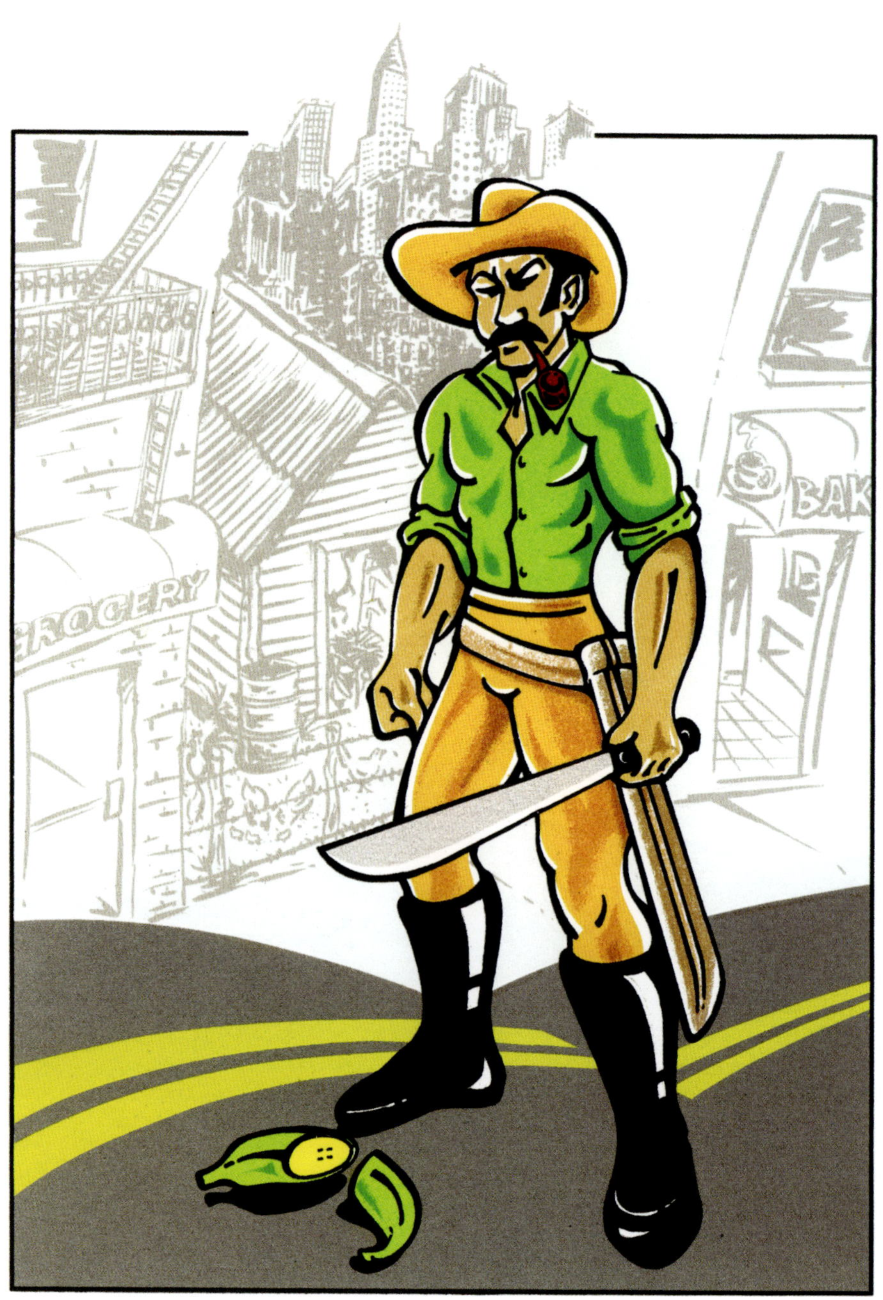

Carlos Almonte, *Vale John*, 2010. Screenprint on BFK Rives, image: 9 × 7 inches; sheet: 15 × 12 inches; edition of twenty-five printed by the artist and Pepe Coronado at Coronado printstudio for the portfolio *Manifestaciones* by the Dominican York Proyecto Gráfica. Courtesy of the artist.

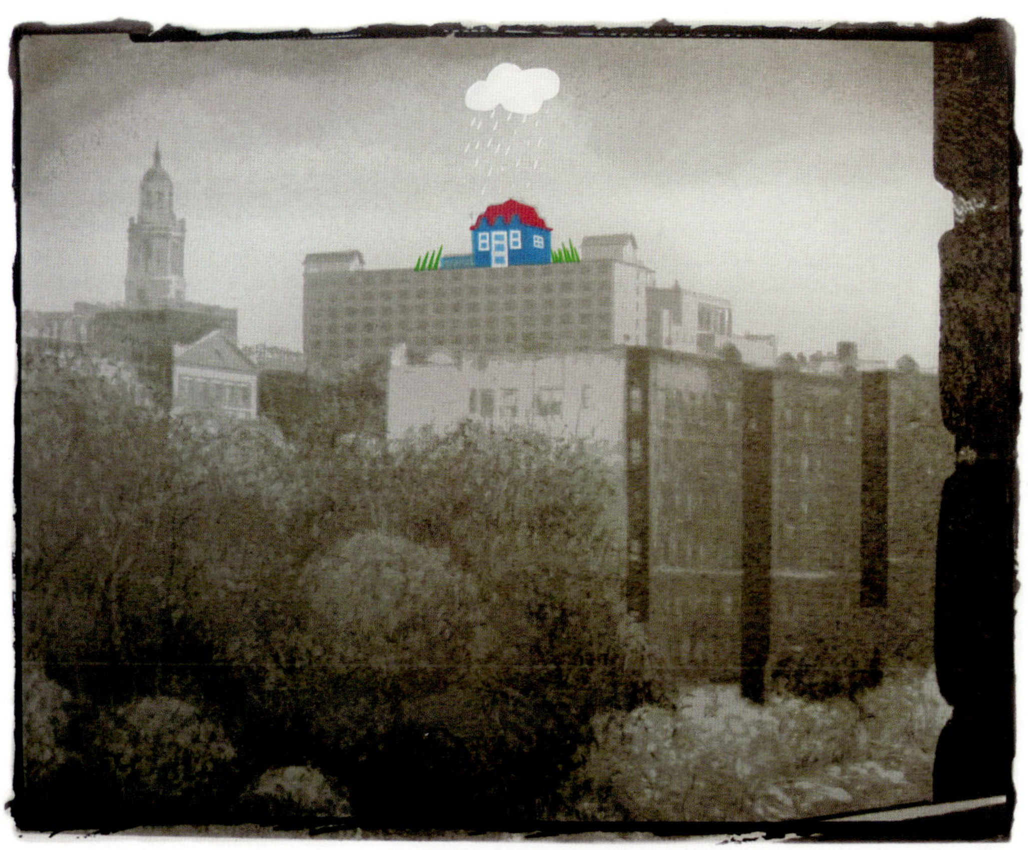

Alex Guerrero, *Vista Psicotrópica*, 2010. Screenprint on BFK Rives, image: 7 × 9 inches; sheet: 12 × 15 inches; edition of twenty-five printed by the artist and Miguel Luciano at Bullrider Studio for the portfolio *Manifestaciones* by the Dominican York Proyecto Gráfica. Courtesy of the artist.

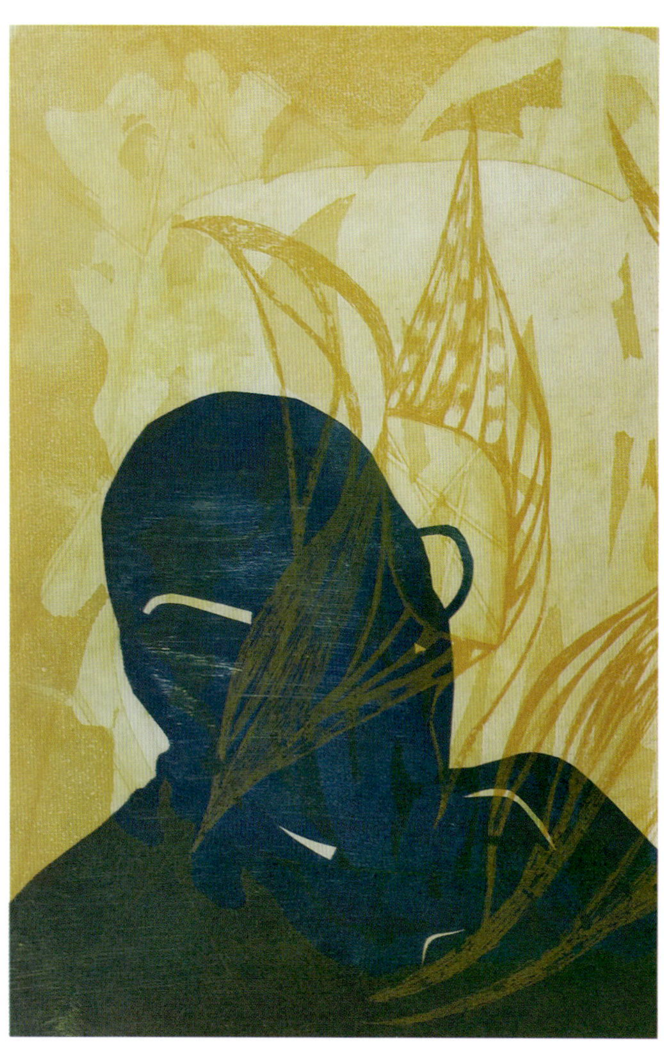

Luanda Lozano, *La Musa de Blackburn*, 2017. Etching, stencil printed on kozuke ivory paper and chine collé, image: 17¼ × 11½ inches; sheet: 22 × 15 inches; edition of thirty, printed by the artist for the Consejo Gráfico portfolio *La Huella Magistral: Homage to Master Printmakers*.

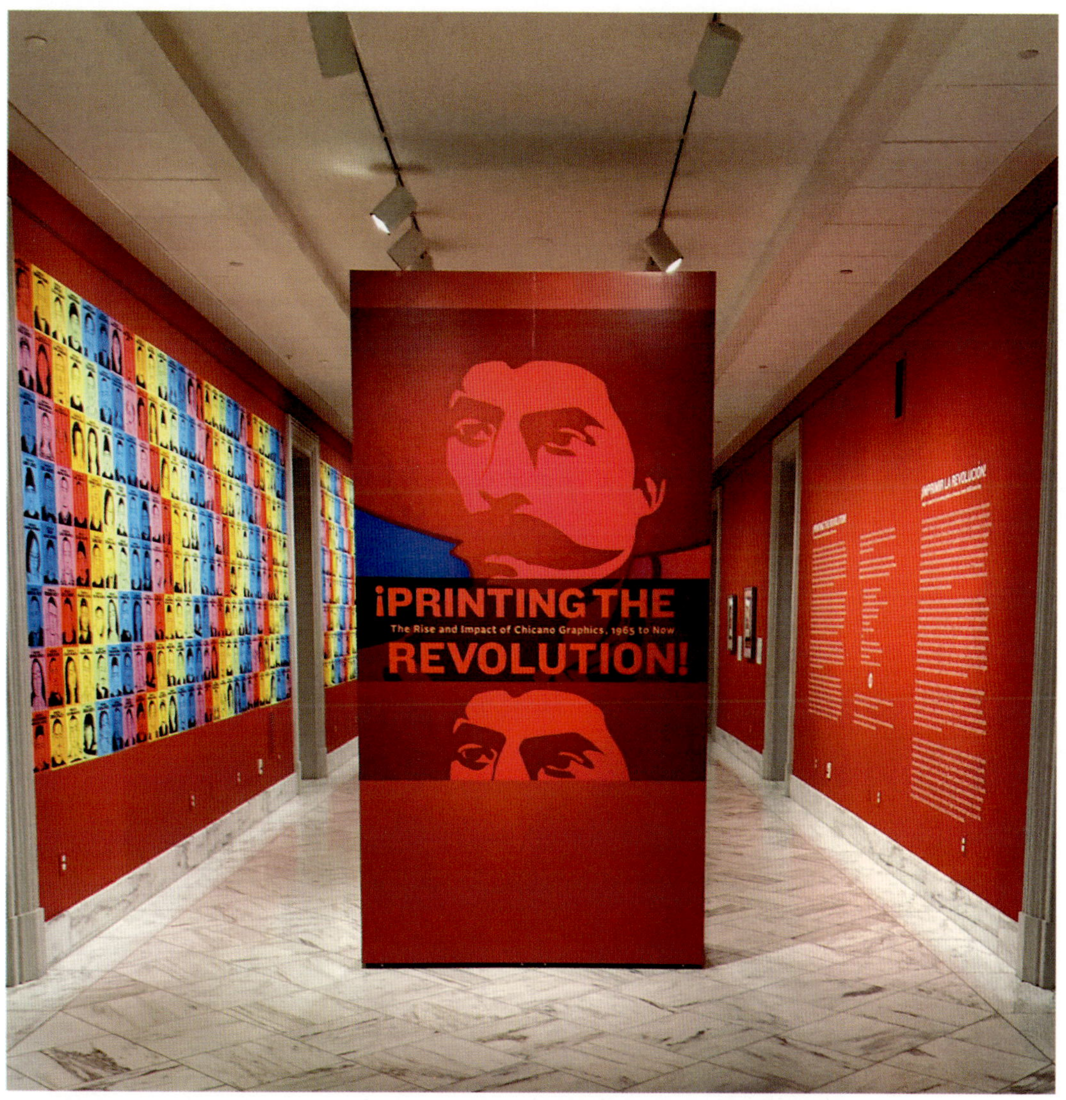

Entrance to *¡Printing the Revolution! The Rise and Impact of Chicano Graphics, 1965 to Now* exhibition at the Smithsonian American Art Museum (November 20, 2020–August 8, 2021). Photo by the author.

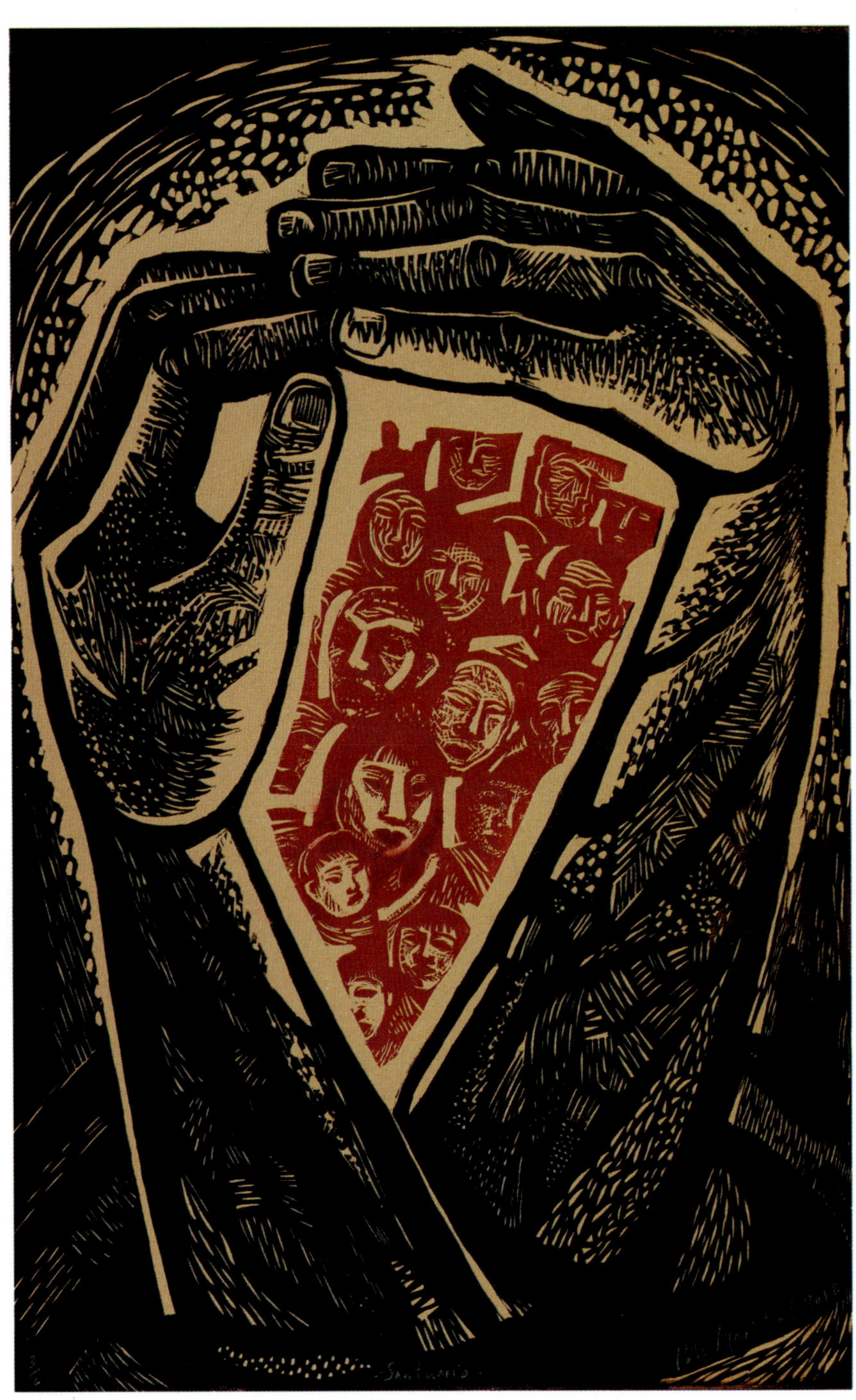

Poli Marichal, *Santuario*, 2018. Linocut on paper, sheet and image: 17¾ × 11¼ inches. Smithsonian American Art Museum, museum purchase through the Frank K. Ribelin Endowment, 2020.32.5. © Poli Marichal. Courtesy of the artist and the Smithsonian American Art Museum.

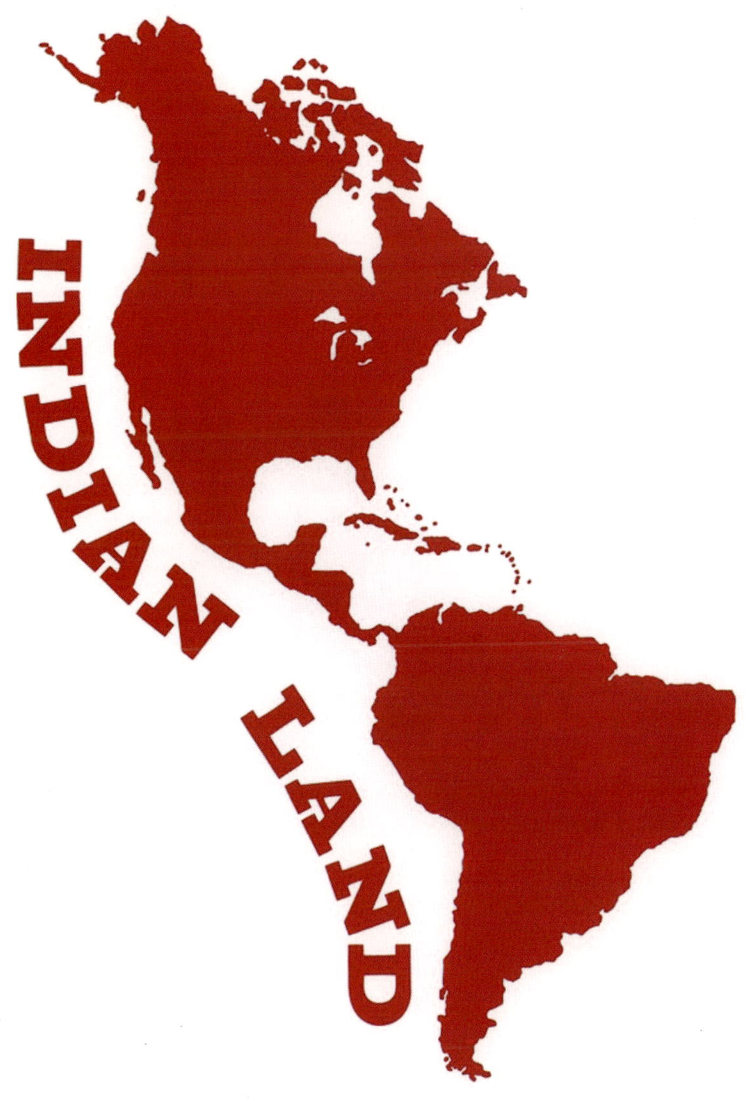

Jesus Barraza and Nancypili Hernandez, *Indian Land*, 2004 (reprinted 2010). Screenprint on paper, sheet and image: 40 × 28 inches. Smithsonian American Art Museum, museum purchase through the Samuel and Blanche Koffler Acquisition Fund, 2020.39.7. © Jesus Barraza and Nancypili Hernandez. Courtesy of the artists.

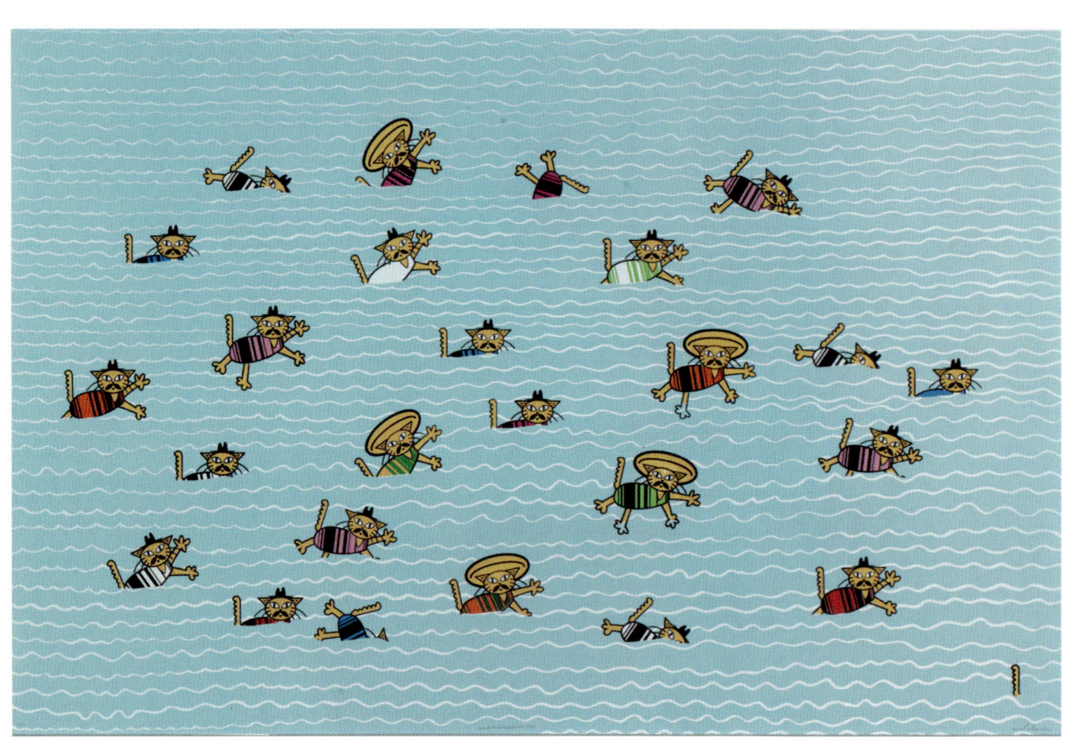

Michael Menchaca, *Cuando el Rio Suena, Gatos Lleva*, 2011. Screenprint on paper, sheet and image: 26 × 40 inches. Smithsonian American Art Museum, Gift of Drs. Harriett and Ricardo Romo, 2019.50.33. © Michael Menchaca. Courtesy of the artist.

grants in search of work. As an artist marked by her own circular migration history, Fernández noticed how the modern American metropolis required undocumented immigrant labor but insisted on making their presence invisible. This concern became the focus of a new body of work in part fostered by Coronado Studio's Latinx artist community in East Austin and its popular residency program Serie Project. But Fernández's concerns over invisibility also signaled the post-9/11 context that shifted the power of policing the border to every corner of the country through the deployment of Immigration and Customs Enforcement, as well as a surging wave of deportations that peaked in 2012, forcing many undocumented residents into the shadows.

The first section of this chapter, "Mestiza Consciousness," traces the artist's return to her mother's homeland and how growing up in Quito suffused her work with an interest in mestizaje, the racial mixtures that make up much of the population of the Americas. Theories of mestizaje, such as those espoused by José Vasconcelos, were likewise littered with problematic notions and, often, racist paradigms meant to devalue the lives of Black and Indigenous populations as they promoted racial mixing to "better" the race in the official discourse of Latin American states. However, Fernández's tactical use of mestizaje, specifically the "mestiza consciousness" of feminist and borderlands writers like Gloria Anzaldúa, symbolically claims space for those subjects who by virtue of their immigration status have been left out of this imperial design. In works such as *Coming of Age (Transformations)* (2008), analyzed in the second section, I look at how Fernández portrays the neoliberal city during the reterritorialization of the nation's borders. *Coming of Age* makes visible the handwriting from a colonial codex as a blueprint for the racial segregation and the mechanisms of invisibility that threaten undocumented migrants. This decolonial maneuver exposes the logic of modernity/coloniality but also questions the disembodied projections of the Eurocentric gaze. In the third section, "Caution," she likewise delinks from these imposed geographies of militarized surveillance in prints such as *CAUTION: Dreamers in/on Sight* (2013), where portraits of Dreamers claim space on a port-of-entry map. Her subject's hybridity as the progeny of colonial violence weaponizes mestizaje against xenophobic territoriality and offers another perspective on using the medium of printmaking to reclaim the Americas.

MESTIZA CONSCIOUSNESS

Quito is nine thousand feet above sea level, and yet it feels like a densely populated valley surrounded by majestic peaks. The Ecuadorian painter Oswaldo Guayasamín depicted the grand scale of the Andean mountain range

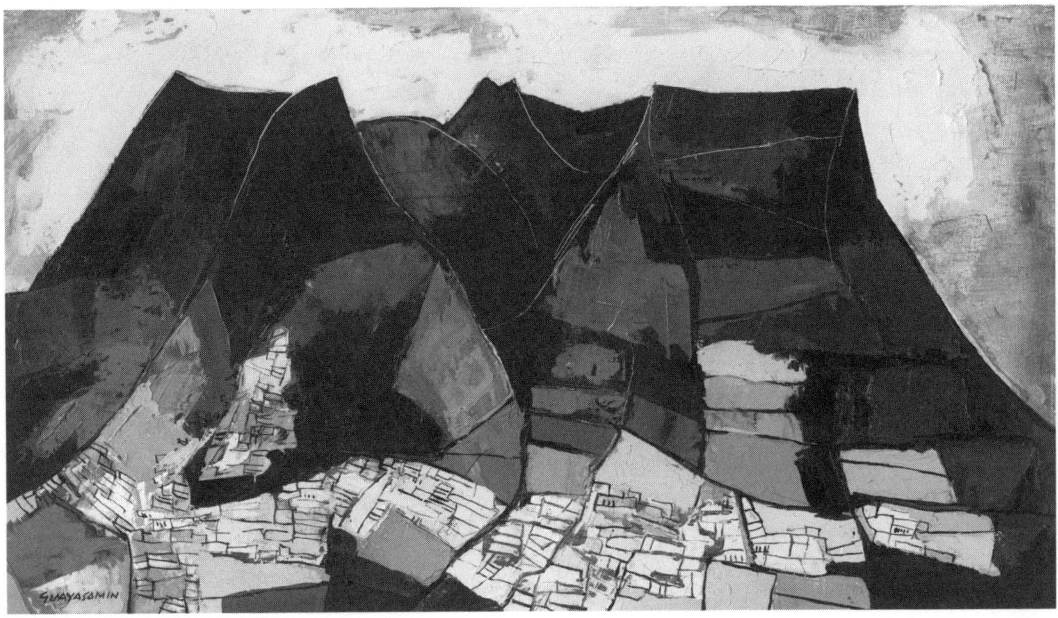

3.2. Oswaldo Guayasamín, *Quito Azul*, n.d. Oil on canvas, 16 × 29½ inches. Courtesy of the estate of Oswaldo Guayasamín and Fundación Guayasamín.

in *Quito Azul* (fig. 3.2). In the painting, the city lies at the base of a tall and menacing slope. Quito's colonial architecture, reduced to the geometric forms of rectangular dwellings, grows and adapts at the mercy of nature's sublime power. Guayasamín contrasted the city's lighter palette with the green, blue, and black hues of the eastern slopes of the Pichincha volcano. The mountain's multiple-point perspectives are marked by the artist's forceful brushwork and dense linework, which crisscross the landscape. The surrounding clouds only heighten the drama of the Andes, which exude a life force of their own and transform the city into a frail, humanlike form lying at its base. *Quito Azul* draws on the language of modernism, cubism, and postimpressionism but shows a precarious modernity for a city still deeply embedded in its colonial history. Moving between these ways of seeing the world—vis-à-vis the modern, the colonial, the Indigenous—was critical to the formation of an artist like Sandra Fernández.

Born in New York to Ecuadorian immigrants, Fernández (b. 1964) moved to Quito with her mother in 1965 when her father enlisted in the US Army. She would remain an only child from that brief union. Fernández grew up in a middle-class family whose house was filled with the books that her grandfather, Leonardo J. Muñoz Muñoz, brought home from his bookstore, Indoamérica, and the precious saint and virgin sculptures of her devout Catholic grandmother, Carlota Quirola Aulestia.[2] Unlike his wife, Muñoz was a staunch atheist, and in 1926 he cofounded the Ecuadorian Socialist Party (Partido Socialista Ecuatoriano), a political position that would cost him persecution and imprisonment. His book *Testimonio de Lucha: Memorias sobre la Historia del Socialismo en el Ecuador* (1988) remains one of the most important first-person accounts of the movement. These material histories rendered Quito a space full of contradictions that played out in the private as much as in the public sphere.

Chief among these contradictions was the teaching of the history of the Geodesic Mission to Ecuadorian schoolchildren. As many scholars have noted, the Geodesic Mission was one of two expeditions that sought to resolve the dispute whether the planet was an oblate spheroid as proposed by Isaac Newton's gravitational theory or a prolate spheroid following the work of René Descartes.[3] In other words, planet Earth is not perfectly round, and Newton predicted a sphere that bulged at the equator, while Cartesian science theorized bulging at the poles. Since the debate raged in the Paris Academy of Sciences of the 1730s, the French and Spanish monarchies worked in tandem, via the Bourbon Compact, to dispatch two expeditions, one to the Arctic led by Pierre-Louis Moreau de Maupertuis, which reached Lapland in 1737 (quickly resolving the matter in favor of Newton), and another to Quito led by French Academy member Louis Godin. Ten Frenchmen and two Spanish military officers were sent to the Spanish Viceroyalty of Peru. Of these Europeans, Charles-Marie de La Condamine is perhaps the best-known figure, having authored popular travel narratives from these voyages. La Condamine became great friends with the Creole scientist, explorer, and governor of the Esmeraldas province, Pedro Vicente Maldonado, who was instrumental in providing cartographic source material and knowledge of the terrain.

The historical significance of Maldonado's 1750 map, which we observed being reissued in 2019, lies in its unusual transatlantic origins. Maldonado traveled to Spain in 1744 with the cartographic manuscripts to produce this map, and the Spanish monarchy agreed to sponsor its publication. Madrid, however, did not possess the advanced technical capacity for this type of map production, and in light of the Bourbon alliance, the Spanish agreed to publish it in Paris at the atelier of Hubert-François Bourguignon d'Anville, brother to the royal geographer of Louis XV. These actions went against Spain's policy of cartographic secrecy relating to its colonies, and in this case the exceedingly profitable mineral resources found in detailed cartographic manuscripts. By 1746, Maldonado arrived in Paris to work on plans for the map with d'Anville and his friend La Condamine. He was made a corresponding member of the French Academy the following year, but before the map could be completed, Maldonado died on a trip to London in 1748. His map was posthumously published in 1750, when the Spanish ambassador pressured d'Anville and La Condamine to submit the printed map, copper plates, and all associated manuscripts to the Spanish Crown. But La Condamine feared that the Spaniards would place the manuscripts in some royal archive that would never see the light of day. He conspired with d'Anville to make two versions of the copper plates. At the time of its printing, the Carta was by far the most precise scientific map of any Latin American region, and in the spirit of Enlightenment, La Condamine wanted to disseminate it widely. But self-interest also motivated his conspiracy: he would publish his famous travelogue *Journal du voyage fait par ordre du roi a l'équateur* in 1751 and would use much of Maldonado's map to produce his own cartographic representation. Through these elaborate efforts, as well as those of the cartographers that followed, Quito came to be known as the city at the center of the world (*mitad del mundo*).[4]

Cultural theorist and literary critic Mary Louise Pratt has argued that European travel and exploration in the eighteenth century helped create an imperial order whereby expansion became more desirable to the people of Europe.[5] Through narrative accounts that enthralled European readers, La Condamine used scientific exploration tainted with the affect of survival literature to disclose the dangers, sickness, animosity of the Natives, and fears of being lost or stranded that his team faced in the Andes, and Pratt argues that such writing was instrumental in shaping moral sentiments to civilize these far-off lands.[6] But the imperial order not only transformed Europe; it created a need for European descendants, the white, elite criollos in the colonies, much like Maldonado, to adapt this discourse for their own self-fashioning. The Creole desire to embrace European scientific discourse and travel writing, from La Condamine to Alexander von Humboldt, served the purpose of justifying a new hierarchical structure in which the Creole class was at the top and would soon rule the newly formed republics.

The 2019 reprinting of the Carta de la Provincia de Quito may initially be read as an attempt to bolster Ecuadorian nationalism, considering that the request came directly from the Office of the President. The idea for a reimpression came about after the copper plates were shown in an exhibition at the Palacio de Gobierno in Quito. The historian Alfonso Ortiz, cultural attaché to the Office of the President, asked the printers at Estampería Quiteña if it might be possible to pull a new impression. In 1947 the Museo Naval de Madrid donated the copper plates to the Republic. In honor of Maldonado, they were sent to the municipal offices of his hometown in Riobamba. By 2018 when Ortiz took up the issue, that tribute had become a matter of national patrimony. Following the restoration of the plates at the Instituto Nacional de Patrimonio Cultural, master printer Sicles Garzón pulled a new edition of thirty-three prints, two of which were sent back to Riobamba; the others would be gifts for official state visits, such as the one given to German president Frank-Walter Steinmeier in 2019. For the historian Ortiz, the map was significant not only for its cartographic precision but also for its ability to make Quiteños feel that they are part of this territory, a historical vision of Quito that is now the Republic of Ecuador.[7] But it would be short-sighted to view the reprinting as solely a matter of national patrimony.

This nationalist gesture constitutes a Francophile attempt to recall, nostalgically, a Eurocentric imperial order in which the Creole elite justified their rule over vast lands and majority Indigenous populations. In his *Idea of Latin America* (2005), Walter Mignolo discusses how the Creole elites became modern vis-à-vis their adoption of the French concept of *latinité*, or Latinidad.[8] Becoming modern forged a postcolonial identity for the Creole elite, who ideologically aligned themselves with European heritage and Europe's civilizing discourses, while differentiating and distancing themselves from the colonial others of African or Indigenous ancestry. This may explain why Maldonado sought recognition from the Council of the Indies, acknowledgment of his service to the Spanish Crown, and affiliation with the Academy of Sciences in Paris.[9] It also explains why the current government of Ecuador, still incapable of fully integrating its Afro and Indigenous populations, reprints this imperial design to embrace its long-standing modernity.

While the imperial order may have succeeded in creating a structure that still exerts its image and power, through objects like the Carta, there is much to say about what it could not control, contain, or comprehend in the mixtures of the region. This is why some scholars view the Geodesic Mission as an "ambiguous legacy."[10] The Ecuadorian novelist Jorge Velasco Mackenzie wrote an award-winning fictional account of the mission titled *En nombre de un amor imaginario* (1996). In the novel, La Condamine's character laments the fact that he does not have the language to truly explain his experience, "De manera que, toda busqueda de las verdades se caracteriza por una ausencia . . . mucho de lo que se sabe del Ecuador de la epoca de la Misión Geodesica tambien es el resultado de la traducción inevitablemente traicionera expresada en mapas y catalogos propios de una ciencia inexacta que ha sido incapaz de liberarse de sus limitaciones humanas."[11] This notion of a treasonous translation and an inexact science is an admission that evokes the ambivalence of incommensurability.[12] Although it has been heralded by some as the historical event that marked the beginnings of a secularization that would lead to the independence and nationalist movements, the mission failed to impose a particular social order because of its inability to acknowledge the racial mixtures of the region. Almost two hundred and fifty years would pass before Ecuador adopted a pluricultural and multiethnic national identity.[13]

Most Ecuadorians today, upwards of 70 percent, identify as mestiza/o, which is certainly the case for the artist.[14] She remarked in our interview, "I am mestiza, a mixture of Spanish and Indian, but I appear more Spanish . . . my features are lighter," and by extension more privileged.[15] The cultural as well as the racial mixture of Amerindian and Spanish was among the earliest themes that preoccupied the artist. In a place like Quito, it was impossible to ignore. Everywhere she turned Indigenous people and their art, ceramics, jewelry, music, and textiles appeared side by side with Spanish colonial painting, sculpture, and architecture. From the age of twelve, she began a snapshot photography practice connecting these worlds with the people in her life. By seventeen, she had her own darkroom. She would continue photography even after starting a sociology degree at the Universidad Central del Ecuador.

The Ecuadorian notion of mestizaje embraced much of Mexican intellectual José Vasconcelos's ideas to restore the racial balance of a nation by promoting interracial marriage to create a mixed race, *la raza cósmica*, that could outmaneuver nations built on the premise of racial purity such as the United States. The art historian Michele Greet has noted how this process of mestizaje "contributed to the eradication of Native languages, customs, and religions" and spurred an artistic and literary movement of *Indigenism* as intellectuals "began to reject the positivist theories of Indigenous racial inferiority that had prevailed in the nineteenth century, maintaining that the roots of Native Americans' problems were economic and ethical rather than biological."[16] The plight of Ecuador's Indians were often articulated in socialist terms, exemplified in the work of Camilo Egas, Eduardo Kingman, and Guayasamín, which Fernández would have seen in school visits to local museums. The subject was also a frequent conversation overheard from her grandfather's involvement in the Partido Socialista Ecuatoriano.

Turning her lens on her local landscape allowed the artist to notice what Mignolo calls the "colonial wound," the hurt that was left from invasive destruction, and the colonial othering that made criollos, mestizos, African diaspora and Indigenous peoples in the Americas subordinate to modern Europeans. Bolivian sociologist Silvia Rivera Cusicanqui has studied the art of Felipe Guaman Poma de Ayala, who penned a twelve-hundred-page letter and illustrated the manuscript with 398 ink drawings for the king of Spain circa 1615.[17] She noticed how his drawings, made less than a hundred years after the arrival of the Spaniards in 1532, exceed what words fail to encompass in describing the drastic changes the Inca experienced under colonial rule. The first part of his account addressed Andean history, philosophy, and ways of life prior to the arrival of the Spanish; the second half detailed the abuses Spaniards committed in the Viceroyalty of Peru, building a persuasive argument for self-government. In drawings such as page 596 (fig. 3.3), a parish priest punishes an Indian seen kneeling before him.[18] The nude Indige-

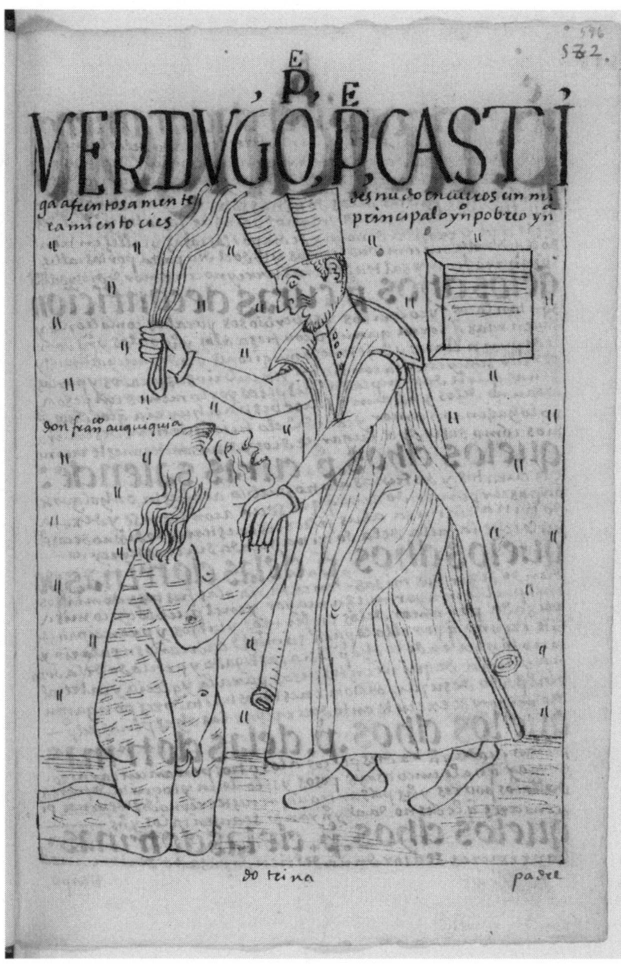

3.3. Felipe Guaman Poma de Ayala, Drawing 233: Executioner: the cruel parish priest metes out punishment indiscriminately, page 596 from *Nueva Corónica y Buen Gobierno* (1615). The Royal Danish Library, GKS 2232 4to. Courtesy of the Royal Library of Denmark.

nous man clasps his hands as if asking for mercy, while the priest lifts his right hand to strike him with a whip. Guaman Poma presented these illustrations as evidence of the cataclysm, or *Pachacuti* in the Quechua language, that turned the Andean world upside down. Rivera Cusicanqui views his drawings as the space where his "ideas unfold about pre-Hispanic indigenous society, about its values and its concepts of time-space, and about the meanings of the bloodbath that was the colonization and subordination of the population and territory of the Andes to the Spanish crown."[19] But the independence movements that followed would eventually push the Spaniards out and leave a new set of masters. For elite Creoles this implied imposing a racial-stratification schema, assimilating purity-of-blood principles from Spain and eventually inflicting an internal colonialism model that persists in Latin America.

One may argue that internal colonialism likewise persists in the US through multiple coexisting colonialities that are acutely felt by Latinx populations who live between the Latin-Saxon divide. The Chicana lesbian poet and theorist Gloria Anzaldúa viewed this experience for border crossers as an open wound—*la herida abierta.* She took up the masculine nationalism of Vasconcelos's mestizaje but resignified the addressee as female: "Being tricultural, monolingual, bilingual, or multilingual, speaking a patois, and in a state of perpetual transition, the *mestiza* faces the dilemma of the mixed breed: which collectivity does the daughter of a dark-skinned mother listen to?"[20] Aligned with Anzaldúa's radical position, Rivera Cusicanqui likewise transforms the homogenizing impulse of mestizaje into one aimed at decolonizing our being. She uses the Aymara concept of *Ch'ixi* to express the contradiction of living and moving between opposite worlds.[21] For the Andean theorist, a liberated mestiza is one free of the shame that comes from her Indian heritage, or perhaps in the case of Anzaldúa, unashamed of her Indian mother.[22] Fernández, too, would later turn toward these forms of mestiza consciousness. This change is likely a result of her own circular migration. In 1987, at the age of twenty-two, she left Ecuador during the oppressive and violent regime of León Febres Cordero (1984–1988).[23] After seeing the forced disappearances of fellow college students, she fled to become a stranger in her native country. These themes would become overwhelming concerns when she relocated to Texas and witnessed the social exclusion of undocumented migrants.

COMING OF AGE

The challenge of representing the subject of "illegality" that circumscribes immigrants' lives has often been taken up by resident artists at the Austin-based residency program Serie Project.[24] Founded in 1993 by the visual artist Sam Coronado (1946–2013), Serie Project invited nearly a dozen artists each year, until the untimely death of its founder.[25] Working side by side with master printers, resident artists produced limited-edition screenprints. By specializing in limited editions, Serie Project built on a radical tradition of collaborative printmaking in US Latinx communities and yet set itself apart as a professional residency program.

> I knew whenever I started this thing that there was a need for it, because I tried to get in to places to go do prints and I could never get in and I knew a lot of people that wanted to do that but it was either you knew somebody or your work was recognized. It was a good starting point and I never thought it was going to last twenty years. I knew there was a need for it. And I knew

> that whatever need it was, it was going to have to be separated from what was going on around us, because we couldn't rely on their support. We at that point were not accepted as printmakers, so I said, well what do we have to lose? What do I have to lose, except time and maybe some money? But I didn't realize how much time and how much money [laughs].[26]

The competitive program insisted on freedom of expression but encouraged a search for identity and belonging among artists of different cultural origins. According to Coronado, at stake was redefining the view of Latinx artists as mere folk or naive artists and intervening in the exclusionary practices of the collaborative-press movement.

For Serie Project's fifteenth anniversary, in 2008, Coronado invited fifteen artists to return for a one-week residency and produce commemorative prints. Coronado personally selected the artists, many of whom had already participated in the Central Texas residency program that operated out of his graphic workshop known as Coronado Studio. The stylistic and thematic range of the projects these artists produced attests to the fact that Coronado did not specify a theme for the anniversary portfolio, but he did make the request that they try to incorporate the number or concept 15 into their work. Unsurprisingly, many of them made an association with the *Quinceañera*, a traditional celebration when a young girl reaches her fifteenth birthday and begins a transition into maturity.

Fernández was among the select anniversary group. She had moved to Austin in 2004. Coronado had invited her to participate in the residency program the following year, when she produced *Enjaulada* (2005), an image of a young girl trapped inside a fragile, triangular cage and surrounded by sewn pieces of handmade paper. Fernández was not new to the graphic arts; in fact she had earned an MFA in Printmaking and Artist Books at the University of Wisconsin–Madison. Much of her work blended printmaking, sewing, and collage and touched on the themes of gender and mestizaje. Drawn by Serie Project's mission of promoting printmaking and the work of underrepresented artists, she soon joined the Board of Directors, thrilled to find a community of artists and an audience that welcomed her interest in identity. In an interview Fernández described the move to Austin as a major turning point in her life: "I felt for the first time at home. I was speaking in Spanish. Everybody spoke Spanish. . . . It was the food, it was the climate. . . . and then I find Sam. I find that amazing place that changed my life."[27]

Inspired by the generative power of his residencies at Self Help Graphics, Coronado had started the printmaking studio in 1991. Shortly thereafter, he began seeking support to establish a residency program. Through a fiscal sponsorship arrangement with La Peña, a larger and more established nonprofit, he secured his first grant from the City of Austin's Cultural Arts Program in 1993 and began inviting artists for residencies.[28] Coronado understood firsthand how the subjective value of quality had regularly been used to exclude minority artists from exhibitions, collections, markets, and residencies.[29] The focus on underrepresented artists paralleled the rise of a prevailing discourse that advocated diversity in American art and trickled public funding into minority-art organizations.

Multiculturalism ushered in a new era of "symbolic acceptance" for minority artists. As a dominant discussion in the art world in the late 1980s and early 1990s, multiculturalism facilitated the crossover for a small number of artists of color whose work began to be shown and acquired at mainstream institutions. *The Decade Show* (1990) and the *Whitney Biennial* (1993) serve as emblematic examples. These measures, however, were short-lived and suffered a drastic backlash, which by the mid-2000s would transform into a postracial, color-blind paradigm. Multiculturalism also engendered criticism from artists on the margin, who implicitly accused others of "selling out." As Malaquias Montoya and Leslie Salkowitz-Montoya put it, "When the doors of museums and galleries opened and invitations were extended, artists went running, despite the fact that Raza communities, which had been the original emphasis for the Chicano Art Movement, rarely frequented museums."[30] The accusation implied that artists were making political compromises in order to achieve gallery representation, exhibitions, or fellowships. The Montoyas advocated an extreme Marxist position that by the 1990s was untenable. Coronado disagreed with their call to separatism; he asserted that artists should make a living from their work, and he strongly believed, much like Sister Karen Boccalero from Self Help Graphics, that prints could offer an alternative opportunity in the art market that was previously unavailable.[31]

Local arts commissions, state agencies, and national endowments made it one of their priorities to fund minority arts organizations during this time. A Minority Assistance Development Grant from the Texas Commission on the Arts and funding from the City of Austin's Cultural Arts Program were critical for getting the Serie Project off the ground. In their first request for program support from the Cultural Arts Program, the city awarded Serie Project $6,344.[32] Although the sum was small, the funding allowed them to hire a master printer and acquire art supplies. The grant required a one-to-one match, which often translated into Coronado supplementing with his own income and donating his labor. In addition, the match stipulated that funds must be generated from print sales and took into account in-kind donations (goods and services). The following year, funding for Serie Project more than doubled with a $10,000 grant from the city and a $4,000 grant from the Texas Commission on the Arts's Minority Economic Development Grant. The funding pattern peaked in 2001–2002, partly because of Austin's tech boom, with a $52,750 grant from the city and a $6,000 Minority Assistance Grant from the Texas Commission.[33] While this may sound like significant operational support, it was only a small fraction of the funding that mainstream art institutions in Austin received. In relation to the uneven development of art funding, the anthropologist Arlene Dávila argues that the multicultural policies became "policies of containment."[34] Instead of legitimating the institutions and creating inclusive definitions of art and cultural production, the politics of multiculturalism framed the projects as oppositional to a "universal" mainstream art and limited their growth and power. Public-grant funding continued to be the core source of Serie Project's general operating budget, further placing the nonprofit in a precarious position in comparison with other local workshops such as the publishers Flatbed Press and Slugfest.[35]

By the time the Serie Project reached its fifteenth anniversary, in 2008, its professional printmaking program had become a nationally recognized institution.[36] For emerging artists such as Carlos Donjuan, Paloma Mayorga, and Michael Menchaca, Serie Project was a rite of passage—an opportunity to be part of an archive/collection that included established artists such as Benito Huerta, Delilah Montoya, and César Martínez. The workshop's geographic location in the Texas borderlands influenced many of its resident artists to take up the themes of migration and trade liberalization. Through their collaborative efforts, artists created limited editions that built a counterhegemonic discourse that challenged assimilationist, racist, and xenophobic policies. The cultural politics of this site of production pushed Fernández into new, uncharted territory. Her work grew increasingly politicized. She focused her attention on the exploitation of immigrant labor, with labor and Indigenism being central concerns of the Ecuadorian socialism that was impressed upon her at an early age.

Her fifteenth-anniversary print *Coming of Age (Transformations)* (2008; fig. 3.4) shows the downtown cityscape and its symbolic north-south divide as viewed from the lower Colorado River. In the foreground, a female doll with a collaged cornhusk dress stands next to a large tree trunk. As if welcoming the viewer, the doll gestures toward a panoramic view of downtown Austin with its skyscrapers, high-rise condos, and its iconic state capitol. Cars drive in on the Congress Avenue Bridge. The full-color foreground and grayscale skyline reinforce a temporal rupture. The artist uncovers the fabricated nature of this multilayered sight (a sixteen-color screenprint) wherein the visible and the inscrutable create an allegorical portrait of a modern American city. *Coming of Age* implies that this spectacle is political. By printing the cityscape devoid of color, Fernández revealed the hidden histories intrinsic in its making.

In contrast to previous accounts of immigrants who were greeted with

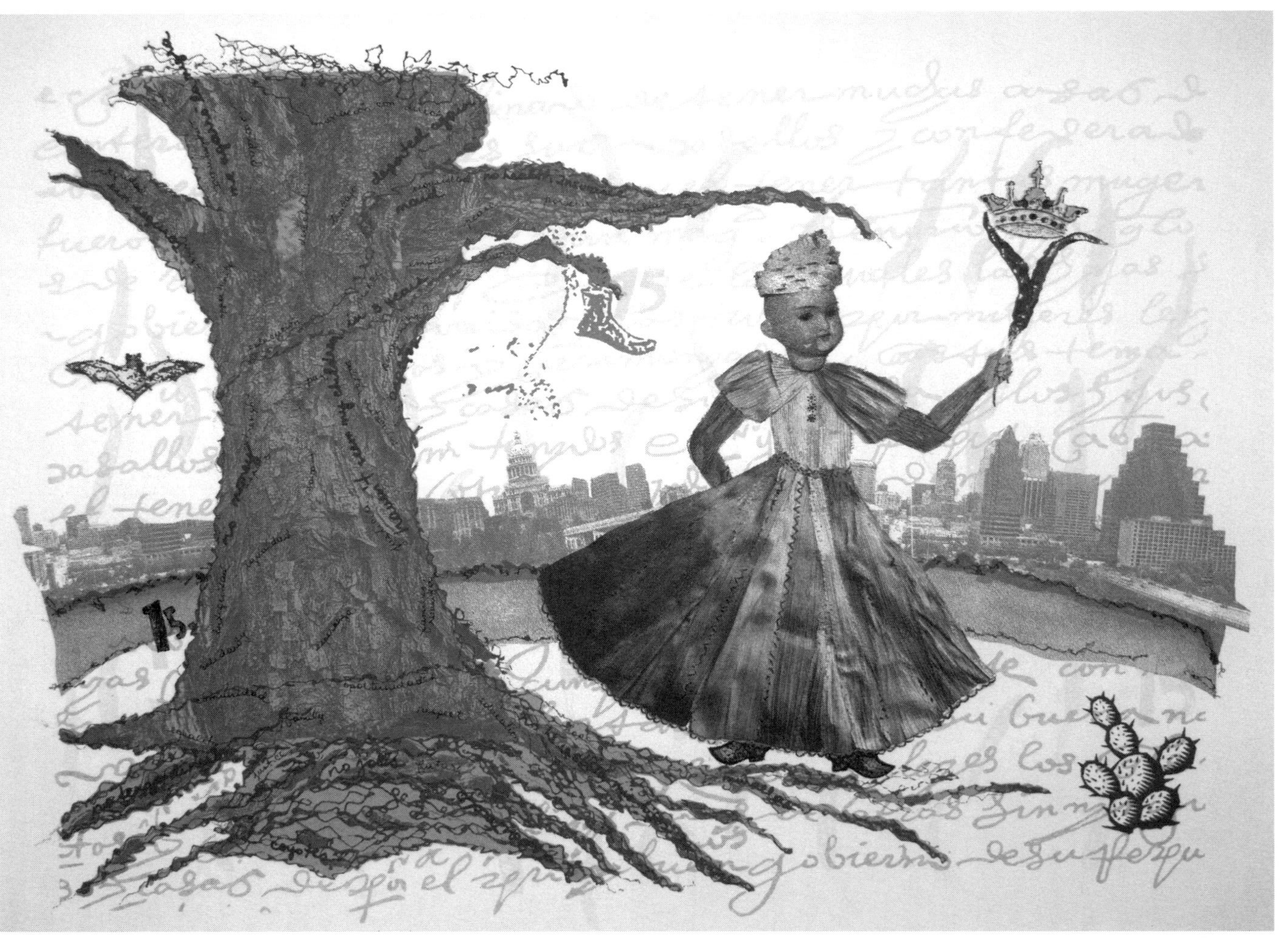

3.4. Sandra C. Fernández, *Coming of Age (Transformations)*, 2008. Screenprint on paper, 24 × 30 inches; edition of fifty. Printed by Brian Johnson at Coronado Studio, Austin, Texas. Courtesy of the artist.

hope by the Statue of Liberty as they entered the Port of New York, Fernández's doll welcomes viewers with caution. The doll raises her crown in the same manner Lady Liberty raises her torch, and yet she does not project a majestic image. Her awkward frontal pose, with one arm bending backward and one shoulder higher than the other, makes her appear to be standing on uneven ground or perhaps magically hovering like a fairy. The paper doll looks to the right and through an authoritative stance seems to halt an incomer before they cross the lower Colorado and enter the city. The artist contrasted the three-dimensionality of the doll's rubbery, rosy face with the flatness and paperlike weight of her dress, perhaps owing to the many interventions she made on the matrix of mylar prior to burning the screen.[37] While the Statue of Liberty holds the torch in her right hand, the doll uses her left and raises by the stem two dried red chili peppers, which balance a jeweled crown. The crown pays homage to Coronado Studio as it mimics its printer's chop.

Carved deeply into the trunk of the tree are messages warning of a foreboding reality in a place that offers little protection for this vulnerable population. Inside the towering form, the artist wrote in bold green lettering about the realities of undocumented life in Austin: "no health insurance," "no money," "*me agarró la migra*."[38] In light green writing she juxtaposed these cautionary tales with the values and aspirations of most newcomers: "equality," "family," "justice," "future." In other words, these aspirations are met with a perpetual threat of deportation. Through the Secure Communities program established by the Department of Homeland Security, the sheriff's office in Austin deported thousands of nonviolent undocumented immigrants. Between 2011 and 2015, local authorities forced the removal of upwards of forty-six hundred people detained through routine investigations such as traffic stops.[39] The collaboration between local and federal law enforcement made it difficult for the undocumented to report crimes or wage theft or assist with investigations; it instilled them with fear, so that they remained in the shadows as they took up jobs in the city as domestics, gardeners, and construction workers.

Fernández's print asks viewers to question how the city's growth requires the labor of these workers. As if welcoming the viewer and the implied immigrant subject, the doll gestures toward a panorama that shows a growing spatial concentration of capital. Yet this picture-perfect cityscape mimics mainstream accounts of economic globalization by obscuring the presence of low-wage labor. Austin, much like the financial centers Saskia Sassen describes in *The Global City* (2001), participates in the production of a specialized high-tech workforce, top-level management, and state-control operations that depend heavily on a low wage and low-profit economic sectors to support the upper sectors of capital.[40] According to the US census, Austin is one of the fastest-growing cities in the nation because of its strong economy and low unemployment rate.[41] Around the time when the artist made *Coming of Age*, the city netted a hundred and ten new residents per day.[42] While most Americans assume that undocumented immigrants are a rural population employed in the farming sector, research shows otherwise. Sixty percent of the eleven million undocumented immigrants reside in twenty metropolitan areas, Austin being the last metro area on this list.[43] Nearly 5 percent of all US workers are undocumented, and while the agriculture sector remains their largest employer, construction, leisure and hospitality, care services (home, children, elderly), and manufacturing employ large numbers of unauthorized workers.[44] In this manner Fernández pointed to the reality that most undocumented immigrants live and work in American cities and disperse about them as restless objects of consumption. An interesting parallel to the subject can be found in the work of the Los Angeles–based artist Jay Lynn Gomez, whose cardboard cutouts, paintings, and prints bring attention to the gardeners, housekeepers, and nannies who care for the affluent families in the westside neighborhoods of Los Angeles.[45]

Light and shadow play off the doll's A-line skirt, creating a topographic terrain that could very well gesture to the desert crossing that many immigrants will make prior to their arrival in the US. Undulating grooves in the husk show an infinitesimal number of verticals and diagonals that make up her unrealistically large body. The doll's elaborate texture may also gesture to the modernist Ecuadorian painter Oswaldo Viteri, a significant influence for the artist.[46] Viteri challenged the pictorial strategies of Indigenism by combining with the local folk objects the international style of *art informel*, creating richly textured canvases transformed through assemblage. The Andean rag dolls, textiles, and ecclesiastical ornaments in his mixed-media paintings "speak of the hybridity derived from Latin America's colonial process."[47] In *Caminantes Somos de la Noche y de la Pena* (1979; fig. 3.5), Viteri divided the square canvas into top and bottom by gluing down a rough texture, likely burlap, its shape resembling a simple peasant square shirt with the arms extended outward. The shirt doubles as an arid landscape, and off center to the right he placed fifteen colorful rag dolls standing shoulder to shoulder. The upper portion of the canvas is a blended sky at dusk that ranges in color from white, light blue to soft yellows to gray and black. Six additional rag dolls balance tightly on the upper-left corner of the night sky, while two others are seen at the bottom of the canvas as if awaiting purgatory. Viteri's richly textured canvases, which called upon the material history of the Andes, served as an important touchstone for the artist.

The triangular motif of the skirt appears consistently throughout Fernández's oeuvre, most noticeably in her "Cucas/Paper Doll" series, which began

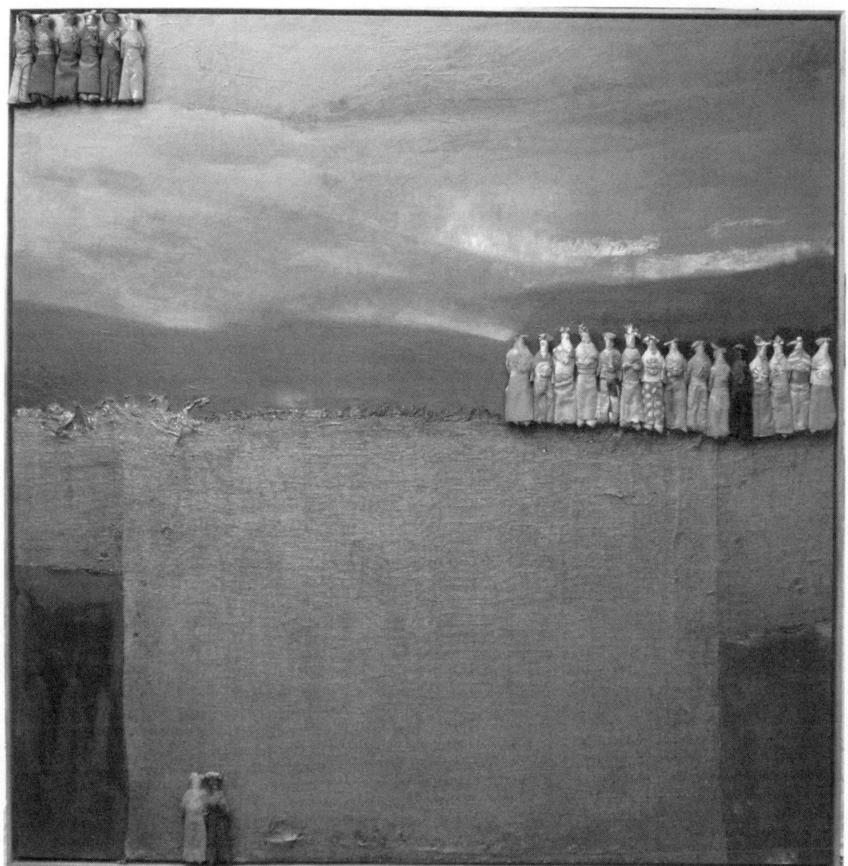

3.5. Oswaldo Viteri, *Caminantes Somos de la Noche y de la Pena*, 1979. Mixed media, 160 × 160 cm. Courtesy of Ileana Viteri.

as early as 1993 following a trip to Cuba.[48] For example, her mixed-media work *Behind What Is Seen* (1998; fig. 3.6) takes that triangular shape. Using paper, book pages, thread, wire, and Xerox copies, the artist fashioned a three-dimensional dress. The blouse is a delicate white with machine-stitched ruffle sleeves. Hidden behind layers of paper, we see the Xeroxed photo of a girl with braided hair. The skirt is a patchwork of printed pages from a book that cascade down on the left and right, while the center is a stitched white apron and just under an almost indiscernible Van Dyke brown print with the face of a child. On the bottom right, an extra piece of paper stitched in red thread holds what appears to be a moth wing, like the little treasures children carry in their pockets. These mixed-media techniques, which came out of her work in artist's books, appear in her prints and also speak to the practice of weaving and sewing she observed growing up with her grandmother. Art historian

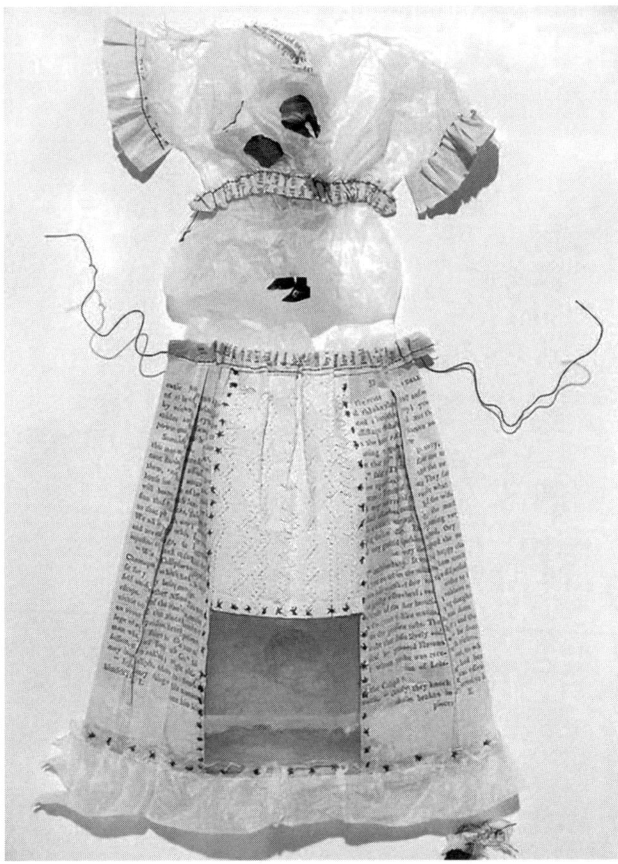

3.6. Sandra C. Fernández, *Behind What Is Seen* ("Paper Doll/ Cucas" series), 1998. Mixed media: paper, book pages, silk thread, wire, color-Xerox copy of an old photograph, Van Dyke printing, machine sewing, and hand stitching, 17½ × 12 × 2¾ inches. Collection of Patricia Nisbet Klingenberg. Courtesy of the artist.

Tatiana Flores has made note that this recurring characteristic in Fernández's work is a "gendered practice of [using] sewing as a surrogate for drawing."[49] In effect the line work mimics the steadiness of machine stitching but grows increasingly fluid and expressive on the roots of the tree in *Coming of Age*. The peculiar dress presents detailed stitching of pink and green thread creating thin zigzag lines. The practice of sewing also points to the gendered labor of immigrants who work in the garment industry, as well as the recent rise in women and unaccompanied minors requesting asylum status at the border.

Coming of Age narrates the story of an American city that becomes a signifier for what Peruvian sociologist Aníbal Quijano calls the "coloniality of power." According to Quijano, the structure of power is colonial, and the coloniality of power is possible only through the "systematic racial division of labor."[50] Fernández positions this Eurocentric model of power as the backdrop of the city with partly legible Spanish script written in light blue cursive. The inscrutable text is an excerpt from the Codex Mendoza, a sixteenth-century document written two decades after the fall of Tenochtitlán (the Aztec capital) and commissioned by the Viceroy Antonio de Mendoza to relay detailed information about the Aztec empire, its economy, and organization (fig. 3.7). For the artist, the Codex Mendoza represents "a permanent reminder of the conquest and the relationship of dominator and dominated that persists when there are conditions of inequality."[51] Fernández's print suggests that Austin operates under a racial logic similar to the one implemented during the colonization of the Americas, ensuring domination through the control of space and labor.

Historical documents confirm that the spatial text of the city was designed to operate under this logic. The Master Plan of 1928 produced a "racial script" foundational to the spatial organization of Austin. According to historian Natalia Molina, "racial scripts" are recurring trends in the production of racial knowledge: "Once attitudes, practices, customs, policies, and laws are directed at one group, they are more readily available and easily applied to other

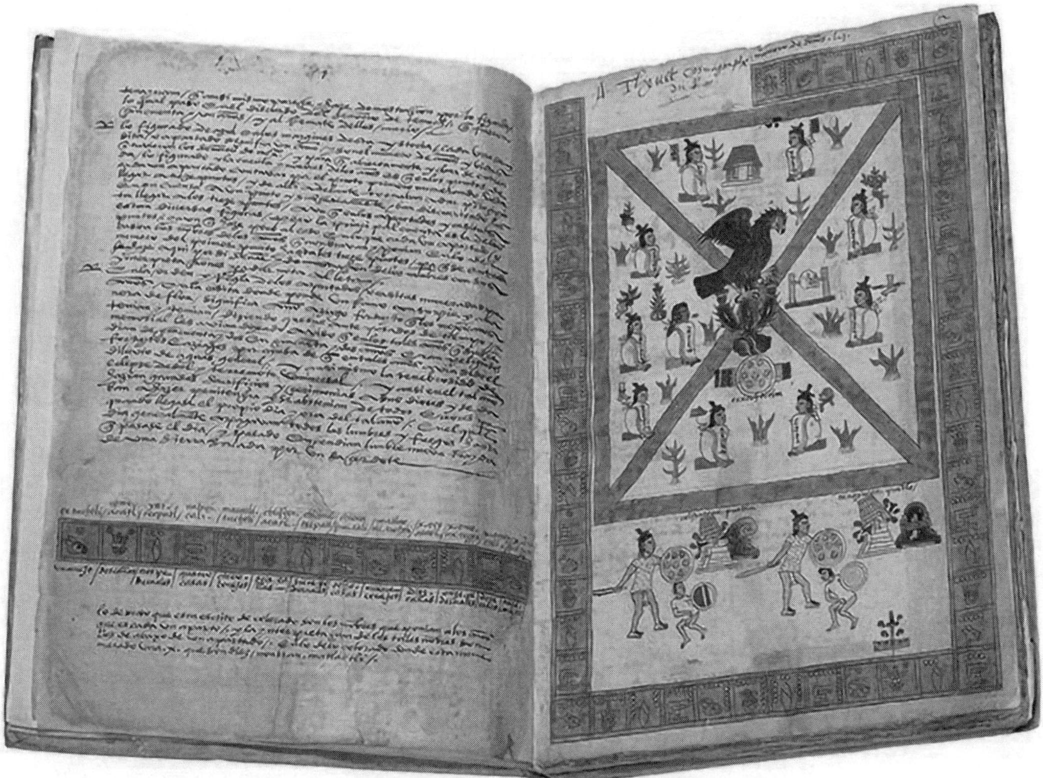

3.7. Codex Mendoza, title page, MS. Arch. Selden A.1, fols. 1v–2r, ca. 1541–1542. Pigment on paper. Courtesy of the Bodleian Library at Oxford University.

groups."[52] The law complied with the "separate but equal" doctrine, confirmed in *Plessy v. Ferguson* (1896) and enabled de jure segregation through an expansion of Jim Crow laws. The master plan displaced 30 percent of Austin's population to the East side by relocating facilities and housing for African American and Mexican families east of East Avenue (now Interstate 35).[53] Many of those displaced were formally enslaved workers (or their descendants) who settled the communities of Clarksville, Wheatville, and Pleasant Hill in West Austin, now among the most exclusive and high-priced neighborhoods in the city.[54] Also displaced was a small but significant immigrant community of Mexican laborers and their families who had settled the area around Republic Square Park, then known as Mexican Park. To enforce Jim Crow, city officials targeted the closure of specific schools, which they justified in the master plan: "It is our recommendation that the nearest approach to the solution of the race segregation problem will be the recommendation of this district [just east of East Avenue and south of the city cemetery] as a *negro district* [author's emphasis]; and that all the facilities and conveniences be provided the negroes in this district as an incentive to draw the negro population to this area."[55] Developers and neighborhood associations embraced the plan by restricting homeownership in downtown and West Austin to whites only. This shameful episode of Austin's history enabled a particular set of mechanisms by which to organize the spatial politics of the city, as well as to make future generations of vulnerable workers necessary but much less visible. The historical treatment and displacement of Mexican and African American workers in this city created a blueprint for how subsequent racialized groups would be treated until they were out of sight or in the shadows of the city.

Coming of Age creates conceptual links between the racial and spatial classification systems of modern Europe with the way American cities organize space and labor along a racial axis, as well as who gets to be visible in these cities. According to Quijano, "One of the fundamental axes of this model of power is the social classification of the world's population around the idea of race, a mental construction that expresses the basic experience of colonial domination and pervades the more important dimensions of global power, including its specific rationality: Eurocentrism."[56] Eurocentrism, as a global hegemonic theory of knowledge, gave way to a hierarchical structure in which women and people of color were considered inferior, closer to nature than to reason. Moreover, this theory of knowledge structures the field of vision, and those closer to nature appear in Fernández's print as objects of the landscape, not as autonomous beings. The artist did not visualize undocumented workers as whole (the landscape is devoid of human figures) but conveys their poignant messages ("Haven't seen my children in 5 years," *me agarró la migra*, or *coyotes*) in the trunk of a large tree. The task of coloniality is to make their presence invisible.

In one of the key texts for borderlands art histories, the cultural critic Claire Fox theorized how trade liberalization in the Western Hemisphere created a problem of representation for the border.[57] While the nation-states encouraged the movement of capital and goods across geopolitical borders or a borderless neoliberal economy, they further restricted the mobility of workers and heavily enforced the boundaries of citizenship. In these highly contentious spatial registers, where literary and artistic representations of the US-Mexico border unfolded, Fox found that national space and its management persisted as central concerns, despite the borderless rhetoric of free trade.[58] The latter, in fact, reinforced the primacy and agency of the border instead of diluting its power. However, it is important to take note of how artists like Fernández interpreted the reterritorialization of the border in the wake of September 11, 2001, when al-Qaeda militants carried out the deadliest suicide attack in US history and immigration surveillance and border security reached unprecedented levels.

Following the attacks, what Fox calls the "capitalist spatial organization" of the US-Mexico border shifted and reorganized its model of power to an expanded notion of the border as being policed in every part of the nation. The new Department of Homeland Security created two immigration enforcement agencies: Immigration and Customs Enforcement (ICE), and Customs and Border Protection (CBP). ICE investigates, detains, and deports undocumented immigrants in the country's interior, while CBP prevents illegal crossings at US ports of entry. The border is thus reterritorialized across the nation at large, making it much easier to restrict mobility and erase the presence of *indocumentados*. Perhaps in contrast to the limited mobility of undocumented workers, Fernández included the icon of a bat to represent the 1.5 million Mexican free-tailed bats that migrate to Austin every spring. The endangered creatures roost under the Congress Avenue Bridge, the diagonal avenue visible on the right side of *Coming of Age*. With its muted yellow wings and faint brown outline, the artist makes a sardonic commentary on Austin's embrace of the Mexican free-tailed bat as an ecotourist attraction and how it differs markedly from the treatment and fate of undocumented Mexican and Central American nationals.

The reterritorialization of the border at large poses a new problem of representation. Fernández was not alone in visualizing the anxious redeployment of national space in this fifteenth-anniversary portfolio. The San Francisco–based Chicana artist Ester Hernandez (b. 1944) was much more explicit in drawing attention to the devastating effects of free trade on Indigenous Mexican farmworkers. In *Sun Raid* (2008; fig. 3.8), she directed viewers to the rural southern communities of Mixtecos, Zapotecos, Triques, and Purepecha, whose farming economy collapsed after the ratification of the North American Free Trade agreement, spurring a wave of migration, only to be met with

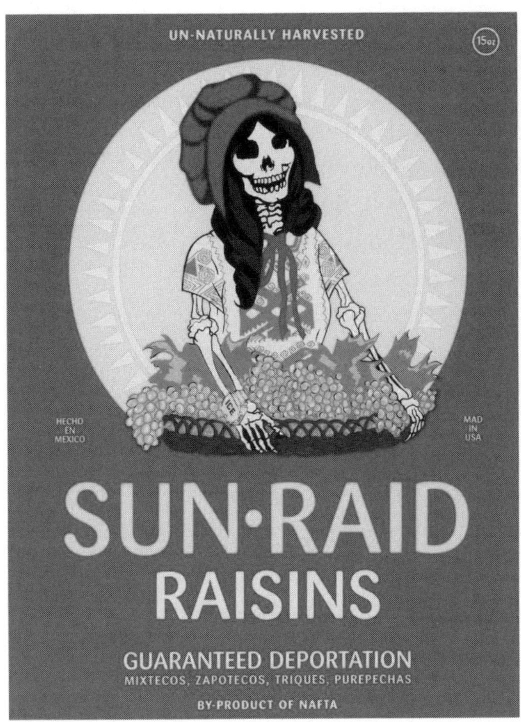

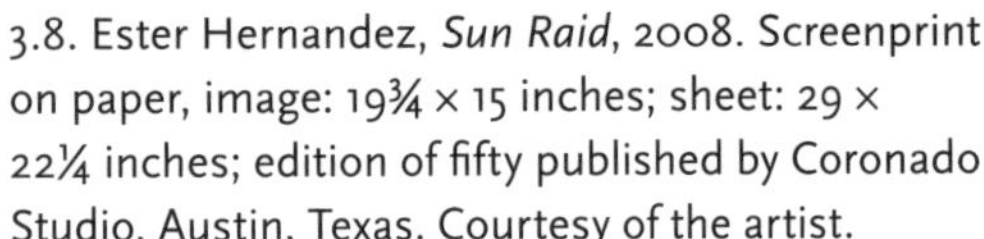
3.8. Ester Hernandez, *Sun Raid*, 2008. Screenprint on paper, image: 19¾ × 15 inches; sheet: 29 × 22¼ inches; edition of fifty published by Coronado Studio, Austin, Texas. Courtesy of the artist.

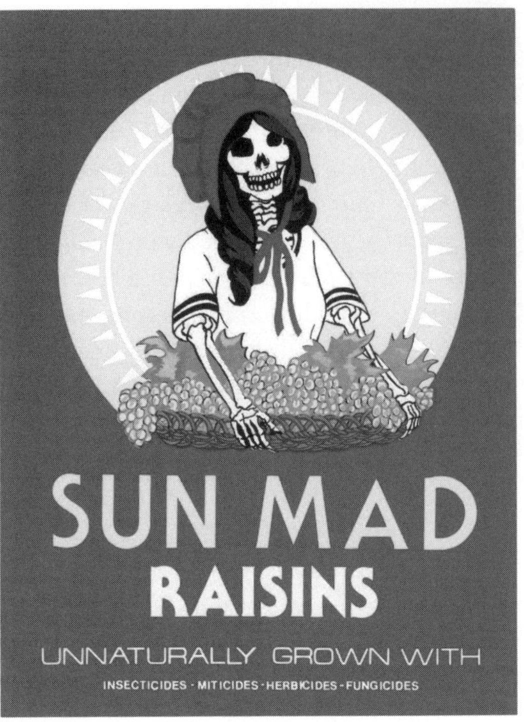

3.9. Ester Hernandez, *Sun Mad*, 1982. Screenprint on paper, image: 20 × 15 inches; sheet: 22 × 17 inches; edition of one hundred published by the artist. Courtesy of the artist.

exceedingly stringent US immigration policies. Hernandez's work is an unapologetic visual statement that denounces US neoliberal policies for ravaging some of the most economically vulnerable communities, forcing their desperate migration north and discarding their right to earn a living through a violent process of deportation. *Sun Raid* builds on her masterpiece, *Sun Mad* (1982; fig. 3.9), a satirical pop-art gesture that catapulted her to national prominence by transforming the Sun Maid Raisins box into an icon of the farmworkers' grape boycott. The vulnerability of the workers is one of personal significance for Hernandez, who grew up as part of a migrant farmworker family in Dinuba, California, and noted, "Slowly I began to realize how to transform the Sun Maid and unmask the truth behind the wholesome figures of agribusiness. *Sun Mad* evolved out of my anger and my fear of what would happen to my family, my community, and to myself."[59]

Sun Raid retains the basic formal elements of the design but alters the maiden to signal agribusiness's new casualties. Hernandez's Posadaesque *calavera* now dons a *huipil*, a traditional garment associated with southern Mexican and Guatemalan Indigenous women.[60] The figure's right-arm bracelet, inscribed with the acronym ICE, warns of her detention by Immigration and Customs Enforcement.[61] Hernandez revisits the trope of the farmworker through the eyes of a new, far more vulnerable workforce who, unable to compete in the international marketplace, have no other recourse but to flee north in search of work. Her sense of location in *Sun Raid*, however, moves beyond the specificity of the US-Mexico border to encompass migrant farming across the United States—in locations as remote as the Pacific Northwest and Vermont's organic farm-to-table movement—which operates under the threat of ICE raids.

While Hernandez's critique of neoliberalism and border enforcement remains firmly grounded in the rural landscape, Fernández shifts viewers' attention to the mechanisms that create "illegality" in the metropolis, where most of the country's eleven million unauthorized workers reside.[62] *Coming of Age* reveals some of the internal borders of the city. Despite the assumptions of sight—the economic growth, the population boom, the creative life of Austin celebrated by geographers like Richard Florida—there are so many hidden barriers for those on the margin of the body politic.[63] *Coming of Age* encourages viewers to question what they cannot see, the underlying structure that divides space and labor. Who gets to live in what part of town? On whom does the building boom rely for labor exploitation? Who makes the beds in that high-rise hotel? Who is more likely to get stopped by police? By including the voices of undocumented workers in the trunk of the tree, Fernández reminds viewers, "The individuals who clean residential homes, care for children while parents go to work . . . cook and wash dishes at the restaurants where we eat . . . and fix roofs around town do not live in another world."[64] They are here, but society has been conditioned not to see them. Her critique of Austin, however, likely extends further as a microcosm enacting state policy. The capital city could well symbolize the state of Texas, a region where ideological neoliberalism shapes state policy. Texas, in the words of sociologist Javier Auyero, "has more immigration detention beds than any other state and also has the largest number of beds operated by private prison companies."[65]

Recent ICE raids, in California, Virginia, North Carolina, Georgia, Kansas, New York, and Texas under the Trump Administration are only a continuation of a deportation machine that began around the time these works were made, earning President Obama the moniker the "deporter-in-chief."[66] The border's spatial mobility makes it abundantly clear that the post-9/11 border is what Mignolo calls a "movable center," where "the power of the center does not depend on geographical representations but, on the contrary, geographical representations are built around the power of the center."[67] In other

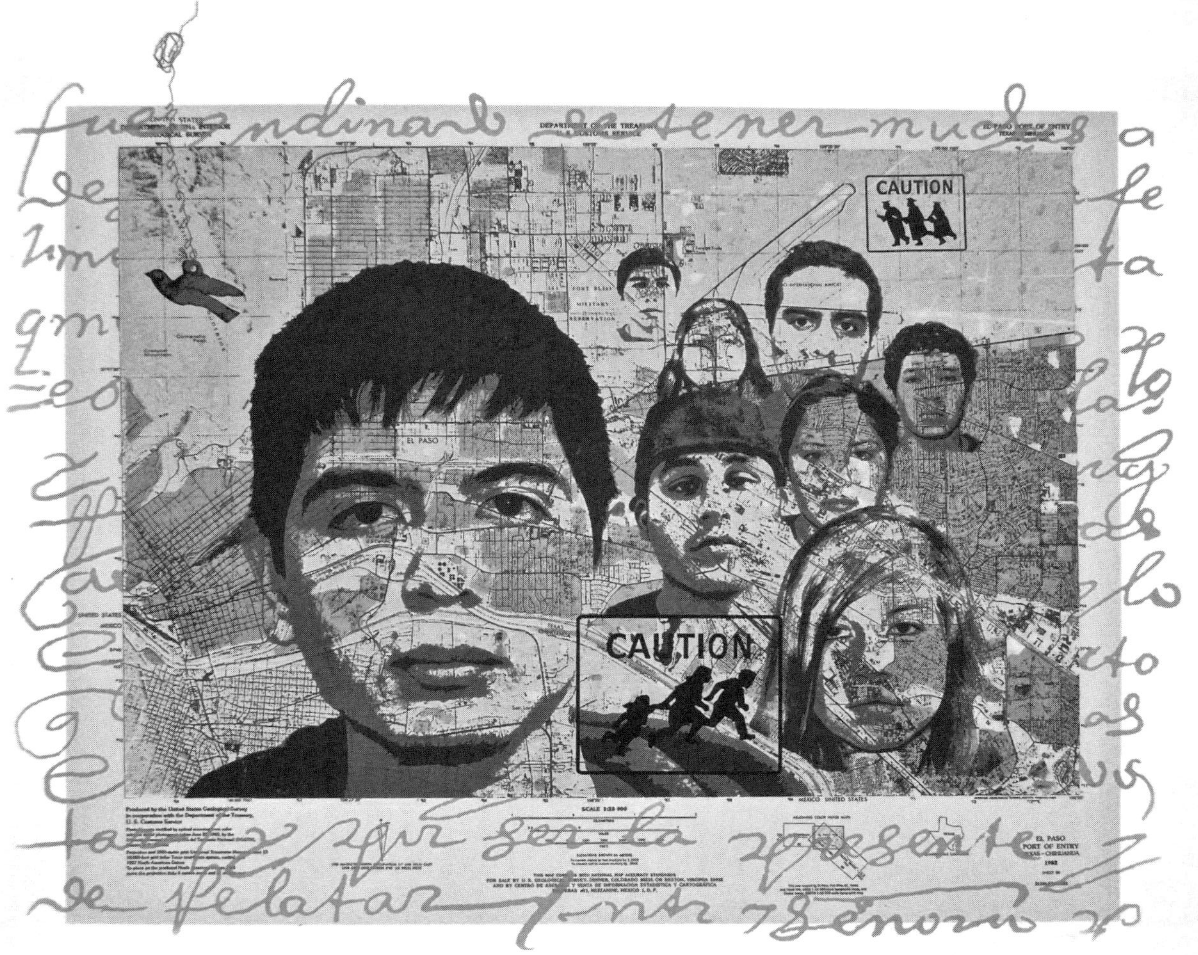

3.10. Sandra C. Fernández, *CAUTION: Dreamers in/on Sight*, 2013. Screenprint and thread on paper, 22 × 30 inches; edition of fifty, printed by Jonathan Rebolloso and Logan Hill at Coronado Studio, Austin, Texas. Courtesy of the artist.

words, in Fernández's work viewers witness how the border does not depend on a static geographic location, but rather how the panorama of the American metropolis is built around the movable border. Insofar as they picture the bordered city and rural farmlands as a site of surveillance, these artists point to the current forms of territoriality that subaltern populations must navigate.

CAUTION

On June 18, 2020, the US Supreme Court blocked President Trump's attempt to end the Deferred Action for Childhood Arrivals (DACA). The immigration policy, issued as an Executive Order under the Obama Administration in 2012, allowed individuals who were brought to the US before their sixteenth birthday to apply for a legal status that protected them from deportation and made them eligible for a work permit. In 2017, the Trump Administration rescinded the program; it proposed to phase out its protections and cited that it was an overreach by the previous administration's executive branch. The young people protected under this policy, known as "Dreamers," reached an estimated eight hundred thousand.[68] Many of them are first-generation college students who, emboldened by their newfound legal status, have created one of the largest immigrant youth activist movements in the United States. Their public image and their stories of resilience and uplift represent a great sense of hope for the eleven million undocumented immigrants who remain in the shadows.

Shortly after the Obama Administration's Executive Order on DACA, Fernández began making work on the Dreamers. The issue was of personal significance, given that many of her students at the University of Texas at Austin were direct beneficiaries of the policy.[69] *CAUTION: Dreamers in/on Sight* (2013; fig. 3.10) shows the blue-tinged portraits of these youth silk-screened over a vintage port-of-entry map of the El Paso–Juárez region. The US Geological Survey produced these maps in the early 1960s in cooperation with US Customs. In this print, Fernández contrasted the map's God's-eye view of the international borderline, including the cadastre used to identify land parcels, with the faces of young people suddenly in the spotlight. The largest portrait on the left shows a young man looking directly at the viewer. At center and suggestive of the print's title is the iconic road sign of a family crossing a highway, but the figures are flipped and run to the right. The sign is discussed at length in chapter 1 through a reading of Ricardo Duffy's *The New Order*. Seven smaller portraits emerge on the right in a series of diagonals and overlaps that may suggest the growing movement of immigrant-youth activism. The artist establishes a triangular composition with the flashpoint

Caution sign, a collaged red aviary *milagro*—a Catholic folk charm intended to plead and give thanks for healing or safe passage—and a refashioned road sign in the upper right with three graduates running triumphantly with their diplomas.

While the voices of the undocumented remained disembodied in the panoramic cityscape of *Coming of Age*, in this work the artist shifted to another representational strategy. The Dreamers are staged front and center. Their unafraid gaze and solemn posture demand acknowledgment. Commenting on this shift, Tatiana Flores noted how the work ponders the "ethics of representation" as Fernández "successfully humanizes a group of anonymous minors who have been victims of circumstances beyond their control."[70] In such a view, Flores frames the intervention to elicit sympathy for these young people. But perhaps there is more at play in this strategy.

By placing their portraits over the borderline, Fernández challenged the disembodied projection of the port-of-entry map with the embodiment of the Dreamers, whose corporeal presence blocks the line of sight. In fact, the subtitle of the work alludes to this maneuver. The strategy recalls the work of the late photographer Laura Aguilar, whose radically vulnerable nude self-portraits counter the frontier ideology of nineteenth-century photographic practices that make up the American West (fig. 3.11). Writing on Aguilar's posthumous retrospective, Macarena Gómez-Barris remarked, "By situating her mestiza body into the folds of land amid the boulders of the Gila Mountains, Aguilar calls forth the historical memory of Spanish colonialism, US colonization, and settler violence."[71] Much like Aguilar's ecological impulse to blend into the landscape and use her embodiment to resist the frontier belief in an empty, free land, Fernández employs the mixed-race Latinx body to visually block the science of cartography used to demarcate territorial borders as well as its political implications for which bodies may enter, exit, and live beyond these entry points.

This shift toward corporeality, forcing the viewer to see those bodies that are prohibited or forbidden, recalls the claiming of space articulated by the late poet Gloria Anzaldúa.[72] "What I want is an accounting with all three cultures—white, Mexican, Indian. I want the freedom to carve and chisel my own face, to staunch the bleeding with ashes, to fashion my own gods out of my entrails. And if going home is denied me then I will have to stand and claim my space, making a new culture—*una cultura mestiza*—with my own lumber, my own bricks and mortar and my own feminist architecture."[73] Both Fernández and Aguilar reclaim that space through the mestiza/o body. The latter put her own body on the line to question the nineteenth-century visuality of photographic practice that claimed the American West, whereas Fernández rendered those chiseled and heroic faces to counter the arbitrary

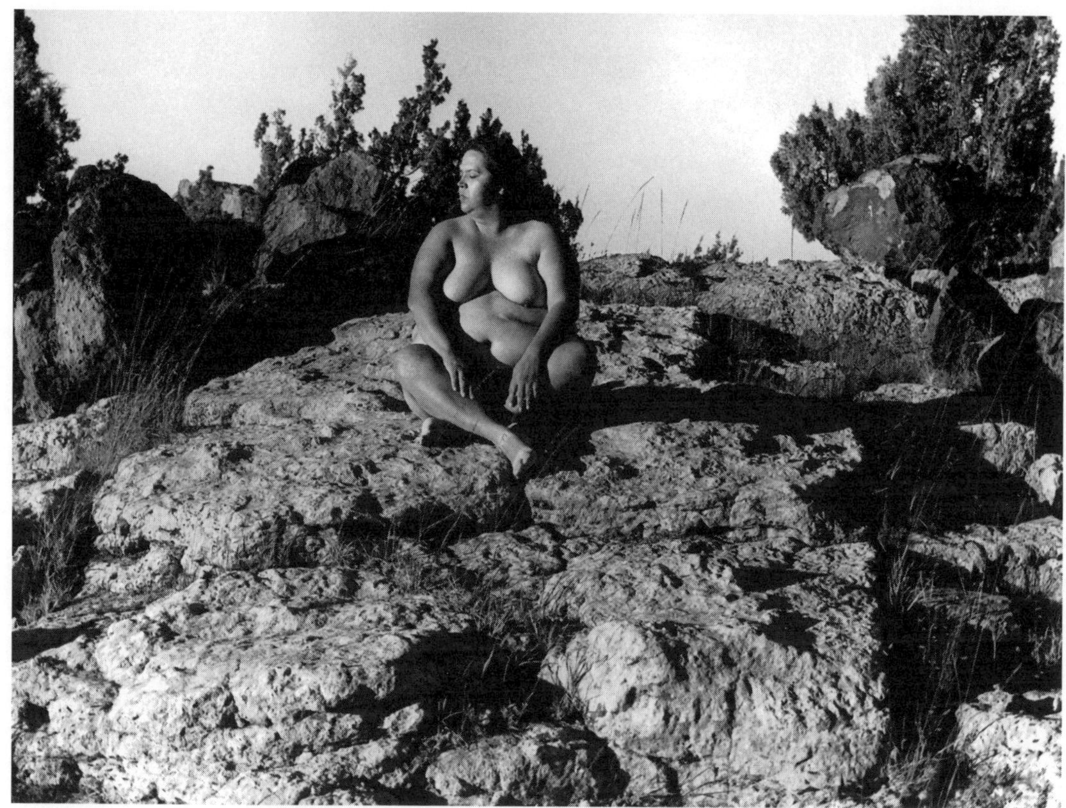

3.11. Laura Aguilar, *Nature Self-Portrait #11*, 1996. Gelatin silver print, 16 × 20 inches. Courtesy of the Laura Aguilar Trust of 2016.

lines on the map and used the medium of printmaking to distribute their colonial logic of exclusion. Fernández's allusion to mestizaje, however, is much more an abstraction. The art historian Holly Barnet-Sánchez noted how the subject of mixed race manifested itself as a "hybrid—formally, conceptually, aesthetically."[74] The formal choices of layering, as if building a palimpsest, allude to the present as well as the historical memory of the region from Spanish colonialism to the Treaty of Guadalupe Hidalgo to the establishment of the Border Patrol.

The Denver-based artist Tony Ortega, also a fellow of the Serie Project/Coronado Studio in Austin, takes a slightly different approach in his figurative and narrative prints on immigration. His screenprint *La Marcha de Lupe Liberty* (2006; fig. 3.12) commemorates the nationwide marches that took place in the spring of 2006 when a House bill introduced by Rep. James Sensenbrenner proposed to make undocumented status a felony subject to prison time, fines, and deportation. Ortega arranged a pyramidal composi-

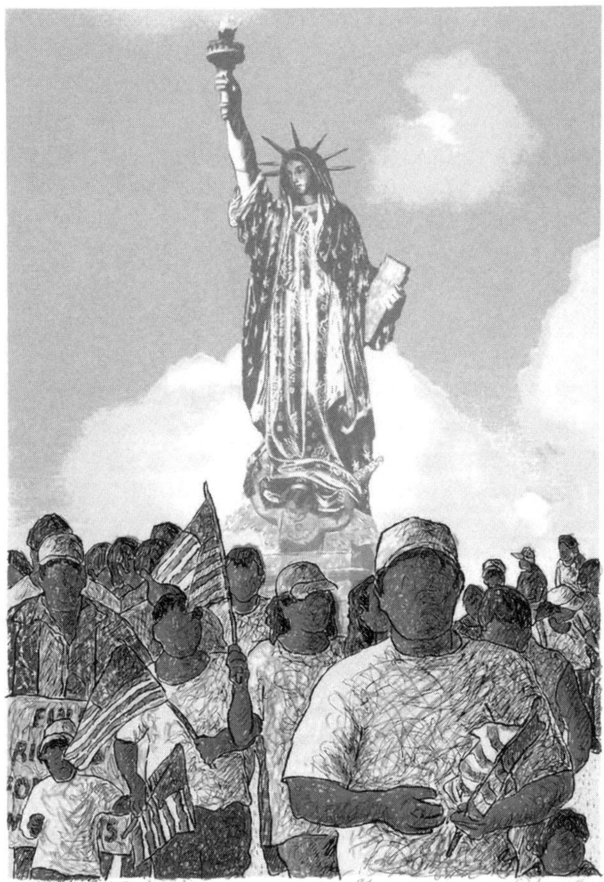

3.12. Tony Ortega, *La Marcha de Lupe Liberty*, 2006. Screenprint on paper, 23 × 16 inches; edition of fifty published by Coronado Studio, Austin, Texas. Courtesy of the artist.

tion with the syncretic icon of Lupe Liberty and a large group of peaceful protesters marching under her image. His impressionistic treatment of the figures makes their representation hover between figuration and abstraction. The nonspecificity of their faces denies viewers something they are already conditioned not to see and in this way makes visible the attitudes and behaviors that shape immigration policy. However, Ortega is keen on showing the racialized Brown bodies of these marchers and in such a way critiquing conceptions of a racially monolithic American homeland and the empty promise written at the base of the Mother of Exiles: "Give me your tired, your poor, your huddled masses yearning to breathe free, the wretched refuse of your teeming shore."[75] Both Ortega and Fernández grapple with this aspect of representing the migrant body and its connection to the border, but they also aim to create dignified portrayals of subjects who have overcome insurmountable odds.

In their reimagining of migrant subjectivity, both artists appeal to icons of faith. Ortega's subjects march under the guidance of a syncretic icon, a patina-green-crowned Virgin carrying the freedom torch. Fernández, on the other hand, turned to the use of the *milagro*. Rather than view this from a strictly religious demonstration of faith, their use of icons mobilized a particular audience who share in this transborder iconography. In *CAUTION*, Fernández used the bird icon perhaps to symbolize freedom and flight, while her earlier print *Coming of Age* employed the *milagro* as a stand-in for the migrant body. Out of strands of pink thread that emanate from the tree, the artist hung a small pink foot to represent a body part often associated with the undocumented who come "by foot" to the United States. The foot is a metonym for the bodies who journey, as well as the physical pain of walking through desolate deserts to reach "the other side." However, by tying the dismembered body part to the branch of the tree, the foot takes on new meaning, as it becomes part of a message board and informal shrine for newcomers.

The foot is a signifier for an array of physical and psychological experiences whose depth there is an inability or unwillingness to represent. How can artists represent that sojourn and the memories of that body? "His first entrance into Texas was scarcely promising. To cross the US-Mexico border, he walked alone in the desert for sixteen days, eating prickly pears and drinking water from the windmill-powered pumps that he came across every couple of days," recalled sociologist Jacinto Cuvi when describing the experience of Santos, a Mexican national who lives in Austin and crossed illegally in the 1960s.[76] Fernández's pink foot is a small gesture, rasterized in a way that eludes identification. If the artist had used a more realistic palette, the foot would shock viewers. Instead, it evokes curiosity like strange fruit hanging from a tree. When a twenty-four-year-old single mother embarked on her journey to Austin, she recalled walking under an oppressive sun: "You couldn't imagine how long we walked to get here! Araceli was just two at the time. . . . *Pero los solazos* [but the sun], the hunger, the thirst. . . . They would give me something to drink, and I would save it for her, for the walk. Everything that they gave me I would save for her."[77] In addition to recalling the physical sensations, this mother, who walked with a child strapped to her back, much like the Native mother in Duffy's *New Order*, expressed the fear and anguish she felt for her child's safety. Her sojourn was nothing short of a miracle.

Fernández's use of the foot to symbolize the subaltern body's inhumane treatment also points to hopeful possibilities. The *milagro* invokes a positive association that the migrant body has value but also that faith has power. When a young Santos decided to leave his family's ranch in the village of Cutzmala de Pinzón and set off from the state of Guerrero, "He left his rancho on foot on a blistering morning in March of 1968 with about thirty dollars in his pocket and a big, fuzzy, northward-pointing dream."[78] Before gaining his permanent-resident status through the Immigration Reform and Control Act of 1986, this Austin resident made the northward trip seventeen times after suffering sixteen deportations. When Cuvi questioned his tenacity, "What were you looking for?" the man replied, "Happiness."[79] Fernández's *milagro* alludes to the tenaciousness that would motivate someone to risk their life again and again to cross the border. Her interest in sewing and mending, visible in the thread that holds the *milagros*, which are often pinned to the robes of a saint or hung with ribbon in shrines, suggests possibilities for rooting and belonging even in a place that is not all that welcoming. Immigrant subjectivity reinvents itself in these works, and eludes narratives of victimization while challenging the "racial scripts" that prevent their acknowledgment as whole beings.

Fernández drew viewers to the abject body of a migrant whose very humanity is placed in question. In the US South, it is difficult to look at a body part hanging from a tree and not conjure images of "racialized spectacle violence" that terrorized Black communities.[80] Lynching and the problematic practice of lynching photography had a dehumanizing effect for victims and a distancing effect for onlookers. The crowds that gathered to witness the hanging or purchase a souvenir photograph of vigilante justice no longer saw a lifeless person.[81] They justified the killing, burning, and dismemberment of bodies because, tied to a tree, the victims became *less than human*. The African American artist Vicki Meek, also a resident artist at Serie Project, alludes to that violence in her print *Ida B. Wells: Telling It Like It Is* (2002; fig. 3.13).[82] The focal point of the horizontal composition is a close-up portrait of Wells, the activist, journalist, and suffragette. The icon glows in the golden light referencing the Yoruba goddess Oshun, and the blue that envelops the figure is an act of protection. Wells's journalistic exposés about lynching and white mob violence brought international attention to these perverse practices in the US South. Meek juxtaposed her portrait with a faint photograph of a lynched victim and a crowd gathered to witness the spectacle. Wells's fearless voice floats above the lifeless body. Likewise, Fernández's disembodied foot may also point to the history of racial violence that deems some bodies, those foreign or nonwhite, as subhuman, forcing viewers to contemplate their role as spectators complicit in this violence.

In addition to the foot, another body part that speaks to the immigrant experience in the US is the tongue. The San Antonio–based Terry Ybañez (b. 1959) began a series in the early 1990s that dealt with language and loss. She had recently completed a master's degree in Bilingual and Bicultural Education at the University of Texas at San Antonio and was grappling with the question, *How do we lose our mother tongue?* Like many Mexican Americans of her generation, she had grown up learning the Spanish of the home but had

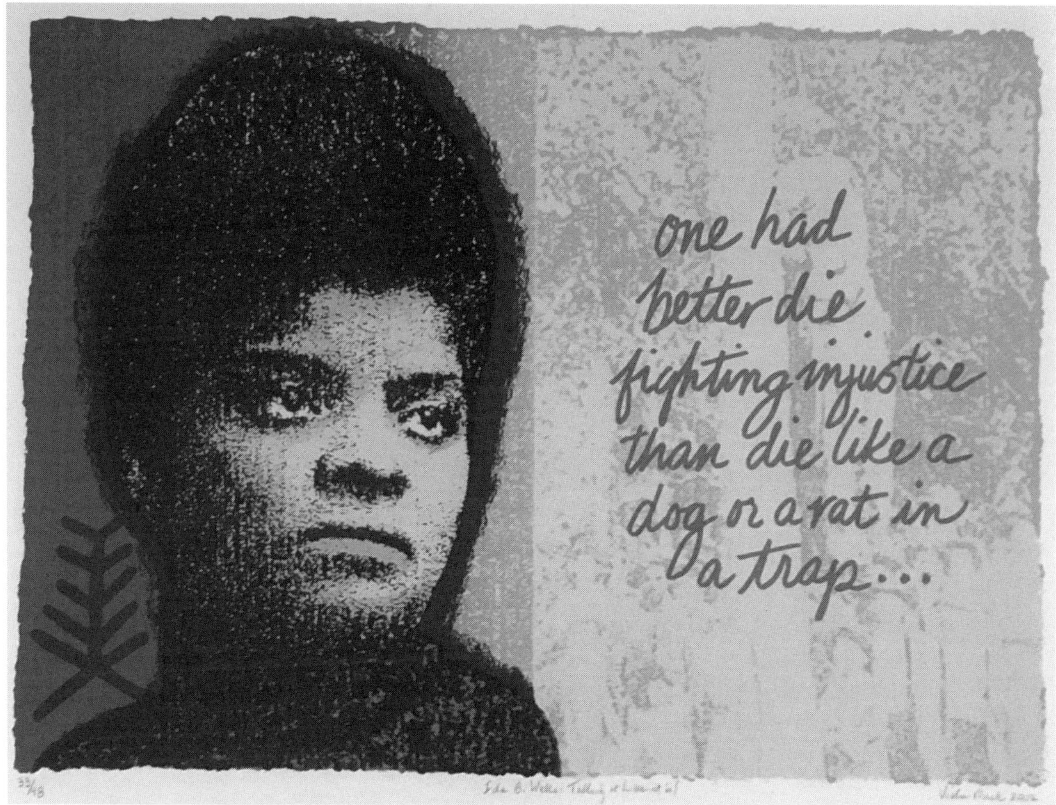

3.13. Vicki Meek, *Ida B. Wells: Telling It Like It Is*, 2002. Screenprint on paper, 16 × 22 inches; edition of fifty published by Coronado Studio, Austin, Texas. Courtesy of the artist.

been punished and forbidden to use the language by the time she entered first grade.[83] The loss of language came with an intense feeling of shame that being Mexican was less worthy than being American.

Coronado invited Ybañez to participate in the residency program in its third year. In the summer of 1996, she spent several days working closely with Dominican master printer Pepe Coronado (see chapter 4) and made a colorful pop art–style screenprint titled *Cutting Tongues* (fig. 3.14). She hoped to capture viewers long enough to think about their relationship to language. Her composition placed two vertical panels side by side with text written on the perimeter. On the left, Ybañez juxtaposed a scissors over red and a tongue over a blue background, creating visual tension between the objects. The scissors' sharp double blades protrude outward in a menacing way. A pink tongue covered in white and pink lingual papillae appears to writhe its body. On the perimeter of the left panel she wrote, "When the Spaniards

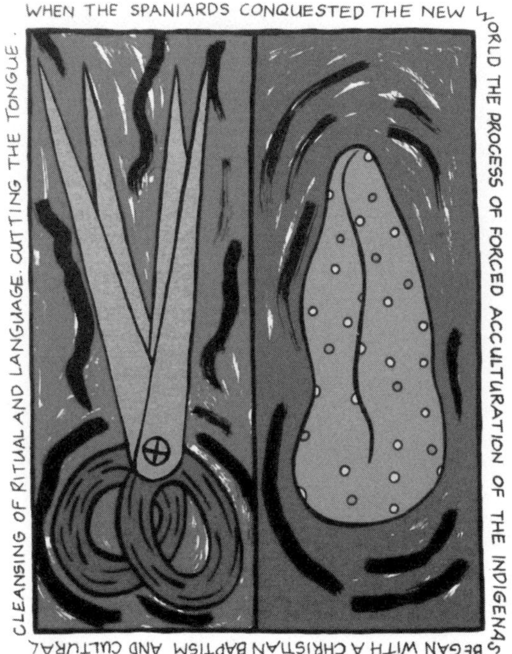

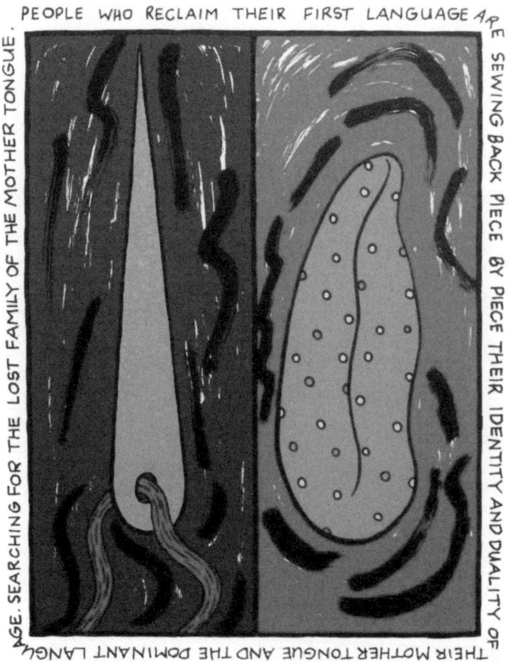

3.14. Terry Ybañez, *Cutting Tongues*, 1996. Screenprint on paper, 11¾ × 18¾ inches; edition of thirty-four published by Coronado Studio, Austin, Texas. Courtesy of the artist.

conquested the New World the process of forced acculturation of the *Indigenas* began with a Christian baptism and cultural cleansing of ritual and language. Cutting the tongue." Ybañez forces the viewer to engage in a reading ritual that questions Western reading practices before the viewer even comprehends her explicit critique of Spanish colonialism and, by extension, Eurocentrism. Ybañez is confident in her use of line, which indicates the movement of her sharp comic book–style objects. Their spiral movement could well reference the speech scroll glyph found in Aztec codices. She deliberately allowed the white of the paper to peer through, creating gestural marks that resemble woodblocks, which she favored during her training in relief printing at Trinity University.

On the right, the artist developed a response to the violent act signified in the previous panel. She placed a needle with thread over a green background and a pink tongue over red. She magnified the needle to such a degree that it takes viewers a moment to decipher what it signifies. On the perimeter of this panel, she wrote: "People who reclaim their first language are sewing back piece by piece their identity and duality of their mother tongue and the dominant language. Searching for the lost family of the mother tongue." Both the panels elicit a somatic response, the feeling of piercing the flesh of an intimate body part. Her work makes viewers reflect how the tongue is a muscle deeply tied to identity formation but out of sight, often taken for granted.

Cutting the Tongue became a series that captured the artist's imagination for several years as she worked to undo the epistemic violence of her childhood schooling.[84] As an adult, Ybañez went through the painful process of relearning her native language. Her basic Spanish of the home had been lost over the years, but she yearned to reclaim its value. She began traveling to Mexico and forcing herself to read and speak Spanish, even when the fear of embarrassment came to the surface. In these trips she took an interest in researching Aztec codices, which referenced the conquest and fall of Tenochtitlán. Unlike the rituals of bloodletting offered to the gods, she found images of Spaniards cutting the tongues of Aztec nobles who refused service to the Spanish Crown.[85] Though these images primarily depicted men, the act of cutting Indigenous tongues resonated with her experience of language acquisition and loss.

While Ybañez is three generations removed from the experiences of her Mexican immigrant grandparents, in the lingual form she captures an archive of coloniality. The abject tongue embodies the painful experiences of speech and silence, memory and erasure cast upon "impossible subjects," and the multigenerational trauma required to mend their mother tongue.[86] Ybañez's critique of Spanish colonialism creates a parallel relationship to the present moment. Her work suggests that the United States engages in a similar process, replacing the baptism with English-only policies that enact a symbolic ethnic cleansing. She likewise points to the construction of hegemony through the violent suppression of other languages and ways of being.

The prints by Fernández, much like *Cutting Tongues*, reinterpret the "colonial wound" through Anzaldúan mestiza consciousness. They explicitly point to what Anzaldúa called the "new mestiza," subjects who inhabit multiple worlds—physical, spiritual, psychic, and sexual. Their work suggests that the bodies of those subject to the weight of coloniality's othering retain possibilities for agency. They imply the abject body can endure and mend its fissures by sewing back what has been lost. Fernández's *milagros* point to a relentless will to search for a better life. Her images of Dreamers physically claim the third space between the imperial design of this borderline. Their bodies interrupt the cartographies of power hidden in the port of entry map.

Fernández likewise hints at the colonial histories and Eurocentric epistemologies that were critical to the formation of the southern border. Under the banner of the Cross, the colonial violence that created the US-Mexico border runs deep, and the viewer can see it emerge in the Spanish translations of the nearly five-hundred-year-old Codex Mendoza. She makes visible the hand of the priest who translated the Nahuatl inscriptions by Indigenous artists that carried detailed information on the structure, economy, and customs of the Aztec people. This manuscript decoded the "savage" for the benefit of the Spanish Crown, and although it was lost to pirates before reaching Spain, the malice of its intent endures, structuring life and labor, free and nonfree bodies, sovereign and nonsovereign nations across all the Americas.

CONCLUSION

Caution: Dreamers in/on Sight was one of the last prints produced at Sam Coronado's workshop. Coronado passed away unexpectedly on November 11, 2013, drawing to a close a twenty-year run for the Central Texas printmaking residency program. His loss left an enormous void in the artist community. In a photograph that documents Fernández's final residency, Coronado and Fernández stand at center proudly holding a proof of the artist's screenprint, printers Jonathan Rebolloso and Logan Hill at their sides (fig. 3.15). Rebolloso was a DACAmented community-college student when he began his apprenticeship with Coronado Studio. Through dedicated mentorship, he would go on to earn the title of Coronado master printer, and, perhaps as a sign of poetic justice, would also have a hand in printing an edition that mirrored his own coming-of-age story. Coronado Studio fostered a search for identity and rootedness in the liminal space of the Texas borderlands. Fernández found refuge and community in this creative laboratory, which gave her the freedom to explore her interests in migration, geography, and race.

Her prints critique US immigration policy and the racial knowledge these policies create on undocumented subjects. Through a meticulous process of layering, her images engage in the decolonial impulse of returning to the past to explain our present, and do so to reimagine an alternative future. In her geographic representations, viewers connect our present-day territories and their anxious policing with a colonial history that divides space and labor along a racial axis. Fernández challenged these stratifications through allusions to the mestiza/o body that block or reveal the Eurocentric episteme of the cartographic gaze. Her abstract metaphors on mestizaje contest xenophobic territoriality by pointing to her subject's hybridity as progeny of colonial violence. Their corporeal disruptions on a map or cityscape claim space and hold colonial histories accountable for their arrival. These gestures challenge geography's disembodied projections.

The Ecuadorian American writer Karla Cornejo Villavicencio's book *The Undocumented Americans* (2020) critiques how those without legal status are

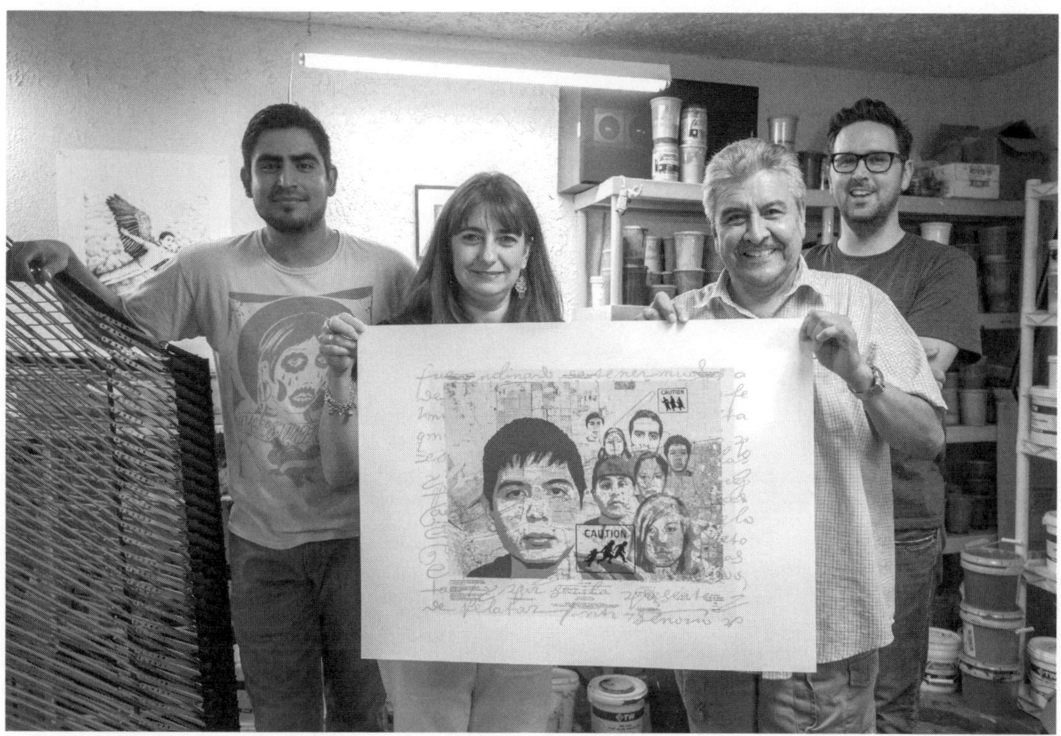

3.15. (*Left to right*) Jonathan Rebolloso, Sandra Fernández, Sam Coronado, and Logan Hill at Coronado Studio, 2013. Photo by Scott David Gordon.

often described in terms of their labor. She notes, "For many years when I have heard nice people try to be respectful about describing undocumented people, I've heard them call us 'undocumented workers' as a euphemism, as if there was something uncouth about being just an undocumented person standing with your hands clasped together or at your sides . . . to describe all of us, men, women, children . . . as workers in order to make us palatable, my god. We were brown bodies made to labor; faces pixelated."[87] The once-DACAmented and Harvard-educated writer makes a well-founded criticism that should be thoughtfully engaged by artists who work and advocate for immigrant rights. Fernández's prints avoid direct allusions to undocumented immigrant labor, though their subjecthood is often implied. However, one way she counters this intense focus on labor is through her attention to children and how they come of age through these precarious conditions. The plight of unaccompanied Central American minors requesting asylum at the southern border was the subject of her latest residency at Self Help Graphics, which resulted in *The Northern Triangle* (2018; fig. 3.16). The print shows a photo stencil of a little girl in a cardboard box, the kind children use to play

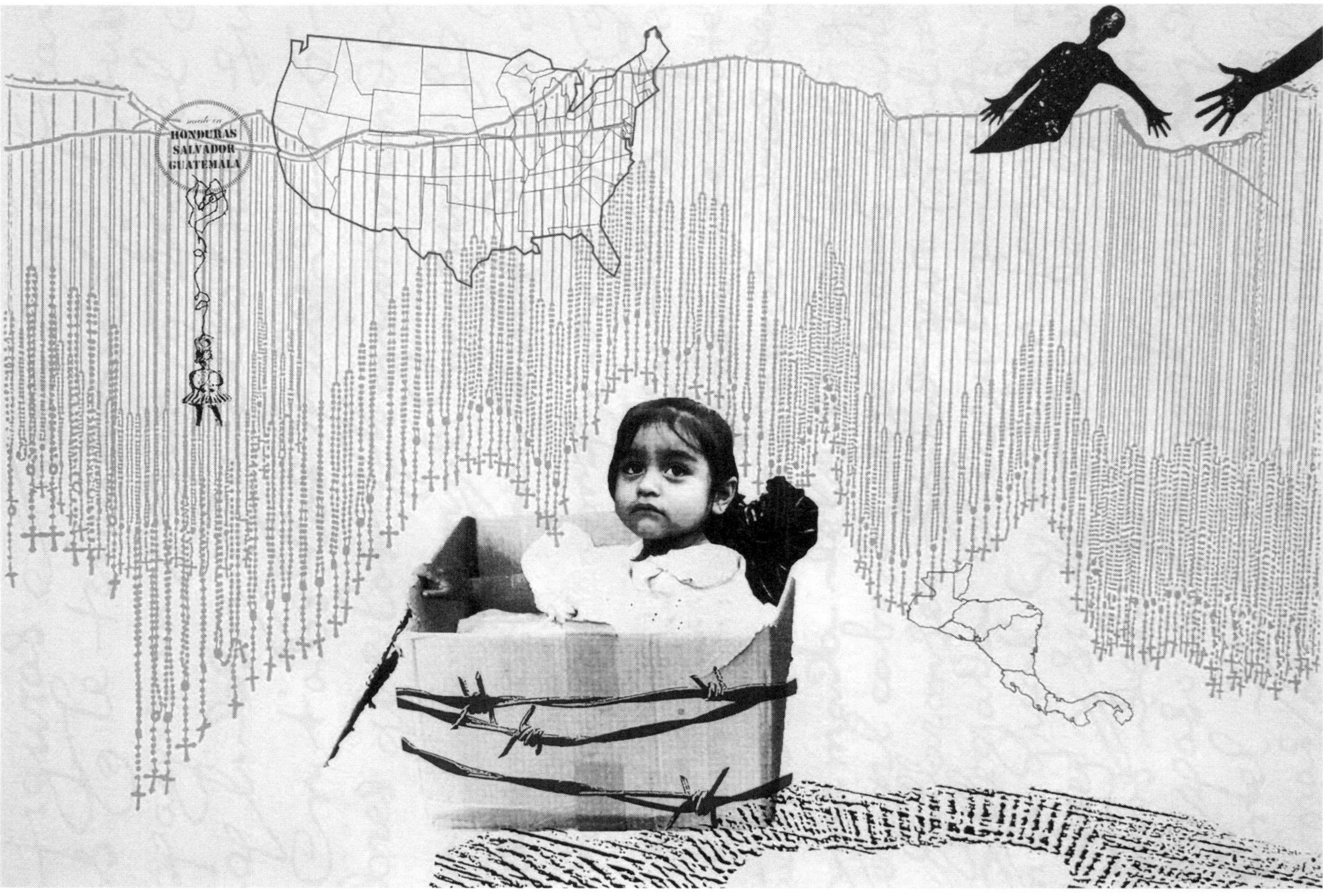

3.16. Sandra C. Fernández, *The Northern Triangle*, 2018. Screenprint on paper, 22 × 30 inches; edition of sixty-four printed by Oscar Duardo and published by Self Help Graphics, Los Angeles. Courtesy of the artist.

pretend. The box is wrapped in red barbed wire and nestled in between a blue outline map of the US and another of Central America. Fernández gestured toward the borderline where these children plead for entry by hanging vertical strands of rosaries as the liminal space between refuge and death. Two silhouettes on the upper right try desperately to grasp and hold hands, perhaps in reference to family separations. Once again, Fernández placed writing from the Codex Mendoza in the backdrop, though its legibility is even more obscure printed in light pink and turned sideways.

While Fernández alludes to the mixed-race bodies and mestiza consciousness of these subjects as in the little girl, their racial ties continue to highlight the mixture of European and Amerindian races, owed in part to the artist's upbringing in Quito. Reflecting on the precedence of these currents in Latin American art, and specifically in the work of Viteri, the art historian Dawn Ades concludes in her now-iconic textbook, "The notion of mestizaje has become central to artistic resistance to colonialism,"[88] and while that concept developed as a way to question the cultural authority of Europe, it also played into mythologizing a Native and Spanish ancestry. The political scientist Juliet Hooker considers Vasconcelos's theory of mestizaje as a key source for Anzaldúa's new mestiza, which selectively borrowed from his notion of racial mixing to unite Latin Americans against white supremacy and, more specifically, US imperialism. However, she notes that Anzaldúa "provides a corrective" by centering the political project of Chicana and queer women and inverting the racial hierarchy by favoring Indigeneity.[89]

Much like Anzaldúa's selective borrowing, Fernández engages in this process of what Hooker calls "mestizaje's travels" by centering the voices of mixed-race undocumented subjects who claim their rightful belonging in this land as the hybrid progeny of colonial and sexual violence. This adoption of borderlands theory likely related to her own lived experience. In an artist statement she noted,

> My Latina roots would be represented through the colorful stitching, while my newfound "American" roots would be reflected in the "flat" images on paper. My latest prints bring my two worlds together, carrying the differences on the same plane. I still utilize the stitch as a drawing tool, but now stitches are embedded within the metal, within the wood. All the competing cultural differences that embody who I am now are finally united, making up a completely new form of expression. It took me twenty-five years to reach this point of integration within myself and my art.[90]

But this mestiza consciousness that traveled from the Andes to the Texas borderlands continues to privilege the Indian and European roots of Latinidad, obscuring the African presence. As such, mestizaje portends a selectively decolonial horizon for the territorial futures of undocumented subjects. Her mestiza territorial futures circumvent the African presence and the history of slavery that shaped modern economies in the Americas. The next chapter shifts this perspective from mestizaje to mulataje by reaffirming the central place of Blackness in the art of the Dominican diaspora. Their engagement with aqueous territorialities and mulatto subjects challenges Latinidad's anti-Blackness and reimagines territorial futures shaped by migrations resulting from European and US interventions in the Caribbean.

CHAPTER FOUR

Aqueous Territorialities

The Dominican York Proyecto Gráfica's Island Dwellers and Water Boundaries

MOSES ROS-SUÁREZ'S 2010 PRINT *El Reggaetón del Bachatero* is among the most playful ways that Dominican American artists envision the ambivalence of being torn between two places (fig. 4.1). On the left, a sepia-toned New York skyscraper appears inside a pyramidal form while bees buzz around the vertical composition. Ros-Suárez (b. 1958), an artist-architect, added tiny ladders on the exterior of the building indicative of social mobility and economic ascent. In contrast, the nostalgic scene on the right evokes the aqueous shifts in color and reflection of the light green Caribbean waters. Ros-Suárez placed a single subject sitting on a hillside that doubles as a floating tropical island with waves moving in and out of its landmass. At center and in his characteristic graphic style, developed from years in the New York graffiti art scene, Ros-Suárez balanced a multiple-perspective dancing figure over a suspension bridge. The bright yellow color at the center of the triptych as well as the diagonal hatch lines that surround the body set a joyous tone, suggesting how Dominican migrants move to the music like the waves in the water that connects both locations. Published under the auspices of the print collective known as the Dominican York Proyecto Gráfica (DYPG), Ros-Suárez's print is one of many efforts by contemporary artists whose work bridges the Dominican Re-

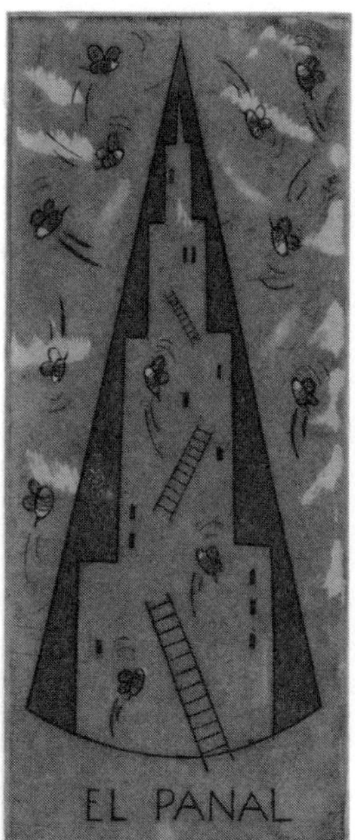

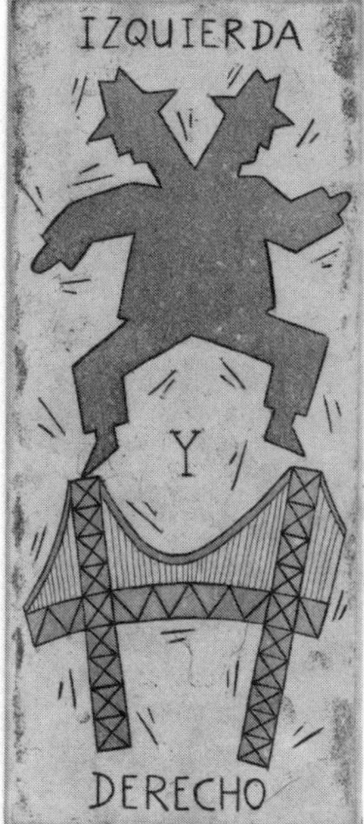

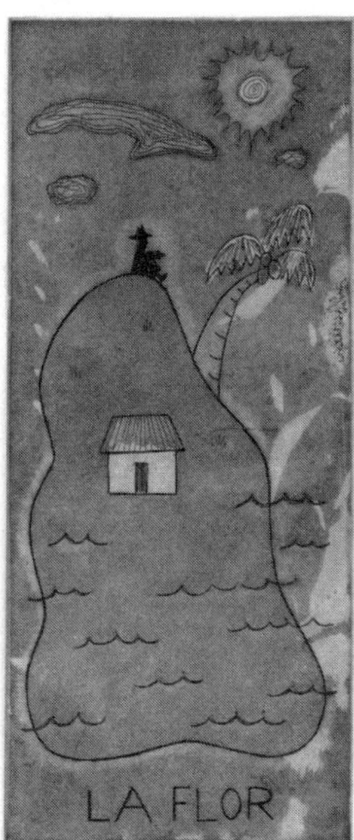

4.1. Moses Ros-Suárez, *El Reggaetón del Bachatero*, 2010. Silk aquatint and chine collé on BFK Rives, image: 7 × 9 inches; sheet: 12 × 15 inches; edition of twenty-five printed by the artist and Luanda Lozano at Manhattan Graphics Center and the Robert Blackburn Printmaking Workshop for the portfolio *Manifestaciones* by the Dominican York Proyecto Gráfica. Courtesy of the artist.

public (DR) and the island of Manhattan to reclaim the once-pejorative moniker "Dominican York," originally coined in reference to Dominican athletes who played on US sports teams and later synonymous with media images of a criminal underclass.[1]

Moved by a shared history of migration and exile, a group of New York–based Dominican artists established the DYPG in January 2010 (fig. 4.2). Their intent was to create an artistic hub for experimentation and exchange that could promote the Dominican graphic tradition in New York City. Soon these artists—who included Pepe Coronado, Yunior Chiqui Mendoza, Carlos Almonte, iliana emilia garcía, Scherezade García, Alex Guerrero, Luanda Lozano, Miguel Luciano, Reynaldo García Pantaleón, René de los Santos, Moses Ros-Suárez, and Rider Ureña—embarked on a series of collaborative printmaking projects that interrogated their experiences in the diaspora. Adopting the label "Dominican York" was more than an act of identification; unsettling the class hierarchies of an elite Santo Domingo (capital city of the DR), the term became a framework to describe the liminal space these individuals inhabit between the island of Hispaniola and the island of Manhattan.

Elsewhere I have argued that the DYPG's strategy of countermapping reveals the geopolitics of US intervention in Hispaniola, describes the subsequent waves of migration, and explores how Dominicans navigate the racial geography of the US.[2] This chapter builds on that research but takes a slightly different approach by focusing on the recurring use of water imagery in the DYPG's inaugural portfolio, *Manifestaciones* (2010). Unlike the previous chapters in the book, which have emphasized delinking from Western conceptions of land to question the excess of current forms of territoriality and nativism, Caribbean-diaspora artists recode geographic representations from the viewpoint of island dwellers who experience water boundaries. They conceive bodies of water (oceans, seas, rivers, channels) as spaces likewise loaded with Western cartography's colonial gaze, mediating the painful entry and exit of islanders, witnesses to the whims of repeated US intervention, and yet offering the hope of a better horizon. Bodies of water do not necessarily operate

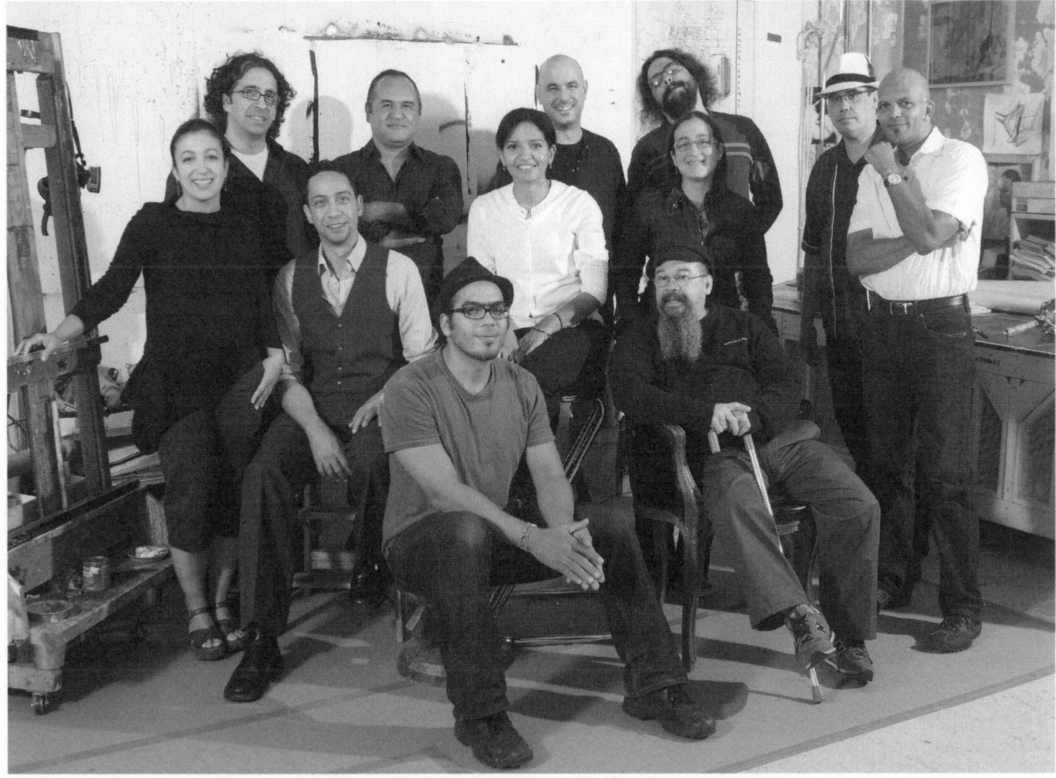

4.2. Members of the Dominican York Proyecto Gráfica at Bullrider Studio, 2010. Front (*L-R*), Rider Ureña, René de los Santos; middle row (*L-R*), Scherezade García, Miguel Luciano, Luanda Lozano, iliana emilia garcía, Carlos Almonte; back row (*L-R*) Alex Guerrero, Yunior Chiqui Mendoza, Pepe Coronado, Reynaldo García Pantaleón, Moses Ros-Suárez. Photo by William Vazquez.

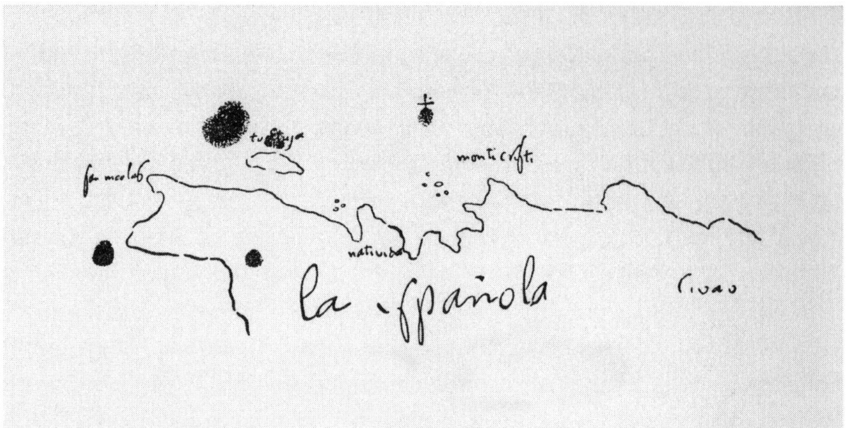

4.3. Christopher Columbus, sketch of northwest coast of Hispaniola, ca. 1492. Reproduced from Leo Bagrow, *History of Cartography*, revised and enlarged by R. A. Skelton (London: C.A. Watts & Co., 1964), 107.

under the same logic of territorial expansion, expropriation, and settlement, but as we will learn, they are policed and bordered just the same. These artists use printmaking to reclaim the Americas for migrant, mixed-race, and Afro-descendant peoples, but their claims to decolonization are not strictly about territory. They force us to consider the human right to mobility in water migrations, to ponder our connection to this life-sustaining and life-taking force, and to acknowledge the history of slavery, which transformed the Caribbean into what the Cuban writer Antonio Benítez Rojo called "the repeating island." This unique perspective, inspired by the island that was home to the first European settlement in the Americas as well as the first slave rebellion, centers the discourse of the Black Atlantic as critical to challenging the colonialist discourse of Latinidad.

The rest of this chapter is divided into four main sections and a conclusion. In the first, "The Origins of a Dominican Print Collective in New York," I map out the origins of the DYPG and their connections to the collaborative atelier models established at Self Help Graphics and Coronado Studio. I foreground the role of artists like master printer Pepe Coronado and intellectuals like Lorgia García-Peña in connecting the borderlands discourse of Chicanx artists to the liminality likewise experienced by Dominican Americans. In the second, "Centering the Black Atlantic," I focus on prints that highlight the complexity of race relations on the island of Hispaniola and how migration to the US reorients the racial geography of these displaced subjects. The third section, "Water Crossings," examines prints that discuss water crossings, noting how migration to the US often involves a dangerous journey to the shores of Puerto Rico, a US territory. The fourth section, "Interventions by Sea," alludes to US military interventions in the Caribbean region.

With a portfolio as large and as conceptually diverse as *Manifestaciones*, which includes a total of twelve prints, it becomes impossible to do justice to each of these works. I do not provide an exhaustive or definitive account of each print, its maker, or even the history of the collective. Instead, I offer a fragmentary reading of one of the most exciting groups to emerge in the last decade in the field of Latinx printmaking. In selecting these prints that emphasize water-based imagery, I hope readers will see how they directly challenge "the territorializing practices of modernity," captured in Christopher Columbus's emblematic drawing of Hispaniola's coastline (fig. 4.3).[3] The Genoese explorer's partial sketch of the island symbolized the Spanish Crown's colonizing imperative to map and control Caribbean ports of entry while blatantly disregarding Native territorialities that had already been charted and named (the island of Hispaniola was then known as Quisqueya). The DYPG's aqueous prints resist the representational and imperial eyes of the West in favor of dialectical images that disclose movement, liminality, and resilience.

THE ORIGINS OF A DOMINICAN PRINT COLLECTIVE IN NEW YORK

The DYPG is itself diasporic in origin. Pepe Coronado and his family left an economically unstable DR in 1989 to settle in Austin, Texas. He had an interest in screenprinting and slowly began building his own business printing T-shirts, Caribe Graphics, which specialized in designs inspired by the culture of the Taíno, an indigenous Caribbean people who were the principal inhabitants of Hispaniola at the time of European contact in the late fifteenth century. He began his artistic education at the Laguna Gloria Art Museum, where one of his instructors, Sam Coronado (1943–2013), a man who incidentally shared Pepe's surname, encouraged his interest in printmaking.[4] Sam Coronado, whose workshop I discussed in the previous chapter, had recently turned his East Austin painting studio into a fine-art printmaking atelier, and he wasted no time recruiting Pepe to become a printer for the workshop.[5] Pepe Coronado served as master printer for the Serie Project's residency program from 1994 to 1997, and introduced many participants to printmaking techniques. During his time at the studio, Pepe worked with dozens of resident artists, including South Central Texas–based painters John Hernandez, César Martínez, Alex Rubio, and Liliana Wilson.

Sam Coronado modeled the Serie Project after the renowned Chicanx flagship workshop Self Help Graphics, which I introduced in chapter 1. The East Los Angeles studio, spearheaded by artists Sister Karen Boccalero, Frank

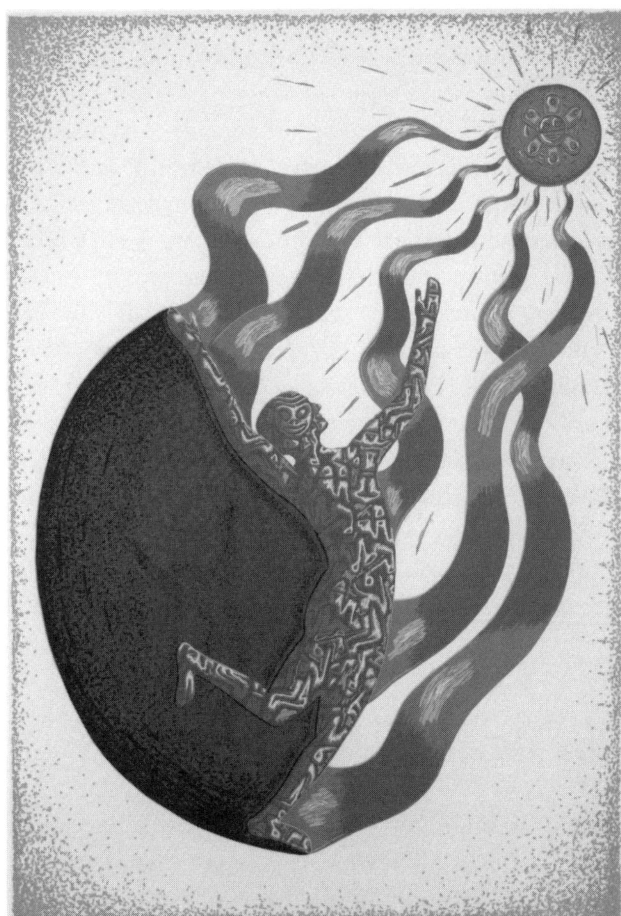

4.4. Pepe Coronado, *Bailando con el Sol*, 1996. Screenprint on paper, 22 × 15 inches; edition of sixty-two printed by José Alpuche and published by Self Help Graphics, Los Angeles. Courtesy of the artist.

Hernández, Milton Jurado, and romantic/artistic couple Carlos Bueno and Antonio Ibañez, officially incorporated in 1973, making it one of the longest-running art workshops in the country, after the Robert Blackburn Printmaking Workshop, in New York (est. 1948), and the Brandywine Workshop and Archives (est. 1972), in Philadelphia.[6] One of Self Help's core initiatives was the Experimental Silkscreen Atelier Program (est. 1983), which supported residencies for emerging artists to collaborate with master printers on limited editions. Sam Coronado was a resident artist in 1988 and 1991 and claimed that his time at Self Help inspired his vision for an Austin workshop. Once Pepe was brought into the fold, Sam also encouraged and recommended the younger artist for a Self Help residency.

Made in collaboration with Self Help Graphics' master printer José (Joe) Alpuche, Pepe Coronado's 1996 print *Bailando con el Sol* (fig. 4.4) contemplates the connection between the sun and an earthbound human figure.

Covered from head to toe in an intricate tribal tattoo drawn from Taíno designs, the figure's outstretched left arm extends toward the red-orange curvilinear rays of the Taíno sun god. Coronado was drawn to the iconography of the Taíno following the quincentennial celebrations of Columbus's arrival on the island of Quisqueya.[7] In our interview, the artist suggested that his Taíno-inspired print series responded to Dominican president Joaquín Antonio Balaguer's Hispanophile regime and in particular criticized the construction of the Columbus Lighthouse Memorial (known as *Faro a Colón*), inaugurated in 1992.[8] "It was just that lack of respect," he explained. "In that courtyard there are these massive lights that at night they turn on, and it's supposed to project the [Christian] cross in the sky, but they built this in one of the poorest neighborhoods in Santo Domingo, displacing tons of people. When they turn it on, the whole *barrio* goes dark, because there is not enough electricity."[9] Coronado's series honored the first inhabitants of the island, who were decimated under that cross.[10]

The artist's residency at Self Help Graphics opened his eyes to the power of collaboration. He was part of the twenty-ninth atelier in 1996, which included artists Sam Baray, Mita Cuaron, Sonya Fe, Eduardo Oropeza, and Ricardo Duffy, who had been invited back to make his iconic print *The New Order*, discussed at length in chapter 1. A draft of a July 1996 letter addressed to Sister Karen and her staff expresses Coronado's gratitude for the residency experience. He writes:

> I just wanted to thank you for the opportunity to have a print made at Self-Help Graphics. I am very satisfied with how the print turned out, and so far it has been received well here in Austin. As a printer, it was also a valuable experience to work with Joe [Alpuche] and Carlos [his assistant]. They were extremely helpful and I learned a lot from working with them. I plan to put some of the techniques I learned into practice at Coronado Studios. I look forward to working with Self-Help Graphics again sometime in the future.[11]

The printmaking techniques and the philosophy of collaboration that Coronado cultivated at Self Help had an enduring influence on his artistic practice. As National Gallery of Art curator E. Carmen Ramos has noted, "The collective spirit Pepe witnessed among Chicanx and other Latino artists would leave a strong impression."[12] In summer 1997, Coronado left Austin for the mid-Atlantic, where he continued honing his skills in printmaking, digital art, and photography, working with Pyramid Atlantic, the Hand Print Workshop International, and as an instructor at the Corcoran College of Arts and Design and the Maryland Institute College of Art.[13] A fortuitous move to New York City in 2006 brought him closer to a network of Dominican American artists, and his vision for the DYPG became not just feasible but necessary.

Most Dominican American printmakers have struggled to make themselves visible in a field dominated by long-standing Nuyorican and Chicanx graphic-art traditions. Groundbreaking exhibitions such as Yasmin Ramirez's 1999 *Pressing the Point* at El Museo del Barrio document the synchronous print activism in US-based Puerto Rican and Chicanx artistic communities during the 1970s.[14] The absence of Dominican artists from that discourse perhaps indicates their relatively late entry into the arena of socially committed Latinx printmaking. Ramos explains:

> Unlike Chicanos and Nuyoricans of the 1960s and 1970s—many of whom were born or raised in the United States and strongly identified with the social movements of this tumultuous period in American (US) history—Dominicans started arriving in the United States in large numbers in the early 1960s, and continued thereafter in a steady stream. Given their "late" arrival, it would take some time before the Dominican American community would come to be known as such.[15]

The DYPG's collective enterprise was partly an effort to stake a claim in this field, as the practitioners were aware that a group initiative had the potential to accomplish more than any one artist could achieve on his or her own. The relative obscurity of the Dominican print tradition also extended back to the island, whose limited infrastructure often required Dominican masters like Rosa Tavárez to seek validation and exhibition opportunities abroad.[16]

Although inspired by Coronado Studio and Self Help Graphics, the intent and operations of the DYPG differed from those studios' on a number of points. First, it is a print collective, similar to collectives such as Los de Abajo in Los Angeles, not a brick-and-mortar workshop that requires overhead and extensive fundraising.[17] "We don't have a studio museum . . . we don't have an art center . . . we don't even have a cultural center," explains Coronado, a state of affairs that forces the DYPG to be "ambulatory, flexible."[18] Second, the DYPG's collaborative portfolios are themed so that they lend themselves to stand-alone exhibitions. And last, since the artists in the group range from emerging to midcareer to established, the collective portfolios open doors for those who are less recognized. Perhaps in contrast to the pioneers of Nuyorican and Chicanx graphic arts—many of whom were self-taught, community-based artists who took a service-based approach to their practice—the DYPG attracted printmakers with art-school training who hoped to compete in the New York art market.[19]

But what I find most striking about this collective vision is that, by naming the pilot project DYPG, the artists geocoded the atelier's production. Taller Boricua in East Harlem (f. 1970), which champions the work of Puerto Rican artists born on the nonsovereign island or in New York, served as an important reference point. In the case of the DYPG, what did it mean for these DR- and New York-born artists to reclaim a term that the Dominican elite associated with a criminal underclass? How would collaborative printmaking respond to the call of defining or debating the Dominican diasporic experience? How could paper and ink conjure nostalgic images of a lost island home within another island? How could DYPG artists use printmaking to attribute spatial meaning to the water crossings they must undertake in the back-and-forth between islands? And what did it mean to inscribe these portfolios with histories seldom written? Prioritizing these issues, the collective turned their attention to the geopolitics of representation, exploring the effects of colonialism, intervention, exile, and racism on those who live between these islands.

Water imagery and an intense interest in geography seemed to pervade most of the prints in this first portfolio. Yunior Chiqui Mendoza (b. 1964) conjured the waters of the Hudson and East rivers in a playful print titled *Bananhattan* (fig. 4.5), which imagines the island of Manhattan as a giant Warholesque banana with a bright red place marker over the Dominican enclave of Washington Heights. Mendoza was a recent transplant to New York after having left his faculty teaching post at the Escuela Nacional de Bellas Artes in Santo Domingo in 2006. It is perhaps no wonder that the New York subway map would appear in his print, crisscrossing land and waterways. René de los Santos (b. 1953) offered a different perspective in his black-and-white woodcut *Cigüita Cibaeña en Nueva York* (fig. 4.6), placing viewers in front of the Upper New York Bay and the George Washington Bridge. We look across the water to a series of tall apartment buildings on the other side of the bridge, but in a magical-realist turn we observe the view from a tree branch on the right, where a Cigüa Palmera (*Dulus dominicus*) sits perched. The national bird of the Dominican Republic is a species unique to the island of Hispaniola, and yet de los Santos imagines it standing watch over the estuary. But this is no ordinary bird. It has the head of a human and the body of a bird, reminiscent of the mythical creatures favored by the Symbolists, and its hair flows directly into the linework that makes up the patchy, windblown sky. Below and at center, a boat sits in the bay, perhaps as a symbol of being able to navigate these waters.

As these artists were coming together to discuss their experiences in diaspora, intellectuals like Lorgia García-Peña were theorizing how the Dominican nation-state projected exclusionary borders around Dominicanidad (Dominicanness) in the form of dictions that denied and obscured the presence of racialized Dominicans. Of particular importance to this study, García-Peña views those forced to migrate and inhabit the liminal identity of Dominican York as subjects of border embodiment.[20] She triangulates those borders

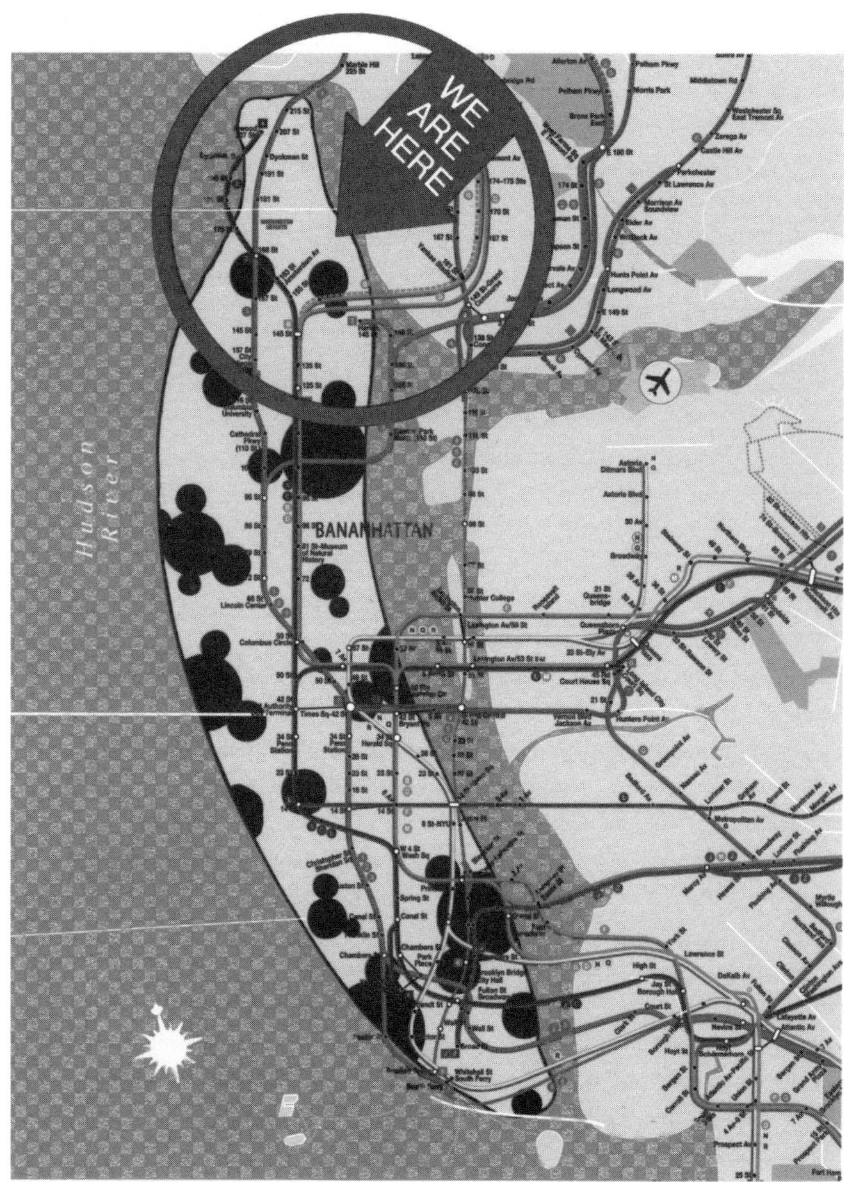

4.5. Yunior Chiqui Mendoza, *Bananhattan*, 2010. Inkjet and screenprint on BFK Rives, image: 9½ × 7 inches; sheet: 15 × 11¼ inches; edition of twenty-five printed by the artist, Reynaldo García Pantaleón, and Pepe Coronado at Coronado printstudio for the portfolio *Manifestaciones* by the Dominican York Proyecto Gráfica. Courtesy of the artist.

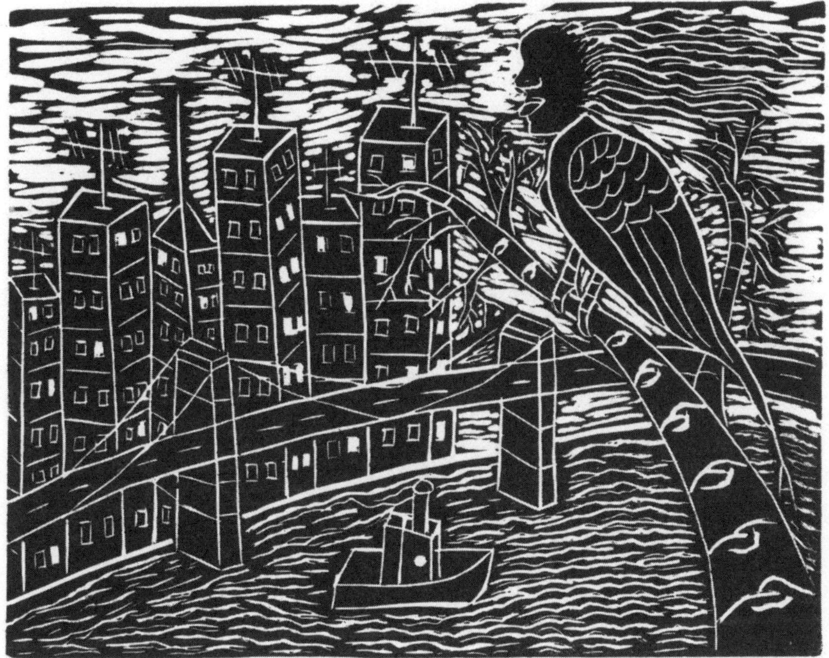

4.6. René de los Santos, *Cigüita Cibaeña en Nueva York*, 2010. Woodcut and screen-print on BFK Rives, image: 7 × 9 inches; sheet: 12 × 15 inches; edition of twenty-five printed by the artist and Pepe Coronado at Coronado printstudio for the portfolio *Manifestaciones* by the Dominican York Proyecto Gráfica. Courtesy of the artist.

between the US, DR, and Haiti in order to stress how these exclusions, often phrased in everyday dictions such as *rayano, prieto,* the sexualized *dominicana,* and *dominicano ausente,* are products of colonial history. Whereas much of borderlands and transnational literature emphasizes geographic points of in-betweenness, García-Peña proposed the racialized Dominican body as both the carrier of the burdens of coloniality and the site of agency that can contradict official discourses of the state and create new forms of belonging.[21] In the next section I look at how DYPG artists helped create what she calls "archives of contradiction" by opposing the marginalization and alterity of racialized Dominican bodies.

CENTERING THE BLACK ATLANTIC

In 2000, the Santo Domingo–born New York artist Scherezade García (b. 1966) represented the Dominican Republic at the Havana Biennial with *Pa-*

raíso, an installation of painted crib mattresses bathed in the light of a palm tree–filled sky. Each mattress featured a barely discernible dark-skinned angel embellished with elaborate and ornamental brushwork.[22] The reflective quality of the plastic-encased mattresses, in conjunction with the skyward-oriented video projection, made the angels appear to emerge out of water. In his catalogue essay for García's exhibition, art historian Edward Sullivan framed the complex visuality of *Paraíso* as a "baroque vision," focusing on formal dynamism; here I wish to discuss how the racialized bodies of the artist's brown-skinned icons commented on the precarious condition of exile and the frailty of paradise.[23]

Born to a politically active family of African, French, and Native American heritage, García immigrated to the US in 1986 to pursue a BFA at the Parsons School of Design. She had recently graduated from the prestigious Altos de Chavón School of Design in La Romana, on the southeast coast of the DR, a site that I will return to in the next section. Through a partnership with Parsons, Altos de Chavón sent a small number of promising students to complete their studies in the US, and García's portfolio earned her a full scholarship. When she arrived in New York in the mid-1980s, there were few Dominican artists in the city. But within a decade, after several waves of *Chavoneros* (alums of Altos de Chavón) settled in the city, Dominicans became a sizable presence in the New York art world. Among them, García credits the performance artist Josefina Báez as a key figure who brought Dominican artists together through festivals, theater performances, and exhibitions.[24] In this creative milieu, García met a number of prominent artists, including German Pérez and Freddy Rodríguez; some of them would become lifelong friends and mentors. However, it was Báez's pioneering efforts to articulate the sentiments of a "flagless nation" and politically reclaim the derogatory term "Dominican York" that were particularly important to island-born artists like García who felt alienated from their homeland. By the time García met Pepe Coronado at a Northern Manhattan Arts Alliance review panel in 2009, New York–based Dominican American artists had made several efforts to work and exhibit collectively, but none of these projects focused on the medium of printmaking.

In *Day Dreaming/Soñando Despierta* (2010; fig. 4.7), García transformed the island of Manhattan into a tropical playground. She intervened in the landscape by superimposing colorful external forms on a panoramic rendering of the city grid. A blue-and-white banana tree rises out of Central Park; two red silhouettes of fruit-shaped airplanes hover over the island, and paper boats imprinted with the facade of a high-rise arrive on its shores. At the bottom of the image García included the profile of a dark-skinned figure. Difficult to discern, at first glance the viewer is likely to read this figure as a landmass, only later to discover facial features in this unknown territory.

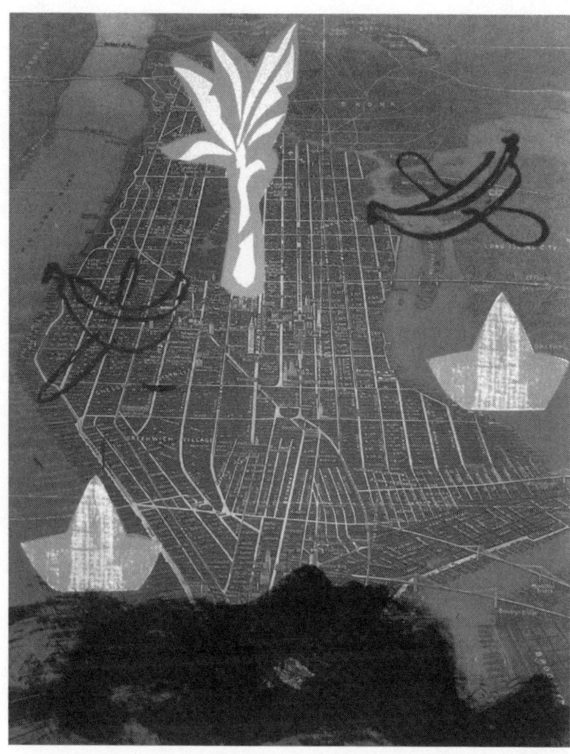

4.7. Scherezade García, *Day Dreaming/Soñando Despierta*, 2010. Screenprint and inkjet on BFK Rives, image: 9 × 7 inches; sheet: 15 × 12 inches; edition of twenty-five printed by the artist, Alex Guerrero, and Pepe Coronado at Coronado printstudio for the portfolio *Manifestaciones* by the Dominican York Proyecto Gráfica. Courtesy of the artist.

García reorients the viewer to a coordinate plane that contrasts the bird's-eye view of the gridded metropolis with the racialized Dominican body. The figure is dark yet translucent, as if the brownish-red ink has been distributed haphazardly across the bottom of the sheet. In an artist statement, García notes, "La gran figura marrón . . . evoca poderosamente la pesadez de un sueño agobiado por el recuerdo. Es un sueño perturbado, enredado en la despiadada claridad y rectitud lineal del mapa." (The great brown figure powerfully evokes the heaviness of a dream overwhelmed by memory. It is a disturbed dream, tangled in the ruthless clarity and linear rectitude of the map.)[25] According to the art historian Abigail Lapin Dardashti, the artist's black angels—a hallmark of her work—are part of a "strategy to develop her critique of colonialism and its legacy, including Trujillo's Indo-Hispanic identity discourse."[26] The dictatorship of Rafael Trujillo (1930–1961) invested in an educational system that promoted Dominicans' Spanish and indigenous roots and dismissed their African heritage in order to distinguish them from Haitians.[27] It was not simply an ideological position: Trujillo's anti-Haitianism enabled extreme forms of state-sanctioned violence, most notably the massacre of more than fifteen thousand ethnic Haitians by machete in October of 1937.[28] In her art, García counters this racist ideology of negrophobia and

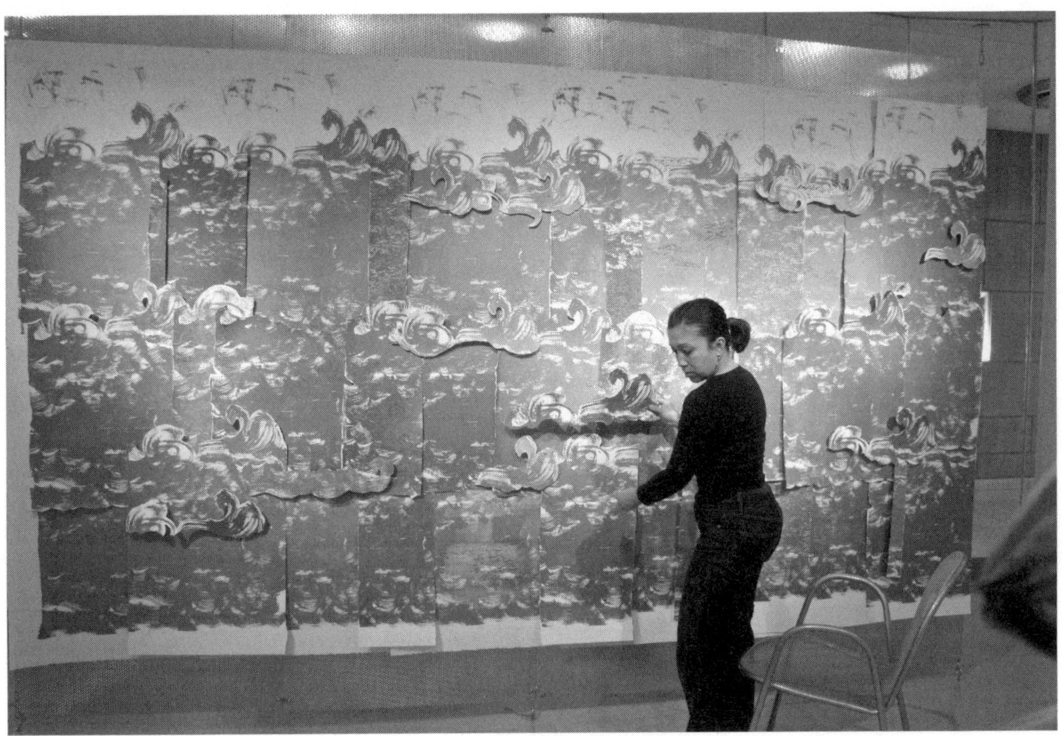

4.8. Scherezade García, *Sea of Wonder*, from the series *Theories of Freedom*, 2011. Screenprint on paper, cutouts, pins, variable dimensions. Courtesy of the artist.

white supremacy with mulatto icons symbolic of a Black and Spanish nation, a more accurate if still-contested view of the DR. Dardashti adds that García's "mulatto/mulatta figures are often submerged in water," as we see in the placement of the figure in New York harbor in *Day Dreaming*, "recalling the Middle Passage and also contemporary migration to the US."[29] Water has been a constant throughout her oeuvre. As the art historian Olga Herrera points out, García conceives of the Atlantic as a "gigantic transcontinental liquid highway of marine routes, mobility, and carrier of ancestral DNA."[30] This sentiment is echoed by artists across the pond like the Ghanaian-born British artist John Akomfrah, who noted, "It is impossible to overstate the significance of the sea in the formation of the African diaspora and Black identity."[31]

Perhaps as a result of her participation in the DYPG, García began extending her experiments in print to her mural practice, which over time transformed from figuration to abstraction and from local concerns to the global implications of diaspora. Her large-scale mural installation *Sea of Wonder*, from the series *Theories of Freedom* (2011; fig. 4.8), collaged silk-screened sheets of paper resembling waves in a monochromatic palette of gray. García animated the sea by adding three-dimensional cutouts coming off the wall to signal the volatile motion of wave crests. In this *Sea of Wonder*, she captured the ambiguity so central to her work. Lapin Dardashti explains that her focus on water "addresses the inevitable physical obstacles faced by Caribbean immigrants coming to the United States, and also identifies the image of a seascape without a horizon as a vision of hope for a better life across the water."[32] Her floating mulatta figure in *Day Dreaming* likewise expresses the dreams of new Caribbean immigrants in Manhattan who yearn to tropicalize this island but also the melancholy of an impossible return. García described the Dominican American's paradoxical position as "*morir soñando*," to dream of love, joy, and possibility but to die nonetheless.[33]

García's submerged mulatta figures center the Black Atlantic in the discourses of Dominicanidad. This poses a direct challenge to much of the island's official discourses of identity, which privilege Spanish and Taíno history, as is the case with many Latin American countries that favor mestizaje. Her oeuvre consistently reminds viewers of what is an undeniable Black heritage, stemming from the DR's ground-zero position, as it was the first territory where slaves were brought from Africa into the New World, but also the longer history of free Blacks who have shaped Dominican culture. Centering the Black Atlantic is an important strategy shared by other Latinx artists of African descent like the Afro-Panamanian artist Arturo Lindsay (b. 1946). Born in Colón, Panama, another historical slave-port city, and reared in Brooklyn, New York, Lindsay developed a series titled *Children of Middle Passage*, which memorialized the many youngsters lost at sea when faced with the brutal conditions of slave ships. For his 2001 residency at the Brandywine Workshop in Philadelphia, the Spelman professor produced ten monochromatic portrait prints of these children.[34] *Oni of Lagos* from the series shows a spectral, black, silhouetted body emerging from a ship (fig. 4.9). Lindsay labored over the subject's delicate facial features, which he made angelic through a pointillist halo and the architectural illusion of an altar. Instruments of confinement such as leg shackles appear as sources of their suffering. By naming the children with a traditional African name tied to a village, Lindsay hopes their lives can be acknowledged and their spirits laid to rest. In these works, García and Lindsay challenge the disavowal of Blackness that continues to plague Latinidad.

In one of his most cited articles, the literary critic Silvio Torres-Saillant reflects on the complexity of racial paradigms in the Dominican Republic.[35] He asks how a society that represents the "cradle of blackness in the Americas" came to be in such denial of its overwhelming Black and mulatto population. For Torres-Saillant, the answer is of course history, particularly how Dominicans navigated the contested sovereignty of their state with Haiti, the US, and Europe. The first event that precipitated the deracialization of Dominicans

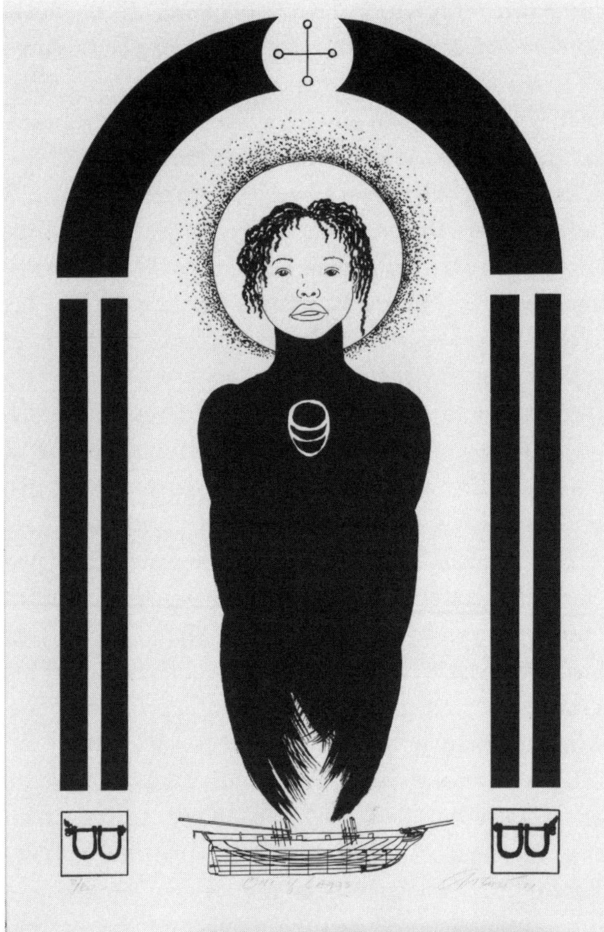

4.9. Arturo Lindsay, *Oni of Lagos*, from the series *Children of Middle Passage*, 2001. Offset lithograph, sheet and image: 22 × 15 inches; edition of eighty published by the Brandywine Workshop, Philadelphia. Courtesy of the artist and the Brandywine Workshop and Archives.

was the decline of the plantation economy and subsequent impoverishment of the colony of Santo Domingo.[36] This economic shift made the hierarchies of race and class, slave and master obsolete, leading to a majority free Black population and the flourishing of interracial marriages. By the seventeenth century, mulattas and mulattos were the ethnic majority in the DR. As a new republic in 1844 seeking official recognition from the US and Europe, the ruling classes sought to distinguish themselves from the "rebellious" nature of Black Haitians, a negrophobic position that Torres-Saillant argues drew significantly from North American sources.[37] But he also noted the presence of Afro-Dominicans who fought bravely against the Spanish in the War of Restoration (1863–1865), when Spain tried to recolonize the fledgling republic.[38] Their most pressing concern was the return of the institution of slavery, which had been abolished as a result of Haiti's efforts to decolonize Hispaniola. The Dominican concept of race, which had practically been decolorized by the end of the nineteenth century, found correspondence in Latin American theories of mestizaje built in opposition to US imperialism.[39] Although these favored mixed race, they nonetheless privileged whiteness or an approximation to whiteness. But it was Trujillo's regime that succeeded in manipulating this open concept of race. Torres-Saillant explains how his regime "gave currency to the term *indio* (Indian) to describe the complexion of people of mixed ancestry," by imposing it through official government documents and willfully eroding the connections to African heritage.[40]

The DYPG artist Miguel Luciano's *Detrás de la Oreja* (2010; fig. 4.10) makes visible this incongruity. How could a country with 90 percent Afro-descendants still identify through Trujillo's *indio* fictions? Luciano's print fea-

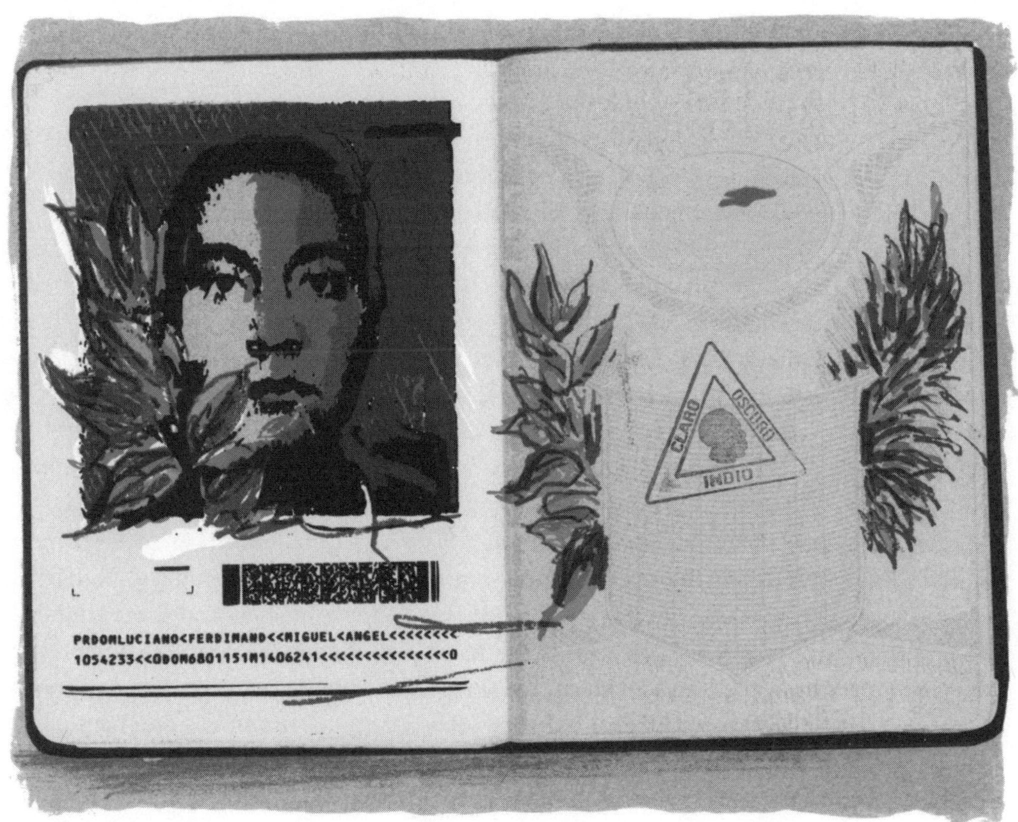

4.10. Miguel Luciano, *Detrás de la Oreja*, 2010. Screenprint and rubber stamp on BFK Rives, image: 7 × 9 inches; sheet: 12 × 15 inches; edition of twenty-five printed by the artist and Alex Guerrero at Bullrider Studio for the portfolio *Manifestaciones* by the Dominican York Proyecto Gráfica. Courtesy of the artist.

tures a Dominican passport opened to the photo page, where the artist's face is composed of three distinct skin tones. The rubber stamp that appears on the following page triangulates the racial terminology of *indio claro* [light-skinned Indian] and *indio oscuro* [dark-skinned Indian] that persists in these government documents, creating a racialized gradation of an essentially fabricated category. The sociologist Ginetta Candelario notes that, since the nineteenth century, the phrase "Black behind the ears" has been part of Dominican vernacular, at once distinguishing the national body from Haitians and reluctantly admitting the predominance of African ancestry among the DR's citizenry.[41] *Detrás de la Oreja*'s embellished tropical passport is another example of the Dominican body resisting an oppressive system of classification. Unable to register the subject's complexion, Luciano (b. 1966) thwarts the system's desire for a racial order that elides Blackness. The experience of leaving his homeland for New York perhaps afforded the artist sufficient physical and psychological distance to question how those vexed terms follow individuals into a new geography.

But another transformation occurs in the consciousness of Dominican migrants that reverses the legacy of the Trujillato. According to García-Peña, a dual exile occurs for Dominicans forced to leave their island nation only to "encounter another form of exile as they become racialized into a US minority."[42] While many Dominican immigrants, including Luciano and García, grew up believing in their "racially Indian and culturally Hispanic" origins, the racial system of this new geography identifies them as Black.[43] Torres-Saillant adds, "It soon becomes obvious to Dominican immigrants that the larger US society does not care to distinguish between them and Haitians," given the one-drop rule that renders them both nonwhite.[44] The 1.5 generation (those who emigrated to the US as children or adolescents) and second generation will most likely self-identify as Black, reversing Trujillo's malevolent negation. This development of a Black or Afro-Latinx consciousness in diaspora leads many artists and return migrants to question the antiquated systems of classification in the DR based on negrophobia and white supremacy. This conscientiousness is particularly strong for Dominican women of color in the US, who must contend with three intersecting matrices of oppression: race, class, and gender. García's *Day Dreaming* exemplifies the "racexile" condition that the spatial sphere projects on the Dominican body. Submerged under water, her dark-skinned mulatta figure daydreams of planting banana trees in Central Park, an intention the artist describes as demonstrating that "We're here to stay."

Another water-based female archetype that emerges in this portfolio is the *ciguapa*. Julia Alvarez begins her short story "The Secret Footprints" with the following description: "On an island not too far away and in a time not

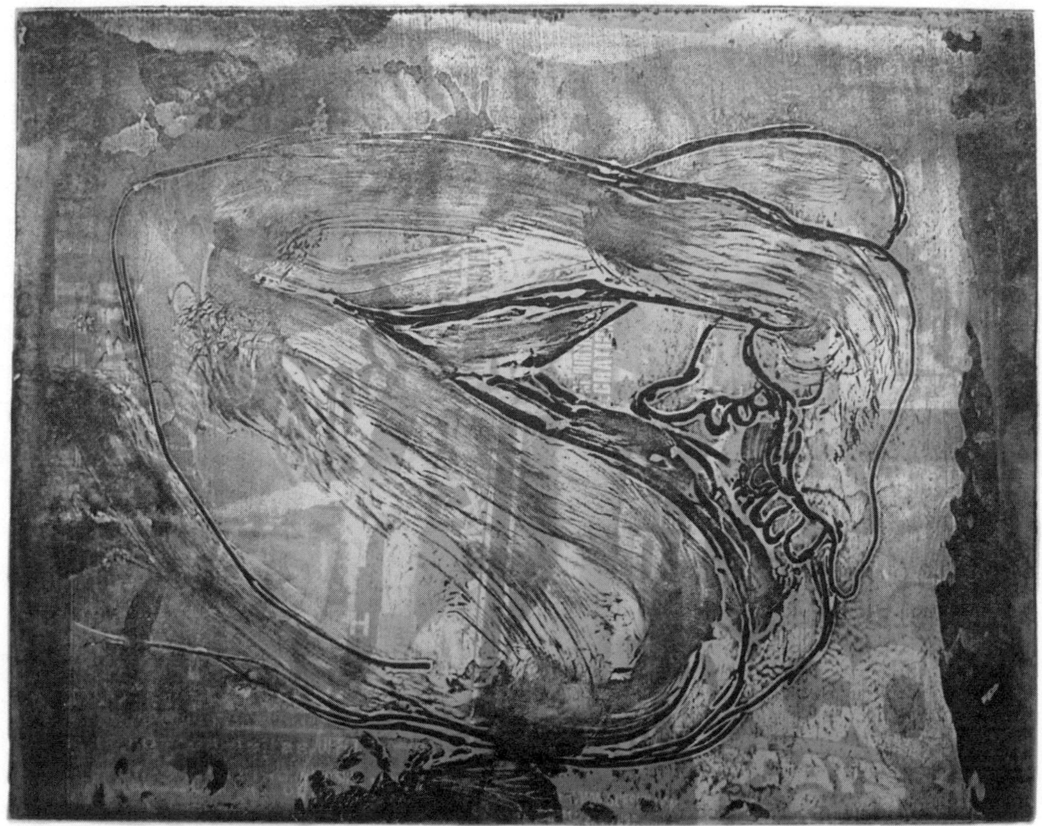

4.11. Rider Ureña, *My Girl on the Floor*, 2010. Inkjet and silk aquatint on BFK Rives, image: 7 × 9 inches; sheet: 12 × 15 inches; edition of twenty-five printed by the artist and Pepe Coronado at Bullrider Studio for the portfolio *Manifestaciones* by the Dominican York Proyecto Gráfica. Courtesy of the artist.

so long ago lived a secret tribe called the ciguapas. They made their homes underwater in cool blue caves hung with seashells and seaweed. They came out on land to hunt for food only at night because they were so fearful of humans."[45] Described as mesmerizing, beautiful creatures with backward pointing feet and long hair, ciguapas are the product of nineteenth-century nationalist and Indigenist literature. Ginetta Candelario explains that writers like Francisco Javier Angulo Guridi, who published *La Ciguapa* in 1866, used the figure to contend with the nation's contradictions of being both colonizer and colonized, enslaver and enslaved, immigrant and native-born.[46] Rider Ureña (b. 1972) conjures her sensual image in a print titled *My Girl on the Floor* (fig. 4.11). Using a digital collage of flyers that advertise erotic dancers and access to voluptuous women as an inkjet print in the background, Ureña overlaid a silk aquatint that made the colorful flyers recede to the point of unreadability. At center, he placed a partial human figure supine. The curvature of the linework suggests that both of the figure's knees are bent and their backward feet hang menacingly over their genitalia. The vivacious surface of the print, with splotches of black, gray, and white ink and visible brushwork, lends the appearance of an underwater scene. Ureña described his reference to the mythical figure as a metaphor for those immigrants who come seeking the American Dream but are easily mislead and lose their way. However, as a multivalent archetypal figure the ciguapa also embodies freedom. She can evade capture like the runaway slave, and in this agentic potential Candelario reads the formulation of a new epistemology: *ciguapear*, a way for the underdog, the vulnerable, the marginal to reject and undermine the machinations of racemaking in Dominican nationalism.[47]

WATER CROSSINGS

Leaving one's island homeland in search of a better life presents a unique set of challenges for many Dominican migrants. Unlike the perilous land journeys discussed in the preceding chapter, Dominicans must face the dangers of water crossings, navigating the treacherous waters of the Mona Passage that connect the Atlantic with the Gulf of Mexico. This stretch of ninety miles, with frigid and choppy waters, has claimed the lives of thousands of men and women hoping to make the undetected journey to the US territory of Puerto Rico and from there eventually to the United States. There are four ways that undocumented Dominicans pursue maritime migration: on the traditional *yola* (large wooden boat), in a smaller boat with a self-employed captain, in an improvised group of family and friends, and finally in a pleasure craft (sailboat or speedboat) for those who can afford the steep price.[48] At least 10 percent of the Dominican Republic's GDP comes from remittances of Dominicans abroad, and this dependence makes the government tacitly condone smuggling, while their navy profits from bribes.[49]

DYPG artist Luanda Lozano (b. 1973) honors these victims of shipwrecks in her etching *Sálvame Santo* (2010; fig. 4.12). The pyramidal portrait composition shows the bust outline of a saint who gazes upwards with a slight tilt of the head. Lozano's confident and organic lines capture the expression of suffering and sacrifice associated with the adoration of saints, as well as the exaggerated gestures of their baroque sculptures. There is a sensual quality to the various marks made on the plate indicating stamping, ruptures, and circular movement. Viewers can almost trace the hand of the artist drawing on the copper plate with bold and fine lines that give a spatial and tactile dimension

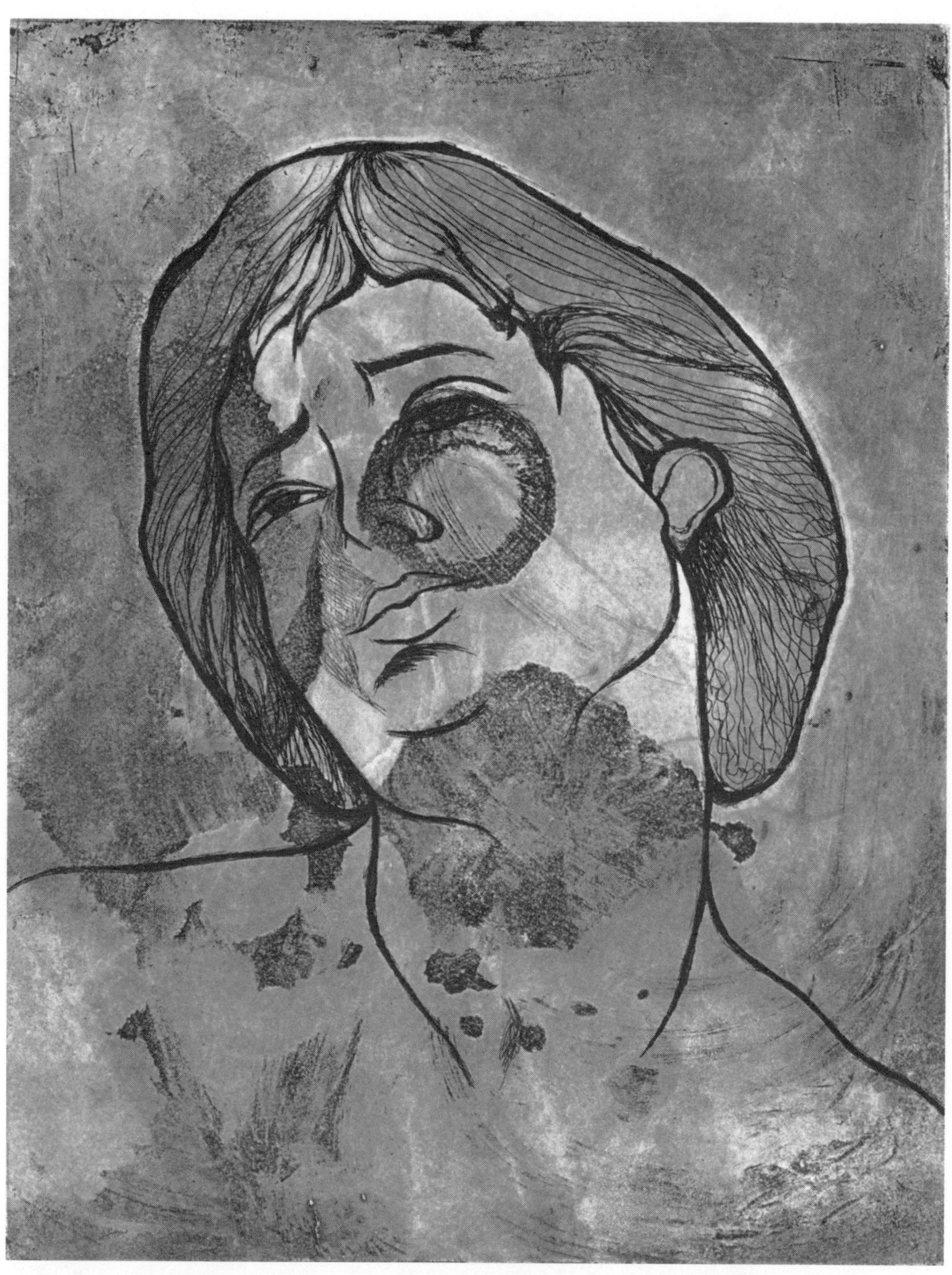

4.12. Luanda Lozano, *Sálvame Santo*, 2010. Etching and chine collé on BFK Rives, image: 7 × 9 inches; sheet: 12 × 15 inches; edition of twenty-five printed by the artist at Manhattan Graphics Center and the Robert Blackburn Printmaking Workshop for the portfolio *Manifestaciones* by the Dominican York Proyecto Gráfica. Courtesy of the artist.

to the subject's flowing hair. But the most dynamic aspect of this small print comes from the painterly layers of aquamarine blues and chine collé emerald greens that create translucent, timeless auras for the religious icon, whose expression recalls the scripture "When you pass through waters, I will be with you; through rivers, you shall not be swept away."[50]

The idea for *Sálvame Santo* came about as Lozano watched a TV segment in which the sole survivor of a shipwreck gave testimony of a tragic night when forty-five fellow passengers on his boat had perished. *Yolas* are typically thirty to forty feet long, eight to twelve feet wide, and can carry upwards of forty passengers.[51] But smugglers typically pack the boats with almost twice as many passengers in order to pocket a minimum of a thousand dollars for each one. These illegal boat rides leave from coastal towns, most prominently Sabana de la Mar, under the cover of night and head east on what is usually a twenty-four-hour journey.[52] They must evade detection by the US Coast Guard as they approach US territorial water limits, as well as the Puerto Rican land-based Border Patrol, the only US Customs and Border Protection agency located outside the continental US.[53] Lozano was visibly moved and teary-eyed as she recounted his story: the man on the television recalled witnessing the boat collapse and seeing how the passengers prayed and begged for safety, some holding dearly to pocket-sized prints of saints, before their bodies entered the water. The most poignant moment that clearly marked her and inspired the work was when the interviewers asked if he would try and do it again, knowing everything he had suffered, lost at sea for ten days before his rescue, and he said, "When I come home and I see my children with no food, of course, I would do it again."[54]

Chronic poverty motivates thousands of Dominicans to risk their lives every year in search of work. As Frank Graziano notes in his ethnographic study of Dominican migrants, "Unemployment, underemployment, the insufficiency of infrastructure and social services, the high cost of food in relation to low income, inadequate housing, and social marginalization all contribute to making yola voyages an attractive escape toward a better future."[55] According to Jorge Duany, Dominicans are the largest and most visible ethnic minority in Puerto Rico and are drawn there by the standard of living, which guarantees higher wages than those available back home.[56] These economic migrants may settle in Puerto Rico or attempt to make their way to the US with the purchase of a fake ID making them eligible to enter the US as Puerto Rican.

Perhaps because of her family's history of migrations, as well as her own journey to the US, this story resonated with Lozano. She was born, along with her twin brother, in the town of Humpata, Angola. Her Dominican parents named her after the capital and largest city of this former Portuguese colony.

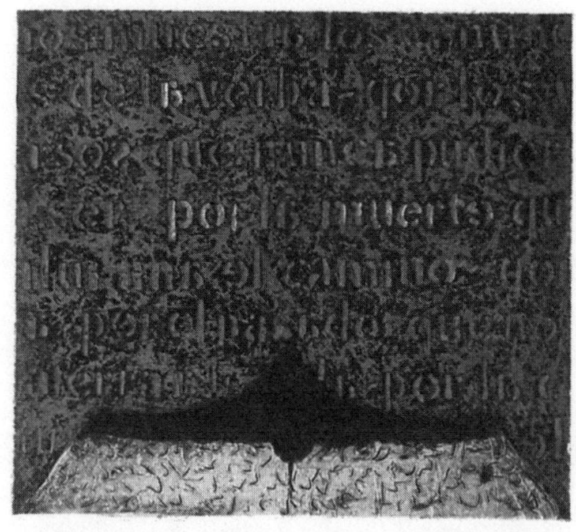

4.13. Ezequiel Taveras, *Cartas III*, from the series *Cartas*, 1998. Etching and chine collé, sheet and image: 12 × 15 inches; edition of twelve printed by the artist. Courtesy of the artist.

Her mother is said to have been pregnant before embarking on this journey to Africa. Lozano's father, an oncologist, had secured a job there through the Missionary Church after finishing his studies in Spain. Lozano's family lived there for about a year and a half and returned to the Dominican Republic just before Angola gained its independence in 1975 and descended into a chaotic civil war. Lozano grew up in the town of San Francisco de Macorís, and her interest in art developed early on as she watched her mother draw patterns for her dressmaking business. She began with after-school art classes and by the time she was in high school she had won a national competition in painting. Altos de Chavón, the school of art in La Romana, the same that Scherezade García attended, was the obvious next step in her development. She described those early college years as pure magic, living in a small community surrounded by artists. After her first printmaking class with Ezequiel Taveras, she knew printmaking was her calling. She grew addicted to the process, working late into the night. She spent so much time in the shop that a cot was set up next to the printing press so Lozano could sleep in the studio.

Taveras (b. 1965) describes Altos de Chavón as the Dominican Bauhaus. Its sprawling campus resembled a Mediterranean villa on a hillside overlooking the Chavón River, where Francis Ford Coppola filmed *Apocalypse Now* (1979).[57] Taveras began teaching at the art school in the early 1990s and would teach at the institution for almost two decades. He was trained at the Escuela Nacional de Bellas Artes in Santo Domingo, where he specialized in printmaking and sculpture, a fortuitous combination that led him to develop highly textured prints such as his series *Cartas* (fig. 4.13). A group critique with Colombian Master Omar Rayo helped launch his international-exhibition trajectory, which recently included representing the Dominican

Republic at the Venice Biennale in 2019. Every graduate of the program describes Altos de Chavón as magical. But Taveras explained the reasons why it was so special.

> He enseñado muchos sitios y en muchos lugares he dado muchos talleres, pero Chavón era especial. Es un sitio, imagínate esto . . . eso era un desierto, y en esa colina, al borde del río, se inventan hacer esta villa que es como una inspiración medieval. Y era como una especie de kibutz [comuna]. Porque quien origina Chavón es un judío. Entonces era una especie de kibutz porque eran las casitas y estaban entonces, talleres de cerámica, talleres de telares, un taller de serigrafía y gráfica, y la escuela de diseño . . . y los muchachos que estudiaban allí vivían, y había muchachos que no salían de allí en seis meses. Tu entraba, comía, dormía y trabajaba. Y nosotros también. Eso daba una sensación muy particular porque entonces teníamos horarios de clase, pero ese horario de clase no era rígido en el sentido de que realmente yo podía estar en aula trabajando con los muchachos hasta la una de la mañana.[58]

It was the synergy between programs, mediums, social classes, and artists that drove the intense production of students at Altos.[59] Five of the artists from the DYPG attended the school: iliana emilia garcía, Scherezade García, Luando Lozano, Miguel Luciano, and Rider Ureña. In such a dynamic environment, students like Lozano flourished. Taveras's printmaking courses introduced her to woodcut, linocut, collagraphs, and intaglio, in the last of which he notes that his student, Lozano, far exceeded her teacher.

The intense two-year program gave her an associate's degree in fine arts, and afterwards Lozano continued her education at the Parsons School of Design, in New York. She arrived in 1992, the year that marked the quincentennial of "discovery." Her friend and fellow Dominican artist Julio Valdez, another recent transplant, introduced her to the African American artist Robert Blackburn (1920–2003). This unexpected encounter allowed Lozano to continue honing her skills in printmaking. At the time Lozano was only a senior at Parsons and unsure that Blackburn would grant such a novice access to the printmaking studio he ran at 55 West 17th Street. Lozano recalled in our interview that he had noticed her hesitation and said, "You can come and use the shop . . . bring your paper and work . . . you don't have to say anything else."[60] Founded in 1947 and active to this day, Blackburn's Printmaking Workshop (PMW) had a reputation for opening the door to artists. Curlee Raven Holton, who was a visiting artist, noted, "For many artists new to the city, the workshop was the only open door that would embrace them regardless of where they had come from or their professional rank."[61] Blackburn's inclusive politics reflected the painful memories of overt racism experienced during his long career but also his dedication to initiating other artists into advancing the medium. As the curator Deborah Cullen, former mentee and executor of his estate explains, "Blackburn's PMW deliberately fostered an environment that juxtaposed artists at different stages of their careers, utilizing a range of formal approaches, and hailing from around the world, to work in lithography, intaglio, relief, and photo processes."[62] Lozano gained experience in all these techniques, but it was the mentorship and camaraderie of the PMW that had the most lasting effects.

Unlike many of her peers, who began to focus on courting gallerists and dealers, Lozano chose to make a name for herself in the printmaking field with the support of her mentors. When I asked her what kept her coming back to the PMW, she said, "Because presses—you can find presses all over the place, but people are the main key."[63] The Peruvian printmaker Claudio Juárez (1938–2001), who had worked with Stanley William Hayter in Paris and resided in New York since the late 1960s, became her primary mentor at the PMW during the 1990s. Known for his technical virtuosity with intaglio techniques, Juárez would pass on this guarded knowledge showing Lozano how to achieve textured surfaces of graduating depth by cutting the copper with acid, those textures and finely graded lines visible in *Sálvame Santo*.[64] In addition to technical rigor, Lozano was inspired by watching fellow artists such as the Nuyorican Juan Sánchez, a Guggenheim Fellow, who could often be seen working on lithographs, and the Puerto Rican artist Javier Cintrón, whom she shared many hours with in the studio.[65] But it was Blackburn's consistent nudging that helped her become an internationally recognized printmaker. Lozano recalled how much he pushed her to participate in competitions and shows: "Bob was all the time telling me, 'There is an exhibition in Holland; get work ready to send in.'" She might hesitate, and he would continue, "Get ready to work, produce the work, and send it."[66] Since then, Lozano has shown her work in every major print exhibition in Sweden, Colombia, Japan, Argentina, France, Poland, Portugal, Bulgaria, Spain, Australia, Taiwan, and Holland.[67]

In 1998, she traveled to Puerto Rico as an invited artist representing the Dominican Republic at the *XII Bienal de San Juan del Grabado Latinoamericano y del Caribe*.[68] Photographs from her archive show Lozano sitting next to Blackburn, one of the members of the jury, while listening to the artists' talks in the galleries (fig. 4.14). Her connection to Blackburn would remain strong until his death and would be the subject of later works, but by the late 1990s she would also begin venturing out to other community spaces and printing at Manhattan Graphics Center. Shown in San Juan, her collagraph and etching *Figuras Fragmentadas por el Tiempo* (1997; fig. 4.15) has an un-

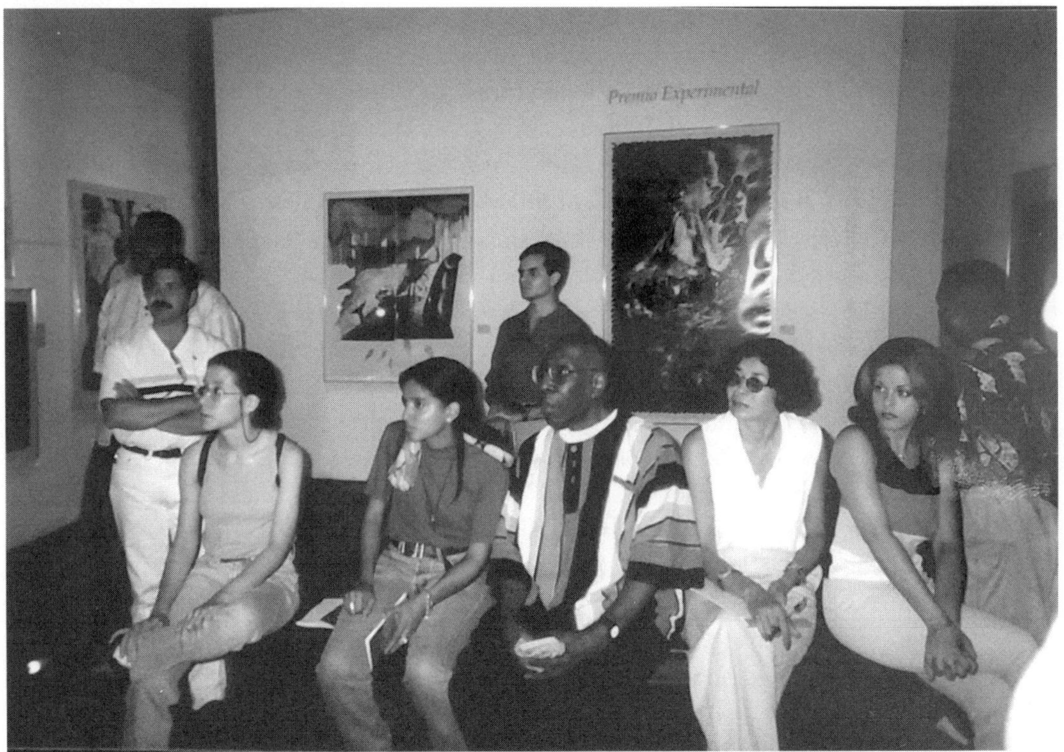

4.14. At center, Luanda Lozano and Robert Blackburn at *XII Bienal de San Juan del Grabado Latinoamericano y del Caribe*, San Juan, Puerto Rico, 1998.

usual, weathered animal-skin shape out of which emerge two small postcard-sized scenes with partial allusions to the human figure. A spiral Taíno symbol graces the top. The Puerto Rican artist Diógenes Ballester served as president of the jury that year and opened his catalogue essay with a historical perspective to explain the significance of these exhibition platforms, "The International Print Biennial and the Triennial tradition has become the principal way those working in the field exchange ideas, recognize the best production of work among graphic artists, reward those whose work is truly magnificent, [and] promote the value of print."[69] Thus it was a major milestone that Lozano had been invited to represent the DR, considering diaspora artists are rarely granted that honor.

Lozano brought all this experience and technical expertise to the nascent DYPG community in 2010. When Moses Ros-Suárez invited her to one of the early meetings, she was excited to have found diasporic artists from her island homeland who shared her passion for printmaking. Lozano's work had never been overtly political or direct at alluding to social issues. She was resistant to the idea that one had to perform a particular identity as an artist or base one's work in the stereotypical tropicalizations expected from artists of the Caribbean. It was a formal position espoused by modernists like Blackburn, a Black artist of Jamaican descent, who "created lyrical, abstract graphic works that dialogued with the many international arenas in which he was interested."[70] Lozano expressed similar sentiments, "I don't consider my art being Caribbean. . . . Caribbean is just a geographic area. . . . There's so many layers in that region."[71] Tatiana Flores and Michelle Ann Stephens, scholars and co-curators of *Relational Undercurrents: Contemporary Art of the Caribbean Archipelago* (2017), argue that the "visual arts are uniquely equipped to bridge the [Caribbean] region's language and cultural divides."[72] For an area often divided by its imperial histories and imposed languages, these scholars stress the vision of the "archipelago," as an assemblage of islands, waterways, and

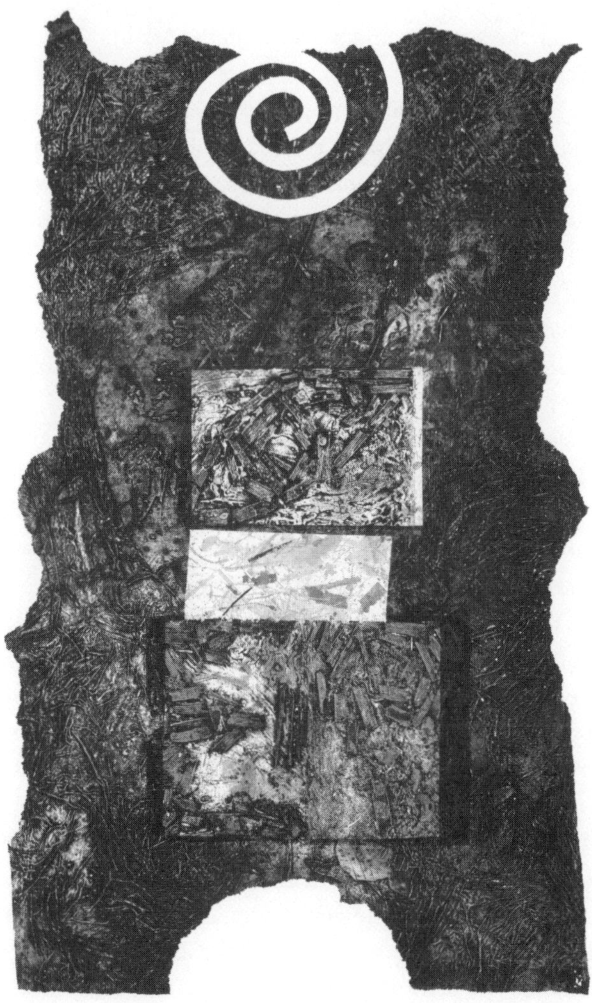

4.15. Luanda Lozano, *Figuras Fragmentadas por el Tiempo*, 1997. Collograph, etching, and chine collé, image and sheet ca. 40 × 25 inches; edition of five printed by the artist at the Robert Blackburn Printmaking Workshop. Courtesy of the artist.

ports, as well as the movement of people and goods that connect these aqueous terrains, including their diasporas on mainland shores.[73]

The prevalence of water-based imagery among these artists attests to this submerged imaginary shared by artists from the Caribbean, regardless of their national, linguistic, or racial identification. In *Relational Undercurrents*, works by Scherezade García, Fausto Ortiz, Tony Capellán, María Magdalena Campos-Pons, Juana Valdés, Andil Gosine, Edouard Duval-Carrié, and David Gumbs drew on these aquatic themes to create broader notions of a shared geography and history. Lozano's oeuvre may not be Caribbean in the representational sense, but *Sálvame Santo* responds to the push-and-pull of these visual sources. It also draws on the influential work of fellow Dominican York artists like the painter and printmaker Julio Valdez (b. 1969) who explore light, space, and the dreamlike qualities of the Caribbean Sea, as his artist statement explains:

> In the Caribbean region, the surrounding waters from the Atlantic Ocean and the Caribbean Sea create a sense of light and space that are at once a blessing and a curse. The same beautiful waters that tourists enjoy as the illusion of paradise and freedom are also experienced as [a] natural "prison," a source of suffering, death and pain for many natives, hoping to improve their lot while risking their lives as they flee their islands in fragile makeshift vessels.[74]

Lozano makes visible that painful experience for all those who have to leave, including herself, as well as the undetermined spatial dimensions of this vibrant living body of water that has seen the likes of Taíno canoes, Spanish armadas, sackings by pirates, aircraft carriers, cruises, *yolas*, and *balsas*.

Much like Sandra Fernández's politicization in Texas, working alongside her DYPG colleagues in New York forced Lozano to allude to the social issues affecting Dominicans in ways that she had not done before and as a result has made her work more accessible to a broader audience. When I asked her which of the DYPG artists she felt her work was in conversation with in this portfolio, she answered without hesitation, "Reynaldo, because we're talking about struggle, and you can tell by his work that this is the second part of the struggle, where you feel trapped for the same reason." A Macorisano, from the same town where Lozano grew up, Reynaldo García Pantaleón's (b. 1967) etching *Amarrao* (2010) speaks to the feeling of being trapped once you reach the other side (fig. 4.16).[75] In our interview, he mentioned seeing droves of young Dominican men leave the island in search of wealth and get caught up in the drug trade. A vicious cycle of drug addiction, incarceration, and deportation kept them trapped. He calls them "la generación perdida," the lost generation.[76]

Lozano's sophisticated use of printmaking techniques far exceeds that of

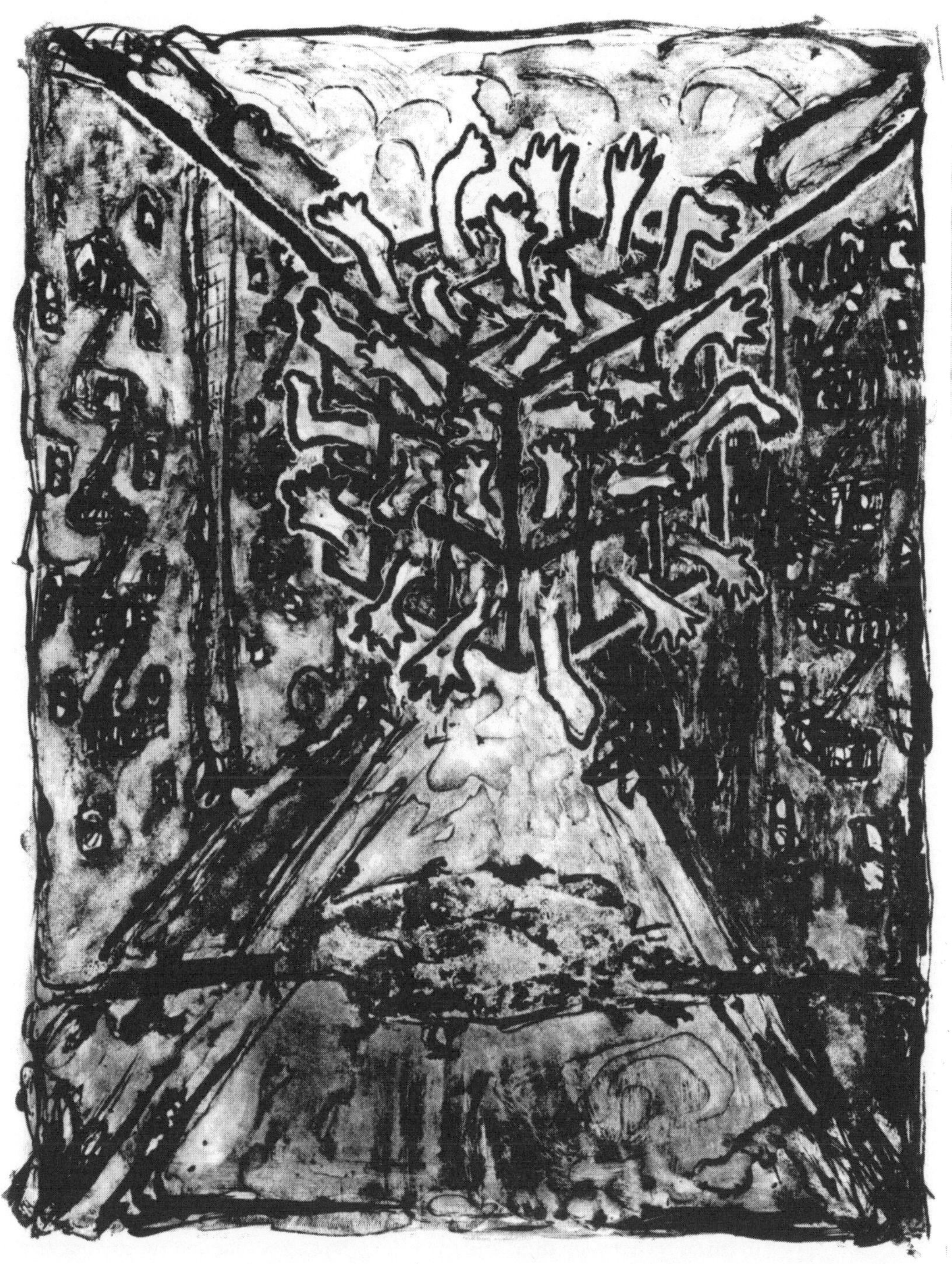

4.16. Reynaldo García Pantaleón, *Amarrao*, 2010. Polymer plate etching on BFK Rives, image: 9¼ × 7¼ inches; sheet: 15 × 12 inches; edition of twenty-five printed by the artist and Pepe Coronado at Coronado printstudio for the portfolio *Manifestaciones* by the Dominican York Proyecto Gráfica. Courtesy of the artist.

her DYPG colleagues, and yet she remains a relatively unknown figure despite having achieved many awards and benchmarks in her career, a painful reality for so many women-of-color artists in this country. While her male counterparts such as Pepe Coronado assume the title "master printer," Lozano prefers to think of herself as *the person behind the curtain*. Most master printers receive that title and recognition after spending many years specializing in their craft and printing impeccable editions for artists who may not be as highly skilled in their media. The fact that there are so few Latina artists with that specialization is nothing short of a crisis, something that needs to be remedied through an institutional pipeline. Lozano has printed many of the editions by artists in the four portfolios so far produced by the DYPG, though her specialization and attention to craftsmanship remain largely unacknowledged. She adds, "Let them talk, let them be the master; it would never be my personality."[77]

INTERVENTIONS BY SEA

It is not surprising that some of the contributors to the DYPG portfolios used this creative opportunity to contest the geopolitics of US intervention. After all, the US has exercised its influence over Hispaniola since the nineteenth century, when the Spanish colony of Santo Domingo came under the aegis of a unified Republic of Haiti. The 1822 unification of the island triggered Spain, France, England, and the US to vie for their economic concerns in the region, especially given the threat of insurrection that a free Black republic represented for the plantation economy. Following the DR's 1844 declaration of independence from Haiti, "the US government sent several commercial agents and one Senate investigating commission to explore the possibility of expanding US economic and military presence in the Dominican territory."[78] In 1869, moreover, President Ulysses S. Grant made a failed attempt to annex the DR to the US in the interest of undermining European colonial rule in the region, following the vision outlined in the Monroe Doctrine.[79] While the project of Manifest Destiny and continental expansion had almost been completed on the mainland, US corporate and government leaders set their sights on the Caribbean.

The Spanish-American War officially opened the door to corporate and military interests and created an asymmetrical power relation that continues to this day. Between 1898 and 1924 the US Marines landed twenty-one times on Caribbean shores.[80] With destabilized governments and an economic downturn during World War I, Hispaniola became much more vulnerable to US intervention. Following a series of political assassinations, including the murder of Haitian president Vilbrun Guillaume Sam, the US sent troops to occupy Haiti from 1915 to 1934. Similarly, political turmoil in the DR resulted in an eight-year US occupation, from 1916 to 1924. During the occupation, the US instituted a Dominican National Guard that trained future military dictator Trujillo, who seized power in 1930.[81] However by 1933 the US shifted their approach, perhaps recognizing the ill effects of gunboat diplomacy, and sought to develop the noninterventionist Good Neighbor Policy, while still retaining a lead in trade and defense and paradoxically supporting the violence and megalomania of Trujillo.[82] However, the Cold War would once again legitimize the use of intelligence and military interventions in the Caribbean. The CIA provided aid to the dissidents of the regime, who assassinated Trujillo in 1961.[83] After the democratically elected leftist government of Juan Bosch was overthrown in a coup in 1963, a civil war ensued and the US invaded Dominican territory once again in 1965 in an effort to install a pro-American anticommunist leader.

I recount these interventions in abbreviated form for readers to understand the difficult position that Dominican American artists find themselves in without access to a robust cultural infrastructure in the DR, forced to migrate to the country that has excessively exercised its hegemony over the region. I can think of no other symbol that more blatantly disregards their right to sovereignty than the presence of the USS *Intrepid* aircraft carrier, the crown jewel of the Intrepid Sea, Air & Space Museum, anchored in the Hudson River in current-day New York City.[84] For Pepe Coronado, who was born in the same year as the 1965 invasion, the ship-turned-museum is a painful reminder of a crucial moment in Dominican history, when the votes of Dominicans and their constitution were effectively crushed with a fleet of US ships and the landing of thousands of US Marines. In April of 1965 supporters of the ousted Juan Bosch launched a revolution with the aim of restoring Bosch's constitutional government. They seized the presidential palace despite counterattacks by loyalists. A few of these rebels belonged to Marxist political circles, but US diplomats and CIA operatives "interpreted the constitutionalist uprising as the potential prelude to a communist takeover."[85] By the end of April, President Lyndon Johnson had ordered a massive deployment of troops by air and sea in order to prevent a "second Cuba." At least twenty-three thousand marines were on site within days. Overwhelmed with the firepower, the rebels had no other choice but to accept an agreement that left power in the hands of Dominican conservatives.[86] President Joaquín Balaguer, a Trujillo acolyte whom I previously mentioned was associated with the Columbus Lighthouse, would assume power again in 1966 and serve multiple terms until 1996.

For the inaugural portfolio, Coronado channeled that anger into his print

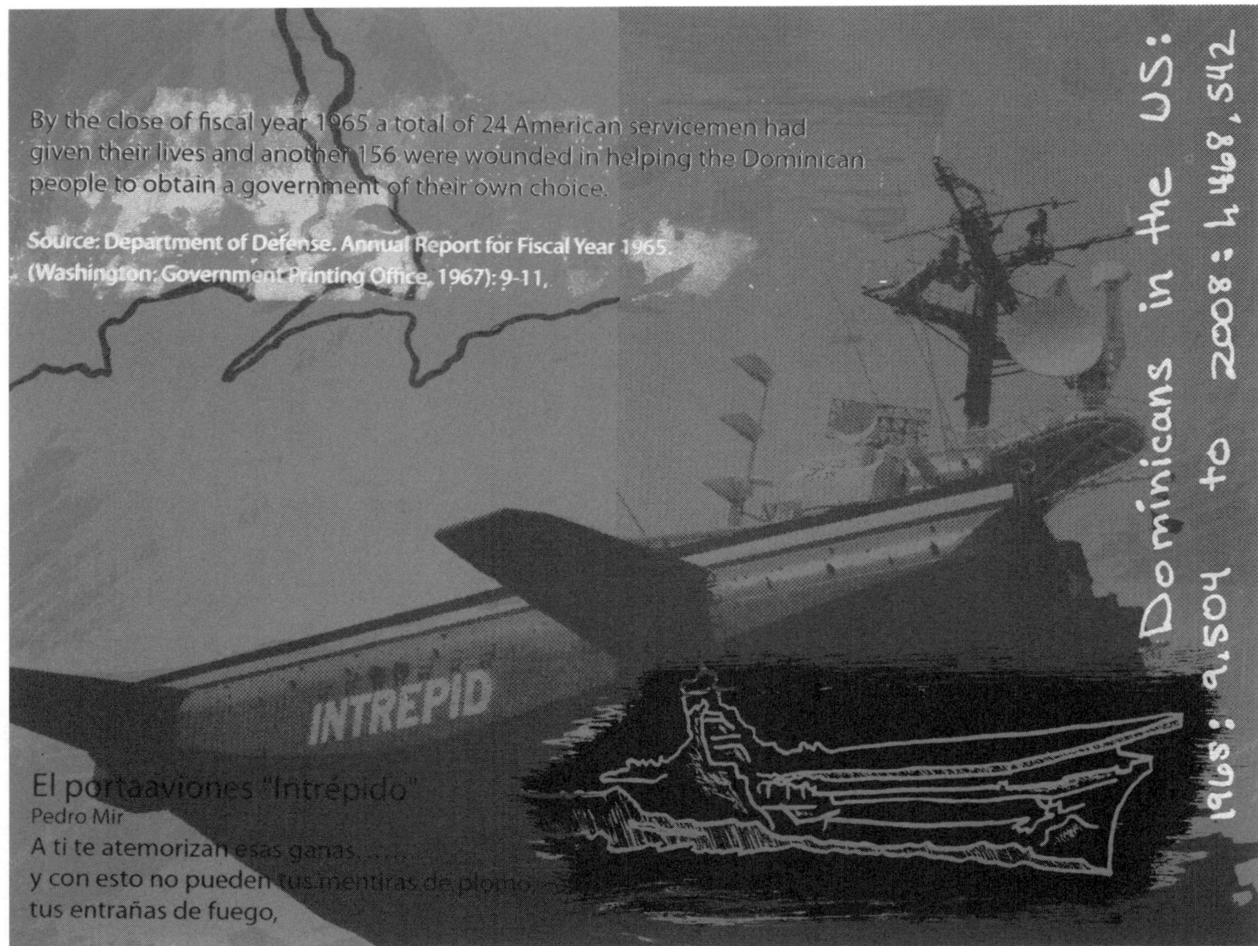

4.17. Pepe Coronado, *Intrépido*, 2010. Screenprint on BFK Rives, image: 7 × 9 inches; sheet: 12 × 15 inches; edition of twenty-five printed by the artist at Coronado printstudio for the portfolio *Manifestaciones* by the Dominican York Proyecto Gráfica. Courtesy of the artist.

Intrépido (2010; fig. 4.17). The golden yellow screenprint consists of a photo stencil of the aircraft carrier with digitally collaged elements that give it the feel of an artist notebook. The horizontal composition is partitioned in half, one side showing the past, the other the present. A partial coastline drawing appears on the upper left with data from the US Department of Defense outlining American casualties and injuries during Operation Power Pack in the name of "helping the Dominican people to obtain a government of their own choice." Coronado contrasted that benevolent rhetoric with the words of the famous Dominican poet Pedro Mir, who in 1962 penned a poem to the *Intrepid* written as if to a monstrous sea creature moved by fear and yet unable to quell the people's cry for justice. The stanza that Coronado draws from states:

A ti te atemorizan esas ganas
de morirse que tienen estos pueblos,
porque van muchos años, muchas elecciones,
muchos millones y muchos prisioneros
y muchas jornadas de sudor no pagado
y demasiado silencio,
y con esto no pueden tus cañones de bronce,
tu coraza de acero,
y con esto no pueden tus mentiras de plomo,
tus entrañas de fuego.[87]

On the bottom right, another view of a hand-drawn *Intrepid* appears, inked in a way mimicking a woodcut or linocut. In his own handwriting the artist added the note: "Dominicans in the US: 1965: 9,504 to 2008: 1,468,542," reflecting his concern with connecting US intervention to the surge in Dominican migration. According to the Migration Policy Institute, the Dominican immigrant population in the US was 12,000 in 1960, and this initial wave, which would increase fivefold by 1970, corresponded to the political and economic upheaval that followed the assassination of Trujillo.[88] During this time, those who left the island were primarily dissidents, students, intellectuals, and middle-class families, but the economic crisis of the 1980s and 1990s spurred waves of economic migrants in search of work opportunities. According to US Census figures, by 2010 there were 879,000 foreign-born Dominicans in the US, and the population grew to 1.2 million by 2019.[89] Coronado's correspondence with Sarah Aponte, chief librarian of the CUNY Dominican Studies Institute Library, attests to the artist's interest in the exponential growth in Dominican emigration but likely also included those of the second generation born on the mainland and those who remain undocumented.[90] That is, while the US was sending troops and meddling in Dominican elections, the island nationals began an exodus, sending ballplayers, musicians, artists, intellectuals, and working-class families to the United States, where their presence is an undeniable reminder of US imperial desire.

Intrépido was the start of a series of works that contemplated the entangled relationship between these two countries that Coronado calls home. In an artist statement he explained: "From trade and commerce going back centuries, to offers of annexation and paternalistic military occupations and interventions, to the current free flow of business, people, tourism, drug traffickers, *peloteros*, and musicians, the two countries have forged an entanglement of political and economic ties that seem to have an inexplicable dynamic."[91] Coronado's *U.S./D.R.: A Love-Hate Relationship* (2012) juxtaposes a map of the United States on the left with a map of the Dominican Republic on the right.[92] The artist intervenes in the standard geographic representation of these locales through seriality and repetition, populating each map with smaller images of the other country. The background is made up of expressionist brushstrokes of light and dark blues that suggest the crashing waves of the gulf dividing these two nations. Coronado binds the two images with chalklike circular arrows that emphasize the movement of people (civilian and military) and goods between the US and the DR. The gold vertical stripes at the center of the diptych highlight the economic interests of trade. In a variation on the theme entitled *U.S./D.R.: A Love-Hate Relationship II* (2012), Coronado opted for a vertical format, placing a map of the DR at the top and an upside-down map of the US at the bottom.[93] The gesture recalls Uruguayan artist and theorist Joaquín Torres-García's iconic drawing *America Invertida* (1943), which reversed the conventional representation of the American continent by positioning Chile and Argentina at the top and omitting the US and Canada altogether. The geographic bodies in Coronado's print are linked at the center through a firing-range target, and the circular arrows moving in a clockwise direction around the target suggest that the orientation of the map is in flux. This graphic composition must have caught the eye of Lorgia García-Peña, who reached out to Coronado in September 2014 for a cover image for her forthcoming book. Her request from September 2014 notably stated, "I would like to use as a cover image for my book your artwork Haiti-Dominican-US map"; she likely had not noticed that Haiti was missing in these early renderings.[94]

I dwell on this omission because the project of envisioning Dominican York, of working through the geopolitics of intervention, was a way for an artist like Coronado to negotiate these complex geographies and histories. It was not an easy or linear path that led to Coronado's 2016 *U.S./D.R. en Relación*, which graced the cover of García-Peña's book, but a process of intense questioning of the intertwined histories of Haiti, the US, and the DR. The DR's

2013 court ruling retroactively revoking the citizenship of thousands of Dominicans of Haitian descent whose parents were undocumented profoundly affected the artist. His 2014 print *Citizenship Revoked* marked the first time the whole island of Hispaniola, both the Dominican and the Haitian side, faced off with the US. But the process of learning about the other half of Quisqueya was also a process of unlearning the discourses of Dominican nationalism that insisted on viewing Haitians as a malevolent force. Curatorial projects that showcased the work of Haitian and Dominican diasporic artists, such as *Consequential Translations* at the Centro Cultural de España in Santo Domingo, further mobilized Coronado's interest in finding common ground between the two cultures.[95] But it was Coronado's collaborative projects with Haitian diasporic artists such as Vladimir Cybil Charlier (b. 1967) that had the most lasting impact on the printmaker. In a 2017 interview, Coronado recalled observing that Haitian artists' visions of Hispaniola were much more complete than his own, as evidenced by Charlier's 2015 screenprint and chine collé *Strange Bath*.[96] The two nations shared music, food, culture, and geography, and yet he "grew up exposed to that negation [or racial hostility toward Haitians] . . . no Dominican knew how to say shit in Creole."[97] It was like discovering the other half of an island that had been denied to you, a half that knew you more intimately than you knew yourself. Through this dialogue with Haitian artists, Coronado's vision of Dominican York grew to encompass a larger Caribbean diaspora.

Coronado's *Intrépido*, which documents the impact of the 1965 US invasion, provides another viewpoint into the aqueous territorialities of the DYPG. The sea is a space of wonder and life, an ancestral connection to Africa, a means by which to flee, but also what makes Hispaniola vulnerable to intervention. *Intrépido* highlights the episodic nature of this ongoing cycle of violence and the reasons it has led to Dominicans becoming the fourth largest Latinx group in the US.

CONCLUSION

I hope readers will be inspired to look much further at the archives of the DYPG than this partial view I have offered from the collective's first portfolio. Of the twelve initial cofounders, only eight remain involved, and the recent changes brought about by the COVID-19 pandemic have further dispersed the group. Some have decided to return permanently to the Dominican Republic. Others, citing personal conflicts, have opted to pull away and refocus on their individual artistic projects. Nonetheless, the DYPG remains an important agent in Latinx printmaking, as it has established a framework for placing Dominican American expressive culture and confronting what scholar Dixa Ramírez calls the "ghosting" of the Dominican Republic from dominant Western discourses.[98] It is important to understand how art history operates as part of these paradigms.

While much of this book has been concerned with delinking from Western conceptions of land to question the excess of current forms of territoriality and nativism, these Caribbean diaspora artists turn the viewer's attention to bodies of water (oceans, seas, rivers, channels) as spaces likewise loaded with violent colonial histories. Their narrative prints speak to stories of navigating these treacherous waters that connect the Dominican diaspora with multiple geographies and temporalities. The island of Hispaniola has had one of the longest histories of being represented through imperial eyes, beginning with that sketch by Columbus and extending further out to the printed maps carried by dozens of explorers, pirates, and slave ships. The portfolio of *Manifestaciones* is a welcome opportunity to see how these artists have endeavored to respond to these territorializing practices through their own eyes with aqueous prints that disclose movement, liminality, and resilience. I will admit that not all of the prints speak to this concern, as is evident in the urban campesino figure in Carlos Almonte's *Vale John* (fig. 4.18), the conceptual print on reflective mylar titled *Dreambox* that alludes to a humble shoe shine box (fig. 4.19) by iliana emilia garcía, and the playful juxtaposition of a blue Caribbean home in the camera-obscura cityscape by Alex Guerrero titled *Vista Psicotrópica* (fig. 4.20). Their differing visions speak to the multiplicity and heterogeneity that characterized every portfolio produced by the collective.

The philosopher Nelson Maldonado-Torres reminds us that the Caribbean is a cornerstone in the decolonial turn, given its history as the site where the colonized subject or "savage" other emerged, where techniques of dehumanization gave way to new economies, and where early revolts by the colonized shook the structure of a modern/colonial world.[99] It is therefore apt to see how artists from the DYPG continue to undo that legacy of coloniality by centering the discourse of the Black Atlantic and framing race as a foremost concern that questions the anti-Haitianism of the DR's nationalist discourse, challenges their racialization in the US, and pushes against the white supremacy of Latinidad. In their quest to elevate the Dominican print tradition and take their place within an expanded Caribbean diaspora, they have forged connections with African American and Latin American artists in New York. This unique history has led many to create an amalgam of artistic genealogies and influences, as observed in Luanda Lozano's contribution to the Consejo Gráfico portfolio titled *La Huella Magistral: Homage to Master Printmakers*, where the profile of her dear mentor Robert Blackburn appears (fig. 4.21).

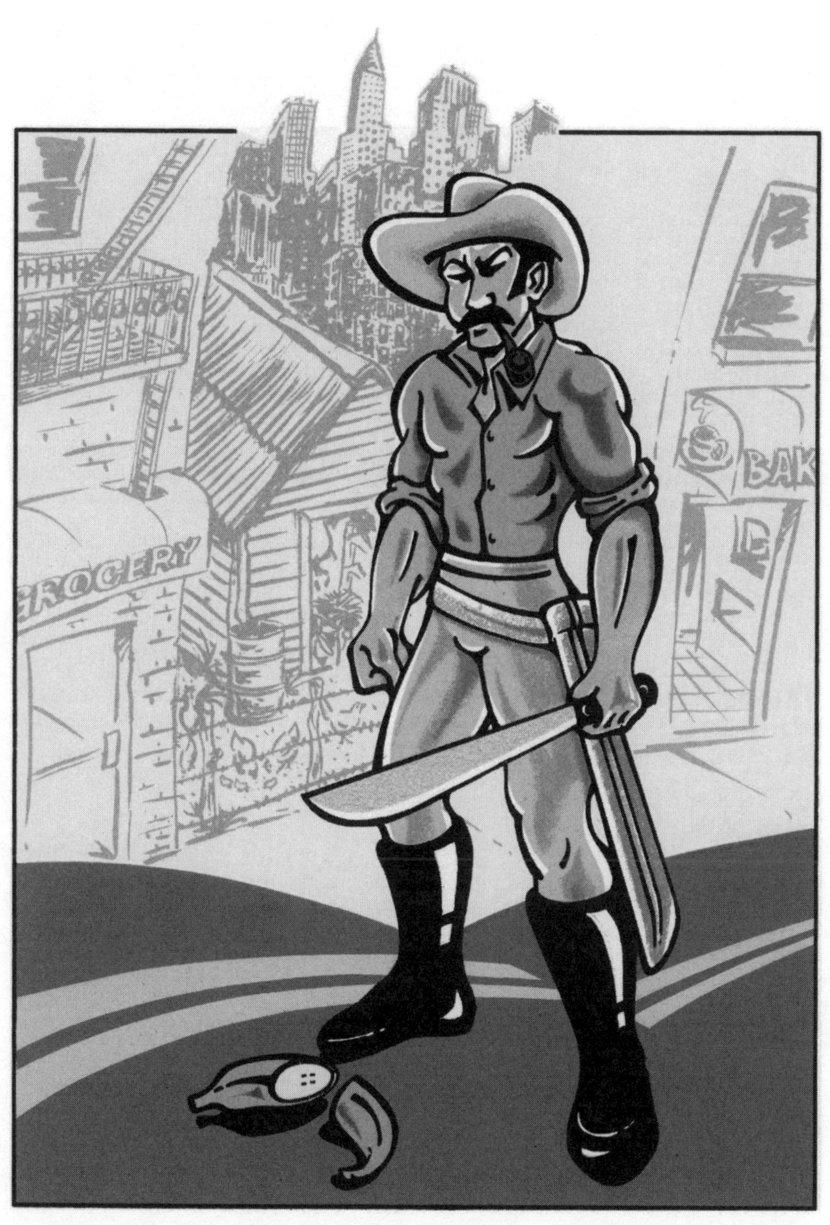

4.18. Carlos Almonte, *Vale John*, 2010. Screenprint on BFK Rives, image: 9 × 7 inches; sheet: 15 × 12 inches; edition of twenty-five printed by the artist and Pepe Coronado at Coronado printstudio for the portfolio *Manifestaciones* by the Dominican York Proyecto Gráfica. Courtesy of the artist.

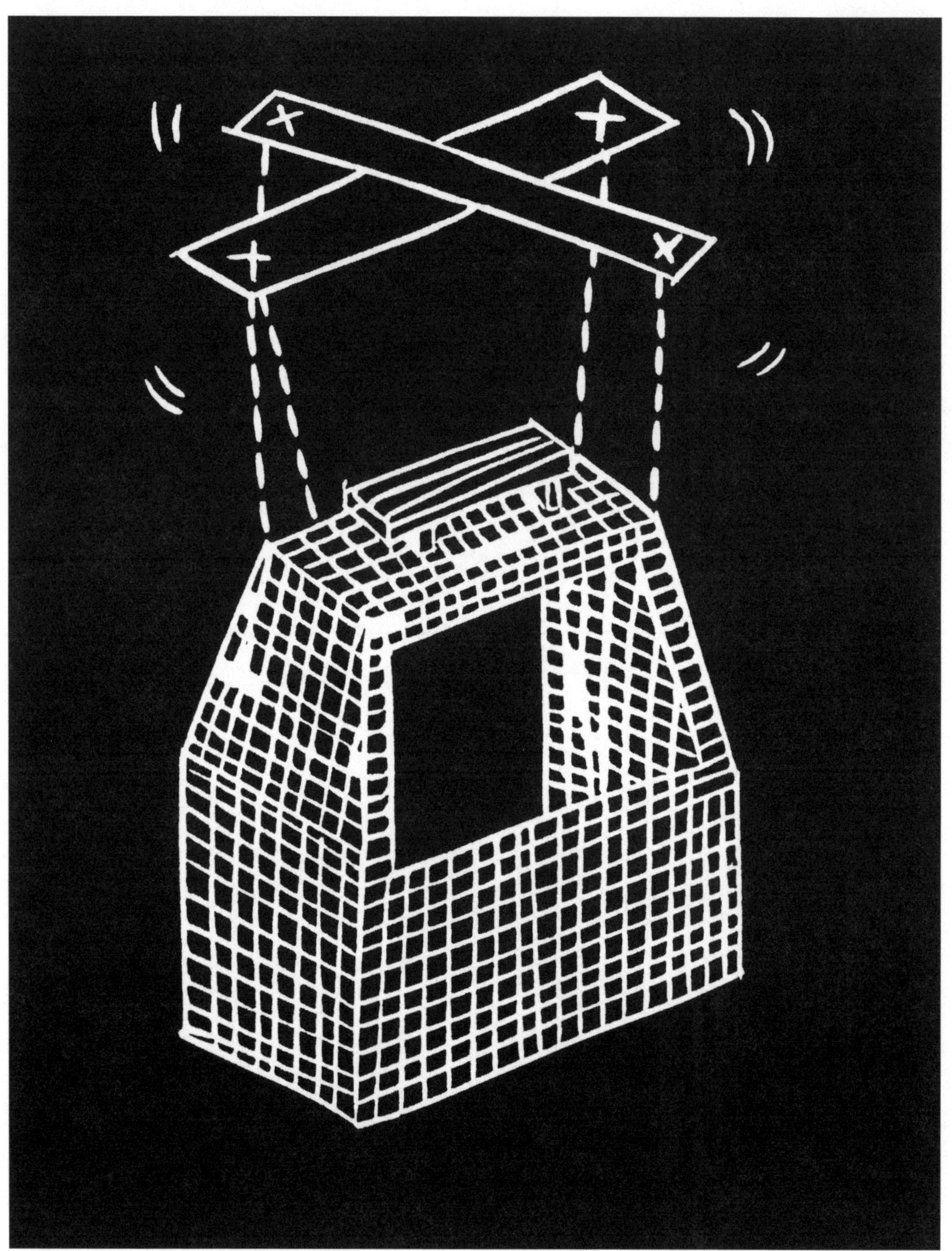

4.19. iliana emilia garcía, *Dreambox*, 2010. Screenprint over reflective mylar and chine collé, image: 9 × 7 inches; sheet: 15 × 12 inches; edition of twenty-five printed by the artist, Alex Guerrero, and Pepe Coronado at Bullrider Studio for the portfolio *Manifestaciones* by the Dominican York Proyecto Gráfica. Courtesy of the artist.

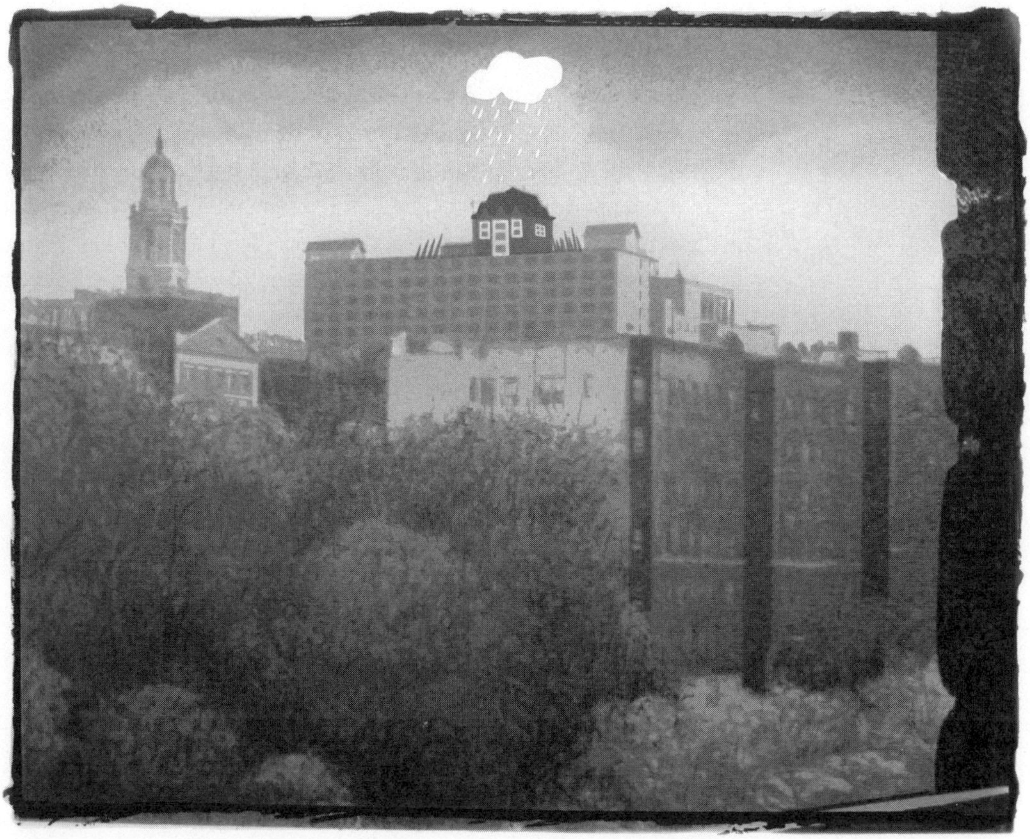

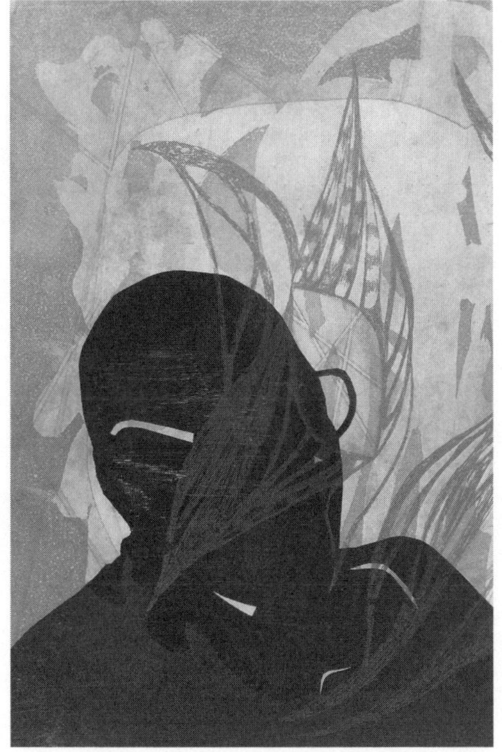

4.20. Alex Guerrero, *Vista Psicotrópica*, 2010. Screen-print on BFK Rives, image: 7 × 9 inches; sheet: 12 × 15 inches; edition of twenty-five printed by the artist and Miguel Luciano at Bullrider Studio for the portfolio *Manifestaciones* by the Dominican York Proyecto Gráfica. Courtesy of the artist.

4.21. Luanda Lozano, *La Musa de Blackburn*, 2017. Etching, stencil printed on kozuke ivory paper and chine collé, image: 17¼ × 11½ inches; sheet: 22 × 15 inches; edition of thirty, printed by the artist for the Consejo Gráfico portfolio *La Huella Magistral: Homage to Master Printmakers*.

DYPG artists have likewise found ways to connect their water crossings to the borderlands experience of many Latinx artists, aware of their difference and yet moved by their shared struggles as immigrants or children of immigrants who experience xenophobia. Their work also signals how the geopolitics of the region has witnessed imperial and neocolonial incursions and how the privilege of sovereignty remains at stake for the future of the Caribbean archipelago.

Conclusion

Revolution on Display

THE PRINTS ANALYZED in this book attest to the urgency with which artists have adopted reproductive technologies to contest the resurgence of xenophobia. Their projects emphasize how these contemporary fears of the foreigner manifest into racial and spatial paradigms that hearken back to colonial times, when Western conceptions of territory were being developed through scenarios of discovery. Aligned with the aims of decolonial aesthetics, they expose the persistence of colonial ideologies in current structures of power, delink from their dominant frameworks, and offer other ways of seeing, thinking, and doing. These artists have revitalized and reclaimed printmaking, a medium that was once complicit in the colonization of lands and peoples of the Americas.

Printmaking helped visualize the territorial ambitions of the West in maps, atlases, travel narratives, romantic landscapes, and images of flora, fauna, and Native populations, but it also projected a particular visual order that could extend the exercise of control over a geographic region. To take up this tradition and expose its role in furthering colonial violence, these contemporary artists are rethinking territoriality in their print projects from various subject positions. Ricardo Duffy emphasized how a return to Native territorialities and an identification with Native heritage can counter the nineteenth-century frontier violence so often romanticized in Marlboro advertising. Relatedly, Enrique Chagoya and poet Alberto Ríos adopted the position of those once deemed cannibals and savages critiquing Western cartographic projections by placing the body at the center of the axis mundi. Their playful maps of the imagination eschew the charged politics of the immigration debate, so closely followed in Duffy's allusion to California's Proposition 187, opening up anarcho-possibilities for skepticism and disobedience. Sandra Fernández, on the other hand, addressed the reterritorialization of the nation's borders after 9/11 and how the shift to nationwide surveillance reactivated the colonial blueprints of racial segregation. Her interest in bringing visibility to the plight of undocumented subjects, and her strategy of reinserting their mixed-race bodies into territorial representations, foregrounds the decolonial aims of a mestiza consciousness that claims a third space for those left out of colonial borders and binaries. The artists in the Dominican York Proyecto Gráfica examined the history of Dominican migration and made visible the imperial desires of US interventions on the island of Hispaniola. They likewise reoriented the discussion of race toward the Black Atlantic, addressing the hemispheric history of slavery in the Americas and countering the legacy of anti-Blackness in Latinidad. Calling attention to liquid highways and fluid identities, the DYPG artists flipped the Western territorial script through water-based imagery that emphasizes movement, liminality, and aqueous spaces that delink from the extractive view of territorial conquest.

In this conclusion, I want to address some of the initial questions I began this study with and explain in further detail the significance of my book's argument. To do so, I will provide an overview and critical reading of the 2020 exhibition *¡Printing the Revolution! The Rise and Impact of Chicano Graphics, 1965 to Now*. This landmark exhibition at one of the country's most prestigious cultural venues, the Smithsonian American Art Museum (SAAM), featured 119 works on paper, many of them recent acquisitions, and surveyed five decades of graphic-art production. It was curated by Carmen Ramos, who at the time was acting chief curator and curator of Latinx art at SAAM and is now chief curator at the National Gallery of Art, with art historian Claudia Zapata serving as the curatorial assistant. There are several reasons why the exhibition helps me address these larger questions about this field. First, it offers a unique lens by which to analyze the institutional critique and avant-garde posture many of these artists adopt. When the historical avant-gardes were absorbed and canonized by art museums, critics like Peter Bürger read this as a failure in their attempts to sublate institutions and bring art closer to life. Is this truly a failure, in the case of Latinx printmaking, when one of the nation's premier cultural palaces acquires and thereby canonizes their work?

Second, the show also provides an opportunity to consider how over the last five decades this medium flourished to become a distinct Latinx cultural tradition in the US with its own canon of major figures, styles, and themes. How did this heterogeneous group of Latinx diasporas, often viewed by the dominant culture as permanently foreign, work toward establishing this longstanding tradition with limited means while battling overt forms of racism in the US art world and classism from their Latin American colleagues? No other racialized minority group has been able to build the vast infrastructure that Latinx printmaking has achieved in the span of fifty years. Third, many of the prints exemplify the desire to reclaim the Americas central to this book's argument. I highlight the politics of territory in the work of Jesus Barraza, Poli Marichal, and Michael Menchaca. With the latter, I signal toward new directions that the next generation of Latinx printmakers are exploring as they extend beyond the limits of the printed medium, adopting digital reproduction techniques and tackling pressing subjects such as climate change and LGBTQ+ rights.

The framework of revolution is admittedly an overused trope in the history of Latin American graphics. Dawn Ades and Alison McClean's *Revolution on Paper: Mexican Prints 1910–1960* and David Kunzle's *Che Guevara: Icon, Myth, and Message* are two prominent examples, but one could cite many others. This lens belies the fact that these print cultures are varied and serve diverse audiences. The political edge has also at times created the illusion that most of the graphic art produced in Latin America is merely propaganda for state ideology, as has often been observed for Taller de Gráfica Popular in Mexico, as well as Editora Política and OSPAAAL (Organization in Solidarity with the People of Africa, Asia and Latin America) in Cuba, which elides artistic agency and renders invisible the diversity of practices that exists in these workshops. The propaganda theory has also caused the work to be dismissed from modernist and avant-garde traditions, an issue that has likewise plagued the field of Latinx printmaking. Art critic Carolina Miranda of the *Los Angeles Times* remarked, "In fine art circles, Chicano printmaking has generally been dismissed as political agitprop connected to the civil rights movements of the 1960s and 1970s, its aesthetic contributions minimized," noting how *¡Printing the Revolution!* highlighted aesthetic innovation, "one that has drawn inspiration from Pop, institutional critique, appropriation, conceptualism and internet art, as much as it has from political printmaking."[1]

Ramos's use of the framework was strategic in that it created a longer lineage for these prints by extending their chronological and geographic parameters. The show was dated *1965 to Now,* but one could see the connections to nineteenth-century figures like the portrait of the Cuban writer José Martí by Salvadoran American artist Oscar Melara and Carlos Cortéz's reclaiming of José Guadalupe Posada as an origin figure for Chicago's Chicano art movement. The framework also projected a larger geographic reach, drawing connections to liberation movements across the hemisphere such as Rupert Garcia's tribute to Che Guevara a year after his assassination in Bolivia, Jos Sances's portrayal of Central America destroying the shark that attempts to consume it as a stand-in for the US, and René Castro's remembrance of the 1973 coup in Chile, which forced him to flee. The work of Juan Fuentes, in particular, extended this geography to a global dimension through formal experimentation that celebrated the checkered black-and-white scarf known as a *keffiyeh*, a symbol of Palestinian nationalism, and the desire to see many Nelson Mandelas as South Africa was still reeling in the violence of apartheid.

The exhibition also beckoned an acknowledgment from Americanists and Latin Americanists that Chicanx (and by extension Latinx) printmaking is a stand-alone field with its own intentions, aesthetics, idiosyncrasies, and actors. Latinx printmakers have on certain occasions been included in American and Latin American print exhibitions, but by and large their work has been absent from the historiography of these fields apart from quick mentions or footnotes. *Proof: The Rise of Printmaking in Southern California* (2011) broke ground in establishing the origins and context of the printmaking renaissance that took place in Southern California workshops such as Tamarind, Gemini G.E.L., and Cirrus Editions. However, studios that privileged the work of artists of color were clearly overlooked. Self Help Graphics is mentioned twice in the text, and twice in the timeline, but only in relation to Sister Corita Kent, who trained Sister Karen Boccalero at Immaculate Heart College. These oversights have likewise been replicated in the Latin American context. Because of nationality and residency restrictions the *Bienal de San Juan del Grabado Latinoamericano* refused admission to US-born Latinx artists until 1981, when the rules were amended by the organizing committee after a very public battle when several artists were turned down in the 1979 biennial.[2] Anyone who viewed *¡Printing the Revolution!* and took the time to read the accompanying catalogue could see that these earlier nominal inclusions did little to represent the scale and history of Latinx printmaking.

While still closely tied to an identity paradigm, the show's revolutionary premise stressed how these artists countered the various forms of oppression that Latinx peoples experience, despite being one of the largest ethnic groups in the US. The spirit of rebellion in their work was not imported from Europe but indigenous to the Americas and fanned a flame through a massive, mobile, and decentralized printed sphere that carried the message about how their life mattered and countered coercive forms of assimilation. Ramos's catalogue essay identified the rejection of melting-pot assimilation, the need to name oneself "Chicana/o," and the growing politicization during the civil-rights movement as the seeds that led artists to produce "visually arresting works that catalyzed a Chicano public coming into awareness of itself."[3] The other popular medium at the outset was muralism, but murals could not be mobilized to the same effect. Posters, prints, calendars, broadsides, comics, and zines could be produced quickly and inexpensively for mass distribution at rallies, community centers, high schools, and college campuses. Drawing on the museum's extensive holdings of Chicanx and Latinx graphic art, *¡Printing the Revolution!* showcased the medium's unique role in reimagining US history and identity and broke ground in bringing needed attention to a graphic-art movement largely overlooked by US museums. Ramos noted in an interview with critic Maximiliano Durón, "histories of Chicanx printmaking are pretty marginalized within the histories of American printmaking . . . when I really started working on this exhibition, looking at museum catalogues on American printmaking. . . . It was shocking."[4] Unlike previous surveys, such as *Just Another Poster?* and *Pressing the Point*, which emphasized the early years of the graphic-arts movement, *¡Printing the Revolution!* looked toward the present, tracking the growth of this printed sphere and its evolution from raw DIY posters to highly technical fine-art limited editions and born-digital projects that helped contextualize and reframe that legacy.

The work placed at the entrance to the exhibition directly alluded to police brutality (fig. 5.1), a bold move for Ramos, who made the decision before the start of protests that marked the police killing of George Floyd and triggered the worldwide decentralized movement of Black Lives Matter. The first works that viewers saw as they entered the gallery were a large-scale wall installation by the Oakland artist Oree Originol titled *Justice for Our Lives* (2014–2020), which consisted of one hundred portraits of BIPOC killed by police, and a 1975 poster *Aquellos Que Han Muerto* by Amado Peña, which marked the senseless killing of a twelve-year-old by police in Dallas. Through this curatorial decision Ramos was able to establish a throughline for the exhibition, noting how many of the social issues that mobilized communities during the civil-rights movement continue well into the present. Originol's project, simple black-and-white portraits that he digitally manipulated from the subject's photographs provided by the families of the deceased, was printed over colorful stock resembling the cyan, magenta, yellow, and key spectrum in color printing and arranged in such a way that it brought to mind a neon installation of interlocked chevrons guiding the viewer toward the next gallery. The project was, and remains, available for the public to download freely through the artist's personal website, an issue that I am certain raised eyebrows for the acquisitions committee.[5] The online distribution also signaled the show's

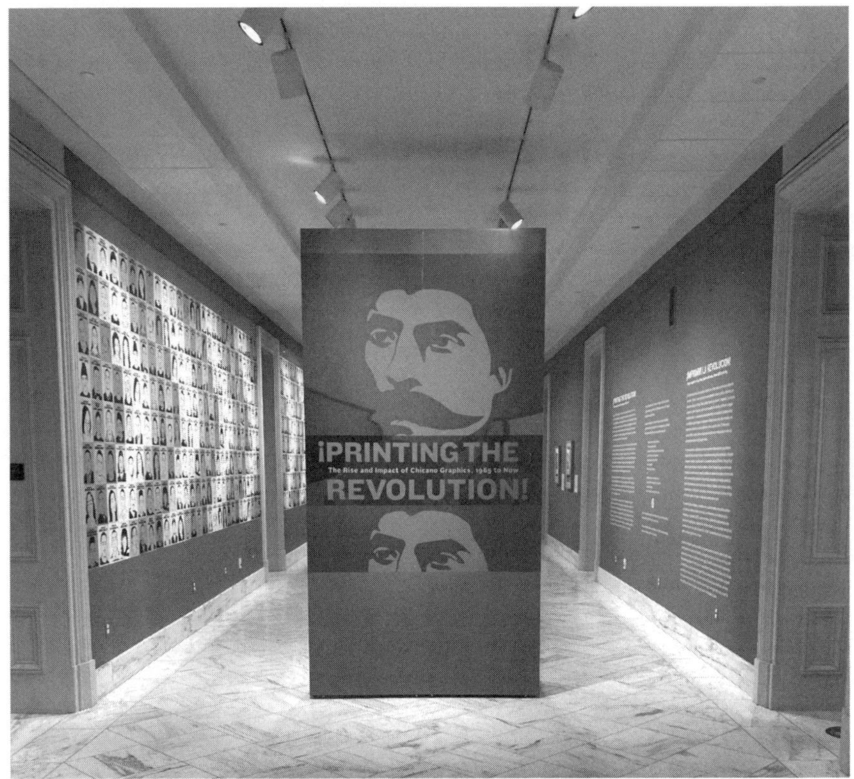

5.1. Entrance to *¡Printing the Revolution! The Rise and Impact of Chicano Graphics, 1965 to Now* exhibition at the Smithsonian American Art Museum (November 20, 2020–August 8, 2021). Photo by the author.

desire to showcase technical innovation and the public engagement of these works, which serve multiple audiences, especially those who may not have access to galleries and museums.

The exhibition opened on November 20, 2020, and closed three days later because of the Smithsonian Institution's decision to shutter its public venues in an effort to curb the spread of the COVID-19 pandemic. *¡Printing the Revolution!* reopened on May 14, 2021, and ran until August 8 of that year. Unfortunately, these closures and interruptions made it extremely difficult for the show to generate press interest, though a few write-ups have appeared and more will likely take place once the exhibition begins its national tour. Readers may recall the controversy generated by Ramos's 2013 exhibition *Our America: The Latino Presence in American Art*. On October 25, 2013, SAAM opened its first large survey of Latinx art, and that same day the *Washington Post* art critic Philip Kennicott wrote a hostile review in which he denounced the exhibition as a "telling symptom of an insoluble problem: Latino art, today, is a meaningless category."[6] Almost immediately artists and scholars used social media to mount counterarguments and show support for the exhibition and its curator. Even those whom I may characterize as militant cultural nationalists, who abhor the term Latina/o/x, joined the ranks in support of the threatened category. Among the vocal critics, the filmmaker Alex Rivera raised salient questions about Kennicott's rhetoric. The *Washington Post* published a polite email exchange between Rivera and Kennicott the following week and offered them an opportunity to further debate the validity of the term. Rivera wrote:

> The problem is that, while critics raise doubts about categories like "Latino art," there's never any discussion of the absence of that work in show after show that keeps groups like Latinos on the margins or excluded entirely from the American conversation. For example, the 2012 Whitney Biennial featured exactly *zero* Latino artists. How can that be a survey of "American art"? . . . It seems like the absence of Latino artists is normal, not newsworthy, but the organizing of our presence causes questions about our existence.[7]

The cleverly amusing debate that ensued between the authors exemplified the unsettled relationship between the art of ethnic minorities and the larger category of American art, as well as the press's general disdain for identity-based exhibitions that call out inequity and racism in the art world as passé.

What most may have missed in the initial review was how much Kennicott marveled at the wall of graphic-art posters included in *Our America*, claiming they possessed "some of the strongest visual invention" in the exhibition. These were hung salon-style and spread out like a wondrous constellation of voices (fig. 5.2): Ignacio Gomez's *Zoot Suit* (2002) occupied a central position with a monumental pachuco gazing upward as the sun sets in Los Angeles; Marcos Dimas's *Lolita Lebrón* (1971) and Ester Hernandez's *Sun Mad* (1982; fig. 3.9) tugged at each side and opened out into a chorus of vibrant and colorful posters that thematized the lives of women, farmworkers, political prisoners, veterans, Native peoples, Afro–Puerto Ricans, the impoverished, and mestizaje. As Kennicott stood before that wall considering its aesthetic prowess, did he wonder: Who made this poster? Where was it printed? Who was the audience? Was it in someone's home or at a local demonstration? What does this wall of printed art signify for Latinx communities in the US? *¡Printing the Revolution!* leaned into all these concerns: the formal and technical innovation, the social history highlighted in the work, the networks and mentorship that make up the field, and the various audiences they serve.

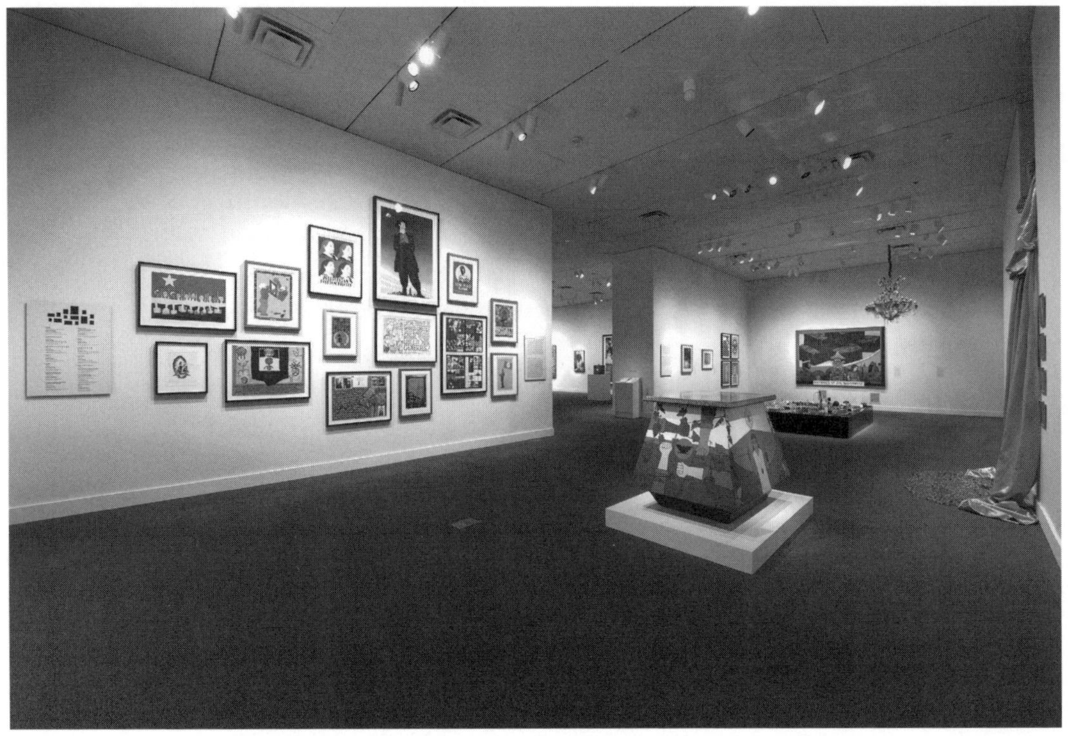

5.2. Wall of graphic art in *Our America: The Latino Presence in American Art* exhibition at the Smithsonian American Art Museum (October 24, 2013–March 2, 2014). Photo by Mildred Baldwin. Courtesy of the Smithsonian American Art Museum.

One significant difference is that *¡Printing the Revolution!* avoided the salon-style display, privileging a unique, intimate experience with each work, save for a few window-pane arrangements, and thereby also elevated their status to fine-art objects. One may ask whether this shift in the status of the object changes the terms of its reception. Does the entrance of these works into the museum collection negate the avant-garde claims of formal innovation and bringing art closer to everyday life? In a section of the show titled "Urgent Images," viewers could witness posters made in support of the United Farm Workers, a land-grant movement, incarcerated youth, and the Third World Strike at San Francisco State University (fig. 5.3). But removed from these contexts of rallies and demonstrations, the exhibition showcased their aesthetic and historical value, which is often overlooked in social-movement history. No one could deny the pop-art aesthetic inherent to Rupert Garcia's screenprint *DDT* (1969), which shows a little girl screaming under large red lettering against a pale blue background. However, it is in the context of museums and galleries that one can actually appreciate how Garcia used the medium of printmaking and the formal strategies of pop to critique the style's unwillingness to address the pressing social issues of the civil-rights movement. An exhibition such as this one demonstrates that these printed objects have multiple lives and that their power can ricochet beyond the specific context in which they were made.

To see the work being acquired and displayed in one of the most prestigious national collections is not a failure of their avant-garde sensibility or a capitulation of the political demands of these social causes. If anything, it is a triumph of subversive maneuvering in which their formal innovation has opened doors to hallowed ground, perhaps without a committee giving much notice to the pointed political commentary in some of these works. I was one of two scholars commissioned to write an essay for the catalogue, and I wrote about how these experimental print practices fostered conceptual iconoclasm. I wanted to show the elasticity of a concept like revolution and how it can dematerialize. I argued, "Their iconoclasm foments an attack on the colonial origins of U.S. nationalism to lay bare the violence of its present-day legacies in a country that has been at war with the Indian, the poor, the immigrant,

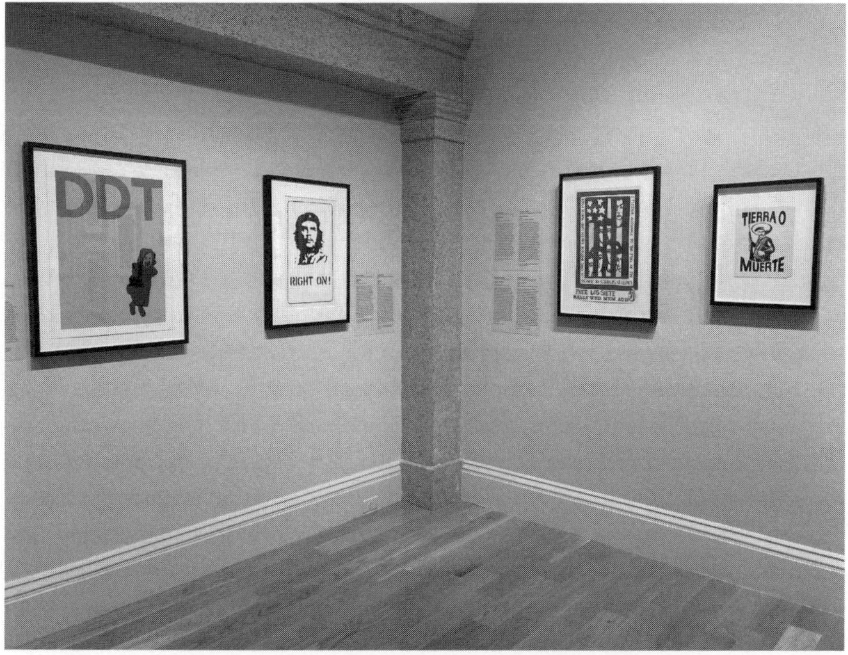

5.3. "Urgent Images" section of *¡Printing the Revolution! The Rise and Impact of Chicano Graphics, 1965 to Now* exhibition at the Smithsonian American Art Museum (November 20, 2020–August 8, 2021). Photo by the author.

the racialized, the queer since its founding."[8] It will be interesting to see how these works continue engaging in these larger conversations beyond the run of the exhibition, when they are seen in permanent-collection galleries and canonized as simply American art.

In chapter 3 of this book, I discussed how multiculturalism provided a brief opening for artists of color to exhibit in mainstream institutions, and how this in turn engendered criticisms in Latinx art spaces where some artists accused others of "selling out." I have yet to hear of that kind of criticism being directed at artists who participated in *¡Printing the Revolution!*, but it is worth clarifying that at least fifty works of the 119 on view were gifted by private collectors, primarily Tomás Ybarra-Frausto, Margaret Terrazas Santos, Ricardo and Harriett Romo, Gilberto Cárdenas, and Dolores García. This anti-market and anti-institutional position is a fallacy that ignores how museum collections work. A vast amount of art in American museums is gifted by collectors, many of them longtime supporters and friends of artists. On occasion they can also be directly gifted by the artist, or by the artist's estate, when a specific request comes along. When purchases do take place, they are a result of intense brokering by curators at the institution, who must run each proposed object through the scrutiny of an acquisitions committee. As I walked through the show with Ramos and Zapata, they discussed the difficulties of making a case for some of the works that they acquired in 2019 and 2020 for the exhibition. The biggest obstacle was not political content or Eurocentric notions of "quality"; it was price point: the works were priced too low, which raised questions about their value. But the problem is, How do we create value when so little of the cultural infrastructure (galleries, dealers, art fairs, museums) is available to Latinx artists, a problem that Arlene Dávila tackles head on in her book *Latinx Art*?[9]

Reclaiming the Americas explored how Latinx artists reinvigorate the medium of printmaking by staging an avant-garde. The word "staging" carries metaphors of performativity and illusion. This is intentional on my part. I see the role of Latinx printmaking studios as akin to a theater in which artists are encouraged to experiment, collaborate, rehearse, play, and even fail. The kind of freedom that Self Help Graphics, Segura Publishing, Coronado Studio, and the DYPG provided the artists in this book led to aesthetic and theoretical breakthroughs in Latinx art but also in regard to articulating a politics of territory. It also led to an engagement with decolonial aesthetics if we consider how their work collectively developed a critique of the print medium and its role in spreading Eurocentric and colonial ideas of land that inform modern-day borders and the racial segregation of our cities. Finally, to stage an avant-garde involves artifice, as we live in a contemporary art world in which no one can fully claim the status of avant-garde. The performance engages the process of mythmaking, which we learned from Duffy is a powerful way to fight erasure.

Returning to Kennicott's dismissive notion that "Latino art is a meaningless category," it is worth considering why the curators of *¡Printing the Revolution!* insisted on using *Chicano Graphics* in the subtitle of the exhibition. According to Ramos, "this exhibition and catalogue use the terms Chicano or Chicanx graphic arts to also denote the institutional and artist networks created during and since El Movimiento that established a context for artists that followed, whether they are Latinx artists with links to other Latin American nations, white allies, card-carrying Chicano activists, or recent Mexican immigrants who may or may not identify as Chicanx."[10] In such a view the title performs an homage to the early artistic networks that originated Chicanx graphics in the Southwest and gives primacy to the narrative outlined in Tere Romo's essay in which she argues that Chicana/o artists developed a new visual lexicon, blending art and activism in support of movement organizations, community art centers, and individual artistic careers.[11] The focus on "Chicano Graphics" also countered the lack of specificity that Kennicott identified in his remarks on *Our America*. However, in its framing of Chicano as the favored category, the exhibition reinforces the idea that printmaking studios were divided along ethnic-identity lines, connotes a masculine identity in the gendered "Chicano," and obscures the diversity of Latinx and non-Latinx cultural producers who helped shape the field. While it shows that Chicanx print networks were inclusive of other groups demonstrating interracial and cross-cultural solidarity in their aesthetics, the frame solidifies what some critics call a "Chicano hegemony," which positions Chicanx art as the dominant narrative and stand-in for the whole of Latinx art.

Of the artists whose work I highlight in the book, Enrique Chagoya, Sandra Fernández, and the DYPG were prominently represented in the exhibition. None of these artists identifies as Chicanx, though we can argue that they all possess strong ties to the Chicanx art community and the larger field of Chicanx art history. Chagoya, who was born in Mexico City and immigrated to the US as a young adult, worked for a number of years at Galería de la Raza in San Francisco's Mission District, where he collaborated with Chicanx artists on exhibition projects. One of his signature amate-paper codices, *The Ghost of Liberty* (2004), was centered in a display case. Born in New York but raised in the city of Quito, Fernández had already built a career for herself exhibiting her prints and mixed-media projects, but it was her collaborations with Mexican American artists in Central Texas's Coronado Studio that allowed her to develop a political edge and brought her into the fold of a larger print network. *¡Printing the Revolution!* featured her large print installation *Mourning and Dreaming on High: Con Mucha Fé* (2014–2018), which included eighteen prints arranged in the shape of a Jerusalem cross that reflected on the criminalization of immigration from the perspective of undocumented youth. The entire portfolio of *Manifestaciones* by the DYPG was on view in a stand-alone display case and, as addressed in chapter 4, the origins of this printmaking collective correspond with Pepe Coronado's experiences working with Chicanx artists at Coronado Studio and through his residency at Self Help Graphics.

In addition to these artists, there were several other works in the exhibition that also addressed themes related to the politics of territory. *Reclaiming the Americas* introduced four methods by which Latinx artists delinked from Western conceptions of territory and brought to light Native, embodied, mestiza, and aqueous territorialities. *Santuario* (2018; fig. 5.4), by the artist Poli Marichal, is a two-color linocut in which a multitude of men, women, and children at center are enveloped in the embrace of two hands. Marichal spent almost two decades working at Self Help Graphics, attuned to the routine ICE raids that threaten undocumented communities in Los Angeles, before relocating back to her native Puerto Rico. Her work does not portray geography per se but invokes many of the ideas surrounding embodied territorialities. Marichal is the daughter of the Spanish painter and printmaker Carlos Marichal, who studied art in Mexico and later formed an integral part of the Centro de Arte Puertorriqueño in Old San Juan, a studio and art school that spearheaded the midcentury Puerto Rican print renaissance. Her use of the linocut technique to tackle the issue of sanctuary during a period of heightened xenophobia unites the aesthetic traditions of Mexico and Puerto Rico, symbolically creating a bridge of solidarity for those desperately seeking refuge. A spiritual connection to nature is another theme that figures largely in her work. The devastation caused by Hurricane Maria, which revealed the vulnerability and precarious position of Puerto Rico, and the growing effects of climate change, led her to produce her tour-de-force linocut assemblage *Hurricane Redux* (2018), which was also acquired by SAAM but not shown in the exhibition.[12]

Native territorialities appeared in the magnificent one-color poster *Indian Land* (2004, reprinted 2010; fig. 5.5) by Jesus Barraza and Nancypili Hernandez. The screenprint depicted the entire Western hemisphere from the Alaskan Peninsula to Patagonia in bright red ink across stark white paper and the bold title written along its Pacific shore. The idea for *Indian Land* came about as Barraza and Hernandez, a longtime Bay Area activist, were making plans for a fundraiser.[13] They thought about the American Indian occupation of Alcatraz Island. On November 20, 1969, Indigenous activists arrived at the former federal prison and began an occupation that lasted a year and a half.[14] At the entrance to the prison, the sign that once read "United States Property"

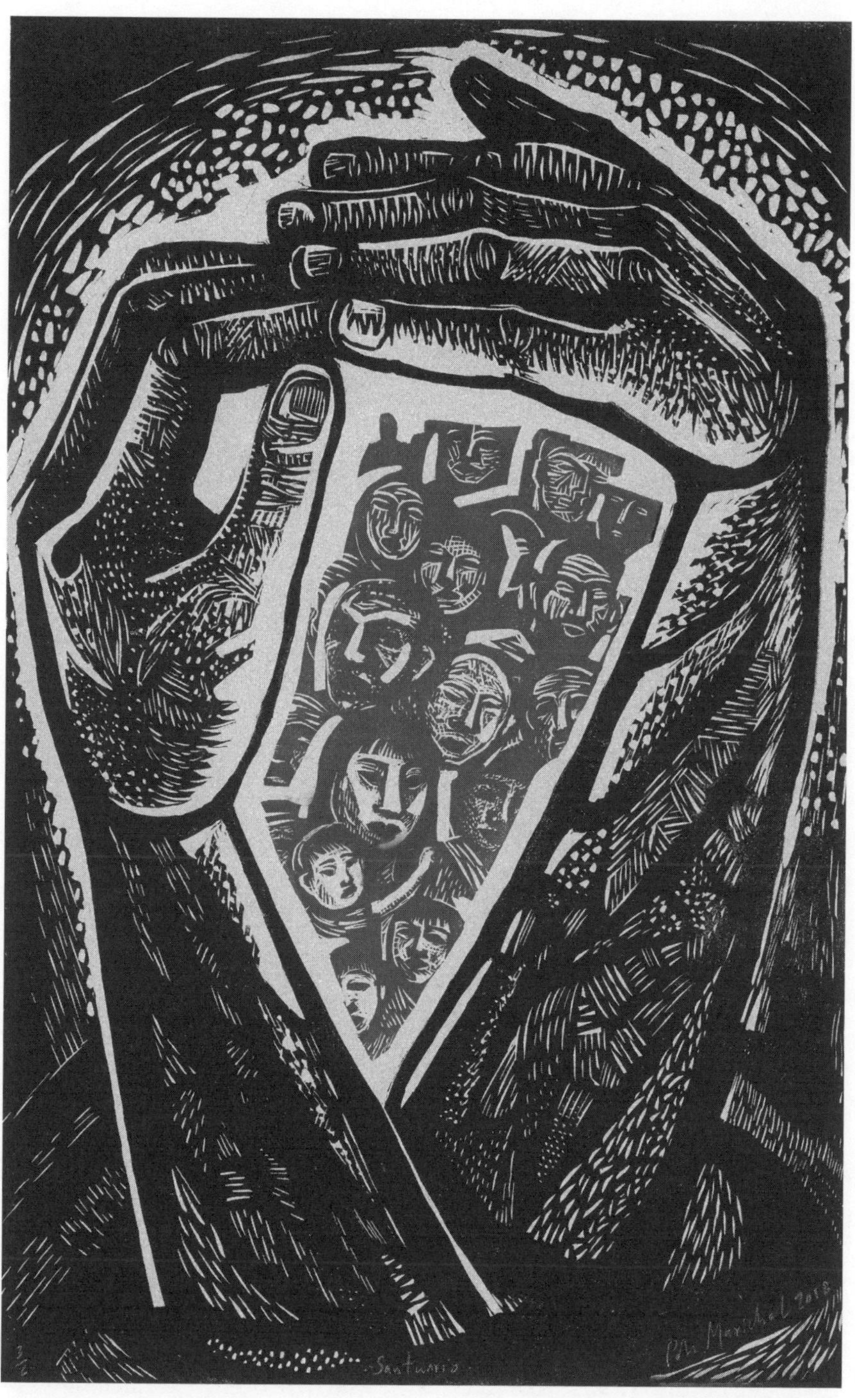

5.4. Poli Marichal, *Santuario*, 2018. Linocut on paper, sheet and image: 17¾ x 11¼ inches. Smithsonian American Art Museum, Museum purchase through the Frank K. Ribelin Endowment, 2020.32.5, © Poli Marichal. Courtesy of the artist and the Smithsonian American Art Museum.

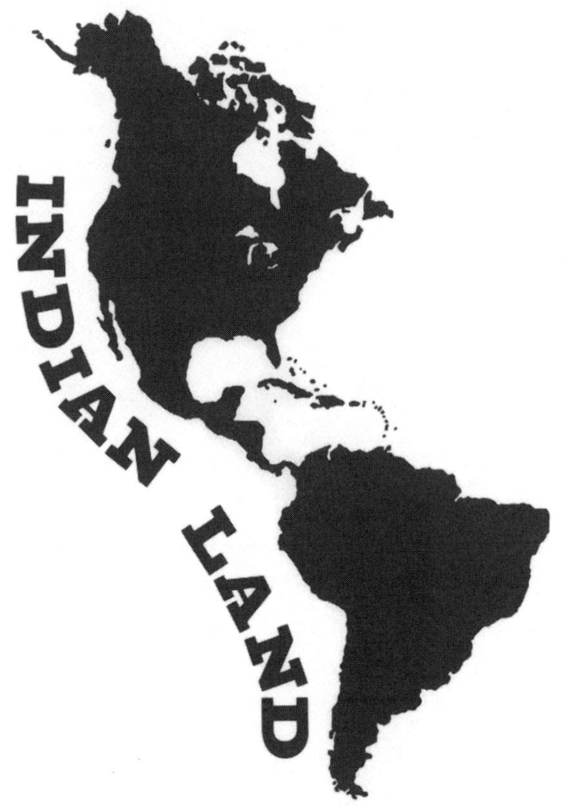

5.5. Jesus Barraza and Nancypili Hernandez, *Indian Land*, 2004 (reprinted 2010). Screenprint on paper, sheet and image: 40 × 28 inches. Smithsonian American Art Museum, museum purchase through the Samuel and Blanche Koffler Acquisition Fund, 2020.39.7. © Jesus Barraza and Nancypili Hernandez. Courtesy of the artists.

was altered to read "United Indian Property" and in larger lettering "Indians Welcome," "Indian Land." Barraza's Indigenous worldview was also heavily influenced by the Zapatista Uprising, when Indigenous communities in the state of Chiapas rose up on January 1, 1994, to protest the enactment of the North American Free Trade Agreement and called for autonomy and self-governance of their communities.[15] "It is through the lens of the Zapatistas' anti-capitalist, anti-colonial, and pro-indigenous philosophy," writes Barraza, "that we strive to make work that serves as symbols of solidarity, and which therefore empowers people struggling for self-determination."[16] *Indian Land* aims to awaken not only the Native communities, from the Mapuche to the Unangan, but also viewers like you and me who have been inculcated in Western concepts of territory for so long they have erased our memory of this view.

Indian Land quickly achieved an unprecedented level of iconicity because of its vast reproduction in books, exhibition catalogues, stickers, pins, tortilla art, and social-media sites, which garnered the attention of critics. The Métis artist and American Indian Studies scholar Dylan Miner called *Indian Land* "the clearest example of hemispheric Xicano indigeneity," which sought to expand the mythical homeland of Aztlán into one of "continental indigenous solidarity."[17] Cornell professor Ella Diaz linked *Indian Land* to the genealogy of Chicano art, tracing its descent from the unassimilable and rebellious philosophy of art collectives like the Royal Chicano Air Force, commenting on how the design, "interrupt[s] the geopolitical borders that guide our understanding of the Western Hemisphere, continuing the RCAF's decolonial message in a new century."[18] *Indian Land* calls for a hemispheric Indigeneity and traces its ideological roots to the Chicano Art Movement, but when it is analyzed as part of a larger sphere of cultural production, such as the prints in this book, one begins to notice how it critiques the very medium of its making. The print challenges the long history of printmaking in early-modern Europe, which envisioned the Americas as Terra Incognita (unknown), Terra Nullius (unclaimed), or Terra Nova (new). Barraza and Hernandez reclaimed the print medium used to diffuse this knowledge of New World peoples and, speaking from the position of *indigena* (Latin, "sprung from the land"), they defy its unknown, unclaimed, new status. From this position, they enunciate other ways of seeing that confront hidden processes that invented Europe's discovery of the New World, and furthermore they promote an identification with Chicanx Indigeneity as a means to decolonize.

While decolonial in its ability to challenge the medium's complicity in the colonization of the Americas, *Indian Land* falls prey to the paradoxical position of reproducing colonial thinking. If Miner's assertion of a hemispheric Chicanx Indigeneity is correct, drawing on the long history of mobilizing Aztlán, the mythical homeland of the Aztecs, then the print performs a reconquest and a reaffirmation in the belief that the land can be owned.[19] These enunciations and images create tensions with Native American groups who may feel their claims to land and painful history of dispossession are being appropriated by new settlers who simulate Indigeneity without actual tribal affiliation or a history of pernicious disenfranchisement. Barraza admits, "I am from this continent and I share the larger land base with the Ohlone people whom I recognize; I am a visitor on their ancestral land."[20] These criticisms bring to light the painful realities of cultural appropriation on the one hand and on the other the detribalized and deterritorialized status of many Latinx artists, like Barraza, who are attempting to recover their Indigenous heritage and view their Indigenization as central to their decolonization.

Some may go so far as to compare this work to the widespread use of land acknowledgments at conferences, museums, universities, and even sporting events. Anthropologists and Indigenous activists Elisa Sobo, Valerie Lambert, and Michael Lambert point out how these land-acknowledgment rituals do little to acknowledge the enduring trauma of dispossession and show no intention of righting that wrong—"The implication is: 'What was once yours is now ours.'"[21] But it is worth clarifying that Barraza and Hernandez produced the work back in 2004, prior to the dominant culture's adoption of land acknowledgments. At the time, Barraza was involved with the Oakland-based print collective Taller Tupac Amaru, which he cofounded with Favianna Rodriguez. The title of their collective reflected their interests in Indigenous history, especially the revolutionary spirit encompassed by the Tupac Amaru Rebellion, and the socially engaged lyrics and Black Panther lineage of the late rapper Tupac Shakur.[22] Given this context, we may speculate that the artists made *Indian Land* with the utopian vision that the land should be returned to its original inhabitants.

I draw attention to this print not to single out the work on the basis of some moral judgment but to ask: How can artists avoid the pitfalls of reproducing colonial thinking in their attempts to reclaim the Americas? And relatedly, how can scholars develop more-nuanced readings of decolonial aesthetics that allow for these contradictions to emerge? This book demonstrates that the politics of territory are quite complicated in the Latinx imaginary. The claims to land are a result of complex identities circumscribed by multiple and often-overlapping colonial histories. There is no us-versus-them as in the resistance paradigm that was so central to the birth of this field. The print projects discussed in this book similarly decenter and delink from Eurocentric conceptions of discovery, but their works may still be embroiled in horizontal cultural battles that are rooted in epistemic violence. That was most apparent in chapter 1, where Ricardo Duffy references the lands of the Southwest and the legend of Apache Leap. He transposes the mythical homeland of the Aztecs, Aztlán, with the land of Apache nations, and inadvertently reproduces the same kinds of settler violence that his work purports to condemn. In chapter 3, I point to a similar paradox that takes place in Sandra Fernández's prints as mestizaje's theories travel from Quito, Ecuador, to the borderlands of Texas. Her works reinsert mixed-race bodies into disembodied geographic projections and claim space for migrant subjects. But the allusions to mestizaje still reference the Spanish and Indigenous past, and likewise inadvertently obscure the African presence in the Americas. These are unresolved issues that add more layers and ambiguity to their thoughtful works and demand more questions from the viewer. Their paradoxical positions serve as an important reminder to scholars working with decolonial frameworks that efforts to decolonize can continue to be haunted by the afterlives of coloniality.

In an essay for the 1993 Whitney Biennial, the performance artist and critic Coco Fusco noted, "the strategy of taking elements of an established or imposed culture and throwing them back with a different set of meanings is not only key to guerrilla warfare; the tactics of reversal, recycling, and subversive montage are aesthetics that form the basis of many twentieth-century avant-gardes."[23] My book adds to the important scholarship generated by *¡Printing the Revolution!* by foregrounding *why* Latinx artists reclaimed the medium of prints, extending their guerrilla warfare further than the civil-rights movement to a historical juncture in the early-modern period when prints helped create hegemonic narratives of art, history, and geography. Their war of images carries that five-hundred-year history of resistance to the domination so tangibly present in Barraza and Hernandez's poster. But I am likewise attentive to Fusco's claim that these forms of engagement carry on the commitments of the avant-garde to continually experiment with form, break with established norms, and technically outpace the art that came before them. I hope readers understand how the artists in this book work with a traditional medium that continues to push boundaries.

This high bar is being met by a newer generation of artists like the printmaker and new-media artist Michael Menchaca (they/them). The San Antonio native was the most represented artist, by number of works, in *¡Printing the Revolution!*, though their humorous prints do not seem to evoke the same political sentiments as those who came of age during the Chicano Movement. Menchaca's printmaking trajectory carries on the spirit of questioning structures of power but completely revamps the iconography of the Chicano protest poster with the aesthetics and narratives of the internet. They explain,

> I have always admired the prints of those legendary Chicano artists of the '60s–'80s and how these were responding to the oppressors and their methods of their time. What I am responding to in my current prints is the unprecedented power that Big Tech companies assert over communities of color and presenting them as the new conquistadors of our time. I recognize that in the present, digital literacy is required of us and therefore I apply a digital sensibility within the production of my prints, something that I hope will provide some distance from the previous generation of printmakers.[24]

Many of their prints evoke the figurative archetypes of Mesoamerican codices, a technique used by artists like Chagoya, but Menchaca embeds the icons with new meaning, and viewers must decipher how these pictograms allude to life in the borderlands. Artists like Menchaca are waging war with techno-capitalism and its ability to spread misinformation. Despite the utopian belief in cyberspace's democratic function, the internet has become the fastest image-reproduction machine, capturing, replaying, and transmitting ideas about belonging.

One of Menchaca's prints invoked the method of aqueous territorialities in describing the liminal space of the Rio Grande. The river, which originates in Colorado and makes its way down the Texas-Mexico border until reaching the Gulf of Mexico, is witness to thousands of migrant crossings each year, some of which result in drownings.[25] Their screenprint *Cuando el Rio Suena, Gatos Lleva* (2011; fig. 5.6) is a humorous representation of what is generally a very somber subject.[26] In the print, a large number of cats who are dressed in Mexican sarapes and sombreros attempt to make their way across a river that the artist abstracts into a pale blue, flat background with wavy white lines that represent water currents. The cats look directly at the viewer; their large mustaches and whiskers animate their frozen and fearful expressions. Some of the cats appear to be avid swimmers, while a few are struggling to stay afloat, and one is completely submerged, the only evidence of its presence a squiggly cat's tail rising from the water. Menchaca began this series of *Gatos* during his undergraduate years at Texas State University–San Marcos, where he learned printmaking with Jeffrey Dell, Brian Johnson, and Elvia Perrin. The idea for the series came from an everyday interaction in their home. Their mother fed the stray cats in the neighborhood, and they noticed how the cats grew dependent on her care and kept reproducing. Menchaca warned her that she needed to stop doing this, and in that moment they realized that they were repeating the anti-Mexican and anti-immigrant rhetoric so pervasive in mainstream media.[27] Their cartoonlike characters also engendered a disturbing and racist question during a group critique: Why does this cat have a "dirty Mexican mustache?"[28] At this point, they realized the icon could reveal behaviors and attitudes on xenophobic territoriality and racism. They began incorporating cats, as well as other animals like the coyote, into their prints as stand-ins for the marginal, outcast, racial other. Their animals performed stereotypical roles in exaggerated form in order to destroy these representations with humor. In *¡Printing the Revolution!*, half of Menchaca's prints were displayed in an arched wall in a window-pane arrangement and overlaid with a video projection of a movable abstract geometry that lent the work an intermedial aesthetic between the printed and the digital. It was the perfect coup de grâce, in which the curators could conclude and demonstrate the lasting power of the revolutionary spirit that has animated this intergenerational graphic-arts movement.

If Menchaca's work is any indication, there is hope that younger artists will continue to delve into the printmaking tradition, altering, experimenting, and extending its reach far beyond what we thought was possible. The extension of print into new media, including augmented reality, social-media distribution, and immersive computer-generated environments, was the subject of Claudia Zapata's essay in the catalogue, in which they wrote:

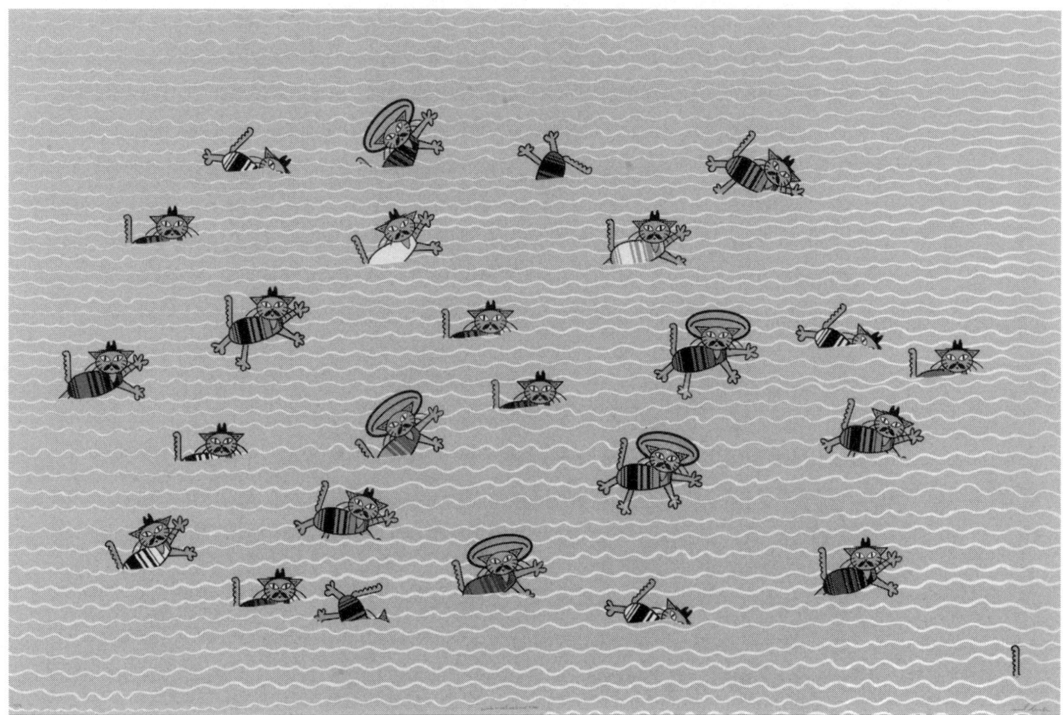

5.6. Michael Menchaca, *Cuando el Rio Suena, Gatos Lleva*, 2011. Screenprint on paper, sheet and image: 26 × 40 inches. Smithsonian American Art Museum, Gift of Drs. Harriett and Ricardo Romo, 2019.50.33. © Michael Menchaca. Courtesy of the artist.

> Chicanx artists have actively participated in each technological paradigm shift, unearthing and connecting these digitally informed efforts to lay the foundation for a new lens of Chicanx study. What is striking is how the rally cries of disruption, empowerment, and resistance of previous generations reverberate in such efforts. This conceptual relationality among critical advancements in technology underscores the shared objective of shaping a decolonial consciousness, to infiltrate and dismantle systems of oppression by whatever means necessary.[29]

Although the technical means and aesthetics are changing, the social-justice issues remain utterly similar to what detonated the social movements of the 1960s. Zapata highlights how this new generation is taking the baton with a decolonial impulse to overturn structures of oppression. While these often are a modus operandi for the dominant culture, they can also be a part of

Latinx cultures, and artists like Julio Salgado are developing pointed critiques of Latinx cultural traditions, such as the *Quinceañera,* that exclude queer youth based on the gendered colonial system that remains firmly in place.[30] Ultimately, *¡Printing the Revolution!* shows that we are only at the beginning of trying to historicize artistic movements that have long been overlooked or dismissed in art history. These scholarly advancements will hopefully compel collectors, curators, gallerists, and scholars to create the infrastructures necessary to sustain this tradition so that these artists cease to be footnotes, afterthoughts, and tokens.

As I conclude this research, we are in the midst of a global pandemic that has brought to light the interconnectedness of our world, and how our survival and the survival of our planet depends on overcoming the severe inequalities drawn about through the "colonial matrix of power." What does it mean to reclaim the Americas at this moment, when so much is at stake including the extinction of our species through environmental violence? What new forms of xenophobia and territoriality will emerge during this century as climate migrants cross borders and oceans in search of food, water, and safety? Overcoming these challenges and visualizing a horizon of justice will require changing our attachments to homeland and nationalism. The artists in this book are sowing these commitments to eradicate our fear of the foreigner, the migrant, the refugee, and to see them as essential to our future.

ACKNOWLEDGMENTS

RECLAIMING THE AMERICAS is the product of a decade of research in which I have benefited immensely from the generosity of archivists, artists, colleagues, curators, scholars, and workshop directors. I would like to begin by acknowledging the countless artists who have invited me to their studios, walked me through their exhibitions, granted me interviews, and opened up their personal archives. I am especially indebted to Enrique Chagoya, Ricardo Duffy, Sandra Fernández, Alberto Ríos, and the artists affiliated with the Dominican York Proyecto Gráfica for the many ways in which their artwork and our conversations inspired my writing. Thanks are also due to many artists and estates who kindly granted permission to reproduce their work: the estate of Laura Aguilar, Jesus Barraza, Louie "the Foot" González, the estate of Oswaldo Guayasamín, Ester Hernandez, Nancypili Hernandez, Consuelo Jimenez Underwood, Pedro Lasch, Arturo Lindsay, Diana Magaloni, Poli Marichal, Emanuel Martinez, Vicki Meek, Michael Menchaca, Dalila Paola Mendez, Kent Monkman, Tony Ortega, Rubén Ortiz Torres, Sandy Rodriguez, Ezequiel Taveras, Oswaldo Viteri, and Terry Ybañez. Working with living artists is as rewarding as it is challenging, and my role models for engagement were the workshop founders and directors who helped shape this field and the reciprocity that exists within these art spaces: Betty Avila, Pepe Coronado, Sam Coronado, Allan Edmunds, Linda Lucero, Domingo Negrón, and Joe Segura. The late Sam Coronado was particularly influential during my formative years of graduate training. It was through my work in the print archives of his workshop that I began to envision the significance of this field to American art history, and I dedicate this book to his memory.

My first exposure to artists working with the medium of printmaking was during my undergraduate years at Sacramento State University. As a studio-art major, I had the good fortune of working with a number of artists affiliated with the Royal Chicano Air Force, a legendary art collective that produced posters in support of the United Farm Workers of America. Their posters have now become iconic images of the labor movement, but when these artists began their graphic-art campaigns in university-based workshops, they were not doing it for fame or glory. Many of them renounced their claims to individualism and sole authorship by signing their work under a collective name. The RCAF became known for the vibrant screenprint production that supported the UFW but also the larger Chicano civil-rights movement for self-determination. Once I began traveling around the country and learning more about the rich history of printmaking in African American, Asian American, Native, and Latinx communities, I realized that their interest in collaborative artmaking was part of a larger trend. The books that touch on the history of printmaking in the United States had completely overlooked one of the most exciting periods of graphic-art production, when artists of color had brought technical innovation and virtuosity to the field, and used it to create new social identities and forms of belonging.

In my dissertation work at the University of Texas at Austin, I examined the significant role that printmaking played in the formation of the discourse of Latinidad ("Latinoness") in the United States. This widely debated and provocative keyword denotes the cultural practices that allowed Latin American–origin groups to be understood as a collective entity in the US, though its history is far more complicated, as you will learn in the pages of this book. Through a study of visual-print culture and its affiliated workshops, I theorized that artists articulate and constitute Latinx identities from "impossible subject" positions, those perhaps most feared by the dominant culture: the political prisoner, the colonial subject, and the undocumented. Moreover, in their quest to create alternative community formations from positions of exclusion, the workshops became engines of identity formation for the largest minority population in the US. I was fortunate to have a dissertation committee that believed in the project and whose expertise represented the broad range of scholarship in American art, American Studies, Latino Studies, and Latin American art to which this work is indebted. Cherise Smith has been an incredibly generous advisor, mentor, and role model. I am especially grateful for how she taught me the value of close reading and challenged me to foreground the machinations of race and racism in art history. Cary Cordova, working at the intersection of American Studies and Latino Studies, prompted me to prioritize the voices of artists as well as the institutional histories of workshops long obscured from art-historical scholarship. Roberto Tejada introduced me to Borderlands Art and Theory, which opened a plethora of interpretive lenses for my scholarship, with particular attention to how contested geographies inform art and identity. Thanks are also due to Eddie Chambers, Andrea Giunta, Julia Guernsey, Frank Guridy, George Flaherty, José Limón, John McKiernan-González, Martha Menchaca, John Morán González, Moyosore Okediji, and Ann Reynolds, for courses, conversations, encouragement, and insightful feedback. The Benson Latin American Collection possessed an embarrassment of riches in my subject field. I am grateful to librarians and archivists such as Julianne Gilland, Margo Gutierrez, Adrian Johnson, and Christian Kelleher for their assistance in locating archival materials and for the opportunity to serve as liaison in the acquisition of the Sam Coronado and Serie Project Inc. papers.

My research would not have been possible without the support of various fellowships. The Inter University Program for Latino Research Mellon Dissertation Fellowship provided a year of funding and, most important, a wonderful cohort of colleagues around the country: Ariel Arnau, Ana Báez, Ryan Mann-Hamilton, Marilu Utomi, and Yvette Martínez-Vu. In 2016, I was awarded a three-year Society of Fellows Postdoctoral Fellowship at Dartmouth College. I would like to thank junior fellows Michael Barany, Yesenia Barragan, Nathalie Batraville, Kate Hall, Yui Hashimoto, Yvonne Kwan, Alex Sotelo-Eastman, Laura McTighe, Garret Nelson, Lakshmi Padmanabhan, Yana Stainova, and Derek Woods as well as senior fellows Mona Domosh, Donald Pease, and Michelle Warren for their investment in my work. Dartmouth was one of the most vibrant intellectual communities I've had the pleasure of being a part of, and I would especially like to thank my Department of Art History colleagues Mary Coffey, who served as my primary mentor, Nicola Camerlenghi, Ada Cohen, Chad Elias, Allen Hockley, Katie Hornstein, Steven Kangas, Sunglim Kim, Kristin O'Rourke, Holly Shaffer, as well as my colleagues in the Program in Latin American, Latino, and Caribbean Studies such as Jorge Cuéllar, Matthew Garcia, Patricia Lopez, Douglas Moody, Eman Morsi, Israel Reyes, and Silvia Spitta. It was during my years at Dartmouth, and through a regime change that instituted draconian anti-immigrant measures, that I started to ponder larger questions about the medium of printmaking and how it had been historically used to distribute the spatial logics of colonization. I became interested in how Latinx artists have reclaimed the medium and used it to create their own representations of territory.

I have presented aspects of my research at various stages of this project and am thankful to these venues for allowing me the opportunity to share my work: the College Art Association Annual Conference, the Latin American Studies Association Conference, the Latino Art Now Biennial Conference, the Latino Studies Association Conference, the Chicano Movement Conference at UC Santa Barbara, and the National Association of Chicana/o Studies Conference. I would also like to thank colleagues across the field who invited me to lecture on the subject, including Jesús Escobar at Northwestern University, Robb Hernández at Fordham University, Pablo González at UC Berkeley, Yolanda Flores at the University of Vermont, Anna Indych-López at CUNY, Gilberto Cárdenas at the University of Notre Dame, and Gina Tarver at Texas State University, San Marcos. Museum venues such as El Museo del Barrio, Mexic-Arte Museum, the Museum of Fine Arts Houston, Pennsylvania Academy of Fine Arts, and the Smithsonian American Art Museum afforded unique opportunities for public presentations. The Permanent Seminar in Latin American Art hosted by the Center for Latin American and Visual Studies at the University of Texas at Austin, the Colloquium for the Study of Latina/o Culture and Theory at CUNY, the New England Consortium for Latino Studies, the Exhibiting and Narrating Latin American and Latino Art seminar hosted by the Getty Foundation's Connecting Art Histories Initiative, and the Notre Dame Young Scholars Symposium led by Charlene Villaseñor Black offered invaluable feedback. I would also like to acknowledge the students in my own classrooms at Dartmouth College and my present institution, the University of Notre Dame, who have been a sounding board and whose curiosity has enriched my thinking. Alondra Alonso, Isabella Di Bono Becerra, Marie Latham, Kendra Lyimo, and Armando Pulido deserve special praise as interlocutors and research assistants.

Portions of this manuscript were previously published. Excerpts from chapter 3 appear in "Immigrant Invisibility and the Post-9/11 Border in Sandra Fernández's Coming of Age," *alter/nativas latin american cultural studies journal* 7 (fall 2017); they are reproduced courtesy of the editor. Portions of chapter 4 were adapted from "The Island within the Island: Remapping Dominican York," *Archives of American Art Journal* 57: 2 (fall 2018): 4–27; and are reproduced courtesy of the University of Chicago Press.

My academic life has been greatly enhanced by finding generous and supportive colleagues in the Department of Art, Art History & Design at the University of Notre Dame. I am especially grateful to Michael Schreffler and Maria Tomasula for serving as my mentors, as well as to art historians Marius Hauknes, Heather Hyde Minor, Robin Rhodes, Elyse Speaks, and Nicole Woods. I feel fortunate to be surrounded by colleagues in studio art and design whose creative practice keeps me engaged with the questions at stake in contemporary art. My colleagues at the Snite Museum of Art, who include David Acton, Joseph Becherer, Bridget Hoyt, Jared Katz, Victoria Perdomo, Ramiro Rodriguez, and Cheryl Snay, are outstanding connoisseurs who have helped cultivate an impressive collection of Latinx art, which I use in my teaching and research. The Institute for Latino Studies spearheaded my recruitment to Notre Dame. I want to thank Luis Fraga, the director, Tatiana Botero, David Cortez, Paloma Garcia-Lopez, Tim Matovina, Marisel Moreno, Xavier Navarro Aquino, Karen Richman, Francisco Robles, Jason Ruiz, and Leonor Wangensteen for fostering such a vibrant intellectual environment.

At the University of Texas Press, it has been a pleasure to work with my editor Kerry Webb, and her team, including Christina Vargas, Ana Cecilia Calle Poveda, and Lynne Ferguson. This book is part of the series "Latinx: The Future Is Now," edited by the illustrious scholars Lorgia García-Peña and Nicole

Guidotti-Hernández, to whom I owe a special thanks for their investment in a book on Latinx art history. This manuscript was greatly enriched through the insightful commentary of two anonymous readers who brought nuance and depth to my claims. I also thank copyeditor Paul Psoinos, proofreader Diane Mankedick, and indexer Sue Gaines for their rigorous work.

Many colleagues helped me develop the project further. My National Center for Faculty Development and Diversity writing group—Jenny Kelly, Kirsten Leuner, and Sarah Orem—provided accountability and support at times of intense revision. My current writing group—Cynthia Cogswell, Marcela Di Blasi, Suzanne Lye, and Michelle Thompson—have likewise provided pillars of support. Our daily check-ins and affirmations have helped me navigate the highs and lows of book authorship and academic life. Robb Hernández and Kency Cornejo have been enduring sources of warm friendship as well as steadfast companions in art pilgrimage, and have commented upon portions of the book manuscript.

My final words of gratitude are to my family. You are the source of my resilience and tenacity. When we left El Salvador in search of safety during the civil war and became immigrants without a map, it was hard to imagine setting roots in a place so far from home and where one day those of us who came as children would be able to pursue the dream of higher education. But you persevered and taught me that home is a movable cartography that we carry with us and that becomes tangible in our cultural expressions. I thank the Reinoza and Fortis families for making me who I am and for always helping me stay connected and grounded when academic positions took me far across the country. My sisters Jennifer Peña and Carolyn Zweben, and cousins Luis Mario Reinoza and Vanessa Kitchens have stood by my side through the most stressful and rewarding periods of this project. Justin Perkins and the Hedges family have been the source of invaluable co-parenting support. And to my beautiful son, Phoenix, this book is your sibling. It has grown as you have grown. My attention to the social history of these works of art, to their decolonial and political aims, is a reflection of the just futures I hope one day you will inherit.

APPENDIX

Latinx Printmaking Workshops and Collectives in the US

Arceo Press and Studio
Founded by René Arceo in 2005
7100 W. Dickens Ave.
Chicago, IL 60707
www.arceopress.com

Bandolero Press
Founded by Carlos Barberena in 2009
Chicago, Illinois
www.bandoleropress.com

Coronado Studio
Founded by Sam Coronado in 1991
Artist residency Serie Project founded in 1993
Current Director: Jill Ramirez
901 Vargas Road
Austin, TX 78741
www.coronadostudio.com
www.serieproject.org

Coronado printstudio
Founded by Pepe Coronado in 2006
901 Vargas Rd.
Austin, TX 78741 (in the former Coronado Studio print shop)
www.coronadoprintstudio.com

Dignidad Rebelde
Founded by Jesus Barraza and Melanie Cervantes in 2007
www.dignidadrebelde.com

Dominican York Proyecto Gráfica
Founded in 2010 by Carlos Almonte (former member), Pepe Coronado, René de los Santos, iliana emilia garcía (former member), Reynaldo García Pantaleón (former member), Scherezade García (former member), Alex Guerrero, Luanda Lozano, Miguel Luciano, Yunior Chiqui Mendoza (former member), Moses Ros-Suárez, and Rider Ureña.
www.dypgrafica.com

El Taller Gráfico
Founded in 1965 by the United Farm Workers of America, AFL-CIO
Keene, California

Instituto Gráfico de Chicago
Founded by Antonio Pazaran, and Ricardo X. Serment in 2010
Chicago, Illinois
www.institutograficodechicago.org

Marimacha Monarca Press
Founded by Sarita Hernández and Moni Pizano Luna in 2017
Chicago, Illinois
saritamaritza.wordpress.com/marimacha-monarca-press

Mono Gráfico Colectivo (formerly Los de Abajo)
Collective members: Kay Brown, Nguyen Ly, Don Newton, Beth Petersen, Marianne Sadowski
724 E. Kensington Road
Los Angeles, CA 90026
Contact: Marianne Sadowski at mariannesadowski@gmail.com

El Nopal Press
Founded by Francesco X. Siqueiros in 1990
109 W. 5th St.
Los Angeles, CA 90013
www.elnopalpress.com

Pájaro Editions
Founded by Juan Fuentes in 2007
1725 Newcomb Avenue
San Francisco CA 94124
www.juanrfuentes.com

Poli Marichal Print Studio
Founded by Poli Marichal in 2018
665 Calle Estado
San Juan, Puerto Rico 00907-3506
www.polimarichal.com

RioMar Studio
Founded by Ramiro Rodriguez and Laurie Rousseau in 2009
120 South Taylor St.
South Bend, IN 46601
www.ramirorodriguez.com

sfernandez Art (Press & Taller)
Founded by Sandra C. Fernández in 2012
8 Molteg Dr.
Parlin, NJ 08859
www.sandrafernandez.info

Self Help Graphics & Art
Founded by Sister Karen Boccalero, Carlos Bueno, and Antonio Ibañez in 1970, incorporated as a nonprofit in 1973
1300 East 1st Street
Los Angeles, CA 90033
www.selfhelpgraphics.com

Segura Arts Studio (formerly Segura Publishing Co.)
Founded by Joe Segura and Lisa Sette
Tempe, Arizona; relocated to South Bend, Indiana in 2013
Active 1981–2018
Archive at Snite Museum of Art, University of Notre Dame
sniteartmuseum.nd.edu

Taller Boricua
Founded by Marcos Dimas, Adrian García, Manuel Otero, Armando Soto, and Martin Rubio in 1969; incorporated as a nonprofit in 1970
Home to the Rafael Tufiño Printmaking Workshop, directed by Nitza Tufiño
1680 Lexington Avenue
New York, NY 10029
www.tallerboricua.org

Taller Arte del Nuevo Amanecer | TANA
Cofounded by Carlos Francisco Jackson and Malaquias Montoya in 2009
1224 Lemen Avenue
Woodland, CA 95776
tana.ucdavis.edu

Taller de Artes Gráficas
Founded by Malaquias Montoya
Active 1974–1981
Oakland, California
www.malaquiasmontoya.com

Taller Mexicano de Grabado
Founded by Rene Arceo, Nicolas de Jesus, Gerardo de la Barrera, Tomas Bringas, Carlos Cortez, Arturo Barrera, and Carlos Villanueva
Renamed in later years Taller Multimedia, Taller Mestizarte, and Casa de la Cultura Carlos Cortez
Chicago, Illinois
Active 1990–ca. 2010

Taller Tupac Amaru
Founded by Jesus Barraza, Estria Miyashiro, and Favianna Rodriguez
Oakland, California
Active 2003–2013

Tamoanchán Print Collective
Founded by Martivón Galindo, Joaquín Dominguez Parada, and Ricardo Portillo, with assistance from Claudia Bernardi; later members included Carlos and Victor Cartagena
Active 1990–2000
Berkeley and San Francisco, California

The Ernest F. De Soto Workshop
Founded by Ernest de Soto
Active 1975–1990
San Francisco, California
www.desotocollection.com

The Great Tortilla Conspiracy
Founded by Art Hazelwood, Jos Sances, René Yañez, and Rio Yañez circa 2006
San Francisco, California
Contact: Jos Sances at jos@unionbug.com

NOTES

INTRODUCTION

1. Atabey is the supreme goddess of the Taínos. She represents fertility and water. Similarly, Yemaya is a water spirit from the Yoruba religion. She is known as the mother of all Orishas.

2. The printmaking exchange was a partnership between Self Help Graphics, the Museum of Latin American Art, the Richardson Center for Global Engagement, and the Taller de Gráfica, in Havana. In 2015, five artists from Self Help Graphics—Margaret Alarcón, Rogelio Gutierrez, Dalila Paola Mendez, Delilah Montoya, and Miyo Stevens-Gandara—were sent to Havana for a one-week residency at the Taller. The following year, five Cuban artists—Yamylis Brito, Carlos del Toro, Dairén Fernández, Aliosky García, and Octavio Irving—participated in a residency at Self Help Graphics. This kind of artistic exchange with Cuba also took place in 1999 at the Brandywine Workshop in Philadelphia.

3. See Bürger, *Theory of the Avant-Garde*, 49, and his article "Avant-Garde and Neo-Avant-Garde."

4. Scott, "La Raza," 14.

5. Scott, "La Raza," 15.

6. Gómez-Barris, "Mestiza Cultural Memory."

7. Gonzales-Day, *Lynching in the West, 1850–1935*, 184.

8. Chagoya, "Lost Continent," 263.

9. For an excellent overview of the visual hybridity of the maps of the *Relaciones Geográficas*, see Mundy, *Mapping of New Spain*.

10. Hansen, "Multiple Visions."

11. Their omission from residencies and their associated exhibitions was among the reasons Carmen Ramos pursued the acquisition of their works for the Smithsonian American Art Museum, noting, "there is a discernible color line that pervades exhibitions that encompass the rise of 'fine art' printmaking during the so-called American print renaissance of the mid-twentieth century." Ramos, *¡Printing the Revolution!*, 25.

12. Coblentz, "Conversation with Joe Segura," 42.

13. One need only look at the first decade of residencies at Tamarind, Gemini GEL, and Universal Limited Art Editions to see how few artists of color made the rosters. Changing that pattern of exclusion required starting new spaces like the Robert Blackburn Printmaking Workshop, Brandywine Workshop, and Self Help Graphics, among others.

14. The spelling of Dominican York or dominicanyork differs across authors. The print collective uses Dominican York. For more on the term, see García-Peña, *Borders of Dominicanidad*, 172.

15. As of this writing, Pepe Coronado relocated to Austin, Texas, in 2020, and along with his colleague and fellow master printer Jonathan Rebolloso is reviving the Coronado Studio name.

16. I borrow the phrase from Tomás Ybarra-Frausto: "To imagine an operative construct of Latino art is to historicize, interpret, and valorize the production of visual artists from the heterogeneous US Latino community, a constituency that includes native-born citizens and immigrants from more than twenty ancestral homelands in South and Central America." Ybarra-Frausto, "Primeros Pasos," 15.

17. For those demographic shifts addressing Latinx migration and a growing ethnic consciousness, see Abreu, *Rhythms of Race*; Cary Cordova, *Heart of the Mission*; Padilla, *Latino Ethnic Consciousness*; Gina Pérez, *Near Northwest Side Story*; Ana Rodríguez, *Dividing the Isthmus*; and Sánchez, *Boyle Heights*.

18. De Genova, "Migrant 'Illegality' and Deportability in Everyday Life." De Genova makes the distinction that it is one thing to study undocumented migrants and another to understand the legal and juridical status through which they relate to the nation-state.

19. Villaseñor Black and Engel, "Why Latinx?"

20. See, for example, Hernandez, *Migra!*; Lee, *America for Americans*; McKiernan Gonzalez, *Fevered Measures*; Menchaca, *Naturalizing Mexican Immigrants*; Molina, *How Race Is Made in America*; and Ngai, *Impossible Subjects*.

21. For histories of anti-Mexican violence, see Gonzales-Day, *Lynching in the West, 1850–1935*; Guidotti-Hernández, *Unspeakable Violence*; and Martinez, *Injustice Never Leaves You*. On repatriation of Mexican Americans in the 1930s, see Balderrama and Rodriguez, *Decade of Betrayal*; Alanís Enciso, *They Should Stay There*.

22. González, Chavoya, Noriega, and Romo, *Chicana and Chicano Art*, 335. Here González alludes to W. E. B. Du Bois's concept of double consciousness.

23. Golash-Boza, *Deported*; Goodman, *Deportation Machine*.

24. Caragol-Barreto, "Aesthetics of Exile"; Dávila, "Culture in the Battlefront."

25. Duany, *Puerto Rican Nation on the Move*; Whalen, *From Puerto Rico to Philadelphia*. This marked difference in their migration history, which shields the group from the specter of illegality, explains their relative absence in this thematic study.

26. Adamson, "Internal Colony as Political Perspective"; Young, *Soul Power*.

27. Lipsitz, "Not Just Another Social Movement," 84.

28. Blackwell, "Contested Histories"; Davalos, *Yolanda M. López*, 28–57; Romo, "Aesthetics of the Message."

29. I develop this critique in my essay "War at Home: Conceptual Iconoclasm in American Printmaking."

30. Zavala, "Latin@ Art at the Intersection."

31. Latorre, *Walls of Empowerment*, 6–7.

32. Thomas, "Generative Networks and Local Circuits."

33. See, for example, their support for the Sandinista cause in Cary Cordova, *Heart of the Mission*, 164–165; and their pan-ethnic appeal for political prisoners in Reinoza, "*No Es un Crimen*."

34. Taller Puertorriqueño's early silkscreen workshop was the subject of a chapter in my dissertation, "Latino Print Cultures in the US, 1970–2008," 87.

35. Exceptions to this pattern include exhibitions (and their catalogues) such as Davidson, *Latin American Posters*; Gabara, *Pop América, 1965–1975*; Heyman, *Posters American Style*; Lennard, *Notes on Solidarity*; and Wye, *Committed to Print*.

36. Ramos, "What Is Latino about American Art?," 36.

37. Noriega, "Orphans of Modernism," 17.

38. Dávila, *Latinx Art*, 25.

39. Dávila, *Latinx Art*, 9.

40. Anreus, Greely, and Sullivan, *Companion to Modern and Contemporary Latin American and Latina/o Art*, xxii.

41. Noriega, Ramírez, and Tompkins Rivas, *Home: So Different, So Appealing*, 17.

42. Goldman, "Between 'Aquí' and 'Allá'"; Romo, "¡Presente!"; Wells, "La Lucha Sigue"; Lyle Williams, *Estampas de la Raza*, 30–31.

43. For a view of his collection, see http://www.desotocollection.com/about.html; and for an interview with Ernest de Soto conducted by Joe Segura, see https://curate.nd.edu/show/fq977s77r37.

44. Tournon, "Usos del Muralismo y Desvíos de la Historia," 256.

45. Orozco, "Adolfo Mexiac en Austin," 27.

46. Mignolo, *Idea of Latin America*, 74.

47. Flores, "'Latinidad Is Cancelled,'" 70.

48. Flores, "'Latinidad Is Cancelled,'" 72.

49. Beltrán, *Trouble with Unity*, 4.

50. Beltrán, *Trouble with Unity*, 5.

51. Beltrán, *Trouble with Unity*, 9.

52. Arrizón, "Mestizaje," 135.

53. Saldaña-Portillo, "Preface," 146–147.

54. Dackerman, "Introduction: Prints as Instruments," 31–32.

55. Rabasa, *Inventing America*, 193.

56. This is not the only representation of cannibalism in the *Carta Marina*. The same can be observed on the Island of Java. For the translation of the legend see Van Duzer, *Martin Waldseemüller's "Carta Marina" of 1516*, 94.

57. *Exploring the Early Americas*. Exhibition interactive presentations: Waldseemüller Maps, the Library of Congress, https://www.loc.gov/exhibits/exploring-the-early-americas/interactives/waldseemuller-maps/cartamarina1516/highlights1516.html.

58. Van Duzer, *Martin Waldseemüller's "Carta Marina" of 1516*, 44–53.

59. Barraza, "Opening the Bundles," https://revistanoj.berkeley.edu/2020/12/14/opening-the-bundles-artists-creating-new-realities-through-spiritual-offerings/.

60. For more on this critical view, see Penn Hilden, "How the Border Lies"; Contreras, *Blood Lines*.

61. Dalila Paola Mendez, interview with the author, October 21, 2021.

62. The Newberry Library exhibition ran from August 28 to November 28, 2020, and was seen by limited audiences because of the public-health restrictions of the COVID-19 pandemic. The curators pivoted some of their programming to vir-

tual formats, which can be seen by visiting https://www.newberry.org/renaissance-invention-portal.

63. Gombrich, "Eastern Inventions and Western Response."

64. Nelson, Cressy, and Karr Schmidt, "Warfare," 157; Zorach, Molà, and Crawford, "Transformation," 165.

65. Cohen-Aponte and Diaz, "Painting Prophecy."

66. "Who are the ones that nourish the earth with their blood? / Who are the ones that produce the rain with their tears? / To whom belong the stars and shells? / To whom the corn? / Who are the humble, joyful ones? / Who are those who need little? / Whose is the water, earth and air? / To whom do we owe this dust and death? / Whom do you come from / and to whom do you return? / We remained without paintings / Without words / Waiting in silence / that the beating of our hearts/ Would convene the creative sounds of the beginning. / To return back to our roots. / To fly over the rainbow of colors/ of a new time." Translation by Diana Magaloni.

67. Gatzambide-Fernández, "Decolonial Options and Artistic/AestheSic Entanglements," 208.

68. Peruvian sociologist Anibal Quijano introduced the concept of "coloniality" in the early 1990s, which helped formulate the language to articulate the decolonial in terms of delinking from coloniality. This differentiated the decolonial from the historical processes of decolonization in places like Asia and Africa that fought for their liberation from colonial rule after World War II. See Quijano, "Coloniality of Power, Eurocentrism, and Latin America."

69. Gómez-Barris, *Extractive Zone*, 5. She continues, "the extractive view sees territories as commodities, rendering land as for the taking, while also devalorizing the hidden worlds that form the nexus of human and nonhuman multiplicity."

70. Gaudio, *Engraving the Savage*; Mignolo, *Darker Side of the Renaissance*, 219–313; Pratt, *Imperial Eyes*.

71. Cohen-Aponte, "Decolonizing the Global Renaissance"; Hyman, "Inventing Painting."

72. Nineteenth- and twentieth-century examples of reclaiming printmaking as a democratic art form abound, from studies with technical specificity to those related to particular locations or conditions of revolution. See, for example, Cushing, *Revolución*; Dolinko, *Arte Para Todos*; Escamilla, *Estética Socialista en México, Siglo XX*; Evans and Donald, *Picturing Power in the People's Republic of China*; Gonzalez, "Hoja Nacionalizada"; Ittman, *Mexico and Modern Printmaking*; Langa, *Radical Art*; Lear, *Picturing the Proletariat*; Lugo, *Xilografía en Puerto Rico, 1950–1986*; Marzio, "Lithography as a Democratic Art"; Williams and Williams, "Early History of the Screenprint."

73. Mignolo and Vazquez, "Decolonial AestheSis"; Mirzoeff, *Right to Look*.

74. Cornejo, "Decolonial Futurisms"; Gómez-Barris, *Extractive Zone*; Laura Pérez, *Eros Ideologies*.

75. Gatzambide-Fernández, "Decolonial Options and Artistic/AestheSic Entanglements," 208.

76. For the important contributions US women of color and queer scholars of color have made to decolonial thought, see the essay by Laura Pérez, "Enrique Dus-

sel's *Ética de Liberación*, US Women of Color Decolonizing Practices, and Coalitionary Politics amidst Difference."

77. Blackwell, Boj Lopez, and Urrieta, Jr., "Introduction to Special Issue Critical Latinx Indigeneities."

CHAPTER ONE. NATIVE TERRITORIALITIES

1. For more on the New World origins of tobacco, see Burns, *Smoke of the Gods*; Kupperman, *Jamestown Project*.

2. The ceramic mural (made in the late 1970s) was based on a photograph of Duffy taken after his return from Morocco. Ricardo Duffy, phone conversation with the author, September 13, 2018.

3. Ricardo Duffy, interview with the author, February 24, 2018, Laguna Beach, California.

4. *Mojado* is a slur, "wetback." Duffy, interview with the author, February 24, 2018.

5. Jerry Rothman taught for more than twenty-five years at California State University, Fullerton, and mentored Chicana/o artists, including ceramist Crispin Gonzalez. http://www.latimes.com/local/obituaries/la-me-jerry-rothman-20140619-story.html https://www.claremont-courier.com/articles/obituaries/t22102-gonzalez.

6. Cathy Curtis, "In Search of . . . Originality: The Conventional Characterizes Laguna Art Institute's Juried Show," *Los Angeles Times*, August 14, 1998. David McQuay, "Give Those Risk-taking Artists a Hand," *Orange County Register*, July 23, 1990.

7. The historiography of SHG extends from articles to exhibition catalogues. Goldman, "Public Voice"; Guzmán, "Art in the Heart of East Los Angeles" and *Self Help Graphics & Art*; Gunckel, "Art and Community in East L.A."; Noriega, *Just Another Poster?*; Saldivar, "Self Help Graphics"; and the anthology *Self Help Graphics at Fifty*, coedited by the author.

8. For more on Sister Karen Boccalero, see Guzmán, "Art in the Heart of East Los Angeles," 6–7.

9. Those connections are highlighted in the following essays and articles: Ramos, "Manifestaciones"; Reinoza, "Printed Proof," 150, and "Island Within an Island"; Lyle Williams, "Without Borders," 25–44.

10. Duffy, interview with the author, February 24, 2018.

11. The snarling jaguar appears in *Curtain Raiser* (1997), about which Duffy has been quoted as saying, "That's my alter ego, in defiance." Cheng, "Looking Both Ways Across the Border; At UC Riverside, Artists Working in Different Media Examine Lives and Cultural Images in the U.S. and Mexico," *Los Angeles Times*, March 24, 2002. *Beaning Indigenous* and *Primavera* can be found at calisphere.org.

12. Ramos, "Printing and Collecting the Revolution," 77.

13. Luis Vargas Santiago's 2019 exhibition *Emiliano: Zapata después de Zapata* explored how the image of this revolutionary icon shaped nationalist discourses and eventually crossed the border and took on new valences in the Chicano Movement. See Vargas Santiago, "Emiliano," 110. Francisco Mora's plate 24, "Emiliano Zapata,

leader of the revolution, on horseback," from the portfolio *Estampas de la Revolución Mexicana,* can be found on the Metropolitan Museum's website.

14. Gaspar de Alba, *Chicano Art,* 166–173.

15. Saldaña-Portillo, "Who's the Indian in Aztlán?" 413.

16. Blackwell, "Geographies of Indigeneity," 157–158.

17. Whiting, *Pop L.A.,* 63.

18. Whiting, *Pop L.A.,* 72.

19. Whiting, *Pop L.A.,* 78.

20. Soja, *Postmodern Geographies,* 242–245.

21. Shirk, "The Real Marlboro Man."

22. In November 1998, Philip Morris and other leading manufacturers signed a master agreement in which they agreed to discontinue the sale and marketing of tobacco products to children, communicate the health consequences of smoking, and pay a fine of approximately $200 billion. For more information or to download the agreement, visit http://www.altria.com/our-companies/philipmorrisusa/tobacco-settlement-agreements/Pages/default.aspx.

23. Slotkin, *Gunfighter Nation,* 16.

24. In another essay, the author compares Duffy's work to the conceptual art of Antonio Caro and Richard Prince. See Reinoza, "War at Home," 110–113.

25. George H. W. Bush, "Address Before a Joint Session of the Congress on the Persian Gulf Crisis and the Federal Budget Deficit," September 11, 1990. George H. W. Bush Presidential Library and Museum, College Station, Texas, https://bush41library.tamu.edu/archives/public-papers/2217.

26. Duffy, interview with the author, February 24, 2018.

27. Patrick J. McDonnell and Dave Lesher, "Clinton, Feinstein Declare Opposition to Prop. 187: Immigration: President Calls Measure Unconstitutional. Senator Admits Her Stance Could Cost Her the Election," *Los Angeles Times,* October 22, 1994; Kenneth B. Noble, "California Immigration Measure Faces Rocky Legal Path," *New York Times,* November 11, 1994.

28. Cathleen Decker and Daniel M. Weintraub, "Wilson Savors Win; Democrats Assess Damage," *Los Angeles Times,* November 10, 1994.

29. "1994 Campaign: The Immigration Issue; California Students Leave School to Protest Alien Ballot Measure," *New York Times,* October 29, 1994.

30. Patrick J. McDonnell, "Prop. 187 Found Unconstitutional by Federal Judge," *Los Angeles Times,* November 15, 1997.

31. Stonard, "Pop in the Age of Boom," 615.

32. Stonard, "Pop in the Age of Boom," 620.

33. Whiting, *Pop L.A.,* 71.

34. For an overview of Garcia's graphic-art production, see Lippard, "Rupert Garcia," 28–31.

35. Jones, "Civil/Rights/Act," 49.

36. Ruben Córdova, "Getting the Big Picture," 179–180, and "Cinematic Genesis of the Mel Casas Humanscape." For more on the place-based context, see Cortez, "Aztlán in Tejas," 36–40.

37. Jones, "Civil/Rights/Act," 22.

38. Whiting, *Pop L.A.,* 77.

39. Carbone, "Exhibit A," 86–88. I bring this to the reader's attention not in or-

der to emphasize a binary between blue-chip artists and the artists of color working in pop that I mention above. Art historians must assume that artists' intentions are fickle and the shifting meaning of their artworks resides largely in the interpretations of changing viewers. This sort of binary easily comes undone when looking at mainstream artists such as Robert Indiana, Edward Kienholz, and Philip Guston, whose work in the 1960s explicitly tackled issues of racial justice.

40. Walker, "Printmaking 1960 to 1990," 80.

41. Warhol and Hackett, *Popism*, 22.

42. Zigrosser, "Serigraph," 477.

43. For many years the Print Council of America did not recognize silk screens/screenprints as original prints.

44. See Dackerman, *Corita Kent and the Language of Pop.*

45. Guzmán, "Art in the Heart of East Los Angeles," 15.

46. Ramos, "What Is Latino About American Art," 35.

47. Lehmbeck, *Proof*; Watson, *Factory Made.*

48. Gabara, "Contesting Freedom," 10–11.

49. Anzaldúa, *Borderlands/La Frontera*, 25.

50. For more on Ortiz Torres, see Chavoya, "Customized Hybrids," 175; Ortiz Torres, *Desmothernismo*; and his retrospective and catalogue published as Botey, *Rubén Ortiz Torres: Customatism.*

51. The photograph was likely taken at the Old Spanish Days Fiesta parade in Santa Barbara.

52. Given that the book's primary argument hinges on desire, it is interesting how José Limon begins his introduction to *American Encounters* with this image. Limón, *American Encounters*, 1.

53. "California was lost to the white man / because gold was in its veins / and life in its sensual body / and Guadalupe lost Hidalgo / and bears walked onto flags. / This is where the Chicano/ manifest-destinyed began." Translation by Louie "the Foot" González.

54. Diaz, *Flying Under the Radar*, 38–39.

55. Mesa-Bains, "Spiritual Geographies."

56. Duffy, interview with the author, February 24, 2018.

57. Crosswhite, "History, Geology, and Vegetation of Picketpost Mountain," 73. See also 50th Congress, 2nd session, H.R. Rep. No. 4099: "General George Stoneman" (February 19, 1889). Serial Set Vol. No. 2675, Session Vol. No. 3.

58. Crosswhite, "History, Geology, and Vegetation of Picketpost Mountain," 73.

59. Barnes, *Arizona Place Names*, 289.

60. Excerpt of transcript of Christine Marin's conversation with Jack August on September 17, 2015; emailed to the author, June 26, 2018. August passed away on January 20, 2017, in Phoenix, Arizona.

61. "Pinal" comes from the Spanish term for pine. The Spaniards named the Apache Indians from this region "Piñaleros." Apache bands included the Aravaipa, Chiricahua, Coyotero, Mimbreño, Mongollon, San Carlos, Tonto, Warm Springs, and Yavapai Apaches.

62. Southeast Arizona Land Exchange and Conservation Act of 2007, H.R. 3301, 110th Congress (November 1, 2007), 19. Accessed August 2, 2018, https://hdl.handle.net/2027/pst.000065502020.

63. Crosswhite, "History, Geology, and Vegetation of Picketpost Mountain," 74–75.

64. Lowe, *Arizona Myths and Legends*, 62.

65. James M. Barney lived from 1874 to 1965 and wrote articles about the history of Arizona. See Barney, "How Apache Leap Got Its Name."

66. Barney, "How Apache Leap Got Its Name."

67. Slotkin, *Gunfighter Nation*, 5.

68. President Grant established the San Carlos Apache Indian Reservation by an executive order on November 9, 1871. By the end of the nineteenth century, the US government had greatly diminished the size of the reservation several times because of the discovery of silver, copper, coal, water, and other natural resources.

69. Apache prisoners of war. Mr. Owen presented the following memorial from S. M. Brosius, agent, Indian Rights Association, relating to the Apache prisoners of war now confined at Fort Sill Military Reservation, Oklahoma, urging that allotments of land be made to the Indians and that they be released from bondage. February 16, 1910. Ordered to be printed. 61st Congress, 2nd session. Serial Set Vol. No. 5657, Session Vol. No. 58, S. Doc. No. 61-366 (1910).

70. Morris, "Crash," 75.

71. Morris, "Crash," 74.

72. Saldaña-Portillo, *Indian Given*, 6.

73. Matthew Weiner, pilot script, "Mad Men," April 3, 2006, p. 35.

74. Mesa-Bains, "Spiritual Geographies," 333.

75. Zamudio-Taylor, "Inventing Tradition, Negotiating Modernism," 343.

76. Saldaña-Portillo, *Indian Given*, 197.

77. Duffy, interview with the author, February 24, 2018.

78. Thanks to Saldaña-Portillo for responding to an excerpt of this chapter at the Latin American Studies Association Conference in Boston, May 2019.

79. Raheja, "Reading Nanook's Smile."

80. Scott Gold, "Artist Behind the Iconic 'Running Immigrants' Image," *Los Angeles Times*, April 4, 2008; Seth Mydans, "One Last Deadly Crossing for Illegal Aliens," *New York Times*, 1991.

81. Kate Morrissey, "Last of Iconic Illegal Immigration Crossing Signs Has Vanished in California," *Los Angeles Times*, February 10, 2018.

82. Roy Cook, "John Hood: Diné Artist, USMC Combat Veteran's Art Is in Smithsonian," n.d. http://www.americanindiansource.com/hoodart.html.

83. John Hood, email to the author, July 27, 2018.

84. Laurel Morales, "For the Navajo Nation, Uranium Mining's Deadly Legacy Lingers," National Public Radio, *Weekend Edition*, April 10, 2016, https://www.npr.org/sections/health-shots/2016/04/10/473547227/for-the-navajo-nation-uranium-minings-deadly-legacy-lingers.

85. Freud, "Uncanny."

86. Bergland, *National Uncanny*, 4.

87. Bergland, *National Uncanny*, 1.

88. O'Sullivan, "Annexation," 5.

89. Philips Galle (1537–1612) produced the widely circulated engraved version as part of *New Inventions of Modern Times (Nova Reperta)*. The series was based on twenty drawings by Stradanus, which the latter sent from Florence to Antwerp,

where the Galle family produced multiple editions popular with scholars and print collectors. Stradanus was the Flemish draftsman and painter Jan Van der Straet (1525–1605), who worked primarily in Italy.

90. Bayers, "U.S. Mint, the Lewis and Clark Bicentennial, and the Perpetuation of the Frontier Myth," 44; Heffernan and Medlicot, "Feminine Atlas?" 113; and Kolodny, *Lay of the Land*, 22.

91. The English-language spelling of Sacagawea's name differs across texts, as Sacagewea, Sakakawea, and Sacajawea. She is thought to have been born around 1788 and died around 1812, although scholars have debated the date and cause of her death.

92. In 1997 the US Congress approved a new $1 coin act; the design process eventually led to the appearance of Sacagawea on the golden dollar coin of the year 2000.

93. Kessler, *Making of Sacagawea*, 23.

94. Kessler, *Making of Sacagawea*.

95. Heffernan and Medlicot, "Feminine Atlas?" 124; Hills, "Picturing Progress in the Era of Westward Expansion," 118.

96. Kessler, *Making of Sacagawea*, 28.

97. Carroll, *Remex*, 35. See also Baddeley, "Engendering New Worlds."

98. Carroll, *Remex*, 171.

99. Chrismas owned Ace Gallery in Vancouver and Los Angeles and retained exclusive rights to sell the series until Warhol's death. One of the paintings in the series sold at auction for $2.4 million in 2016. Sotheby's, *Contemporary Art Day Auction* (November 2016), online catalogue, http://www.sothebys.com/en/auctions/ecatalogue/2016/contemporary-art-day-auction-n09573/lot.139.html.

100. Sotheby's, *Contemporary Art Day Auction* (November 2016).

101. For primary sources on the Wounded Knee Occupation, see Russell Means, "Desperation Is the Cause of Occupation," *Wassaja*, February–March 1973, 4; as well as front-page news coverage such as "Armed Indians Seize Wounded Knee, Hold Hostages," *New York Times*, March 1, 1973; and "Occupation of Wounded Knee Is Ended," *New York Times*, May 9, 1973.

102. The film is adapted from the James Fenimore Cooper historical novel *The Last of the Mohicans: A Narrative of 1757* (1826).

103. Vizenor, *Manifest Manners*, 18.

104. Schimmel, "Inventing the 'Indian,'" 186.

105. Schimmel, "Inventing the 'Indian,'" 161–162.

106. For more on the artist, see Laura Pérez, *Eros Ideologies*, 179–191; Pérez and Leimer, eds., *Consuelo Jimenez Underwood: Art, Weaving, Vision*.

107. Barron, "Making of *Made in California*," 43.

108. Roberta Smith, "Memo to Art Museums: Don't Give up on Art," *New York Times*, December 3, 2000.

109. Christopher Knight, "Thematically Overwrought: 'Made in California' Looks to Both Art and Kitsch to Force New Contexts on the Image of the Golden State," *Los Angeles Times*, October 23, 2000.

110. Howard Fox, "Many Californias, 1980–2000," 270.

CHAPTER TWO. EMBODIED TERRITORIALITIES

1. "Remarks Made by the President, Prime Minister Tony Blair of England (via satellite), Dr. Francis Collins, Director of the National Human Genome Research Institute, and Dr. Craig Venter, President and Chief Scientific Officer, Celera Genomics Corporation, on the Completion of the First Survey of the Entire Human Genome Project," The White House, Office of the Press Secretary, June 26, 2000, https://www.genome.gov/10001356/june-2000-white-house-event.

2. Hanley, "Segura Reborn at University of Notre Dame," n.p.

3. Joe Segura, interview by Amelia Malagamba, June 12, 2007, Institute for Latino Studies, University of Notre Dame.

4. Rabasa, *Inventing America*, 93.

5. According to the print documentation, Chagoya and Ríos worked on the portfolio July 3–8, 2000. By September of that year, master printer Joe Freye and printer John Altomare had completed the limited edition of sixty portfolios.

6. Joe Segura, interview by the author, November 18, 2016, Segura Arts Studio.

7. Joe Segura, interview by the author, November 18, 2016, Segura Arts Studio.

8. Enrique Chagoya, telephone interview by the author, December 13, 2017. (Hereafter "Chagoya, telephone interview.")

9. Enrique Chagoya, oral-history interview with Paul Karlstrom, Archives of American Art, Smithsonian Institution, Washington, DC, July 25–August 6, 2001.

10. Paglen, "Experimental Geography," 31.

11. I thank my friend Michael Barany for pointing out the pervasiveness of the theorem in the history of mathematics. For a sample of various proofs, see Loomis, *Pythagorean Proposition*, as well as more recent scholarship such as Posamentier, *Pythagorean Theorem*.

12. Mondrian, "Toward the True Vision of Reality (1941)," 12.

13. Mignolo, *Darker Side of the Renaissance*, 226.

14. Kanas, *Star Maps*, 19–22.

15. Mignolo, *Darker Side of the Renaissance*, 230–231.

16. Pickles, *History of Spaces*, 80.

17. The poem was reprinted with an alternative title, "Clemente and Ventura Show Themselves, If Just for a Moment, in Their Son," in Ríos's *Theater of Night*.

18. Taylor, "Remapping Genre through Performance," 1417.

19. Taylor, "Remapping Genre through Performance," 1418.

20. For more on the *Mapa de Cuauhtinchan*, see the beautifully illustrated volume *Cave, City, and Eagle's Nest*, edited by Carrasco and Sessions.

21. Enrique Chagoya, oral-history interview with Karlstrom.

22. Hanley, "Visual Culture of the Nacirema."

23. Mignolo, *Darker Side of the Renaissance*, 266–270.

24. Schreffler, "Vespucci Rediscovers America," 304.

25. For more on de Bry's engravings of John White's watercolors, see Kuhlemann, "Between Reproduction, Invention and Propaganda."

26. Gaudio, *Engraving the Savage*, xvii.

27. Staden, *Hans Staden's True History*, 137.

28. Mignolo, *Darker Side of the Renaissance*, 278.

29. Andrade, "Anthropophagous Manifesto," 466.
30. Andrade, "Anthropophagous Manifesto."
31. Taylor, "Remapping Genre through Performance," 1420.
32. The show traveled to several venues, including the Rochester Art Center, The Albuquerque Museum, the Colby College Museum of Art, and Museum London. Nato Thompson, "In Two Directions," 13.
33. Thompson, "In Two Directions," 15–23.
34. Paglen, "Experimental Geography," 31.
35. Paglen, "Experimental Geography," 28.
36. For two recent surveys on the map as art since World War II, see Harmon, *Map as Art*, and her previous anthology, *You Are Here*.
37. Pearce, "Review of Experimental Geography," 65.
38. Foster, "Real Fictions," 170.
39. Foster, "Real Fictions," 173.
40. Chagoya, telephone interview.
41. NASA, "Space Debris and Human Spacecraft."
42. The poem continues: "It's somebody in the humming telephone lines./ It's somebody inside all those white envelopes./ The earth and the sky,/ We fill them with our dead."
43. For more on these mythical creatures, see Van Duzer, *Sea Monsters on Medieval and Renaissance Maps*.
44. Chagoya enjoys employing such Disney characters as Mickey Mouse and Donald Duck to critique consumer culture. As a student of economics at the Universidad Nacional Autónoma de Mexico, he read *How to Read Donald Duck* (1971) by Chileans Armando Mattellart and Ariel Dorfman, in which they argue that Disney's comics are in fact imperialist and ideological. The book quickly became a best–seller in Latin America and was republished dozens of times.
45. Wood, *Power of Maps*, 7.
46. Rabasa, *Inventing America*, 181.
47. Rabasa, *Inventing America*, 192.
48. Rabasa, *Inventing America*, 208.
49. Rabasa, *Inventing America*, 181.
50. Taylor, *Archive and the Repertoire*, 54.
51. Taylor, *Archive and the Repertoire*, 55.
52. Bhagat and Mogel, *An Atlas of Radical Cartography*, 6.
53. Greeley, "Enrique Chagoya," 5.
54. Jennifer González, "Introduction," n.p.
55. Seda, "Decolonizing the Body Politic," 136.
56. Gómez-Peña, "Disclaimer," 154.
57. Sheren, "Coco Fusco and Guillermo Gómez-Peña's *Cage Performance* and La Pocha Nostra's *Mapa Corpo*," 69.
58. Sheren, *Portable Borders*, 61.
59. Claire Fox, *Fence and the River*, 122.
60. *Mapa/Corpo 2: Interactive Rituals for the New Millennium*, performed June 13, 2007, at Centro Cultural Recoleta, Buenos Aires. Video documentation, Hemispheric Institute, http://hidvl.nyu.edu/video/000549498.html.
61. Bhagat and Mogel, *Atlas of Radical Cartography*, 6.

62. Ríos, *Smallest Muscle in the Human Body.* The book was a finalist for the National Book Award. To read the poem online, visit https://www.poetryfoundation.org/poems/48353/some-extensions-on-the-sovereignty-of-science.

63. Ríos and Wootten, "Edge in the Middle," 57.

64. The red stamps on each print are what Chagoya calls an "afterimage." Chagoya, telephone interview.

65. I call it "epistemic violence" because European colonization of space involved the suppression of native territorialities. Mignolo describes how the colonization of space functions on cognitive and pragmatic levels: cognitive because it can suppress other ways of seeing and pragmatic because its distribution through the printing press overpowered the handmade painted codices. It is also important to point out that since the sixteenth century, Native artists have adopted the civilizing technologies of mapping and used them to further Native rationalizations of space. Mignolo, *Darker Side of the Renaissance,* 242, 250–253.

66. Joe Segura, interview by the author, November 18, 2016, Segura Arts Studio.

67. The Snite Museum of Art at the University of Notre Dame holds a complete archival collection of limited editions produced at the studio, an incredible resource that I hope others will access for exhibitions and/or research. The university took control of the remaining inventory of prints, which currently remain in storage.

68. Chagoya, quoted in Kathan Brown, *Why Draw a Live Model?* (San Francisco: Crown Point Press, 1997), 12.

CHAPTER THREE. MESTIZA TERRITORIALITIES

1. Safier, *Measuring the New World,* 5.

2. Sandra Fernández, interview with the author, January 11, 2019, Quito, Ecuador. His unusual last name is owed to the fact that his father, David Muñoz, married his niece Tomasa Muñoz. For more on his biography see https://rodolfoperezpimentel.com/munoz-munoz-leonardo-j/.

3. I have synthesized much of the Geodesic Mission history from the following sources: Capello, "From Imperial Pyramids to Anticolonial Sundials"; Ferreiro, *Measure of the Earth;* and Safier, *Measuring the New World.*

4. Capello, *City at the Center of the World,* 58–59.

5. Pratt, *Imperial Eyes,* 3.

6. Pratt, *Imperial Eyes,* 17.

7. Ana Cristina Alvarado, "El Primer Mapa de la Provincia de Quito se volvió a estampar," *El Comercio,* February 22, 2019.

8. Mignolo, *Idea of Latin America,* 58.

9. Safier, *Measuring the New World,* 128.

10. Safier, *Measuring the New World,* 8.

11. "Inasmuch as every search for the truth is characterized by an absence . . . much of what we know of Ecuador from the time of the Geodesic Mission is also the result of translations that are inevitably betrayed in maps and catalogues of an inexact science which is incapable of liberating itself from its human limits." Translation by the author.

12. Handlesman, "En nombre de un amor imaginario y los origenes de la República del Ecuador," 176.

13. This was a major victory for Indigenous- and Afro-Ecuadorian-rights groups when the 1998 constitution recognized national identity as pluricultural.

14. According to census results from 2001, an estimated 78 percent of the population self-identify as mestizo (mixed), 10 percent as white, 6 percent as Indigenous, and 5 percent as Afro-Ecuadorian, with smaller percentages as Black and mulatto. See endnote 1 in Radcliffe, "Representing the Nation," 209.

15. Fernández, interview with the author, February 13, 2019, Parlin, New Jersey.

16. Greet, *Beyond National Identity*, 14–15.

17. The manuscript is called *The First New Chronicle and Good Government* and is housed at the Royal Danish Library in Copenhagen. It can be accessed virtually by visiting http://www5.kb.dk/permalink/2006/poma/info/en/frontpage.htm.

18. To view the image visit: http://www5.kb.dk/permalink/2006/poma/596/en/text/.

19. Rivera Cusicanqui, *Ch'ixinakax utxiwa*, 15–16.

20. Anzaldúa, *Borderlands/La Frontera*, 100.

21. Rivera Cusicanqui, *Ch'ixinakax utxiwa*, 64–67.

22. Rivera Cusicanqui and Veronica Gago, "Entrevista: Orgullo de ser mestiza," *Página 12*, July 30, 2010, https://www.pagina12.com.ar/diario/suplementos/las12/13-5889-2010-07-30.html.

23. Flores, "Latino Art and the Immigrant Artist," 168.

24. According to anthropologist Nicholas de Genova, there is a distinction between "studying undocumented people, on the one hand, and studying 'illegality.'" The state determines the parameters of citizenship through a historical and juridical process based on inclusions and exclusions. I contemplate the representation of "impossible subjects" with this distinction in mind: people are not "illegal," though they may be undocumented. De Genova, "Migrant 'Illegality' and Deportability in Everyday Life," 422.

25. For more on Coronado, see Tatiana Reinoza, "CORONADO, SAM ZARAGOSA, JR.," *Handbook of Texas Online* (http://www.tshaonline.org/handbook/online/articles/fcozw), Texas State Historical Association, April 28, 2015.

26. Sam Coronado, interview with the author, March 6, 2013, Austin, Texas.

27. Fernández, interview with the author, February 13, 2019, Parlin, New Jersey.

28. La Peña served as an umbrella organization and provided fiscal sponsorship for the first seven years of Serie Project, until the latter received their nonprofit status.

29. For an insightful commentary on the issue of quality, see the work of cultural critic Alicia Gaspar de Alba, *Chicano Art Inside/Outside the Master's House*, 166–173. For more on Coronado, see Reinoza, "Printed Proof," 145–155.

30. Montoya and Salkowitz-Montoya, "Critical Perspective on the State of Chicano Art."

31. As an example of his willingness to work within the system and effect change, Coronado designed a Christmas card for Governor George W. Bush, and several artists accused him of accommodationist politics. During the exhibit at the Governor's Mansion, Coronado requested that his wall label state his full name, and for nationality: "Chicano, born in 1946."

32. Serie Project, Inc. Records, Benson Latin American Collection, University of Texas Libraries, The University of Texas at Austin.

33. Serie Project, Inc. Records, Benson Latin American Collection, University of Texas Libraries, The University of Texas at Austin.

34. Dávila, "Culture in the Battlefront," 168–169.

35. The collaborative-press model arrived rather late to the capital city. In the early 1990s, Austin was home to a small number of for-contract publishers and one independent collaborative workshop, Flatbed Press. Founded by master printer Katherine Brimberry and Mark L. Smith, Flatbed went on to specialize in intaglio, relief, lithography and monotype printing. Flatbed offered contract printing, an active schedule of printmaking classes, shop rentals, studio space, gallery rentals, and partnerships with local colleges. Coronado Studio followed the for-contract print shop model and also rented to fledgling poster makers who specialized in gig posters for Austin's vibrant music scene. A third collaborative workshop, Slugfest, began operating in 1992 but officially opened as a lithography, intaglio, and relief studio in 1996 with Margaret Simpson and Thomas Druecker at the helm. Flatbed has published and sells Fernández's prints, while Vamp and Tramp Booksellers sells her artists' books.

36. In 2008, Serie Project/Coronado Studio hosted the biennial conference for Consejo Gráfico, the national print alliance of Latinx workshops. The University of Texas at Austin's Center for Mexican American Studies co-hosted a symposium, and Mexic-Arte Museum opened a large graphic-art exhibition featuring work from each of these workshops.

37. Fernández, email to the author, October 14, 2015.

38. The writing requires close looking and may not be visible in the image provided. Me agarró la migra translates to "I was caught by the immigration police."

39. Auyero, *Invisible in Austin*, 16.

40. Sassen, *Global City*, 4–5.

41. Between 2010 and 2014, Austin's population grew by nearly 16 percent: http://www.texastribune.org/2015/05/21/interactive-texas-population-growth-2010-2014/. The job-creation growth rate has been over 3 percent annually since 2010: http://www.forbes.com/sites/joelkotkin/2015/10/06/the-cities-americans-are-thronging-to-and-fleeing/.

42. Tate, "Austin, Texas, in Socio-Historical Context," 22.

43. Tata Bahrampour, "Most Unauthorized Immigrants Live in Urban Areas, Study Shows," *Washington Post*, February 9, 2017.

44. Jens Manuel Krogstad, Mark Hugo Lopez, and Jeffrey S. Passel, "Majority of Americans Say Immigrants Mostly Fill Jobs U.S. Citizens Do Not Want," *Pew Research Center*, June 10, 2020, https://pewrsr.ch/2MoaLEx.

45. Weschler, *Domestic Scenes*, 8. See also Brody, "Painting Labor."

46. The artist and I visited Viteri's home and studio in January of 2019. It is a private museum. The first floor houses Viteri's collection of Ancient and Colonial Andean art and religious relics, and the second floor contains a carefully organized collection of Viteri's art and archives.

47. Cecilia Suárez, "Viteri, Oswaldo," *Benezit Dictionary of Artists*, Oct. 31, 2011.

48. Fernández, phone conversation with the author, May 25, 2017.

49. Flores, "Latino Art and the Immigrant Artist," 171.

50. Quijano, "Coloniality of Power, Eurocentrism, and Latin America" 536.

51. Fernández, email to the author, October 14, 2015.

52. Molina, *How Race Is Made in America*, 7.

53. For more information on the Master Plan of 1928, see Koch and Fowler, *City Plan for Austin, Texas* (Austin: Department of Planning, 1928), 57; and the analysis by Amanda Gray, "Modern Displacements: Urban Injustice Affecting Working-Class Communities of Color in East Austin" (M.A. thesis, University of Texas at Austin, 2013), 29–37.

54. Tate, "Austin, Texas, in Socio-Historical Context," 28.

55. Koch and Fowler, *City Plan for Austin, Texas*.

56. Quijano, "Coloniality of Power, Eurocentrism, and Latin America" 533.

57. Claire Fox, *Fence and the River*, 4–5.

58. Claire Fox, *Fence and the River*, 11.

59. Hernandez as quoted in Heyman, *Posters American Style*, 166.

60. *Calaveras* are skeletal figures often associated with *Día de los Muertos* and popularized by the Mexican illustrator and engraver José Guadalupe Posada (1852–1913). *Huipiles* are usually woven on a back-strap loom, and their intricate patterns suggest site specificity and ethnic origin.

61. As opposed to the US Border Patrol, created through an appropriations act in 1924, which enforced US Customs and Immigration laws in the border zone particularly with checkpoints along the US-Mexico border.

62. Jeffrey Passel and D'Vera Cohn, "20 Metro Areas Are Home to Six-in-Ten Unauthorized Immigrants in U.S.," *Pew Research Center*, February 9, 2017, http://www.pewresearch.org/fact-tank/2017/02/09/us-metro-areas-unauthorized-immigrants/.

63. Florida, *Rise of the Creative Class*.

64. Auyero, *Invisible in Austin*, 4.

65. Auyero, *Invisible in Austin*, 16.

66. John Burnet and Lakshmi Singh, "ICE Says Recent Immigrant Raids Are Business as Usual," National Public Radio, *All Things Considered*, February 11, 2017. Eyder Perlata, "National Council of La Raza Dubs Obama 'Deporter-in-Chief,'" NPR, March 4, 2014.

67. Mignolo, "Movable Center," 266.

68. For a discussion of DACA's impact, see Abrego, "Renewed Optimism and Spatial Mobility," 192–207.

69. From 2008 to 2015, Fernández served as Assistant Professor of Printmaking at the University of Texas at Austin. For a recent CV, visit the artist's website. https://www.sandrafernandez.info/cv. Flores, "Latino Art and the Immigrant Artist," 170.

70. Flores, "Latino Art and the Immigrant Artist," 170.

71. Gómez-Barris, "Mestiza Cultural Memory," 80.

72. The art historian Holly Barnet-Sánchez was the first to point out this connection between Fernández's work and Anzaldúa. Barnet-Sánchez, "Sandra C. Fernández," 312.

73. Anzaldúa, *Borderlands/La Frontera*, 44.

74. Barnet-Sánchez, "Sandra C. Fernández," 314.

75. This is an excerpt of the Emma Lazarus poem *The New Colossus* (1883) located at the pedestal of the Statue of Liberty.

76. Cuvi, "Santos," 45.

77. Dunning-Lozano, "Inés," 84.

78. Cuvi, "Santos," 44.

79. Cuvi, "Santos," 45.

80. Cassandra Jackson uses the term "racialized spectacle violence" to discuss the racially motivated vigilante mob killings that terrorized Black and other minorities and reinforced white supremacy. Jackson, *Violence, Visual Culture, and the Black Male Body*, 77–101.

81. For a critical approach to lynching photography, see Gonzales-Day, *Lynching in the West, 1850–1935*.

82. I would like to thank my art-history student Kendra Lyimo for drawing my attention to this print with her incisive writing for the Artura.org database.

83. Terry Ybañez, interview with the author, November 8, 2015.

84. Ybañez, interview with the author, November 8, 2015.

85. Ybañez, interview with the author, November 8, 2015.

86. Ngai, *Impossible Subjects*, 5.

87. Cornejo Villavicencio, *Undocumented Americans*, 12–13.

88. Ades, *Art in Latin America*, 299–300.

89. Hooker, *Theorizing Race in the Americas*, 189.

90. Fernández, artist statement, in Barnet-Sánchez, "Sandra C. Fernández," 325.

CHAPTER FOUR. AQUEOUS TERRITORIALITIES

1. The spelling "Dominican York" or "dominicanyork" differs across authors. I have chosen to use "Dominican York" to signal the name of the print collective and its emphasis on place making. For more on the term, see García-Peña, *Borders of Dominicanidad*, 172.

2. Reinoza, "Island Within an Island," 4–27.

3. Pickles, *History of Spaces*, 91.

4. The Laguna Gloria Art Museum was originally housed in the Clara Driscoll Villa, on the shore of Lake Austin. In 1996, the museum moved its primary exhibition space downtown and renamed itself the Austin Museum of Art. (The art school remained on the grounds of the historic villa.) Laguna Gloria is now part of the kunshalle known as The Contemporary Austin. For more on Sam Coronado, see Reinoza, "Printed Proof," 145–155; and "Coronado, Sam Zaragosa, Jr.," in *Handbook of Texas Online*, http://www.tshaonline.org/handbook/online/articles/fcozw.

5. The terms "silk screening," "screenprinting," and "serigraphy" refer to the same printmaking technique. However, serigraphy is often reserved for fine-art prints.

6. For more on Blackburn's workshop, see Cullen, "Robert Blackburn," *Robert Blackburn Legacy*, and *Robert Blackburn*.

7. Artist statement, Arts Westchester Exhibit, 2010. Pepe Coronado Papers, Archives of American Art, Smithsonian Institution.

8. Coronado identifies the Balaguer regime and the economic violence that it unleashed on the working class as the reason his family left the DR. Pepe Coronado, interview by the author, June 16, 2017, East Harlem, New York. For an insight-

ful discussion of the Columbus Lighthouse and the criticisms it generated, see Dixa Ramírez, *Colonial Phantoms,* 115–123.

9. Coronado, interview by the author, June 16, 2017.

10. Coronado felt validated in this choice of subject matter. In an interview with the author, he recalled that Sister Karen told him she was intrigued by the work and happy to "finally see something that is not another *Virgen de Guadalupe*." Pepe Coronado, interview by the author, June 16, 2017.

11. Coronado, thank-you letter to Self Help Graphics, Coronado Papers, Archives of American Art, Smithsonian Institution.

12. Ramos, "*Manifestaciones,*" n.p.

13. Coronado, interview by the author, June 16, 2017.

14. Ramírez and Estrada, *Pressing the Point.*

15. Ramos, "*Manifestaciones,*" n.p.

16. Rosa Tavárez (b. 1939) is one of the most accomplished Dominican painters and engravers. She studied at the National School of Fine Arts and taught at various schools for over thirty-five years, including Altos de Chavón between 1983 and 1988. In 2000, she founded La Casa del Grabado, a center she hopes will document the history of Dominican graphic arts. I am grateful to Ezequiel Taveras for bringing her work to my attention. See the retrospective catalogue Ditrén, *Rosa Tavárez.*

17. A print collective is made up of artists who collaborate on printmaking projects, including portfolios, exhibitions, and more, but also maintain their own individual artistic practices. A print workshop, on the other hand, whether commercial or fine-art, is the engine of production and often invests in print projects as a publisher. Among the DYPG artists, Coronado and Rider Ureña each own and maintain their own workshop, while other artists like Moses Ros-Suárez and Luanda Lozano work out of cooperative spaces like the Robert Blackburn Printmaking Workshop and Manhattan Graphics.

18. Coronado, interview by the author, June 16, 2017.

19. For an example of community-based poster artists, see Reinoza, "*No Es un Crimen,*" 239–256.

20. García-Peña, *Borders of Dominicanidad,* 4.

21. García-Peña, *Borders of Dominicanidad,* 6.

22. Art critic Benjamin Genocchio claims that the Black childlike figures are "composite self-portrait(s) of the artist and her daughter." See Genocchio, "With Expectations of a Better Life," *New York Times,* December 17, 2006, Scherezade García Papers, Archives of American Art, Smithsonian Institution.

23. Sullivan, "From Here to Eternity," 2.

24. For more on Báez, see García-Peña, "Performing Identity, Language, and Resistance," 28–45; Stevens, "Home Is Where Theater Is," 29–48; and Torres-Saillant and Hernández, *Dominican Americans,* 130–134.

25. García, artist statement, in *Manifestaciones/Dominican York Proyecto Grafica,* n.p. Translation by the author. This work in particular is in conversation with García's exhibition *Morir Soñando* (2008) in Santo Domingo's District & Co. Gallery. Her artist statement for the exhibition reads: "The young mestizo figure is central in my storytelling. Through the mixing of races, religious and new values embodied in the mestizo, the figure represents consequences of the discovery of America, an innovation and atrocity. These consequences are ever present in the everyday life of

any Spanish Caribbean islander, passing by the ruins of the Cathedral of the Spanish Empire, just next to an American fast-food chain, accompanied by the sound of merengue music." Scherezade García, email communication with the author, May 3, 2018.

26. Lapin Dardashti, "El Dorado," 83.

27. In her sociological study of Dominican racial identity, Ginetta E. B. Candelario observes, "Even during the most politically unstable times, the Dominican government acted to protect the archeological evidence of the country's Hispanic and indigenous heritages, as the colonial-era buildings became national monuments and pre-Columbian artifacts and remains became archeological treasures. By contrast, there was no language in any of the legislation relating to the research, preservation, display, and diffusion of knowledge about the country's African heritages and artifacts." See Candelario, *Black Behind the Ears*, 105. For more on the Antillean obsession with Taíno iconography and its tendency to disavow Blackness, see Román, "Indians Are Coming!," 102; and Duany, *Puerto Rican Nation on the Move*, 261. For a fascinating study on how the Trujillato adopted the excess of masculinity, militarism, gift exchange, kinship, and even witchcraft to ensure absolute fidelity and fear from the rural and urban poor, see Derby, *Dictator's Seduction*.

28. For eyewitness accounts, see Roorda, Derby, and González, *Dominican Republic Reader*, 281–285.

29. Lapin Dardashti, "El Dorado," 83.

30. Herrera, "Introduction," 13.

31. John Akomfrah in "London," *Art in the Twenty-First Century*, Season 10, September 18, 2020. https://art21.org/watch/art-in-the-twenty-first-century/s10/john-akomfrah-in-london-segment/

32. Lapin Dardashti, "Tracing the Ocean," 29.

33. García, interview by the author, June 16, 2017. *Morir soñando* is also a tropical drink made in the DR that combines fresh orange juice and milk. I am grateful to Ginetta Candelario for making me aware of the wordplay in this phrasing.

34. See entry Arturo Lindsay in Artura.org: https://artura.org/Detail/entity/1602.

35. Torres-Saillant, "Tribulations of Blackness."

36. Torres-Saillant, "Tribulations of Blackness," 134.

37. Torres-Saillant, "Tribulations of Blackness," 129.

38. Torres-Saillant, "Tribulations of Blackness," 130.

39. Torres-Saillant, "Tribulations of Blackness," 136–137.

40. Torres-Saillant, "Tribulations of Blackness," 139.

41. Candelario traces the origin of the phrase to a nineteenth-century poem by Juan Antonio Alix. See *Black Behind the Ears*, 1–5.

42. García-Peña, *Borders of Dominicanidad*, 173.

43. Candelario, *Black Behind the Ears*, 2.

44. Torres-Saillant, "Tribulations of Blackness," 141.

45. Julia Alvarez, "Secret Footprints," *Baltimore Sun*, March 14, 2001.

46. Candelario, "La ciguapa y el ciguapeo," 102.

47. Firelei Báez's *Ciguapa* series (2005–2015) is an excellent example of overturning a maligned mythical figure into one of agentic potential. For more on Báez, see Alvarado, "Flora and Fauna Otherwise."

48. Graziano, *Undocumented Dominican Migration*, 36–41.

49. Graziano, *Undocumented Dominican Migration*, 10.

50. Isaiah 43:2.

51. Graziano, *Undocumented Dominican Migration*, 36.

52. For oral-history accounts of *yola* trips, see Ricourt, "Reaching the Promised Land."

53. In 1987, the United States Border Patrol established a station in Aguadilla, Puerto Rico, known as the Ramey Station to prevent the arrival of undocumented Dominican migrants who travel by boat to the coast of Puerto Rico. The Ramey Station is responsible for overseeing 730 miles of coastline between Puerto Rico and the US Virgin Islands. https://www.cbp.gov/border-security/along-us-borders/border-patrol-sectors/ramey-sector-aguadilla-puerto-rico.

54. As retold by Luanda Lozano, interview with the author, January 29, 2021.

55. Graziano, *Undocumented Dominican Migration*, 13.

56. Duany, "Dominican Migration to Puerto Rico."

57. The founder of Altos de Chavón is the Austrian-born American industrialist Charles Bluhdorn, who owned the conglomerate Gulf and Western, parent company to Paramount Pictures. He is largely responsible for initiating the tourism industry to the Dominican Republic, having developed renowned golf courses and resorts in the area. He hoped the island would be a primary site for Hollywood filmmaking.

58. "I have taught at many sites and given many workshops at different locations, but Chavón was special. It's a place—imagine this: this was a desert, and on this hillside bordering the river they think to make this villa that is like a medieval inspiration. And it was like a type of kibbutz [commune]. Because the founder of Chavón is Jewish. So it was this type of kibbutz because of the little houses, and then you had the ceramic workshop, the textile workshop, the serigraphy and graphic workshop, and the school of design . . . and the young folks who studied there lived there, and there were many who didn't leave in six months. You went in, ate, slept, and worked. And we did too. That gave a very particular sensation, because we had a schedule of classes; but that schedule was not strictly enforced, in the sense that I could be in the classroom working with the students until 1:00 in the morning." Ezequiel Taveras, interview with the author, February 22, 2021. Translation by the author.

59. Michael Scatturro, "Altos de Chavón: Where Dominican Republic's Richest and Poorest Paint Side by Side," *Guardian*, April 2, 2015. https://www.theguardian.com/world/2015/apr/02/altos-de-chavon-dominican-republic-arts-school-rich-poor.

60. As retold by Luanda Lozano, interview with the author, January 29, 2021.

61. Holton, "Robert Blackburn, A Modernist," 13.

62. Cullen, *Robert Blackburn: Passages*, 93.

63. Luanda Lozano, interview with the author, January 29, 2021.

64. Unlike engraving, which requires cutting into the copper with a tool or burin, etching requires drawing with an etching needle over a waxy or resin-coated plate. The plate is then immersed in an acid bath, which eats away, or bites, the copper, creating those drawn lines. Anthony Griffiths describes it as extremely unpredictable in nature, and such unpredictability can be a draw for many artists hoping to experiment. Griffiths, *Prints and Printmaking*, 56–57.

65. Many of these artists can be seen in the documentary *Lasting Impres-*

sions: Robert Blackburn's Printmaking Workshop, https://www.youtube.com/watch?v =xWzRc5M6eqY.

66. As retold by Luanda Lozano, interview with the author, January 29, 2021.

67. For more on her exhibition history and awards, see https://luandalozano .com/cv.

68. Other invited artists from the DR included José Castillo, Nelson Ceballos, Pascal Meccariello, Radhamés Mejía, Belkis Ramírez, Raúl Recio, Luz Severino, Rosa Tavárez, Ezequiel Taveras, and Julio Valdez. Moses Ros-Suárez and Elia Alba were included via the open-call submission process. See Ballester, "*Perspectives*," 212–225.

69. Ballester, "Perspectives," 7. For more on the history of the *Bienal de San Juan*, see González, "Politics of Display"; Mari Carmen Ramírez, "Stamping (Molding) Marks," 14–21; and Reinoza and González, "Island as a Bridge."

70. Cullen, *Robert Blackburn*, 110.

71. Luanda Lozano, interview with the author, January 29, 2021.

72. Flores and Stephens, "Relational Undercurrents," 15.

73. Flores and Stephens, "Relational Undercurrents," 26.

74. Julio Valdez, artist statement in the monograph Palomero, *Julio Valdez*, 122.

75. Brotherton and Barrios, *Banished to the Homeland*.

76. Reynaldo García Pantaleón, interview with the author, December 15, 2021.

77. Luanda Lozano, interview with the author, January 29, 2021.

78. Candelario, *Black Behind the Ears*, 45. Roorda also discusses the goal of setting up a US naval base in Samaná Bay as an objective of these envoys beginning in 1854; see Roorda, *Dictator Next Door*, 242.

79. See, for example, the transcript of Grant's 1870 State of the Union address in Roorda, Derby, and González, *Dominican Republic Reader*, 158; see also Nelson, *Almost a Territory*.

80. Maingot and Lozano, *United States and the Caribbean*, 2.

81. Roorda, *Dictator Next Door*, 21.

82. Roorda, *Dictator Next Door*, 22.

83. Roorda, *Dictator Next Door*, 242. Military historian Theresa Kraus writes: "The day after the Dominican leader's death, the Caribbean Ready Amphibious Squadron (TG 44.9), permanently stationed in the Caribbean since Castro seized power in 1959, was patrolling off Ciudad Trujillo and planning for a possible hostile landing on Dominican shores. Additional forces, previously alerted, were en route to the Caribbean. Those forces included 2 additional amphibious squadrons with approximately 5,000 Marines embarked, 3 aircraft carriers—*Intrepid* (CVA 11), *Shangri-La* (CVA 38), and *Randolph* (CVA 15)—1 submarine, and about 50 surface combatants and 280 aircraft." See "Prelude to the Storm: The United States Navy and the Dominican Republic, 1959–1964," in U.S. Naval Historical Center, *Caribbean Tempest: The Dominican Republic Intervention of 1965*, colloquium held January 9, 1990, https://www.history.navy.mil/research/library/online-reading-room /title-list-alphabetically/c/caribbean-tempest.html.

84. The USS *Intrepid* had a long history of operations. It was launched in 1943, during World War II, and was used strategically as part of the Pacific Fleet, fighting against the Japanese navy. The *Intrepid* operated in the Caribbean from Guantanamo Bay to Santo Domingo and was sent for three deployments to Vietnam in the

1960s. The ship was eventually decommissioned, in 1974, and in 1982 the *Intrepid* opened its doors to the public at Pier 86 on the Hudson River, where it remains today. Visit https://www.intrepidmuseum.org/.

85. Grow, *US Presidents and Latin American Interventions*, 79.

86. Grow, *US Presidents and Latin American Interventions*, 81.

87. "You are scared by the longing / for death among those peoples, / for many years have gone by, many elections, / many millions and many prisoners / and many working days of unpaid sweat / and too much silence, / and this is too much for your bronze cannons, / your steel armor-plating, / too much for your leaden lies, / your fiery bowels." Pedro Mir and Donald D. Walsh, "To the Aircraft Carrier Intrepid," *The American Poetry Review* 5, no. 1 (1976): 36–37. Translation by Donald D. Walsh.

88. Erin Babich and Jeanne Batalova, "Immigrants from the Dominican Republic in the United States," Migration Policy Institute, April 15, 2021. https://www.migrationpolicy.org/article/dominican-immigrants-united-states-2019.

89. Babich and Batalova, "Immigrants from the Dominican Republic in the United States."

90. Coronado, email correspondence with Sarah Aponte, "RE: una pregunta," November 9, 2010, Coronado Papers, Archives of American Art, Smithsonian Institution. The Migration Policy Institute estimates that there are 191,000 unauthorized immigrants from the DR in the US. The Pew Research Center estimated there were 2.1 million Dominicans living in the US by 2017, a figure that includes foreign-born and US-born with Dominican ancestry.

91. Coronado, artist statement and checklist, *Crossing Borders* folder, Coronado Papers, Archives of American Art, Smithsonian Institution.

92. To view this work, please visit https://www.dypgrafica.com/here-there.

93. To view this work, please visit https://www.coronadoprintstudio.com/product-page/us-dr.

94. García-Peña, correspondence with Pepe Coronado, September 3, 2014, Coronado Papers, Archives of American Art, Smithsonian Institution.

95. *Consequential Translations* featured the work of twenty-eight Haitian and Dominican artists based in New York City. Organized by Coronado and Carlos Jesus Martinez Dominguez, the exhibition aimed to build solidarity when Dominicans of Haitian descent were being stripped of their citizenship rights. The Centro Cultural de España hosted the exhibition from May 8 through June 23, 2015.

96. You can see the print by visiting https://www.coronadoprintstudio.com/a-strange-bath.

97. Coronado, interview by the author, June 16, 2017. There are communities of Creole speakers in the DR, particularly those closer to the DR-Haiti border, as well as those working closely with Haitian migrants.

98. Dixa Ramírez, *Colonial Phantoms*, 5–11.

99. Maldonado-Torres, "On Metaphysical Catastrophe, Post-Continental Thought, and the Decolonial Turn," 247.

CONCLUSION

1. Carolina Miranda, "Great Tortilla Conspiracy and the Legacy of Chicano Graphics," *Los Angeles Times*, February 6, 2021.

2. Reinoza and González, "Island as a Bridge," 184.

3. Ramos, "Printing and Collecting the Revolution," 24.

4. Ramos in conversation with Maximiliano Durón, "New Exhibition on Printmaking by Chicanx Artists Looks to Expand Who Tells U.S. History," *ARTnews*, March 2, 2021, https://www.artnews.com/art-news/news/chicano-graphics-exhibition-smithsonian-american-art-museum-1234585128/.

5. To download the images, visit https://www.oreeoriginol.com/justiceforourlives.

6. Philip Kennicott, "Art Review: 'Our America' at the Smithsonian," *Washington Post*, October 25, 2013.

7. Philip Kennicott and Alex Rivera, "Critic vs. Artist: What 'Latino Art' Means," *Washington Post*, November 3, 2013.

8. Reinoza, "War at Home," 106.

9. See also Dávila, Davalos, and Reinoza, "Creating Infrastructures of Value."

10. Ramos, "Printing and Collecting the Revolution," 30.

11. Romo, "Aesthetics of the Message," 72.

12. To view the work, please visit https://americanart.si.edu/artwork/hurricane-redux-116198.

13. Jesus Barraza, artist statement, March 3, 2015. https://melaniecervantes.tumblr.com/post/112678875290/printing-indian-land-stickers-to-promote-a-new.

14. Julian Brave NoiseCat, "Why Alcatraz Matters to Native Americans," *New York Times*, November 20, 2019.

15. Barraza and Cervantes, "*Empujando Tinta*."

16. Barraza, "Signs of Solidarity."

17. Aztlán is the mythical homeland of the Aztecs. Oral histories and manuscripts describe their migration from an island homeland named Aztlán and how they were led by Huitzilopochtli to the central valley of Mexico to found their city of Tenochtitlán in 1325. For more on Aztlán, see Fields and Zamudio-Taylor, *Road to Aztlán*. For his reading of *Indian Land*, see Miner, *Creating Aztlán*, 209–210.

18. Diaz, *Flying Under the Radar with the Royal Chicano Air Force*, 6.

19. Miner, *Creating Aztlán*, 186. For more on this critical view, see Penn Hilden, "How the Border Lies"; and Contreras, *Blood Lines*.

20. Barraza, "Signs of Solidarity," 212.

21. Elisa Sobo, Valerie Lambert, and Michael Lambert, "Land Acknowledgments Meant to Honor Indigenous People Too Often Do the Opposite—Erasing American Indians and Sanitizing History Instead," *Conversation*, October 7, 2021. https://theconversation.com/land-acknowledgments-meant-to-honor-indigenous-people-too-often-do-the-opposite-erasing-american-indians-and-sanitizing-history-instead-163787.

22. Born Lesane Parish Crooks, West Coast rap artist Tupac Shakur was renamed after this heroic figure by his mother, who was active in the New York chapter of the Black Panther Party. Túpac Amaru (1545–1572), the last reigning Inca monarch, waged war against the Spaniards from his seat in Vilcabamba. He was eventually captured and hanged in a central square of Cuzco. Two hundred years after his murder, a new insurgent movement took on his name in the viceroyalty of Peru and led the Túpac Amaru Rebellion (1780–1782). For more on the iconoclasm caused by the rebellion, see Ananda Cohen-Aponte, "Genealogies of Revolutionary

Iconoclasm from Tupac Amaru to Central Park," in *Age of Revolutions* (October 9, 2017), https://ageofrevolutions.com/2017/10/09/genealogies-of-revolutionary-iconoclasm-from-tupac-amaru-to-central-park-pt-i/.

23. Fusco, "Passionate Irreverence," 34.

24. Michael Menchaca, correspondence with the author, October 30, 2020.

25. Zolan Kanno-Youngs, "Death on the Rio Grande: A Look at a Perilous Migrant Route," *New York Times*, June 8, 2019.

26. The title references the proverb "Cuando el rio suena, agua lleva," which is often translated in English as "Where there's smoke, there's fire."

27. Michael Menchaca, interview by Patricia Ruiz Healy in *Michael Menchaca: Vignettes from San Antonio* (San Antonio: Ruiz Healy Art, 2018), n.p.

28. Menchaca, interview by Patricia Ruiz Healy.

29. Zapata, "Chicanx Graphics in the Digital Age," 131.

30. For more on queer of color critiques in Latinx art see Robb Hernández, *Archiving an Epidemic*, and "Unfinished: Death Worlds of Homombre LA."

BIBLIOGRAPHY

Abrego, Leisy. "Renewed Optimism and Spatial Mobility: Legal Consciousness of Latino Deferred Action for Childhood Arrivals Recipients and their Families in Los Angeles." *Ethnicities* 18, no. 2 (2018): 192–207.

Abreu, Christina. *Rhythms of Race: Cuban Musicians and the Making of Latino New York City and Miami, 1940–1960*. Chapel Hill: University of North Carolina Press, 2015.

Acuña, Rodolfo. *Occupied America: The Chicano's Struggle toward Liberation*. San Francisco: Canfield Press, 1972.

Adamson, Morgan. "Internal Colony as Political Perspective: Counterinsurgency, Extraction, and Anticolonial Legacies of '68 in the United States." *Cultural Politics* 15, no. 3 (2019): 343–357.

Ades, Dawn. *Art in Latin America: The Modern Era, 1820–1980*. New Haven: Yale University Press, 1989.

Alanís Enciso, Fernando S. *They Should Stay There: The Story of Mexican Migration and Repatriation During the Great Depression*. Translated by Russ Davidson. Chapel Hill: University of North Carolina Press, 2017.

Alvarado, Leticia. "Flora and Fauna Otherwise: Black and Brown Aesthetics of Relation in Firelei Báez and Wangechi Mutu." *Latin American and Latinx Visual Culture* 1, no. 3 (July 2019): 8–24.

Andrade, Oswald de. "The Anthropophagous Manifesto." In *Inverted Utopias: Avant-Garde Art in Latin America*, translated by Héctor Olea, 466. New Haven: Yale University Press in association with the Museum of Fine Arts Houston, 466–467. Originally published as "Manifesto antropófago," *Revista de antropofagia* 1, no. 1 (São Paulo, 1928): 3, 7.

Anreus, Alejandro, Robin Adèle Greeley, and Megan A. Sullivan. *A Companion to Modern and Contemporary Latin American and Latina/o Art*. Hoboken, NJ: Wiley-Blackwell, 2022.

Anzaldúa, Gloria. *Borderlands/La Frontera: The New Mestiza*. 3rd edition. San Francisco: Aunt Lute Books, 2007.

Arrizón, Alicia. "Mestizaje." In *Keywords for Latina/o Studies*. Edited by Deborah Vargas, Nancy Raquel Mirabal, and Lawrence La Fountain-Stokes, 133–136. New York: New York University Press, 2017.

Auyero, Javier, ed. *Invisible in Austin: Life and Labor in an American City*. Austin: University of Texas Press, 2015.

Baddeley, Oriana. "Engendering New Worlds: Allegories of Rape and Reconciliation." In *The Visual Culture Reader*, edited by Nicholas Mirzoeff, 382–388. New York: Routledge, 1998.

Balderrama, Francisco, and Raymond Rodriguez. *Decade of Betrayal: Mexican Repatriation in the 1930s*. Albuquerque: University of New Mexico Press, 1995.

Ballester, Diógenes. "Perspectives on the XII San Juan Biennial of Latin American and the Caribbean Printmaking at the Transition to the 21st Century." In *XII Bienal de San Juan del Grabado Latinoamericano y del Caribe*, exhibition catalogue, 7–18. San Juan: Instituto de Cultura Puertorriqueña, 1998.

Barnes, Will C. *Arizona Place Names*. Tucson: University of Arizona Press, 1960.

Barnet-Sánchez, Holly. "Sandra C. Fernández: Fractured Layers of Dreams and Memories and Hope for the Future." *A Contra Corriente: A Journal on Social History and Literature in Latin America* 13, no. 2 (Winter 2016): 311–326.

Barney, James M. "How Apache Leap Got Its Name." *Arizona Highways* 11, no. 6–7 (August 1935): 20–21.

Barnitz, Jacqueline. *Twentieth-Century Art of Latin America*. Austin: University of Texas Press, 2001.

Barraza, Jesus. "Opening the Bundles: Artists Creating New Realities Through Spiritual Offerings." *Revista N'oj* 2 (December 2020). https://revistanoj.berkeley.edu/2020/12/14/opening-the-bundles-artists-creating-new-realities-through-spiritual-offerings/.

———. "Signs of Solidarity: The Work of Dignidad Rebelde." *ASAP/Journal* 3, no. 2 (May 2018): 208–216.

Barraza, Jesus, and Melanie Cervantes. "*Empujando Tinta*: The Work and Politics of Dignidad Rebelde." *Aztlán: A Journal of Chicano Studies* 41, no. 2 (Fall 2016): 209–220.

Barron, Stephanie. "The Making of *Made in California*." In *Made in California: Art, Image, and Identity, 1900–2000*, edited by Stephanie Barron, Sheri Bernstein, and Ilene Susan Fort, 27–47. Berkeley: University of California Press and Los Angeles County Museum of Art, 2000.

Bayers, Peter L. "The U.S. Mint, the Lewis and Clark Bicentennial, and the Perpetuation of the Frontier Myth." *Journal of Popular Culture* 44, no. 1 (2011): 37–52.

Beltrán, Cristina. *The Trouble with Unity: Latino Politics and the Creation of Identity*. New York: Oxford University Press, 2010.

Bergland, Renée L. *The National Uncanny: Indian Ghosts and American Subjects*. Hanover, NH: University Press of New England, 2000.

Bhagat, Alexis, and Lize Mogel, eds. *An Atlas of Radical Cartography*. Los Angeles: Journal of Aesthetics and Protest Press, 2007.

Blackwell, Maylei. "Contested Histories: Las Hijas de Cuauhtémoc, Chicana Feminisms and Print Culture in the Chicano Movement, 1968–1973." In *Chicana Feminisms: A Critical Reader*, edited by Gabriela Arrendondo, Aida Hurtado, Norma Klahn, Olga Najera-Ramírez, and Patricia Zavella, 59–89. Durham, NC: Duke University Press, 2003.

———. "Geographies of Indigeneity: Indigenous Migrant Women's Organizing and Translocal Politics of Place." *Latino Studies* 15, no. 2 (2017): 156–181.

Blackwell, Maylei, Floridalma Boj Lopez, and Luis Urrieta, Jr. "Introduction to Special Issue Critical Latinx Indigeneities" *Latino Studies* 15, no. 2 (2017): 126–137.

Botey, Mariana. *Rubén Ortiz Torres: Customatism*, with texts by C. Ondine Chavoya, José Falconi, and Cuauhtémoc Medina. Mexico City: Museo Universitario Arte Contemporáneo, 2019.

Brody, David. "Painting Labor: Ramiro Gomez's Representations of Domestic Work." *Women's Studies Quarterly* 45, no. 3 *Precarious Work* (Fall/Winter 2017): 154–159.

Brotherton, David C., and Luis Barrios. *Banished to the Homeland: Dominican Deportees and Their Stories of Exile*. New York: Columbia University Press, 2011.

Bürger, Peter. "Avant-Garde and Neo-Avant-Garde: An Attempt to Answer Certain Critics of Theory of the Avant-Garde," *New Literary History* 41 (2010): 695–715.

———. *Theory of the Avant-Garde*. Translated by Michael Shaw. Minneapolis: University of Minnesota Press, 1984.

Burns, Eric. *The Smoke of the Gods: A Social History of Tobacco*. Philadelphia, PA: Temple University Press, 2007.

Candelario, Ginetta E. B. *Black Behind the Ears: Dominican Racial Identity from Museums to Beauty Shops*. Durham, NC: Duke University Press, 2007.

———. "La ciguapa y el ciguapeo: Dominican Myth, Metaphor, and Method." *Small Axe* 20, no. 3 (November 2016): 100–112.

Capello, Ernesto. *City at the Center of the World: Space, History, and Modernity in Quito*. Pittsburgh, PA: University of Pittsburgh Press, 2011.

———. "From Imperial Pyramids to Anticolonial Sundials: Commemorating and Contesting French Geodesy in Ecuador." *Journal of Historical Geography* 62 (2018): 37–50.

Caragol-Barreto, Taína. "Aesthetics of Exile: The Construction of Nuyorican Identity in the Art of El Taller Boricua." *Centro Journal* 17, no. 2 (Fall 2005): 6–22.

Carbone, Teresa. "Exhibit A: Evidence and the Art Object." In *Witness: Art and Civil Rights in the Sixties*, edited by Teresa Carbone and Kellie Jones, 80–108. New York: Brooklyn Museum and Monacelli Press, 2014.

Carrasco, David, and Scott Sessions, eds. *Cave, City, and Eagle's Nest: An Interpretive Journey through the Mapa de Cuauhtinchan No. 2*. Albuquerque: University of New Mexico Press, 2007.

Carroll, Amy Sara. *REMEX: Toward an Art History of the NAFTA Era*. Austin: University of Texas Press, 2017.

Chagoya, Enrique. "A Lost Continent: Writings Without an Alphabet." In *The Road to Aztlán: Art from a Mythic Homeland*, edited by Virginia M. Fields and Victor Zamudio-Taylor, 262–273. Los Angeles: Los Angeles County Museum of Art and University of New Mexico Press, 2001.

Chavoya, C. Ondine. "Customized Hybrids: The Art of Rubén Ortiz Torres and Lowriding in Southern California." *CR: The New Centennial Review* 4, no. 2 (Fall 2004): 141–184.

Coblentz, Cassandra. "A Conversation with Joe Segura." In *Right to Print: Segura Publishing Company*, edited by Lucy Flint, 41–48. Scottsdale, AZ: Scottsdale Museum of Contemporary Art, 2007.

Cohen-Aponte, Ananda. "Decolonizing the Global Renaissance: A View from the Andes." In *The Globalization of Renaissance Art: A Critical Review*, edited by Daniel Savoy, 67–94. Leiden: Brill, 2017.

Cohen-Aponte, Ananda, and Ella Maria Diaz. "Painting Prophecy: Mapping a Polyphonic Chicana Codex Tradition in the Twenty-First Century." *English Language Notes* 57, no. 2 (October 2019): 22–42.

Contreras, Sheila. *Blood Lines: Myth, Indigenism, and Chicana/o Literature*. Austin: University of Texas Press, 2008.

Cordova, Cary. *The Heart of the Mission: Latino Art and Politics in San Francisco.* Philadelphia: The University of Pennsylvania Press, 2017.

Córdova, Ruben C. "The Cinematic Genesis of the Mel Casas Humanscape, 1965–1967." *Aztlán: A Journal of Chicano Studies* 36, no. 2 (Fall 2011): 51–87.

———. "Getting the Big Picture: Political Themes in the Humanscapes of Mel Casas." In *Born of Resistance: Cara a Cara Encounters with Chicana/o Visual Culture,* edited by Scott L. Baugh and Victor A. Sorell, 172–189. Tucson: University of Arizona Press, 2015.

Cornejo, Kency. "Decolonial Futurisms: Ancestral Border Crossers, Time Machines, and Space Travel in Salvadoran Art." In Robb Hernández et al., *Mundos Alternos: Art & Science Fiction in the Americas,* 21–31. Riverside, CA: UCR ARTSblock, 2017.

Cortez, Constance. "Aztlán in Tejas: Chicano/Chicana Art from the Third Coast." In *Chicano Visions: American Painters on the Verge.* Boston, MA: Bulfinch Press, 2002.

Crosswhite, Frank S. "History, Geology, and Vegetation of Picketpost Mountain." *Desert Plants* 6, no. 2 (1984): 73–80.

Cullen, Deborah T. "Robert Blackburn: American Printmaker." PhD diss., The City University of New York, 2002.

———. *Robert Blackburn: Passages.* College Park: The David C. Driskell Center at the University of Maryland, 2014.

———. *The Robert Blackburn Legacy: The Printmaking Workshop at Forty-Five.* Newark, NJ: Newark Public Library, 1994.

Cushing, Lincoln. *Revolución: Cuban Poster Art.* San Francisco, CA: Chronicle Books, 2003.

Cuvi, Jacinto. "Santos: The Gold Hunter." In *Invisible in Austin: Life and Labor in an American City,* edited by Javier Auyero, 42–58. Austin: University of Texas Press, 2015.

Dackerman, Susan, ed. *Corita Kent and the Language of Pop.* Cambridge, MA: Harvard Art Museums, 2015.

———. "Introduction: Prints as Instruments." In *Prints and the Pursuit of Knowledge in Early Modern Europe,* exhibition catalogue, 19–35. Cambridge: Harvard Art Museums and Yale University Press, 2011.

Dardashti, Abigail Lapin. "El Dorado: The Neobaroque in Dominican American Art." *Diálogo: An Interdisciplinary Studies Journal* 20, no. 1 (Spring 2017): 73–87.

———. "Tracing the Ocean: Transnational Movement in Scherezade García's Murals, 1997–2018." In *Scherezade García: From This Side of the Atlantic,* edited by Olga Herrera, 25–31. Washington, DC: Art Museum of the Americas, 2020.

Davalos, Karen Mary. *Yolanda M. López.* Los Angeles, CA: UCLA Chicano Studies Research Center Press, 2008.

Davidson, Russ, and David Craven, eds. *Latin American Posters: Public Aesthetics and Mass Politics.* Santa Fe: Museum of New Mexico Press, 2006.

Dávila, Arlene. "Culture in the Battlefront: From Nationalist to Pan-Latino Projects." In *Mambo Montage: The Latinization of New York,* edited by Agustín Lao-Montes and Arlene Dávila, 159–180. New York, NY: Columbia University Press, 2001. (First published as "Culture in the Battleground: From Nationalist to Pan-Latino Projects." *Museum Anthropology* 23, no. 3 [2000]: 26–41. https://doi.org/10.1525/mua.2000.23.3.26.)

———. *Latinx Art: Artists, Markets, and Politics.* Durham, NC: Duke University Press, 2020.

Dávila, Arlene, Karen Mary Davalos, and Tatiana Reinoza. "Creating Infrastructures of Value: Self Help Graphics and the Art Market, an interview with Arlene Dávila conducted by Karen Mary Davalos and Tatiana Reinoza." In *Self Help Graphics at Fifty: A Cornerstone of Latinx Art and Collaborative Artmaking*, edited by Tatiana Reinoza and Karen Mary Davalos, 257–269. Oakland: University of California Press, 2023.

Deer, Sarah, Bonnie Clairmont, and Carrie A. Martell. *Sharing Our Stories of Survival: Native Women Surviving Violence.* Lanham, MD: AltaMira Press, 2008.

De Genova, Nicholas. "Migrant 'Illegality' and Deportability in Everyday Life." *Annual Review of Anthropology* 31 (2002): 419–447.

Derby, Lauren. *The Dictator's Seduction: Politics and the Popular Imagination in the Era of Trujillo.* Durham, NC: Duke University Press, 2009.

Diaz, Ella M. *Flying Under the Radar with the Royal Chicano Air Force: Mapping a Chicano/a Art History.* Austin: University of Texas Press, 2017.

Ditrén, María Elena. *Rosa Tavárez: Territorios de la pasión y la memoria, 1963–2013.* Santo Domingo, Dominican Republic: Museo de Arte Moderno, 2014.

Dolinko, Silvia. *Arte Para Todos: La Difusión del Grabado como Estrategia para la Popularización del Arte.* Buenos Aires, Argentina: Fundación Espigas, 2003.

Donahue-Wallace, Kelly. "Picturing Prints in Early Modern New Spain." *The Americas* 64, no. 3 (2008): 325–349.

Duany, Jorge. "Dominican Migration to Puerto Rico: A Transnational Perspective." *Centro Journal* 17, no. 1 (Spring 2005): 243–268.

———. *The Puerto Rican Nation on the Move: Identities on the Island and in the United States.* Chapel Hill: University of North Carolina Press, 2002.

Dunning-Lozano, Jessica. "Inés: Mothering in the Margins." In *Invisible in Austin: Life and Labor in an American City*, edited by Javier Auyero, 80–98. Austin: University of Texas Press, 2015.

Escamilla, Ricardo Pérez. *Estética Socialista en México, Siglo XX.* Mexico City: Museo de Arte Carrillo Gil, 2003.

Evans, Harriett, and Stephanie Donald. *Picturing Power in the People's Republic of China: Posters of the Cultural Revolution.* Lanham, MD: Rowman and Littlefield, 1999.

Exploring the Early Americas. Exhibition interactive presentations: Waldseemüller Maps, the Library of Congress, https://www.loc.gov/exhibits/exploring-the-early-americas/interactives/waldseemuller-maps/cartamarina1516/highlights1516.html.

Ferreiro, Larrie D. *Measure of the Earth: The Enlightenment Expedition That Reshaped Our World.* New York, NY: Basic Books, 2011.

Fields, Virginia, and Victor Zamudio-Taylor, eds. *The Road to Aztlán: Art from a Mythic Homeland.* Los Angeles, CA: Los Angeles County Museum of Art, 2001.

Flores, Tatiana. "'Latinidad Is Cancelled': Confronting an Anti-Black Construct." *Latin American and Latinx Visual Culture* 3, no. 3 (2021): 58–79.

———. "Latino Art and the Immigrant Artist: The Case of Sandra C. Fernández," *Diálogo* 18, no. 2 (2015): 167–172.

Flores, Tatiana, and Michelle A. Stephens, eds. "Relational Undercurrents: Toward an Archipelagic Model of Insular Caribbean Art." In *Relational Undercurrents:*

Contemporary Art of the Caribbean Archipelago, 15–89. Long Beach, CA: Museum of Latin American Art, 2017.

Florida, Richard. *The Rise of the Creative Class: And How It's Transforming Work, Leisure, Community, and Everyday Life*. New York, NY: Basic Books, 2002.

Foster, Hal. "Real Fictions." *Artforum International* 55, no. 8 (April 2017): 166–174.

Fox, Claire F. *The Fence and the River: Culture and Politics at the U.S.–Mexico Border.* Minneapolis: University of Minnesota Press, 1999.

Fox, Howard. "Many Californias, 1980–2000." In *Made in California: Art, Image, and Identity, 1900–2000*, edited by Stephanie Barron, Sheri Bernstein, and Ilene Susan Fort, 235–271. Berkeley: University of California Press and Los Angeles County Museum of Art, 2000.

Freud, Sigmund. "The 'Uncanny.'" In The Standard Edition of the Complete Psychological Works of Sigmund Freud, Volume XVII, 217–256. London: The Hogarth Press, 1919.

Fusco, Coco. "Passionate Irreverence." In *English Is Broken Here: Notes on Cultural Fusion in the Americas, 25–36*. New York, NY: The New Press, 1995.

Gabara, Esther, ed. "Contesting Freedom." In *Pop América, 1965–1975, 10–19*. Durham, NC: Nasher Museum of Art at Duke University, 2018.

García-Peña, Lorgia. *The Borders of Dominicanidad: Race, Nation, and Archives of Contradiction*. Durham, NC: Duke University Press, 2016.

———. "Performing Identity, Language, and Resistance: A Study of Josefina Báez's Dominicanish." *Wadabagei* 11, no. 3 (October 2008): 28–45.

Gaspar de Alba, Alicia. *Chicano Art Inside/Outside the Master's House: Cultural Politics and the CARA Exhibition*. Austin: University of Texas Press, 1998.

Gatzambide-Fernández, Rubén. "Decolonial Options and Artistic/AestheSic Entanglements: An Interview with Walter Mignolo." *Decolonization: Indigeneity, Education & Society* 3, no. 1 (2014): 196–212.

Gaudio, Michael. *Engraving the Savage: The New World and Techniques of Civilization*. Minneapolis: University of Minnesota Press, 2008.

Giunta, Andrea. *Avant-Garde, Internationalism, and Politics: Argentine Art in the Sixties*. Durham: Duke University Press, 2007.

Golash-Boza, Tanya. *Deported: Immigrant Policing, Disposable Labor, and Global Capitalism*. New York, NY: New York University Press, 2015.

Goldman, Shifra. "Between 'Aquí' and 'Allá': Thirty Years of the Taller Boricua." In *Homenaje Alma Boricua, XXX Aniversario: Taller Alma Boricua Portfolio Exhibition*, edited by Diógenes Ballester, 20–27. San Juan, Puerto Rico: Museo de las Americas, 2001.

———. "A Public Voice: Fifteen Years of Chicano Posters." *Art Journal* 44, no. 1 (Spring 1984): 50–57.

Gombrich, E. H. "Eastern Inventions and Western Response." *Daedalus* 127, no. 1 (January 1998): 193–205.

Gómez-Barris, Macarena. *The Extractive Zone: Social Ecologies and Decolonial Perspectives*. Durham, NC: Duke University Press, 2017.

———. "Mestiza Cultural Memory: The Self-Ecologies of Laura Aguilar." In *Laura Aguilar: Show and Tell*, edited by Rebecca Epstein, 79–85. Los Angeles, CA: UCLA Chicano Studies Research Center Press, 2017.

Gómez-Peña, Guillermo. "Disclaimer." *TDR: Drama Review* 50, no. 1 (Spring 2006): 149–158.

Gómez-Peña, Guillermo, Enrique Chagoya, and Felicia Rice. *Codex Espangliensis: From Columbus to the Border Patrol*. San Francisco: City Lights Books, 2000.
Gonzales-Day, Ken. *Lynching in the West, 1850–1935*. Durham: Duke University Press, 2006.
González, Jennifer. "Part V. Border Visions and Immigration Politics." *Chicana and Chicano Art: A Critical Anthology*, edited by Jennifer A. González, C. Ondine Chavoya, Chon Noriega, and Terezita Romo. Durham: Duke University Press, 2019.
———. "Introduction." In *Codex Espangliensis: From Columbus to the Border Patrol*. San Francisco: City Lights Books, 2000.
González-González, María del Mar. "La Hoja Nacionalizada: DIVEDCO's Graphic Arts." *Aztlán* 42, no. 1 (Spring 2017): 163–178.
———. "The Politics of Display: Identity and the State at the San Juan Print Biennial, 1970–1981." PhD diss., University of Illinois at Urbana-Champaign, 2013.
Goodman, Adam. *The Deportation Machine: America's Long History of Expelling Immigrants*. Princeton, NJ: Princeton University Press, 2020.
Gordon, Avery. *Ghostly Matters: Haunting and the Sociological Imagination*. Minneapolis: University of Minnesota Press, 1997.
Graziano, Frank. *Undocumented Dominican Migration*. Austin: University of Texas Press, 2013.
Greeley, Robin. "Enrique Chagoya." *Bomb* 74 (Winter 2001): 4–5.
Greet, Michele. *Beyond National Identity: Pictorial Indigenism as a Modernist Strategy in Andean Art, 1920–1960*. University Park: Pennsylvania State University Press, 2009.
Griffiths, Anthony. *Prints and Printmaking: An Introduction to the History and Techniques*. Berkeley: University of California Press in association with the British Museum, 1996.
Grow, Michael. *US Presidents and Latin American Interventions: Pursuing Regime Change in the Cold War*. Lawrence: University Press of Kansas, 2008.
Guidotti-Hernández, Nicole. *Unspeakable Violence: Remapping US and Mexican National Imaginaries*. Durham, NC: Duke University Press, 2011.
Gunckel, Colin. "Art and Community in East L.A.: Self Help Graphics & Art from the Archive Room." *Aztlán: A Journal of Chicano Studies* 36, no. 2 (Fall 2011): 157–170.
Guzmán, Kristen. "Art in the Heart of East L.A.: A History of Self Help Graphics and Art, Inc., 1972–2004." PhD diss., University of California, Los Angeles, 2005.
———. *Self Help Graphics & Art: Art in the Heart of East Los Angeles*. 2nd edition. Edited by Colin Gunckel. Los Angeles, CA: UCLA Chicano Studies Research Center, 2014.
Handlesman, Michael. "En nombre de un amor imaginario y los origenes de la República del Ecuador." *Guaraguao* 15, no. 38 (Winter 2011): 167–181.
Hanley, Sarah Kirk. "Segura Reborn at University of Notre Dame." In *Images of Social Justice from the Segura Arts Studio*. South Bend, IN: Snite Museum of Art, 2016.
———. "Visual Culture of the Nacirema: Chagoya's Printed Codices." *Art in Print* 1, no. 6 (March–April 2012): 3–15. https://artinprint.org/article/visual-culture-of-the-nacirema-chagoyas-printed-codices/.
Hansen, Trudy. "Multiple Visions: Printers, Artists, Promoters, and Patrons." In *Printmaking in America: Collaborative Prints and Presses, 1960–1990*, 32–69. New York: Harry N. Abrams, 1995.

Harmon, Katherine. *The Map as Art: Contemporary Artists Explore Cartography*. New York, NY: Princeton Architectural Press, 2009.

———. *You Are Here: Personal Geographies and Other Maps of the Imagination*. New York, NY: Princeton Architectural Press, 2004.

Heffernan, Michael, and Carol Medlicot. "A Feminine Atlas? Sacagewea, the Suffragettes, and the Commemorative Landscape in the American West, 1904–1910." *Gender, Place, and Culture: A Journal of Feminist Geography* 9, no. 2 (2002): 109–131.

Hernandez, Kelly Lytle. *Migra! A History of the U.S. Border Patrol*. Berkeley: University of California Press, 2010.

Hernández, Robb. *Archiving an Epidemic: Art, AIDS, and the Queer Chicanx Avant-Garde*. New York: New York University Press, 2019.

———. "Unfinished: The Death Worlds of *Homombre LA*." In *Self Help Graphics at Fifty: A Cornerstone of Latinx Art and Collaborative Artmaking*, edited by Tatiana Reinoza and Karen Mary Davalos, 135–163. Oakland: University of California Press, 2023.

Herrera, Olga U., ed. "Introduction." In *Scherezade García: From This Side of the Atlantic*, exhibition catalogue. Washington, DC: Art Museum of the Americas, 2020.

Heyman, Therese Thau. *Posters American Style*. Washington, DC: Smithsonian American Art Museum, 1998.

Hills, Patricia. "Picturing Progress in the Era of Westward Expansion." In *The West as America: Reinterpreting Images of the Frontier, 1820–1920*, edited by William H. Truettner, 97–147. Washington, DC: Smithsonian Institution Press, 1991.

Holton, Curlee Raven. "Robert Blackburn, A Modernist: My Personal Story." In *Robert Blackburn: Passages*. College Park: The David C. Driskell Center at the University of Maryland, 2014.

Hooker, Juliet. *Theorizing Race in the Americas: Douglass, Sarmiento, DuBois, and Vasconcelos*. New York, NY: Oxford University Press, 2017.

Hyman, Aaron. "Inventing Painting: Cristóbal del Villalpando, Juan Correa, and New Spain's Transatlantic Canon." *Art Bulletin* 99, no. 2 (April 2017): 102–135.

Ittman, John, ed. *Mexico and Modern Printmaking: A Revolution in the Graphic Arts, 1920–1950*. Philadelphia, PA: Philadelphia Museum of Art, 2006.

Jackson, Cassandra. *Violence, Visual Culture, and the Black Male Body*. New York, NY: Routledge, 2011.

Jones, Kellie. "Civil/Rights/Act." In *Witness: Art and Civil Rights in the Sixties*, edited by Teresa Carbone and Kellie Jones, 11–55. New York, NY: Brooklyn Museum and Monacelli Press, 2014.

———. *Now Dig This! Art and Black Los Angeles, 1960–1980*. Los Angeles, CA: Hammer Museum, 2011.

Kanas, Nick. *Star Maps: History, Artistry, and Cartography*. 2nd edition. Cham, Switzerland: Springer International Publishing AG, 2019.

Kessler, Donna. *The Making of Sacagawea: A Euro-American Legend*. Tuscaloosa: University of Alabama Press, 1996.

Kolodny, Annette. *The Lay of the Land: Metaphor as Experience and History in American Life and Letters*. Chapel Hill: University of North Carolina Press, 1975.

Kuhlemann, Ute. "Between Reproduction, Invention and Propaganda: Theodor de Bry's Engravings after John White's Watercolours." In *A New World: England's First View of America*, edited by Kim Sloane, 79–92. London: British Museum, 2007.

Kupperman, Karen O. *The Jamestown Project*. Cambridge, MA: Harvard University Press, 2007.

Langa, Helen. *Radical Art: Printmaking and the Left in 1930s New York.* Berkeley: University of California Press, 2004.

Latorre, Guisela. *Walls of Empowerment: Chicana/o Indigenist Murals of California.* Austin: University of Texas Press, 2008.

Lear, John. *Picturing the Proletariat: Artists and Labor in Revolutionary Mexico, 1908–1940.* Austin: University of Texas Press, 2017.

Lee, Erika. *America for Americans: A History of Xenophobia in the United States.* New York, NY: Basic Books, 2019.

Lehmbeck, Leah, ed. *Proof: The Rise of Printmaking in Southern California.* Los Angeles, CA: Getty Publications and the Norton Simon Museum, 2011.

Lennard, Debra. *Notes on Solidarity: Tricontinentalism in Print.* New York, NY: James Gallery, 2019.

Limón, José. *American Encounters: Greater Mexico, the United States, and the Erotics of Culture.* Boston, MA: Beacon Press, 1998.

Lippard, Lucy. "Rupert Garcia: Face to Face." In *Rupert Garcia: Prints and Posters, 1967–1990*, exhibition catalogue, 13–42. San Francisco, CA: Fine Arts Museums of San Francisco.

Lipsitz, George. "Not Just Another Social Movement: Poster Art and the Movimiento Chicano." *Just Another Poster? Chicano Graphic Arts in California*, edited by Chon A. Noriega, 71–89. Santa Barbara: University Art Museum, University of California, 2001.

Loomis, Elisha. *The Pythagorean Proposition: Its Demonstrations Analyzed and Classified and Its Bibliography of Sources for Datá of the Four Kinds of Proofs.* 2nd edition. Ann Arbor, MI: Edwards Brothers, 1940.

Lowe, Sam. *Arizona Myths and Legends: The True Stories Behind History's Mysteries*, 2nd edition. Guilford, CT: TwoDot, 2016.

Lugo, Flavia Marichal. *La Xilografía en Puerto Rico, 1950–1986.* San Juan: Universidad de Puerto Rico, 1987.

Lugones, Maria. "Heterosexism and the Colonial/Modern Gender System." *Hypatia* 22, no. 1 (2007): 186–209.

Maingot, Anthony, and Wilfredo Lozano. *The United States and the Caribbean: Transforming Hegemony and Sovereignty.* New York, NY: Routledge, 2005.

Maldonado-Torres, Nelson. "On Metaphysical Catastrophe, Post-Continental Thought, and the Decolonial Turn." In *Relational Undercurrents: Contemporary Art of the Caribbean Archipelago*, edited by Tatiana Flores and Michelle Stephens, 247–259. Long Beach, CA: Museum of Latin American Art, 2017.

Manifestaciones: Dominican York Proyecto GRAFICA. New York, NY: CUNY Dominican Studies Institute Gallery, 2010.

Mapa/Corpo 2: Interactive Rituals for the New Millennium. Performed June 14, 2007 at Centro Recoleta, Buenos Aires, Argentina. Hemispheric Institute, http://hidvl.nyu.edu/video/000549498.html.

Markey, Lia, ed. *Renaissance Invention: Stradanus's Nova Reperta.* Evanston, IL: Northwestern University Press, 2020.

Martinez, Monica Muñoz. *The Injustice Never Leaves You: Anti-Mexican Violence in Texas.* Cambridge, MA: Harvard University Press, 2018.

Marzio, Peter. "Lithography as a Democratic Art: A Reappraisal." *Leonardo* 4, no. 1 (1971): 37–48.

McKiernan Gonzalez, John. *Fevered Measures: Public Health and Race at the Texas-Mexico Border, 1848–1942.* Durham, NC: Duke University Press, 2012.

Menchaca, Martha. *Naturalizing Mexican Immigrants: A Texas History*. Austin: University of Texas Press, 2011.

Mesa-Bains, Amalia. "Spiritual Geographies." In *The Road to Aztlán: Art from a Mythic Homeland*, edited by Virginia Fields and Victor Zamudio-Taylor, 332–341. Los Angeles, CA: Los Angeles County Museum of Art and University of New Mexico Press, 2001.

Mignolo, Walter D. *The Darker Side of the Renaissance: Literacy, Territoriality, & Colonization*. 2nd edition. Ann Arbor: University of Michigan Press, 2003.

———. *The Idea of Latin America*. Malden, MA: Blackwell Publishing, 2005.

———. "The Movable Center: Geographical Discourses and Territoriality During the Expansion of the Spanish Empire." In *The Latin American Cultural Studies Reader*, edited by Ana del Sarto, Alicia Rios, and Abril Trigo, 262–290. Durham, NC: Duke University Press, 2004.

Mignolo, Walter, and Rolando Vazquez. "Decolonial AestheSis: Colonial Wounds/Decolonial Healings." *Social Text: Periscope* (July 15, 2013). https://socialtextjournal.org/periscope_article/decolonial-aesthesis-colonial-woundsdecolonial-healings/.

Miner, Dylan. *Creating Aztlán: Chicano Art, Indigenous Sovereignty, and Lowriding Across Turtle Island*. Tucson: University of Arizona Press, 2014.

Mir, Pedro and Donald D. Walsh. "To The Aircraft Carrier Intrepid." *The American Poetry Review* 5, no. 1 (1976): 36–37.

Mirzoeff, Nicholas. *The Right to Look: A Counterhistory of Visuality*. Durham, NC: Duke University Press, 2011.

Molina, Natalia. *How Race Is Made in America: Immigration, Citizenship, and the Historical Power of Racial Scripts*. Berkeley: University of California Press, 2014.

Mondrian, Piet. "Toward the True Vision of Reality (1941)." In *Mondrian and His Studios: Colour in Space*, edited by Francesco Manacorda and Michael White, 11–15. London: Tate Publishing, 2014.

Montoya, Malaquias, and Lezlie Salkowitz-Montoya, "A Critical Perspective on the State of Chicano Art." *Metamorfosis* 3, no. 1 (Spring–Summer 1980): 3–7. [Reprinted in Jacinto Quirarte, *Chicano Art History: A Book of Selected Readings*, 120–124. San Antonio: Research Center for the Arts and Humanities, University of Texas at San Antonio, 1984.]

Morris, Kate. "Crash: Specters of Colonialism in Contemporary Indigenous Art." *Art Journal* 76, no. 2 (Summer 2017): 70–80.

Mundy, Barbara E. *The Mapping of New Spain: Indigenous Cartography and the Maps of the Relaciones Geográficas*. Chicago, IL: University of Chicago Press, 1996.

Muñoz, José Esteban. *The Sense of Brown*. Edited by Joshua Chambers-Letson and Tavia Nyongó. Durham, NC: Duke University Press, 2020.

NASA. "Space Debris and Human Spacecraft." May 26, 2021. https://www.nasa.gov/mission_pages/station/news/orbital_debris.html.

Nelson, David, Jennifer Cressy, and Suzanne Karr Schmidt, "Warfare." In *Renaissance Invention: Stradanus's Nova Reperta*, edited by Lia Markey, 153–158. Evanston, IL: Northwestern University Press, 2020.

Nelson, William Javier. *Almost a Territory: America's Attempt to Annex the Dominican Republic*. Newark: University of Delaware Press, 1990.

Ngai, Mae. *Impossible Subjects: Illegal Aliens and the Making of Modern America*. Princeton, NJ: Princeton University Press, 2004.

Noriega, Chon A. "The Orphans of Modernism." In *Phantom Sightings: Art After the Chicano Movement*, exhibition catalogue, 16–45. Los Angeles, CA: Los Angeles County Museum of Art, 2008.

———, ed. *Just Another Poster? Chicano Graphic Arts in California*, exhibition catalogue. Santa Barbara: University Art Museum, University of California, 2001.

Noriega, Chon A., Mari Carmen Ramírez, and Pilar Tompkins Rivas. *Home—So Different, So Appealing*, exhibition catalogue. Los Angeles, CA: UCLA Chicano Studies Research Center Press with Los Angeles County Museum of Art and the Museum of Fine Arts Houston, 2017.

Orozco, Sylvia. "Adolfo Mexiac en Austin." In *Libertad de Expresión: Adolfo Mexiac*, edited by Blanca Garduño Pulido. Mexico City: Instituto Nacional de Bellas Artes/Museo Casa Estudio Diego Rivera y Frida Kahlo, 1998.

Ortíz Torres, Rubén, and Tyler Stallings. *Desmothernismo: A Survey of Work from 1990 to 1998*, exhibition catalogue. Santa Monica, CA: Smart Art Press and Huntington Beach Art Center, 1998.

O'Sullivan, John L. "Annexation." *United States Magazine and Democratic Review* 17, no. 1 (July–August 1845): 5–10.

Padilla, Felix. *Latino Ethnic Consciousness: The Case of Mexican Americans and Puerto Ricans in Chicago*. Notre Dame, IN: University of Notre Dame Press, 1985.

Paglen, Trevor. "Experimental Geography: From Cultural Production to the Production of Space." In *Experimental Geography: Radical Approaches to Landscape, Cartography, and Urbanism*, exhibition catalogue, 27–33. Edited by Nato Thompson. Brooklyn, NY: Melville House and Independent Curators International, 2008.

Palomero, Federica. *Julio Valdez*. New York: FTC Group, 2009.

Pearce, Margaret Wickens. "Review of Experimental Geography: Radical Approaches to Landscape, Cartography, and Urbanism." *Cartographic Perspectives* 70 (2011): 64–66.

Penn Hilden, Patricia. "How the Border Lies: Some Historical Reflections." In *Decolonial Voices: Chicana and Chicano Cultural Studies in the Twenty-First Century*, edited by Arturo Aldama and Naomi Quiñonez, 152–176. Bloomington: University of Indiana Press, 2002.

Pérez, Gina M. *The Near Northwest Side Story: Migration, Displacement, & Puerto Rican Families*. Berkeley: University of California Press, 2004.

Pérez, Laura E. "Enrique Dussel's *Ética de Liberación*, US Women of Color Decolonizing Practices, and Coalitionary Politics Amidst Difference." *Qui Parle: Critical Humanities and Social Sciences* 18, no. 2 (2010): 121–146.

———. *Eros Ideologies: Writings on Art, Spirituality, and the Decolonial*. Durham, NC: Duke University Press, 2019.

Perez, Laura E. and Ann Marie Leimer, eds. *Consuelo Jimenez Underwood: Art, Weaving, Vision*. Durham: Duke University Press, 2022.

Pickles, John. *A History of Spaces: Cartographic Reason, Mapping, and the Geo-coded World*. New York: Routledge, 2004.

Ponce de León, Jennifer. *Another Aesthetics Is Possible: Arts of Rebellion in the Fourth World War*. Durham, NC: Duke University Press, 2021.

Posamentier, Alfred. *The Pythagorean Theorem: The Story of Its Power and Beauty*. Amherst, NY: Prometheus Books, 2010.

Pratt, Mary Louise. *Imperial Eyes: Travel Writing and Transculturation*. 2nd edition. New York, NY: Routledge, 2008.

Quijano, Aníbal. “Coloniality of Power, Eurocentrism, and Latin America.” *Nepantla: Views from the South* 1, no. 3 (2000): 533–580.

Quirarte, Jacinto. *Chicano Art History: A Book of Selected Readings.* San Antonio: Research Center for the Arts and Humanities, University of Texas at San Antonio, 1984.

Rabasa, José. *Inventing America: Spanish Historiography and the Formation of Eurocentrism.* Norman: University of Oklahoma Press, 1993.

Radcliffe, Sarah. “Representing the Nation.” In *Mapping Latin America: A Cartographic Reader,* edited by Jordana Dym and Karl Offen, 207–210. Chicago, IL: University of Chicago Press, 2011.

Raheja, Michelle. “Reading Nanook’s Smile: Visual Sovereignty, Indigenous Revisions of Ethnography, and ‘Atanarjuat (The Fast Runner).’” *American Quarterly* 59, no. 4 (2007): 1159–1185.

Ramírez, Dixa. *Colonial Phantoms: Belonging and Refusal in the Dominican Americas, from the 19th Century to the Present.* New York, NY: New York University Press, 2018.

Ramírez, Mari Carmen. “Stamping (Molding) Marks.” In *Poly/Graphic San Juan Triennial: Latin America and the Caribbean.* San Juan, Puerto Rico: Instituto de Cultura Puertorriqueña, 2004.

Ramírez, Yasmin, and Henry Estrada. *Pressing the Point: Parallel Expressions in the Graphic Arts of the Chicano and Puerto Rican Movements.* New York, NY: El Museo del Barrio, 1999.

Ramos, E. Carmen. “Manifestaciones: Expressions of Dominicanidad in Nueva York.” In *Manifestaciones: Dominican York Proyecto GRAFICA,* exhibition catalogue. New York, NY: CUNY Dominican Studies Institute Gallery, 2010.

———. “Printing and Collecting the Revolution: The Rise and Impact of Chicano Graphics, 1965 to Now.” In *¡Printing the Revolution! The Rise and Impact of Chicano Graphics, 1965 to Now,* exhibition catalogue, 23–69. Washington, DC: Smithsonian American Art Museum and Princeton University Press, 2020.

———. *¡Printing the Revolution! The Rise and Impact of Chicano Graphics, 1965 to Now.* Washington, DC: Smithsonian American Art Museum and Princeton University Press, 2020.

———. “What Is Latino About American Art?” In *Our America: The Latino Presence in American Art,* exhibition catalogue, 33–69. Washington, DC: Smithsonian American Art Museum, 2014.

Reinoza, Tatiana. “Collecting in the Borderlands: Ricardo and Harriett Romo’s Collection of Chicano Art.” MA thesis, University of Texas at Austin, 2009.

———. “The Island Within an Island: Remapping Dominicanyork.” *Archives of American Art Journal* 57, no. 2 (Fall 2018): 4–27.

———. “Latino Print Cultures in the US, 1970–2008.” PhD diss., University of Texas at Austin, 2016.

———. “*No Es un Crimen*: Posters, Political Prisoners, and the Mission Counterpublics.” *Aztlán: A Journal of Chicano Studies* 42, no. 1 (Spring 2017): 239–256.

———. “Printed Proof: The Cultural Politics of Ricardo and Harriett Romo’s Print Collection.” In *A Library for the Americas: The Nettie Lee Benson Latin American Collection,* edited by Julianne Gilland and José Montelongo, 145–155. Austin: University of Texas Press, 2018.

———. “War at Home: Conceptual Iconoclasm in American Printmaking.” In

¡Printing the Revolution! The Rise and Impact of Chicano Graphics, 1965 to Now, edited by E. Carmen Ramos, 105–127. Washington, DC: Smithsonian American Art Museum and Princeton University Press, 2020.

Reinoza, Tatiana, and María del Mar González-González, "The Island as a Bridge: Reconceptualizing the *Trienal Poli/Gráfica de San Juan.*" Dossier edited by Andrea Giunta. *Caiana: Revista de Historia del Arte y Cultura Visual del Centro Argentino de Investigadores de Arte* 11 (Fall 2017). http://caiana.caia.org.ar/template/caiana.php?pag=articles/article_2.php&obj=287&vol=11.

Ricourt, Milagros. "Reaching the Promised Land: Undocumented Dominican Migration to Puerto Rico." *Centro Journal* 19, no. 2 (Fall 2007): 224–243.

Ríos, Alberto. *The Smallest Muscle in the Human Body.* Port Townsend, WA: Copper Canyon Press, 2002.

———. *The Theater of Night.* Port Townsend, WA: Copper Canyon Press, 2005.

Ríos, Alberto, and Leslie A. Wootten. "The Edge in the Middle: An Interview with Alberto Ríos." *World Literature Today* 77, no. 2 (July–September 2003): 57–60.

Rivera Cusicanqui, Silvia. *Ch'ixinakax utxiwa: On Practices and Discourses of Decolonization.* Translated by Molly Geidel. Medford, MA: Polity Press, 2020.

Rodríguez, Ana Patricia. *Dividing the Isthmus: Central American Transnational Histories, Literatures, and Cultures.* Austin: University of Texas Press, 2009.

Rodríguez, Pedro, and Antonio Martorell. *The Role of Paper: Affirmation and Identity in Chicano and Boricua Art.* San Antonio, TX: Guadalupe Cultural Arts Center, 1999.

Román, Miriam Jiménez. "The Indians Are Coming! The Indians Are Coming! The Taíno and Puerto Rican Identity." In *Taíno Revival: Critical Perspectives on Puerto Rican Identity and Cultural Politics,* edited by Gabriel Haslip-Viera, 101–138. Princeton, NJ: Markus Wiener Publishers, 2001.

Romo, Tere. "Aesthetics of the Message: Chicana/o Posters, 1965–1987." In *¡Printing the Revolution! The Rise and Impact of Chicano Graphics, 1965 to Now,* edited by E. Carmen Ramos, 71–103. Washington, DC: Smithsonian American Art Museum and Princeton University Press, 2020.

———. "¡Presente! Chicano Posters and Latin American Politics." In *Latin American Posters: Public Aesthetics and Mass Politics,* edited by Russ Davidson, 51–63. Santa Fe: Museum of New Mexico Press, 2006.

Roorda, Eric Paul. *The Dictator Next Door: The Good Neighbor Policy and the Trujillo Regime in the Dominican Republic, 1930–1945.* Durham, NC: Duke University Press, 1998.

Roorda, Eric Paul, Lauren Derby, and Raymundo González, eds. *The Dominican Republic Reader: History, Culture, Politics.* Durham, NC: Duke University Press, 2014.

Ruiz-Healy, Patricia. *Michael Menchaca: Vignettes from San Antonio.* San Antonio, TX: Ruiz Healy Art, 2018.

Safier, Neil. *Measuring the New World: Enlightenment Science and South America.* Chicago, IL: University of Chicago Press, 2008.

Saldaña-Portillo, María Josefina. *Indian Given: Racial Geographies Across Mexico and the United States.* Durham, NC: Duke University Press, 2016.

———. "Preface." *Aztlán: A Journal of Chicano Studies, Dossier: Revisiting Mestizaje Twenty Years Later,* 46, no. 2 (Fall 2021): 145–148.

———. "Who's the Indian in Aztlán? Re-Writing Mestizaje, Indianism, and Chicanismo from the Lacandón." In *The Latin American Subaltern Studies Reader*, edited by Ileana Yamileth Rodríguez et al., 402–423. Durham, NC: Duke University Press, 2001.

Saldivar, Reina Prado. "Self-Help Graphics: A Case Study of a Working Space for Arts and Community." *Aztlán: A Journal of Chicano Studies* 25, no. 1 (2000): 167–181.

Sánchez, George. *Boyle Heights: How a Los Angeles Neighborhood Became the Future of American Democracy*. Oakland: University of California Press, 2021.

Sassen, Saskia. *The Global City: New York, London, Tokyo*. Princeton, NJ: Princeton University Press, 1991.

Schimmel, Julie. "Inventing the 'Indian.'" In *The West as America: Reinterpreting Images of the Frontier, 1820–1920*, edited by William Truettner, 149–189. Washington, DC: Smithsonian Institution Press, 1991.

Schreffler, Michael J. "Vespucci Rediscovers America: The Pictorial Rhetoric of Cannibalism in Early Modern Culture." *Art History* 28, no. 3 (June 2005): 295–310.

Scott, Amy. "La Raza: Photography, Race, and Place in the American West." In *La Raza*, edited by Colin Gunckel, 12–25. Los Angeles, CA: UCLA Chicano Studies Research Center Press, 2020.

Seda, Laurietz. "Decolonizing the Body Politic: Guillermo Gómez-Peña's *Mapa/Corpo 2*: Interactive Rituals for the New Millennium." *TDR* 53, no. 1 (Spring 2009): 136–141.

Sheren, Ila. "Coco Fusco and Guillermo Gómez-Peña's *Cage Performance* and La Pocha Nostra's *Mapa Corpo*: Art of the [Portable] Border." *Hemisphere: Visual Cultures of the Americas* 3, no. 1 (2010): 58–79.

———. *Portable Borders: Performance Art and Politics on the U.S. Frontera Since 1984*. Austin: University of Texas Press, 2015.

Shirk, Adrian. "The Real Marlboro Man." *Atlantic*, February 17, 2015. https://www.theatlantic.com/business/archive/2015/02/the-real-marlboro-man/385447/.

Slotkin, Richard. *Gunfighter Nation: The Myth of The Frontier in Twentieth-Century America*. Norman: University of Oklahoma Press, 1998.

Smith, Roberta. "Memo to Art Museums: Don't Give Up on Art." *New York Times*, section 2, page 1. December 3, 2000.

Soja, Edward W. *Postmodern Geographies: The Reassertion of Space in Critical Social Theory*. New York, NY: Verso, 1989.

Staden, Hans. *Hans Staden's True History: An Account of Cannibal Captivity in Brazil*. Edited and translated by Neil L. Whitehead and Michael Harbsmeier. Durham, NC: Duke University Press, 2008.

Stevens, Camilla. "'Home Is Where Theater Is': Performing Dominican Transnationalism." *Latin American Theater Review* 44, no. 1 (Fall 2010): 29–48.

Stonard, John-Paul. "Pop in the Age of Boom: Richard Hamilton's 'Just What Is It That Makes Today's Homes So Different, So Appealing?'" *The Burlington Magazine* 149, no. 1254 (September 2007): 607–620.

Sullivan, Edward. "From Here to Eternity: *Paraíso* and Other Recent Works by Scherezade García." In *Paraíso*, exhibition catalogue. Havana, Cuba: Casa de la Cultura, Galería Carmelo González, 2000.

Tarver, Gina McDaniel. *The New Iconoclasts: From Art of a New Reality to Conceptual Art in Colombia, 1961–1975*. Bogotá: Universidad de los Andes, Facultad de Artes y Humanidades, Departamento de Arte, Ediciones Uniandes, 2016.

Tate, Maggie. "Austin, Texas, in Socio-Historical Context." In *Invisible in Austin: Life and Labor in an American City*, edited by Javier Auyero, 20–41. Austin: University of Texas Press, 2015.

Taylor, Diana. *The Archive and the Repertoire: Performing Cultural Memory in the Americas*. Durham, NC: Duke University Press, 2003.

———. "Remapping Genre through Performance: From 'American' to 'Hemispheric' Studies." *PMLA* 122, no. 5 (October 2007): 1416–1430.

Thomas, Mary. "Generative Networks and Local Circuits: Self Help Graphics and the Visual Politics of Solidarity." In *Self Help Graphics at Fifty: A Cornerstone of Latinx Art and Collaborative Artmaking*, edited by Tatiana Reinoza and Karen Mary Davalos, 77–103. Oakland: University of California Press, 2023.

Thompson, Nato. "In Two Directions: Geography as Art, Art as Geography." In *Experimental Geography: Radical Approaches to Landscape, Cartography, and Urbanism*, exhibition catalogue, 13–25. Brooklyn, NY: Melville House and Independent Curators International, 2008.

Torres-Saillant, Silvio. "The Tribulations of Blackness: Stages in Dominican Racial Identity." *Latin American Perspectives* 25, no. 3 (May 1998): 126–146.

Torres-Saillant, Silvio, and Ramona Hernández. *The Dominican Americans*. Westport, CT: Greenwood Press, 1998.

Tournon, Annabela. "Usos del Muralismo y Desvíos de la Historia: La Conexión Chicana del Grupo 65." In */Synchronicity/Contacts and Divergences in Latin American and U.S. Latino Art: 19th Century to the Present*, edited by Doris Bravo and Tatiana Reinoza, 247–256. Austin: The University of Texas at Austin, 2012.

US Naval Historical Center. *Caribbean Tempest: The Dominican Republic Intervention of 1965*. Colloquium January 9, 1990. https://www.history.navy.mil/research/library/online-reading-room/title-list-alphabetically/c/caribbean-tempest/html.

Van Duzer, Chet. *Martin Waldseemüller's "Carta Marina" of 1516: Study and Transcription of the Long Legends*. Cham, Switzerland: Springer Open, 2020.

———. *Sea Monsters on Medieval and Renaissance Maps*. London, England: The British Library, 2013.

Vargas-Santiago, Luis. "Emiliano: Framing Zapata's Migrations through Greater Mexico in Mexico City's Museo del Palacio de Bellas Artes." *Latin American and Latinx Visual Culture* 3, no. 1 (2021): 109–119.

Villaseñor Black, Charlene, and Emily Engel. "Why Latinx?" *Latin American and Latinx Visual Culture* 3, no. 2 (2021): 5–10.

Villavicencio, Karla Cornejo. *The Undocumented Americans*. New York, NY: One World, 2020.

Vizenor, Gerald. *Manifest Manners: Post-Indian Warriors of Survivance*. Hanover, NH: University Press of New England, 1994.

Walker, Barry. "Printmaking 1960 to 1990." In *Printmaking in America: Collaborative Prints and Presses, 1960–1990*, edited by Elaine M. Stainton, 70–95. New York, NY: Harry N. Abrams, 1995.

Warhol, Andy, and Pat Hackett. *Popism: The Warhol 60s*. New York, NY: Harcourt Brace Jovanovich, 1980.

Watson, Steven. *Factory Made: Warhol and the Sixties*. New York, NY: Pantheon Books, 2003.

Wells, Carol. "La Lucha Sigue: From East Los Angeles to the Middle East." In *Just Another Poster? Chicano Graphic Arts in California*, edited by Chon A. Noriega, 172–201. Santa Barbara: University Art Museum, University of California, 2001.

Weschler, Lawrence. *Domestic Scenes: The Art of Ramiro Gomez*. New York, NY: Harry N. Abrams, 2016.

Weyl, Christina. *The Women of Atelier 17: Modernist Printmaking in Midcentury New York*. New Haven, CT: Yale University Press, 2019.

Whalen, Carmen Teresa. *From Puerto Rico to Philadelphia: Puerto Rican Workers and Postwar Economies*. Philadelphia, PA: Temple University Press, 2001.

Whiting, Cécile. *Pop L.A.: Art and the City in the 1960s*. Berkeley: University of California Press, 2006.

Williams, Lyle, ed. "Without Borders." In *Estampas de la Raza: Contemporary Prints from the Romo Collection*, exhibition catalogue, 25–44. San Antonio, TX: McNay Art Museum and University of Texas Press, 2012.

Williams, Reba, and Dave Williams. "The Early History of the Screenprint." *Print Quarterly* 3, no. 4 (1986): 287–321.

Wood, Denis. *The Power of Maps*. New York, NY: Guilford Press, 1992.

Wye, Deborah. *Committed to Print: Social and Political Themes in Recent American Printed Art*. New York, NY: Museum of Modern Art, 1988.

Ybarra-Frausto, Tomás. "Primeros Pasos: First Steps Toward an Operative Construct of Latino Art." In *Our America: The Latino Presence in American Art*, edited by E. Carmen Ramos, 13–31. Washington, DC: Smithsonian American Art Museum, 2014.

Young, Cynthia. *Soul Power: Culture, Radicalism, and the Making of a US Third World Left*. Durham, NC: Duke University Press, 2006.

Zamudio-Taylor, Victor. "Inventing Tradition, Negotiating Modernism: Chicana/o Art and the Pre-Columbian Past." In *The Road to Aztlán: Art from a Mythic Homeland*, edited by Virginia Fields and Victor Zamudio-Taylor, 342–357. Los Angeles, CA: Los Angeles County Museum of Art and University of New Mexico Press, 2001.

Zapata, Claudia. "Chicanx Graphics in the Digital Age." In *¡Printing the Revolution! The Rise and Impact of Chicano Graphics, 1965 to Now*, edited by E. Carmen Ramos, 128–156. Washington, DC: Smithsonian American Art Museum and Princeton University Press, 2020.

———. "The Future Is Feminist: How the Maestras Atelier Transformed Self Help Graphics." In *Self Help Graphics at Fifty: A Cornerstone of Latinx Art and Collaborative Artmaking*, edited by Tatiana Reinoza and Karen Mary Davalos, 107–134. Oakland: University of California Press, 2023.

Zavala, Adriana. "Latin@ Art at the Intersection." *Aztlán: A Journal of Chicano Studies* 40, no. 1 (2015): 125–140.

Zigrosser, Carl. "The Serigraph, A New Medium." *Print Collector's Quarterly* 28, no. 4 (December 1941): 442–477.

Zorach, Rebecca, Luca Molà, and Matthew James Crawford, "Transformation." In *Renaissance Invention: Stradanus's Nova Reperta*, edited by Lia Markey, 163–168. Evanston, IL: Northwestern University Press, 2020.

INDEX

Page numbers in italic type indicate information contained in images or image captions.

acculturation, forced, 142–145, 194–196. *See also* assimilationist ideology, countering

Ades, Dawn, 149, 193

African American art/artists: anti-racist themes of, 44, 142, 164–168; coalitional work, 11–12; Robert Blackburn workshop, 156, 174–175, *176*, 186. *See also* African heritage

African heritage: Black Atlantic discourse, 28, 153–155, 164–165, 186, 192; Creole elite rejection of, 119; Dominican rejection of, 154, 163–164, 165–168; in racial mixing ideology, 14–15, 18, 149–150, 206

Aguilar, Laura, 4, 138–139

Akomfrah, John, 164

Albers, Josef, 84

Alcatraz occupation (1969), 202, 204

"Allegory of America" (Galle after Stradanus), *62*, 63

Almonte, Carlos, 152, *153*, 186, *187*

Alpuche, José (Joe), 156–157

Altomare, John, 100

Altos de Chavón School of Design, La Romana, Dominican Republic, 162, 173–174

Alvarez, Julia, 168–169

Alÿs, Francis, 90

Amarrao (García Pantaleón), 178, *179*

America Invertida (Torres-García), 105, 184

American icons in Latinx art, 43, 47, 63–64, 95, 140–141. *See also* cowboy mythos and imagery; Marlboro imagery

"American" identity, 98–100

American Indian, The (Russell Means) (Warhol), 65–67

American Indian Series, The (Warhol, series), 65–67

American Ocean/Cuba (Chagoya and Ríos), 93–97, *98*

Andes Mountains, 113, 114, 115–116

Andrade, Oswald de, 88–90

Angola, 172–173

Angulo Guridi, Francisco Javier, 169

"animatives," 83

Anreus, Alejandro, 13

anthropocentrism, 22, 24

anthropophagy, 89. *See also* cannibalism

anti-immigration discourse, 2, 7, 9, 25, 42, 47, 139–140. *See also* xenophobia and nativism

Anzaldúa, Gloria: "claiming of space" concept, 138; and mestizaje consciousness and border crossing, 15, 47, 115, 122; "new meztiza" concept, 145, 149

Apache Indians, 52–55. *See also* Apache Leap

Apache Leap, 52–54, 57–59, 206

Aponte, Sarah, 183

Aquellos Que Han Muerto (Peña), 195

aqueous territorialities, 18–19, 208. *See also* water

Arizona Highways, 54, *55*

Arizona State University (ASU), 5, 74

Arizona Volunteers, 54

art history field, Eurocentrism of, 11, 12

art informel style, 128

artists of color, marginalization of in mainstream art, 5–6, 12–14, 34, 44, 46, 124–125, 194–198, 200–201

Asian American artists, 11–12

Asian Celestial Map (Chagoya and Ríos), 79, 101

assemblage techniques, 128

assimilationist ideology, countering, 10, 64, 69, 125, 194–195. *See also* acculturation, forced

Atabey (Taíno deity), 1

Atlas (Mercator), *26*, 95, 105
Atlas of Radical Cartography, An (Bhagat and Mogel, eds.), 98–99, 105
August, Jack, 52
Austin, Tex., 123, 124–128, 133, 135. *See also* Coronado Studio
Austin Museum of Art, 235n4
authority, rejection of and delinking, 20–22, 24
Auyero, Javier, 135
avant-garde moments and concepts, 3, 10–11, 77, 88, 192–193, 200–201
axis mundi concept, 79, 108, 192
Azaceta, Luis Cruz, 6
Aztec culture/cultural icons, 21, 47–49, 64, 84, 131, 144–146. *See also* Aztlán (Aztec ancestral homeland)
Aztlán (Aztec ancestral homeland), 26, 35, 52, 58–59, 97, 205, 206

Báez, Josefina, 162
Bailando con el Sol (Coronado, P.), 156–157
Balaguer, Joaquín Antonio, 157, 181
Ballester, Diógenes, 176
Bananhattan (Mendoza), 159, *161*
Baray, Sam, 157
Barletti, Don, 59
Barnet-Sánchez, Holly, 139
Barney, James Mitchell, 54
Barnitz, Jacqueline, 3
Barraza, Jesus, 18, 202, 204–206
Barron, Stephanie, 69, 70
Beaning Indigenous (Duffy), 33
Behind What Is Seen (Fernández), 129–130
Beltrán, Cristina, 15
Benítez Rojo, Antonio, 154
Bergland, Renée, 61
Bernardi, Claudia, 6
Bhagat, Alexis, 98, 105
Bienal de San Juan del Grabado Latinoamericano y del Caribe (XII, 1998), 175–176, 194
Birmingham Race Riot (Warhol), 44, *45*
Black Atlantic discourse, 28, 153–155, 164–165, 186, 192
Blackburn, Robert, 156, 174–175, *176*, 186
Black heritage. *See* African American art/artists; African heritage
Black Lives Matter movement, 195
Black Man and Flag (Garcia, R.), 44
Bluest Eyes, The (Morrison), 61
Bluhdorn, Charles, 238n57
Boccalero, Karen, 5, 32–33, 46, 124, 155, 194
Border Patrol, 40, 41
"border pop," 26, 35, 47, 67, 69–70
borders and border crossing: border culture and resistance paradigm, 9; dangers of, 41, 59–60, 170–172, 178, 186, 208; embodiment of and map imagery, 100–109; immigrant crossing "caution" sign, 59, 69, 137–138; North American Free Trade Agreement (NAFTA), impact of, 35, 47, 65, 100–101, 133–135, 204; reterritorialization/mobility of, 27, 76, 102, 111, 115, 133–134, 137, 192; water as boundary/border, 153–154, 159, 164–165, 170–172, 178, 186, 208. *See also* caution sign (immigrant crossing)
border security: fences/walls, 59–60; US Border Patrol, 40–41, 100, 139, 172, 234n61, 238n53; US Customs and Border Protection (CBP), 133, 172; US Department of Homeland Security, 127, 133; US Immigration and Customs Enforcement (ICE), 9, 115, 133, 135
Bosch, Juan, 181
Bouguer Pierre, 113
Boy's Art (Kozloff, series), 91
Brandywine Workshop, Philadelphia, 12, 156, 165, 220n2, 220n13
Briefe and True Report of the New Found Land of Virginia, A (Harriot), 86–87
Brimberry, Katherine, 233n35
Bueno, Carlos, 5, 32, 156
Bürger, Peter, 3, 193
Burnett, Leo, 39
Burning Gas Station (Ruscha, series), 44
Bush, George H. W., 41
Bush, George W., 103
Bustamante, Nao, 65

calavera (representational skull), 41, 42
California: anti-immigration efforts, 15, 42, 47, 59–60, 192; representative imagery of, 37–39, 43, 49–50, 69–70
California Department of Transportation (Caltrans), 59

California Taco (Ortiz Torres), *49*
Caminantes Somos de la Noche y de la Pena (Viteri), 128, *129*
Campos-Pons, María Magdalena, 178
Candelario, Ginetta, 168, 169, 237n27
cannibalism, 17–18, 63, 84–90
Capellán, Tony, 178
Carbone, Teresa, 44
Cárdenas, Gilberto, 200
Caribbean culture and identity, influence of, 19, 153–155, 165, 177–178, 186. *See also* Creole elites and cultural hierarchies; Dominican Republic (DR), overviews
Carroll, Amy Sara, 65
Carta de la Provincia de Quito y de sus Adyacentes, *112*, 113–114, 117–119
Carta Marina (Fries after Waldseemüller), 85–86
Carta Marina (Waldseemüller), *16*, 17–18
Cartas III and *Cartas* series (Taveras), 173–174
cartography/maps and territorial politics: cartographic gaze concept, 81–82, 110–111, 146, 153–154; Earth shape debate and mapping expeditions, 117–118; Eurocentric manipulation of, 79, 90–92, 102–109; phenomenological approach to, 77–83, 89–98; radical cartography as activism, 76, 98–100, 104–105; and territorial colonialism and delinking, 2–4, 17–19, 24–26, 31–35, 109–110
cartoon characters in pop art, 47, 95
Casas, Mel, 44
Castro, René, 194
Casualties of Modernity (Monkman), 56–57
Catlin, George, 67
CAUTION: Dreamers in/on Sight (Fernández), *136*, 137–139, 146
caution sign (immigrant crossing), 59, 67, 69, 137–138. *See also CAUTION: Dreamers in/on Sight* (Fernández)
Ceballos, Michelle, 102
Ceci N'Est Pas une Pipe (Magritte), 66
Center for Land Use Interpretation, 90, 91
Central Texas, 114–115. *See also* Austin, Tex.
Central Texas printmaking residency program, 123, 146. *See also* Serie Project at Coronado Studio
Centro de Arte Puertorriqueño, San Juan, Puerto Rico, 202
ceramic arts, 31–32
Chagoya, Enrique: artistic refutation of Eurocentric cartography, 92–101, 104–109; background, 75; border pop and cultural identity, 47–49; collaboration with Ríos, overviews, 75–77, 109–111; on loss of precolonial books and manuscripts, 4; and map embodiment concept, 102; overviews, 192; and phenomenological approach to cartography, 77–85, 89–98; in *¡Printing the Revolution!* (exhibition), 201. *See also* Chagoya (Enrique), works by; Chagoya and Ríos, works by
Chagoya (Enrique), works by: *Codex Espangliensis* (Gómez-Peña and Chagoya), 102; *Crossing I*, *47*, *48*; *Ghost of Liberty, The*, 201; *Governor's Nightmare, The*, 47, *48*, 49; *Le Cannibale Moderniste*, 84–85; *Road Map*, 101. *See also* Chagoya and Ríos, works by
Chagoya and Ríos, works by: *American Ocean/ Cuba*, 93–97, 98; *Asian Celestial Map*, 79, 101; *Genome Map*, *72*, 73, 74, 111; *Theorem*, 77–80, 82, 83, 98; *Trash World*, 92–93; *Upside Down World Map*, 105–107; *You Are Here* (portfolio), 26–27, 74, 92, 98, 105, 109–110
Charlier, Vladimir Cybil, 185
Chavoneros (alumni of Altos de Chavón), 162
Che Guevara: Icon, Myth, and Message (exhibition), 193
Chicano movement, 5, 33
Chicanx art and cultural identity, 5, 9, 11–12, 193, 198, 201–202
children of immigrants/slaves, 9, 41, 61, 137, 141, 147–149, 165
Children of Middle Passage (Lindsay, series), 165, *166*
Chiricahua Apache people, 54–55
Chrismas, Douglas, 65
cigarettes, 40. *See also* Marlboro imagery; smoking and tobacco
ciguapa (mythological creature), 168–170
Cigüa Palmera (*Dulus dominicus*), 159, *161*
ciguapear concept, 170
Cigüita Cibaeña en Nueva York (De los Santos), 159, *161*

Cintrón, Javier, 175
Cirrus Editions (workshop), 5, 194
Citizenship Revoked (Coronado), 185
City of Austin Cultural Arts Program, 124–125
civil rights movement, US, 7–8, 34–35, 193
Clinton, Bill, 73–74
coalitions (interethnic) in printmaking, 11–12. *See also* collaborative workshops
Codex Boturini, 97
Codex Espangliensis (Gómez-Peña and Chagoya), 102
Codex Mendoza, 130–131, 146, 149
Codex Rodriguez-Mondragón (Rodriguez, S., series), 21
codices, ancient American, 4
Cold War, 8, 94, 181
collaborative workshops, 4–5, 11–12, 46–47, 233n35. *See also* print workshops
collectives. *See* print collectives
Collectors Press Lithography, San Francisco, 13
colonialism: coloniality concepts, 24–26, 130–131, 223n68; "colonial wound" and legacy of trauma, 1–2, 27, 55–56, 120–121, *xiv*; colonization as cultural cannibalism, 84–85; internal, 14, 121–122; modern persistence of, 209–210; settler colonialism, 17, 35, 47, 49, 58. *See also* decolonization and delinking; Eurocentrism
Columbus, memorialization of, 157
Columbus Lighthouse Memorial (*Faro a Colón*), 157, 181
Coming of Age (*Transformations*) (Fernández), 115, 125–128, 135
Congress Avenue Bridge, Austin, 125, 133
Consequential Translations (exhibition), 185
consumer culture themes, 40, 42–43, 46, 47, 230n44
Cook, Roy, 60
Corazón de la Tierra (Mendez), 1–2, 19, *xiv*
Córdova, Ruben, 44
Coronado, Pepe: and Coronado Studio, 6, 221n15; and DYPG, 6–7, 152, *153*, 158–161; early career and Serie Project residency, 155–157; and resentment over US interventions in DR, 181–185; and Scherezade García, 162, 180; and Terry Ybañez, 143
Coronado, Sam, 6, 122–124, 146, *147*, 155–156
Coronado Studio, 6–7, 114–115, 123–124, 201. *See also* Coronado, Sam; Serie Project at Coronado Studio
Cortés, Hernán, 64, 74–75
Cortéz, Carlos, 193–194
COVID-19 pandemic, 185, 196, 222–223n62
cowboy mythos and imagery, 39–41, 57, 64. *See also* frontier mythologies and imagery; Marlboro imagery
craft-revival movement, 31
Creole elites and cultural hierarchies, 14, 118, 119, 121
criollos, 118
Critical Latinx Indigeneities (field of study), 26
Crossing I (Chagoya), 47, *48*
crossings. *See* borders and border crossing
Cuando el Rio Suena, Gatos Lleva (Menchaca), 208, *209*
Cuaron, Mita, 157
Cuba and Latinx art, 2, 93–95, 193–194
Cuban Missile Crisis, 94–95
Cucas/Paper Doll (Fernández, series), 128–129
Cuellar, Rodolfo "Rudy," 14
Cuevas, José Luis, 13
CUNY Dominican Studies Institute, 183
Curtain Raiser (Duffy), 224n11
Cutting the Tongue (Ybañez, series), 145
Cutting Tongues (Ybañez), 143–145
Cuvi, Jacinto, 141–142

dangers of border crossings, 41, 59–60, 170–172, 178, 186, 208
d'Anville, Hubert-François Bourguignon, 117
Dávila, Arlene, 12, 125, 200
Day Dreaming/Soñando Despierta (García, S.), 162, *163*, 165, 168
DDT (García, Rupert), 198–199
Debord, Guy, 90
de Bry, Theodore, 86–87
Decade Show, The (exhibition), 124
decolonization and delinking: artists approaches to, 2–3, 18–24, 92–101, 104–109; and decolonial theory/framework, 24–26, 200–201; and paradox of reclamation, 205–210
Deferred Action for Childhood Arrivals (DACA), 137

De Genova, Nicholas, 221n18, 232n24
delinking. *See* decolonization and delinking
Dell, Jeffrey, 208
De los Santos, René, 152, *153*, 159, *161*
deportations, 9, 115, 127, 133, 135, 142
Descartes, René, 117
De Soto, Ernest (and workshop), 13
De Stijl (design style), 77
Detrás de la Oreja (Luciano), 167–168
detribilization/deterritorialization, 18, 58, 205
Diasporicans, 10. *See also* Nuyoricans (Puerto Rican diasporans)
Diaz, Ella, 52, 205
digital sensibility concept, 207
Dig These (Duffy), 30–31
Dimas, Marcos, 197
diseases, European, 21
Disney characters in Latinx art, 47, 95
displacement. *See* dispossession and displacement, imagery of
dispossession and displacement, imagery of, 4, 19–21, 41–42, 52–53, 55–57, 205–206
DNA and human genome sequencing, 72, 73–74
Dominicanidad (Dominicanness), 159, 165
Dominican Republic (DR), overviews, 180, 181, 183–184, 237n27. *See also* Dominican York Proyecto Gráfica (DYPG)
"Dominican York" label, 6–7, 151–152, 162
Dominican York Proyecto Gráfica (DYPG): artists in *¡Printing the Revolution!* (exhibition), 201; collective vision of and approaches to African heritage, 161–168; evolution and formation of, 6–7, 151–152, 155–161; future outlook, 185–190; impact and legacy of, 28, 200; interventions in, geopolitical impacts of, 180–185; mythical water figure as immigrant metaphor, 168–170; overviews, 192; perspectives on water as border and territoriality, 170–180
Donjuan, Carlos, 125
DR (Dominican Republic). *See* Dominican Republic (DR), overviews
Dreambox (garcía, i), 186, *188*
Dreamers (under DACA), 137–138
Druecker, Thomas, 233n35
drug trade, 178
Duany, Jorge, 172
Duffy, Ricardo: background and early years, 31; on Karen Boccalero, 32–33; overviews, 26, 191–192, 206; SHG atelier residencies, 33, 157. *See also* Duffy (Ricardo), works by
Duffy (Ricardo), works by: *Beaning Indigenous*, 33; *Curtain Raiser*, 224n11; *Dig These*, 30–31; *Primavera*, 33; *Veni Vidi Vici*, 31–32. *See also New Order, The* (Duffy)
Durón, Maximiliano, 195
Duval-Carrié, Edouard, 178

Earth shape debate and mapping expeditions, 117–118
Ecuador and mestiza consciousness, 115–122, 125
Editora Política (publisher/printer), 193
Egas, Camilo, 120
1848 (González L.), 50–52
El Museo del Barrio, New York, 158
El Paso Walmart shooting (2019), 9
El Reggaetón del Bachatero (Ros-Suárez), 151–152
Emiliano (Vargas-Santiago), 224–225n13
Engel, Emily, 8
engraving *v.* etching processes, 238n64
Enjaulada (Fernández), 123
En nombre de un amor imaginario (Velasco Mackenzie), 119
Ernest F. De Soto Workshop, San Francisco, 13
Estampas de La Raza (exhibition), 10
Estampas de la Revolución Mexicana (Mora), 33
Estampería Quiteña (workshop), 114, 118
etching *v.* engraving processes, 238n64
Etymologiae (Isidore of Seville), 108–109
Eurocentrism: in art history study, 11, 12; of cartographic gaze, 146, 153–154; of colonial printmaking, 3; and Creole elite identity, 119; and decolonial framework, 24–26, 200–201; extraction from other cultures, 19–21; manipulation of epistemic cartography/geography, 79, 90–92, 102–109; and politics of territory, 17–19, 21–24; in racial classification, 132; and rise of Latinx cultural identity, 8. *See also* colonialism
exceptionalism, American, 19–21, 41–42
exhibitions, evolution of in Latinx art, 10–13
expansionism themes, 33–35, 37, 41, 55, 57, 64
Experimental Geography (exhibition), 90
"experimental geography" concept, 27, 91, 98, 110

Experimental Silkscreen Atelier Program of SHG, 5, 26, 46, 156–157
extractive model of territorial conquest, 21, 24–25, 192

Factory, The (workshop), 47
Fe, Sonya, 157
Febres Cordero, León, 122
feminism, 10, 25, 115, 138
Fernández, Sandra C.: background and family, 114–115, 116–117; and mestiza consciousness, 12–122; overviews, 27–28, 192, 206; photography work, 120; in *¡Printing the Revolution!* (exhibition), 201–202; Serie Project residency, 123, 125. *See also* Fernández (Sandra C.), works by
Fernández (Sandra C.), works by: *Behind What Is Seen*, 129–130; *CAUTION: Dreamers in/on Sight*, *136*, 137–139, 146; *Coming of Age (Transformations)*, 115, 125–128, 135; *Cucas/Paper Doll* (series), 128–129; *Enjaulada*, 123; *Mourning and Dreaming on High*, 201–202; *Northern Triangle, The*, 147–149
Ferus Gallery, Los Angeles, 43
Figuras Fragmentadas por el Tiempo (Lozano), 175–176, *177*
Florence, Ariz., 52, 54
Florentine Codex (document), 21
Flores, Tatiana, 14–15, 129–130, 138, 177
Floyd, George, 195
for-contract printer/workshop model, 233n35
Fort Marion, Fla., 55
Foster, Hal, 92
Fox, Claire, 104, 133
Fox, Howard, 70–71
fresco painting, 3
Freud, Sigmund, 60
Freye, Joe, 100
Fries, Lorenz, 85–86
"From the Life of Don Margarito" (Ríos), 81–82, 83, 90
frontier mythologies and imagery, 35, 39–41, 43, 56–58, 64, 74
Fuentes, Juan, 194
Fusco, Coco, 206–207

Gabara, Esther, 47
Galería de la Raza, San Francisco, 201
Galle, Philips (and Theodoor), 19, *20*, *62*, 63
Gallegos, Pete, 12
García, Dolores, 200
garcía, iliana emilia, 152, *153*, 174, 186, *188*
García, Rupert, 13, 43–44, 194, 198–199
García, Scherezade, 152, *153*, 161–165, 174, 178
García Pantaleón, Reynaldo, 152, *153*, 178, *179*
García-Peña, Lorgia, 159, 161, 168, 184–185
Gaudio, Michael, 86
Gemini G.E.L. (workshop), 5, 46–47, 194, 220n13
gender topics: bias in printing arts and academia, 5, 25–26, 178, 180; and colonial legacy of trauma, 1–2, 8, 19, 25–27, 55–56, 120–121, 210, *xiv*; feminism, 10, 25, 115, 138; gendered art techniques, 129–130; and Native/Indigenous territorialities, 61–69, 103
Genome Map (Chagoya and Ríos), *72*, *73*, 74, 111
Geodesic Mission, Franco-Hispanic, 113, 114, 117–118, 119
geometric projection, 77–82
"ghosting" of Dominican Republic, 186
ghostliness imagery, 61, 63
Ghost of Liberty, The (Chagoya), 201
Giunta, Andrea, 3
Global City, The (Sassen), 127
globalization, 65, 101, 104, 127
Godin, Louis, 113, 117
Goldman, Shifra, 13
Gombrich, Ernst, 20–21, 22
Gomez, Ignacio, 197
Gomez, Jay Lynn, 128
Gómez-Barris, Macarena, 4, 24, 138, 223n69
Gómez-Peña, Guillermo, 102, 103, 104
Gonzales-Day, Ken, 4
González, Jennifer, 9, 102
González, Luis "Louie the Foot," 50–52, 64–65
Good Neighbor Policy of US, 181
Gosine, Andil, 178
Governor's Nightmare, The (Chagoya), 47, *48*, 49
Grant, Ulysses S., 180, 227n68
Great Depression, 9
Greeley, Robin Adèle, 13, 101
Greet, Michele, 120
Griffiths, Anthony, 238n64
Grupo 65, Mexico City (art group), 13

Guaman Poma de Ayala, Felipe, 120–121
Guayasamín, Oswaldo, 115–116, 120
Guerrero, Alex, 152, *153*, 186, *189*
Guevara, Che, 194
Gumbs, David, 178
Günther, Ingo, 91

Haiti, 163, 165–168, 180–185, 186
Hamilton, Richard, 42–43
Hand Print Workshop International, 157
Hanley, Sarah Kirk, 84–85
Hansen, Trudy, 4
haptic experiences, 106–108
Harriot, Thomas, 86
Havana Bicentennial (2000), 161–162
Hayter, Stanley William, 175
Hernandez, Ester, 133–135, 197
Hernández, Frank, 32, 156
Hernandez, John, 155
Hernandez, Nancipili, 202, 204–206
Hill, Logan, 146, *147*
Hispaniola, 6–7, 152, 153–155, 180–185, 186, 192
Hollywood (Ruscha), 37, 43
Holt, Nancy, 91
Holton, Curlee Raven, 174–175
Home—So Different, So Appealing (exhibition), 13
Hood, John, 59, 60
Hooker, Juliet, 149
Huerta, Benito, 125
human genome sequencing, 72, 73–74
Humanscape 68 (*Kitchen Spanish*) (Casas), 44
Humanscapes (Casas, series), 44
Humor in Xhicano Arte 200 Years of Oppression 1776–1976, 14
Hurricane Maria, 202
Hurricane Redux (Marichal, P.), 202

Ibañez, Antonio, 5, 32, 156
Ida B. Wells: Telling It Like It Is (Meek), 142, *143*
Idea of Latin America (Mignolo), 119
"illegality" concepts, 122, 135
Immaculate Heart College, Los Angeles, 5, 32, 194
immigrant crossing sign, 59, 69, 137–138
Immigration and Naturalization Service (INS), 42
immigration issues: anti-immigration discourse and policies, 2, 7, 9, 25, 42, 47, 59–60, 139–140; Austin overview, 127–128; border crossers and embodiment of American identity, 98–101; exploitation art themes, 125; urban undocumented population profile, 135. *See also* borders and border crossing
Immigration Reform and Control Act of 1986, 142
Indian Land (Barraza and Hernandez, N.), 202, 204–206
Indians, American. *See* Native Americans (North American Indians)
Indigenism movement, 120
indio (Indian), 167–168
indio oscuro (dark-skinned Indian), 168
Instituto Nacional de Patrimonio Cultural, 118
intaglio techniques, 175
interethnic/racial artist networks, 11–12
interracial marriage. *See* mestizaje ideology
Intrépido (Coronado, P.), *182*, 183, 184, 185
invisibility/cultural erasure of migrants, 114–115, 132, 135, 140
Isidore of Seville, 108

Jackson, Cassandra, 235n80
Jean Baptiste (Charbonneau) (son of Sacagawea), 63–64
Jim Crow Laws, 132
Jiménez, Luis, 6, 13
Jimenez Underwood, Consuelo, 67–68
Johns, Jasper, 46
Johnson, Brian, 208
Jones, Kellie, 44
Jones Act of 1917, 10
Jones-Hogu, Barbara, 44
Journal du voyage fait par ordre du roi à l'équateur, 118
Juan y Santacilia, Jorge, 113
Juárez, Claudio, 175
Jurado, Milton, 156
Just Another Poster? (exhibition), 10, 195
Justice for Our Lives (Originol), 195–196
Just What Is It That Makes Today's Homes So Different, So Appealing? (Hamilton), 42–43

Kearny Street Workshop, San Francisco, 12
Kennicott, Philip, 196–197, 201
Kent, Corita, 5, 32, 46, 194

Kessler, Donna, 64
King, Charles Bird, 67
Kingman, Eduardo, 120
Klett, Mark, 5
Knight, Christopher, 70
Kozloff, Joyce, 91
Kraus, Theresa, 239n83
Kuitca, Guillermo, 91
Kunzle, David, 193

La Casa del Grabado, 236n16
La Ciguapa (Angulo Guridi), 169
La Condamine, Charles Marie de, 113, 117–118, 119
La Huella Magistral (Lozano), 186, *189*
La Marcha de Lupe Liberty (Ortega), 139–141
Lambert, Michael, 206
Lambert, Valerie, 205–206
land dispossession, 42
land reclamation themes, 33–34
language, loss of, 142–145
Lapin Dardashti, Abigail, 163, 164, 165
La Pocha Nostra (performance troupe), 102–105
La Raza (magazine), 4
La Raza Silkscreen Center, San Francisco, 11–12, 13
Las Casas, Bartolomé de, 29
Lasch, Pedro, 98–100
Last of the Mohicans (film), 65
Latin American and Latinx Visual Culture, 8
Latin American art *v.* Latinx art, 13–15, 17
Latinidad, 3, 14–15, 17, 119–120. *See also* mestizaje ideology
"Latinidad Is Canceled" (Pelaez Lopez, cultural campaign), 15
Latinx Art (Dávila), 12, 200
Latinx art/artists, overviews: Chicanx art and cultural identity, 5, 8–9, 11–12, 193, 198, 201–202; cultural/professional infrastructure, evolution of, 34–35; etymology and evolution of term, 7–8; heterogeneity of canons in, 7–10, 12–13; marginalization of, 12–14, 196–198, 200–201. *See also* printmaking and Latinx cultural identity
La Tira de la Peregrinación (Codex Boturini), 97
Latorre, Guisela, 11
Le Cannibale Moderniste (Chagoya), 84–85
Leo Burnett Worldwide, 39
LGBTQ issues. *See* queer perspectives
Libertad de Expresión (Mexiac), 13–14
Lichtenstein, Roy, 44, 46
Life magazine, 44, *45*
Lindsay, Arturo, 165, *166*
Lipsitz, George, 10
Lolita Lebrón (Dimas), 197
Lorde, Audre, 109
Los Angeles County Museum of Art (LACMA), 21, 33, 69–70. *See also Los Angeles County Museum on Fire, The* (Ruscha)
Los Angeles County Museum on Fire, The (Ruscha), 44, *45*
Los Angeles Times, 59, 70, 193
Los de Abajo (print collective), 158
Lowe, Sam, 54
Lozano, Luanda, 152, *153*, 170–172, 174, 175–180, 186, *189*
Lucero, Linda, 12
Luciano, Miguel, 152, *153*, 167–168, 174
Luna, Violeta, 102, 103
lynchings and racialized spectacle violence, 4, 142

Made in California (exhibition), 33, 69–70
Mad Men (television program), 39, 57
Magaloni, Diana, 21–22, 24, 96
Magritte, René, 66
Maldonado, Pedro Vicente, 113–114, 117–118
Maldonado-Torres, Nelson, 186
Malinche, legend of, 64–65
Manifestaciones (DYPG portfolio), 153, 155, 186
Manifest Destiny, 35, 58, 61–63
"Manifesto Antropófago" (Andrade), 88–90
Mapa Corpo (La Pocha Nostra, performance art presentation), 102–105
Map of Cuauhtinchan, 82–83
Map of Tenochtitlán (Cortés), 74–75
maps/mapping. *See* cartography/maps and territorial politics
Marichal, Carlos, 202
Marichal, Poli, 202, *203*
Marin, Christine, 52
Marlboro imagery, 30–31, *32*, 35, 39–40, 42–43, 50, 56–61
Marquez, Vicencio, *99*, 100
Martí, José, 193

Martínez, César, 125, 155
Martinez, Emanuel, 33
Marxism, 124
Maryland Institute College of Art, 157
masculinist ideologies, 61, 66
Master Plan of 1928, Austin, Tex., 131–132
Maupertuis, Pierre-Louis Moreau de, 117
Mayorga, Paloma, 125
McClean, Alison, 193
Means, Russell, 65–66
Meek, Vicki, 142, *143*
Melara, Oscar, 12, 193
Menchaca, Michael, 125, 206–208, *209*
Mendez, Dalila Paola, 1–2, 19, *xiv*
mending imagery, 144–145. *See also* sewing/stitch art
Mendoza, Antonio de, 131
Mendoza, Yunior Chiqui, 152, *153*, 159, *161*
Mercator, Gerhard, 95, *96*, 105
Mesa-Bains, Amalia, 58
mestiza consciousness, evolution of, 27–28, 115–122, 149–150
mestizaje ideology: concepts of, overviews, 115; and cultural identities, 14, 119–120; mixed-race identity as resistance to colonialism, 149; promotion of, 14–15, 17; roots of and colonialism, 18
mestizos/as. *See* mestiza consciousness, evolution of
Mexiac, Adolfo, 13–14
Mexican culture, commodification of, 49–50
Mexican free-tailed bats in Austin, 133
Mexicanidad, 3
Mignolo, Walter, 14, 25, 79, 85, 88, 119, 120, 135, 223n67
Migration Policy Institute, 183
milagros (folk charm) imagery, 138, 141, 142, 145
militarization of border, 9
Miner, Dylan, 205
Mir, Pedro, 183
Miranda, Carolina, 193
mixed-media art, 128, 129
Mogel, Lize, 90, 98, 105
Molina, Natalia, 131–132
Mona Passage (strait), 170
Mondrian, Piet, 79, 84
Monet, Claude, 84
Monkman, Kent, 55–57
Montoya, Delilah, 125
Montoya, Malaquias, 124
Mora, Francisco, 33
Morris, Kate, 55–57
Morrison, Toni, 61
Mourning and Dreaming on High (Fernández), 201–202
Mujeres Artistas del Suroeste, Texas (art network), 14
mulattos/as, 14, 164–166
multiculturalism and artists of color, 124–125, 200
Muñoz, Leonardo J., 116–117
mural art/artists, 3, 30–31, 164–165, 195
Museo Naval de Madrid, 118
My Girl on the Floor (Ureña), 169–170
mythologies. *See* frontier mythologies and imagery; savage/savagery myth and imagery

NAFTA (North American Free Trade Agreement). *See* North American Free Trade Agreement (NAFTA)
NASA, 92–93
nationalism, xenophobic, 8, 61, 194, 199–200
National Uncanny, The (Bergland), 61
Native Americans (North American Indians): Alcatraz occupation 1969, 202, 204; Apache Leap, 52–54, 57–59, 206; dispossession and displacement of, 60, 61; Warhol's print series, 65–67
nativism and xenophobia, 8–9, 42, 50, 153, 191
negrophobia, 163–164, 166, 168
neoliberalism: and embodied geography, 90–92, 98, 102, 110–111; impact on borders and mobility, 133–137; and NAFTA, 64–65
nepantla concept, 26
"new mestiza" concept, 145
New Order, The (Duffy): and gendered territories, 61, 63–64, 67; in *Made in California* exhibition, 69–70; overview, 26; and pop/border art concepts, 35–37, *36*, 39–43, 50; racial perspectives on frontier mythologies, 52, 57–58, 60
Newton, Isaac, 117
New York Times, 70
nonobjective art, 78–79
Noriega, Chon, 12, 13, 14

North American Free Trade Agreement (NAFTA), 35, 47, 64–65, 100–101, 133–135, 204
Northern Triangle, The (Fernández), 147–149
Nosie, Wendsler, Sr., 52–53
Nova Reperta (Galle after Stradanus, series), 19–21, *62*, 63, 86
Nuyoricans (Puerto Rican diasporans), 10, 158

Ocampo, Manuel, 38–39
"omphalos syndrome," 79
one-drop rule in US, 15, 168
Oni of Lagos (Lindsay), 165, *166*
Operation Bootstrap, 10
Operation Gatekeeper, 59–60
Operation Power Pack, 183
Organization in Solidarity with the People of Africa, Asia and Latin America (OSPAAAL), 193
Originol, Oree, 195–196
Oropeza, Eduardo, 157
Orozco, José Clemente, 3
Orozco, Sylvia, 14
Ortega, Tony, 139–141
Ortiz, Alfonso, 118–119, 178
Ortiz Torres, Rubén, 49–50
Our America (exhibition), 196–197, *198*, 201

Paglen, Trevor, 77, 90, 91, 92
Paraíso (García, S.), 162
Partido Soicialista Ecuatoriano, 120
Pearce, Margaret Wickens, 91
Pelaez Lopez, Alan, 15
Peña, Amado, 195
Pérez, German, 162
Pérez, Laura, 25
performance art and embodied geography, 102–105
Perrin Elvia, 208
Persian Gulf crisis, 41
Phillip Morris, Inc., 31, 40, 57. *See also* Marlboro imagery
photography and colonialism, 3–4
Picasso, Pablo, 83–84
Pickles, John, 81
Piper, Adrian, 90
Plessy v. Ferguson, 132
Pocahontas, 101
police brutality theme, 195–196
Poly/Graphic San Juan Triennial (exhibition), 10
Pop América (exhibition), 44
pop art aesthetic, 40, 42–50, 65–67, 134, 143, 198–199. *See also* "border pop"
portable border concept, 102, 103–104
Portable Borders (Sheren), 104
Posada, José Guadalupe, 194
Pratt, Mary Louise, 118
Pressing the Point (exhibition), 10, 158, 195
Primavera (Duffy), 33
print collectives, 158–159, 236n17. *See also* printmaking and Latinx cultural identity
¡Printing the Revolution! (exhibition): art/artist highlights, 201–204; display strategies, 198–199; Latinx art culture identity debate, 196–198, 200–201; overviews, 14, 192; revolutionary framework associations, 193–196, 198–200; significance and legacy of, 192–193
printmaking and Latinx cultural identity: future outlook, 207–210; as instrument of territorial colonization/decolonization, 2–4, 17–19, 24–26, 31–35, 109–110. *See also* print workshops
Prints and the Pursuit of Knowledge in Early Modern Europe (exhibition), 17
print workshops: Brandywine Workshop, Philadelphia, 12, 156, 165, 220n2, 220n13; collaborative workshops, 4–5, 11–12, 46–47, 233n35; evolution of and overviews, 2, 4–7, 10–14; print collectives, 158–159, 236n17; Robert Blackburn Printmaking Workshop, 156, 174–175, 220n13. *See also* Self Help Graphics & Art (workshop)
Project 1521 (podcast), 21
Proof: The Rise of Printmaking in Southern California (exhibition), 194
Proposition 187, California (Save Our State campaign), 15, 35, 42, 59–60, 192
Puerto Rico: art legacy of, 10, 11, 15, 202; Dominican water crossings to, 154–155, 170, 172
Pyramid Atlantic, 157
Pythagorean theorem, 77–79, 80, 83

queer perspectives, 15, 19, 25–26, 149, 210
Quijano, Aníbal, 130, 132
Quinceañeras, 123
Quirola Aulestia, Carlota, 117

Quisqueya (Hispaniola), 157
Quito, Ecuador, *112*, 113–114, 115–119
Quito Azul (Guayasamín), 116

Rabasa, José, 17, 75, 95
racial mixing concept, 14–15, 18, 115, 120, 149–150, 206. *See also* mestizaje ideology
racism: in art history disciplines, 11, 12; artists of color, marginalization of in mainstream art, 5–6, 12–14, 34, 44, 46, 124–125, 194–198, 200–201; Dominican rejection of African heritage, 154, 163–164, 165–168; profiling, 9; racial scripting, 131–132, 142; segregation, 131–132. *See also* racial mixing concept
"Rainbow/Arco de Tiempo" (Magaloni, poem), 21–22, 24, 96
Rainbows, Grizzlies, and Snakes, Oh My! (Rodriguez, S.), 21, *23*
Ramírez, Dixa, 186
Ramírez, Mari Carmen, 13, 14
Ramirez, Yasmin, 158
Ramos, E. Carmen, 12, 46, 157–158, 192, 193–197, 220n11
rape as allegory, 65
Raqs Media Collective, 90
Rauschenberg, Robert, 2, 46
Rayo, Omar, 173
Rebolloso, Jonathan, 146, *147*, 221n15
reclaiming Americas. *See* decolonization and delinking
Reinoza, Tatiana, 199–200
Relational Undercurrents (exhibition), 177–178
religion and colonialism, 14, 141, 144, 157, 172
Renaissance Invention (exhibition), 19
reterritorialization/mobility of borders, 27, 76, 102, 111, 115, 133–134, 137, 192
"reverse modernism," 83–84
revolution framework and themes, 193–196
Revolution on Paper (exhibition), 193
Richard E. Peeler Art Center, DePauw University, 80
Ringgold, Faith, 6
Rio Grande River, 208
Ríos, Alberto: artistic refutation of Eurocentric cartography, 92–100, 104–109; background, 75–76; collaboration with Chagoya, overviews, 76–77, 109–111; overviews, 192; and phenomenological approach to cartography, 77–83, 89–98. *See also* Ríos (Alberto), works by
Ríos (Alberto), works by: "From the Life of Don Margarito," 81–82, 83, 90; "Some Extensions on the Sovereignty of Science," 107–108; "Venus Trombones, The," 79. *See also* Chagoya and Ríos, works by
Risseeuw, John, 5
Rivera, Alex, 197
Rivera, Diego, 3
Rivera Cusicanqui, Silvia, 120, 121
Road Map (Chagoya), 101
Robert Blackburn Printmaking Workshop, 156, 174–175, 220n13
Rodriguez, Elizabeth Anne, 54–55
Rodriguez, Favianna, 206
Rodríguez, Freddy, 162
Rodriguez, Sandy, 21, *23*
Role of Paper, The (exhibition), 10
Romo, Ricardo and Harriett, 200
Romo, Tere, 13, 201
Rosenquist, James, 44
Ros-Suárez, Moses, 151–152, *153*, 176
Rothman, Jerry, 31
Route Guide (Lasch), 99
Royal Chicano Air Force (RCAF), 205
Rubio, Alex, 155
Ruscha, Ed, 37–38, 43, 44, 45, 46

Sabana de la Mar, Dominican Republic, 172
Sacagawea, 63–64
Saldaña-Portillo, María Josefina, 15, 57, 58–59
Salgado, Julio, 210
Salkowitz-Montoya, Leslie, 124
Sálvame Santo (Lozano), 170–172, 175, 178
Sam, Vilbrun Guillaume, 181
Sance, Jos, 194
Sánchez, Juan, 175
San Francisco de Macorís, Dominican Republic, 173
Santa Monica Mountains, 37, 43
Santo Domingo, Dominican Republic, 152
Santos, Margaret Terrazas, 200
Santos's border crossing story (anonymous), 141–142

Santuario (Marichal, P.), 202, *203*
Sassen, Saskia, 127
satire and immigrant right activism, 47–50
savage/savagery myth and imagery, 17–18, 40–41, 57–58, 67, 86–90
Save Our State campaign, 42, 47
"scenarios of discovery," 97–98
Schimmel, Julie, 67
Schreffler, Michael, 86
Scott, Amy, 4
screenprinting, 5, 43–47
Sea of Wonder (García, S.), 164–165
Seda, Laurietz, 103
Segura, Joe: background, 74–75; and Chagoya/Ríos collaboration, 75–76; workshop and residency programs, Arizona State University, 5–6; on *You Are Here* portfolio, 109. *See also* Segura Publishing Company
Segura Arts Studio, 109–110
Segura Publishing Company, 74–75, 100, 109–110, 200; establishment of, 6
Self Help Graphics & Art (workshop): background and history, 5, 32–33; Experimental Silkscreen Atelier Program, 26, 46, 156–157; impact and legacy of, 200; influence on Serie Project development, 155–156
Sensenbrenner, James, 139
"separate but equal" doctrine, 132
September 11, 2001, attack, 102, 133
Serie Project at Coronado Studio, 6, 115, 124–125, 143, 146, 155–156
serigraphy. *See* screenprinting
Sette, Lisa, 6, 74
settler colonialism, 17, 35, 47, 49, 58
sewing/stitch art, 67–69, 129–130, 142, 144–145
Shakur, Tupac, 206
Sheren, Ila, 103–104
SHG. *See* Self Help Graphics & Art (workshop)
Shirk, Adrian, 40
Sicles Garzón, Roberto Arnoldo, 114, 118–119
Sifuentes, Roberto, 102, 103
Sigüenza, Herbert, 12
Simpson, Margaret, 233n35
Smith, Mark L., 233n35
Smith, Roberta, 70
Smithsonian American Art Museum (SAAM), 192–193, 196–197
smoking and tobacco, 29–31, 40. *See also* Marlboro imagery
Sobo, Elisa, 205–206
socialism, 117, 120
social issues and protest movements, 34–35
Soja, Edward, 38
"Some Extensions on the Sovereignty of Science" (Ríos), 107–108
"space junk," 92–93
Spanish-American War, 180–181
"spiritual geographies," 52
Staden, Hans, 86, 88
Statue of Liberty, 139–141
Steinmeier, Frank-Walter, 119
Stephens, Michelle Ann, 177
Stonard, John-Paul, 43
Stoneman, George, 52, 54
Stradanus, Johannes, 19–21, *62*, 63, 86
Straet, Jan van der. *See* Stradanus, Johannes
Strange Bath (Charlier), 185
Sullivan, Edward, 162
Sullivan, John L., 63
Sullivan, Megan, 13
Sun Mad (Hernandez, E.), 134, 197
Sun Raid (Hernandez, E.), 133–135
Superior, Ariz., 52, 54–55
survivance concept, 67

Taíno culture and iconography, 1, 155, 157, 176, 178, *xiv*
Taller Boricua, Manhattan (gallery and workshop), 158–159
Taller de Gráfica Popular, Mexico City (workshop), 33, 193
Taller Experimental de Gráfica, Havana (workshop), 1
Taller Puertorriqueño, Philadelphia (workshop), 12
Taller Tupac Amaru, Oakland (print collective), 206
Tamarind Institute, Albuquerque, 5, 13, 194, 220n13
"T and O map," 108
Tarver, Gina McDaniel, 3
Tavárez, Rosa, 158

Taveras, Ezequiel, 173–174
Taylor, Diana, 82–83, 97–98
technological advancements, influence of: in colonialist extractive model, 24–25; in European history, 19–21; technocapitalism, 207–208
terminology: *calaveras* (skeletal figures), 234n60; *huipiles* (traditional Indigenous garments), 234n60; Latinx, 7–8; *milagros* (folk charm) imagery, 138, 141, 142, 145; *mojado*, 224n4; "Pinal," 226n61; *yolas* (large wooden boats), 170, 172
Terrae Novae Tabula (Fries after Waldseemüller), 85
Terra Nullius concept, 22, 42
Testimonio de Lucha (Muñoz), 117
Texas Commission of the Arts, 124–125
textile art, 67–69
"Their Manner of Praying with Rattles About the Fire" (de Bry after White), 86, *87*
Theorem (Chagoya and Ríos), 77–80, 82, 83, 98
Theories of Freedom (García, S., series), 164
"The Secret Footprints" (Alvarez), 168–169
Thomas, Mary, 11
Thompson, Nato, 90, 91
Tierra o Muerte (Martinez, E.), 33–34
tobacco and smoking, 29–31, 40. *See also* Marlboro imagery
Tompkins Rivas, Pilar, 13, 14
Torres-García, Joaquín, 184
Torres-Saillant, Silvio, 165, 167
Trash World (Chagoya and Ríos), 92–93
Trujillo, Rafael Leónidas, 163, 167–168, 181, 183
Trump Administration, 137
Tupi Indians, 86–87
Turrell, James, 6

Ulloa, Antonio de, 113
Undocumented Americans, The (Villavicencio), 146–147
Unforgettable Guerrilla Tania, The (Grupo 65), 13
"Union" (Ríos), 74
Unite (Jones-Hogu), 44
Universal Limited Art Editions (ULAE) (worshop), 220n13
University of Notre Dame, 109–110
Untitled (*Ethnic Map of Los Angeles*) (Ocampo), 38–39
Upside Down World Map (Chagoya and Ríos), 105–107
urban segregation/fragmentation, 38–39
Ureña, Rider, 152, *153*, 169–170, 174
"Urgent Images" (section of *¡Printing the Revolution!*), 198–199
US Border Patrol, 40–41, 100, 139, 234n61, 238n53
US Customs and Border Protection (CBP), 133, 172
US Department of Homeland Security, 127, 133
U.S./D.R.: A Love-Hate Relationship (Coronado, P.), 184
U.S./D.R. en Relación (Coronado, P.), 184–185
US Immigration and Customs Enforcement (ICE), 9, 115, 133, 135
USS *Intrepid*, 181

Valdés, Juana, 178
Valdez, Julio, 174
Vale John (Almonte), 186, *187*
Vamp and Tramp Booksellers, 233n35
Vargas-Santiago, Luis, 224–225n13
Vasconcelos, José, 14, 115, 120, 122, 149
Velasco Mackenzie, Jorge, 119
Veni Vidi Vici (Duffy), 31–32
"Venus Trombones, The" (Ríos), 79
Vespucci, Amerigo, 63, 86
Viesulas, Romas, 5, 32
Villaseñor Black, Charlene, 8
Villavicencio, Karla Cornejo, 146–147
violence of conquest, colonial: printmaking's connection to, 24–25, 191–192; "racialized spectacle violence," 4, 142; rape of Indigenous, 1–2, 18, 65, 149–150; savage myth as justification for, 17–18, 40–41, 57–58, 67, 86–90
Virgen de los Caminos (Jimenez Underwood), 67–69
Virgin of Guadalupe, 67
Vista Psicotrópica (Guerrero), 186, *189*
visual excess technique, 42
Viteri, Oswaldo, 128, *129*, 149
Vizenor, Gerald, 66–67
Voulkos, Peter, 31

Waldseemüller, Martin, 17–18
Walker, Barry, 46
Warhol, Andy, 44, *45*, 46–47, 65–66

War of Restoration, Spanish, 166
Washington Post, 196–197
water: as boundary/border, 153–154, 159, 164–165, 170–172, 178, 186, 208; imagery, 18–19, 94–96, 164–165, 168–170, 177–178, 208–210; as route for foreign interventions, 180–185
Watts Rebellion, 44
Weems, Carrie Mae, 6
Wells, Carol, 13
West as America, The (exhibition), 67
White, John, 86–87
Whiting, Cécile, 37–38, 43, 44
Whitney Biennial (exhibition), 70, 124, 197, 206–207
Williams, Lyle, 13
Wilson, Liliana, 155
Wilson, Pete, 42
Witness: Art and Civil Rights in the Sixties (exhibition), 44
Wolffer, Lorena, 65
women. *See* gender topics
Wood, Denis, 95
workshops, print. *See* print workshops
World Processor (Günther), 91
Wounded Knee occupation, 65

xenophobia and nativism, 8–9, 42, 50, 153, 191

Ybañez, Terry, 142–145
Ybarra-Frausto, Tomás, 200, 221n16
Yemaya (Yoruba deity), 1, 19
yolas (large wooden boats), 170, 172
Yoruba culture and iconography, 1, 19, 142, 178, *xiv*
You Are Here (Chagoya and Ríos, portfolio), 26–27, 74, 92, 98, 105, 109–110

Zapata, Claudia, 192, 208–210
Zapata, Emiliano, 33–35
Zapatista Uprising 1994, 204
Zigrosser, Carl, 46
Zoot Suit (Gomez), 197
Zuñiga, Francisco, 13